A TOUR *of the* SUMMA

A TOUR *of the* SUMMA

By PAUL J. GLENN

TAN BOOKS AND PUBLISHERS, INC.
Rockford, Illinois 61105

IMPRIMATUR: ✠ JOSEPH E. RITTER, S.T.D.

ARCHBISHOP OF ST. LOUIS—SEPT. 26, 1960

Fifth Printing, 1978

Printed and bound in the United States of America

TAN BOOKS AND PUBLISHERS, INC.
P. O. Box 424
Rockford, Illinois 61105

1978

TO ALL PRIESTS WHOSE EARLY STUDIES
WERE MADE AT SAINT CHARLES SEMINARY
COLUMBUS, OHIO

PREFACE

We may adapt a remark of St. Thomas Aquinas, and apply it to his own great work, the *Summa Theologica:* not everyone has talent to master this work; not everyone has a taste for the study it requires; not everyone has time to devote to such study.

The present book has been written for the many talented persons who wish to know the *Summa* but who lack inclination or opportunity to spend years of sustained effort learning it.

This book is a turnpike trip through the wide region known as the *Summa Theologica* of St. Thomas Aquinas. A turnpike is only a ribbon of trail through a territory in which every square mile is filled with sights to see, people to know, and places to visit. But a turnpike trip cannot pause for these interesting and valuable things; it must rush on, content with affording a full length view of the lay of the land in a succession of rewarding glimpses.

A Tour of the Summa is not a translation, not a digest, not a selection of parts called basic, or best. It is a journey through the entire *Summa* from beginning to end, and it furnishes a tourist's view of the scope and content of that master work. It is a condensed paraphrase of the essential teaching of the *Summa,* so presented as to enable the reader to turn instantly to the exact locus in St. Thomas for full treatment of each point discussed.

The *Summa Theologica* is the most important of the many works with which St. Thomas—great Dominican scholar and saint of the thirteenth century—enriched the world. St. Thomas died before completing this work, but it was rounded out by compilation from earlier writings of his; this completing part is called the Supplement.

The *Summa* consists of three Parts and the Supplement. The second part has two distinct sections. Each part is divided into questions. Each question is divided into articles. Each article is preceded by objections, and followed by replies to the objections. Names and symbols for the parts are these:

A reference to the *Summa* is made thus: Ia IIae, q. 6, a. 2. This means: First Part of the Second Part, question 6, article 2.

The present work holds strictly to the major divisions of the *Summa*, but omits objections and replies to objections. The parts here are those of the *Summa* itself. The questions are indicated by numbered marginal headings, the articles by numbered paragraphs under these headings. To find in this book the locus indicated above, look up Ia IIae, run down the marginal headings to 6, and consult paragraph 2 under that heading.

CONTENTS

[Ia]
THE FIRST PART
Questions 1-119

[Ia IIae]
The FIRST PART *of*
THE SECOND PART
Questions 1-114

[IIa IIae]
The SECOND PART *of*
THE SECOND PART
Questions 1-189

[IIIa]
THE THIRD PART
Questions 1-90

Contents

[IIIa Suppl.]
SUPPLEMENT TO
THE THIRD PART
Questions 1-99

[Ia]

THE FIRST PART

[*Questions 1-119*]

GOD AND HIS ATTRIBUTES

(QUESTIONS 1 TO 26)

1. SACRED DOCTRINE

1. Man's most urgent need is to know truths about God. Some of these truths can be known by philosophy, that is, by thinking them out. Other truths about God are made known to man by divine revelation. And indeed divine revelation is required for the proper understanding of all truths about God, even those which philosophy teaches. For without revelation man could not know *quickly* and *accurately* the naturally knowable truths about God so as to make these truths the rule and guide for his responsible life right from the start. Therefore, philosophy is not enough for man; divine revelation is required.

2. Truths about God manifested by divine revelation constitute sacred doctrine or supernatural theology. Sacred doctrine is a true science. For a science is a body of truths established with certitude, and sacred doctrine is a body of truths imparted on God's own authority, and hence established with absolute certitude.

3. Sacred doctrine is a single science rather than a group of related sciences, for it brings all its truths into the one precise focus of *what is divinely revealed*.

4. Sciences are speculative or practical. A speculative science contemplates truth; it fixes on what is so. A practical science considers what is to be done in consequence of the truths it contemplates; it fixes on what to do. Sacred doctrine is both speculative and practical, but it is primarily a speculative science, for its chief effort is to teach men truths about God.

5. Under either aspect, speculative or practical, sacred doctrine is the most noble of sciences. On the speculative side, it treats of the noblest object, that is, God himself, and it affords the most nobly satisfying certitude because it speaks with God's own authority. On the practical side, sacred doctrine is the noblest of sciences because it guides man to the noblest goal—God and everlasting happiness.

6. Sacred doctrine is wisdom. Wisdom involves deep knowledge of a valuable end to be attained together with a suitable and pleasing plan for attaining it. Sacred doctrine gives man the deepest knowledge

of his infinitely valuable end, and stirs and directs him to attain it.

7. The object of sacred doctrine, that is, its subject matter and also its special focus of attention, is God. All truths manifested by sacred doctrine are either truths about God or truths about creatures in reference to God.

8. The principles, that is, the basic truths, of sacred doctrine are the articles of faith. Sacred doctrine does not argue about these principles, as philosophy does, to show that they are in accord with reason; sacred doctrine presents these truths on God's authority and proceeds to draw other truths from them by study and reasoning.

9. Holy Scripture is a source of divine revelation, and hence a source of sacred doctrine. Scripture sometimes imparts a truth by figurative language, but not in such wise as to confuse us. This is right, for truth is often taught most effectively by making comparison with material and familiar things, that is, by using a figure of speech such as a simile or metaphor.

10. Sometimes scripture uses a term with an extension of meaning or a spiritual implication, as when St. Paul (Heb. 10:1) calls the Old Law a figure of the New Law. Here the term "the Old Law" receives the added meaning of a forecast or promise. It is suitable that scripture should thus manifest its richness by conveying in literally true words an abundance of implied meanings or suggestions.

2. THE EXISTENCE OF GOD

1. It is sometimes said that the truth of God's existence is self-evident, and hence neither needs a proof nor admits one. Now, a truth may be self-evident in two ways: (a) in itself and to the human mind; or (b) in itself, but not to the human mind. If you know the meaning of the words circle and roundness, you need no proof for the statement, "A circle is round." Indeed, no proof is possible, for a proof is to make a thing more evident, and nothing can make this statement more evident than the words in which it is expressed. Knowing what a circle is, you know that roundness belongs to it; when you say "circle" you are already saying "round." Here, then, is a truth that is self-evident both in itself and also self-evident to your mind. But if you did not clearly know the meaning of the words circle and roundness, the statement, "A circle is round" would not be self-evident to your mind, although it would still be, in itself, a self-evident truth. Now, the truth of the statement "God exists" is self-evident in itself; for God is necessarily existent; existence is as truly identified with God as roundness is identified with a circle. If the ideas God and existence, with their implications, were as quickly and perfectly available to the human

mind as are the ideas circle and roundness, we should not need, and could not have, a reasoned proof for the existence of God. But, as a fact, we have not this prompt and perfect knowledge of God and existence. Thus, while the truth that God exists is self-evident in itself, it is not self-evident to the human mind. For man, this truth needs to be evidenced or proved.

2. Can we prove that God exists? Yes, we can. We can reason out this truth. There are two ways of reasoning a thing out. First, we may so perfectly know a cause that we can reason out what its effect must be; this is *a priori* reasoning. Secondly, we may know an effect better than we know its cause, and by studying the effect we can work back to know the cause that produced it; this is *a posteriori* reasoning. In proving the existence of God we use *a posteriori* reasoning.

3. There are five notable ways of reasoning out the truth that God exists. The first way is by considering motion in the world. Where there is motion, there is a mover, and ultimately a first mover, itself unmoved. This is God. The second way is by considering the chains of effecting causes that exist in the world. Things here are produced by their causes; these causes in turn were produced by their causes, and so on. Ultimately, there must be a first cause which is itself uncaused. This is God. The third way is by considering the contingency of things in the world. Contingent things do not have to exist; they are nonnecessary; they come into existence, and undergo change, and pass away. Now, contingent things demand as their ultimate explanation a noncontingent being, a necessary being. This is God. The fourth way is by considering the scale of perfection manifest in the world. Things are more or less good, more or less noble, and so on. Now, where there is good and better and still better, there must at last be a best which is the source and measure of goodness all along the line. And where there is noble and nobler and still more noble, there must ultimately be a noblest which is the standard by which all lesser degrees of nobleness can be known and given their rating. In a word, where there are degrees of perfection, there must ultimately be absolute perfection. This is God. The fifth way is by considering the order and government seen in this world. Things act in a definite way and were manifestly designed to act so; through their nature (that is, their active or operating essence) they are governed in their activities. Thus there are design and government in the world. Hence there are ultimately a first designer and first governor. And since both design and government involve intelligence, there must be governor and designer who is the first and absolute intelligence. This is God.

3. THE SIMPLICITY OF GOD

1. When we speak of God's simplicity we speak of the fact that God is not composed of parts, or compounded of elements. In God there is no composition or compounding of any kind. First of all, in God there is no material composition, for God is not material or bodily. A body is subject to motion and change, but God is the unmoved First Mover, and the changeless necessary being. Further, a body is always in the state of potentiality, that is, capable of being acted on by causes, and God is in no wise capable of being affected by any causes. For God is the First Cause; there is no cause prior to God or independent of him that could act upon him. In God there is no passive potentiality at all; God is pure actuality. Therefore, in God there is no material composition, and no composition of potentiality and actuality.

2. Since God is not a body, he is not composed as all bodies are of primal matter (the element common to all bodies; the element by which a body is bodily) and substantial form (the substantial determinant in each body which makes it an existing body of its essential kind). In God there is no composition of matter and form.

3. Since God is not a body, he is not composed, as a body always is, of an essence or nature concreted in an individual subject. A body *has* its nature or working essence; we cannot say that a body *is* its nature. But God does not *have* anything; if he did, he would be in potentiality towards having it, and he would receive it from some prior being. But there is no being prior to the First Being. God is pure actuality. God *is* his own essence, his own nature, his own life, his own Godhead, and whatever else may be thus predicated of him. Therefore, in God there is no compounding of a nature with the individual subject which has that nature.

4. And God is his own existence. Creatures, bodily or spiritual, are composed of essence (which receives existence) and existence (which is received by essence to make an existing creature). But since God is the First Being, there is nothing prior to him from which his essence could receive existence. God does not receive anything of his being. God is necessary being; it is God's essence to exist. In God, essence and existence are absolutely one and the same. Therefore, God is not a compound of essence and existence.

5. We understand and define a creature by knowing the general essential class of things to which it belongs (its *genus*) and adding to that class the special difference by which it is essentially distinguished from other members of its class (its *specific difference*). Thus we understand an organism as belonging to the general class of *body*, and as

6

marked off from body-as-such by the fact that it has *life*. Hence we say that an organism is compounded or composed of bodiliness and life as of genus and specific difference. Now, God is not a member of a class of things from which he is marked off by specific difference. God is absolute and unique. In God, therefore, there is no composition or compounding of genus and difference.

6. Nor is God composed of substance and accidentals. A substance is a reality that is naturally suited to exist *as itself*, and not as the mark or determinant of some other thing. An accidental (or, in older language, an accident) is a reality that is suited to exist *as of something other than itself*. An apple is a substance. The size, color, weight, position, temperature, flavor, etc., of the apple are existing realities, but they are not "on their own" so to speak; they exist *as of the apple*, not *as themselves*. Accidentals are said to inhere in the substance which they mark or qualify; hence a creatural substance is said to be composed of substance and inhering accidentals. Now, a creatural substance *has* accidentals; it stands in potentiality to receive them, and to undergo a change in them. But God is not in potentiality to receive or undergo anything in his substantial being. God is pure actuality. Therefore, there are in God no accidentals at all. All that God has, God *is*. Hence in God there is no compounding or composition of substance and accidentals.

7. Thus it is manifest that God is not composed of parts or elements of any kind. In other words, God is absolutely simple. We might know this truth at once from the fact that whatever is compounded or composed is subsequent to its elements or parts, and also subsequent to the action of the cause which brings the parts together. But God is the First Being; God is not subsequent to anything. Nor is God subject to the action of any cause. It follows, therefore, that God is absolutely simple and uncomposed. God is pure actuality, God is also absolute simplicity.

8. The absolutely simple God cannot be the part or element of anything else. For God is the First Cause, acting primarily and essentially. But what is an element or part of a compound cannot act primarily and essentially; only the completed compound can act so. Therefore God is not a part or element of anything else. Hence it is absurd to think of God as a "world soul" or even as primal matter.

[*Note:* As we shall see later, God's absolute simplicity in being and essence in no wise conflicts with the subsistence of the simple divine essence in the three distinct Persons of the Blessed Trinity.]

4. THE PERFECTIONS OF GOD

1. The first being must be self-existent, for it is *first;* there is nothing prior to it from which existence could be received. Now, self-existent being, or pure actuality, exists by its unbounded excellence or perfection. Pure actuality means absolute perfection. Therefore, God is absolute perfection. Consider the point in another way. There are perfections in creatures—being, life, knowledge, etc. All these perfections have been conferred on creatures and, in the first instance, these perfections were conferred by one who had them to confer; that is, the First Cause. These perfections must be in the First Cause in a manner suited to its pure actuality; that is, the perfections must exist in God absolutely, as identified with his divine essence. Therefore, God is pure or absolute perfection.

2. For the perfections of creatures cannot be in God as accidentals; as we have seen, God has no accidentals. They cannot be in God as parts, for God is pure simplicity and has no parts. These perfections can be in God only as identified with his essence. This is what theologians mean when they say that creatural perfections are in God *eminently.*

3. Creatures are *like* to God by analogy, inasmuch as creatures have perfections in a limited way, while these perfections are in God unlimitedly and eminently as identified with his very essence, being, and substance.

5. GOODNESS

1. A thing has goodness in so far as it can be the goal of a desire or tendency. That is called good which answers an appetite or appetency. Now, a thing can be the goal of a tendency by the fact that it is a thing at all, that it has being. Hence goodness and being are really the same thing. But logically, that is, in the way of human understanding, there is a distinction between goodness and being; for we can think of being without noticing that it is desirable or good. Therefore, between goodness and being, there is not a *real* distinction (as between thing and thing), but there is a *logical* distinction (as between distinct mental approaches to the same thing).

2. Hence it is evident that our idea of being is prior to our idea of goodness; for we are aware of a being as such before we are aware that it is necessarily good.

3. A thing is good in so far as it has positive being; positive being is perfection or actuality. For perfection is desirable, and desirability defines goodness.

4. Goodness has the character of a final cause, for it is an end-in-

view; it invites or attracts, and thus far causes the action which seeks to attain it.

5. Positive being (and hence perfection or actuality) is found in the essence of a thing, in its mode of being, in its specific kind, and in its tendency to its end. Therefore we discern goodness in a reality, in its mode, in its species, and in its direction to its end, goal, or purpose.

6. Good may be classified as the *seemly or virtuous,* the *pleasing,* and the *useful.*

6. THE GOODNESS OF GOD

1. God is the cause of all creatural being, and therefore he is the cause of all goodness in creatures. Finite things, each in its way and measure, manifest the goodness of God. God is absolute goodness. As such, he is the first producing (or effecting) cause, and the ultimate final cause (or goal) of all created goodness, that is, of all creatures.

2. God is the supreme good. Creatural goodness is always imparted, and by that fact is limited goodness. Creatural goodness cannot approach to the unlimited goodness of God.

3. Only God is essentially good, for God alone is necessary being and necessary goodness. Creatures *have* goodness. God *is* goodness.

4. Since God's goodness is the cause of goodness in things, creatures are properly called good by reason of the divine goodness.

7. THE INFINITY OF GOD

1. When we call God infinite, we mean that God is not limited in any way whatever. All creatures are finite or limited. For creatures *receive* their being and their perfections, and whatever is received is measured and limited by the giver or by the capacity of the receiver. Now, God's being is not received; God is self-existent being. There is nothing prior to God from which he could receive anything. Hence nothing can mark or limit God; nothing can set boundaries to God's self-existing perfection; nothing can diminish that perfection, nothing can add to it. A perfection that can neither be diminished nor increased is necessarily boundless or infinite. Hence, God is infinite in perfection. As God is absolute being, God is absolute infinity.

2. God alone is infinite. Creatures have what is called potential infinity inasmuch as there is no fixed limit to the possibility of succession and variation in them. A lump of wax is a finite thing with a finite shape, but there is no limit to the number or variety of shapes that may be given to it. At any moment, the number of shapes it has

received is a finite number; potential infinity attaches only to the shapes not yet received. Again, an abstract number may be multiplied or divided without limit, although at any instant in the process of multiplying or dividing, the number is a finite number. This type of infinity is actual infinity. Actual infinity is absolute. It excludes all potentiality. It can neither be increased nor diminished. Actual infinity is pure actuality. God alone is pure actuality; hence God alone is actual infinity.

3. No bodily thing can be infinite. For bodily infinity would be infinity in size, and size is always measurable; that is, size is always finite. Even a mathematical body must be thought of as contained within its lines and surfaces.

4. There cannot be an actually infinite number. A number has potential infinity, for it can be endlessly multiplied or divided. But actual infinity is incapable of being multiplied or divided. What is actually infinite cannot be increased or diminished, but a number can always be added to or lessened.

8. THE EXISTENCE OF GOD IN THINGS

1. God is present to things as an agent (that is, doer, performer, effecting cause) is present *to* and *in* the action and the effect which it produces. God is the source of all actuality in creatures; He must, then, be in creatures to produce and preserve this actuality; for creatural actuality is not self-producing or self-preserving. Creatures depend essentially on God both for production and preservation. God is in all things in the most perfect manner, not limited by the things nor identified with them.

2. God is in all places, actual and possible, for God is infinite. If any possible place could exclude God, it would impose a limit on the illimitable; it would impose a finiteness on the infinite. Since this is impossible, it follows that God is everywhere. God is not limited by the place in which he is, for God is not contained in a place as a body is. God's presence in a place does not block out a creature from occupying that place.

3. The mode or manner by which God is in places and things is threefold: (a) God is in all things by his power, as exercising absolute rule there; (b) God is in all things by his presence, as perfectly knowing the things and disposing them by his providence; (c) God is in all things by his essence as creator and preserver.

4. Only God can be everywhere, for only God is infinite and absolute. God is in all things and all places by the whole of his undivided being, not part here and part there, for God is not made of

parts. Thus God is present everywhere absolutely, and such presence belongs to the absolute being alone.

9. THE IMMUTABILITY OF GOD

1. Immutability means changelessness. That God is changeless follows upon his infinity and his absolute actuality. What is changeable is, to that extent, perfectible, and God is absolutely perfect. What is changeable is finite, for change means loss or gain, increase or diminishment, and God is infinite. What is changeable is in the state of potentiality (the state of "can be") and in God there is no potentiality at all; God is not in the state of "can be"; God IS. Therefore God is immutable or changeless. This does not mean that God is in a kind of frozen fixity. Changelessness in God is sheer perfection. It means that God is without any lack which a change could fill up, and that God is pure actuality which can suffer no loss by change.

2. God alone is immutable, for only God is infinite and absolutely actual. Every creature is in some way changeable, for a creature is finite or limited, and what is limited can conceivably have its limits extended or contracted. All things other than God are thus marked by potentiality. God who is pure actuality is absolutely changeless.

10. THE ETERNITY OF GOD

1. Eternity is the complete possession of boundless perfection, all at once, without beginning, succession, or end, and therefore without any *before* and *after*.

2. Since God is immutable, he is not subject to time which consists of continuous change. And since God is infinite, he is not limited by the terminations called beginning and ending.

3. Only God is eternal, for only God is immutable and infinite. Some creatures are called eternal in the meaning that they will never end; such are spiritual beings. And even bodily things are called eternal in the sense that they are not quickly or visibly affected by time; thus we speak of "the eternal hills." But strictly speaking, eternity belongs to God alone, and is identified with the essence of God.

4. Eternity, as duration, differs essentially from time. Time is a matter of before and after, of past and future, but eternity is an all-perfect changeless present. Eternity is an immutable, everlasting *now*. Thus eternity involves infinity, and so is identified with the pure actuality of God. We can know what eternity means, but we cannot picture it in imagination. Every attempt to envision eternity in imagination results merely in a lengthened view of imaginary time.

And time, as we have just noticed, is essentially different from eternity, and even opposite to it.

5. Time is a continuous succession of events or movements (therefore, of changes) which can be numbered, and considered with reference to before and after. But eternity is without succession or movement, and involves no aspects of before and after. Besides time and eternity there is a duration called *eviternity* that we ascribe to spiritual creatures (souls, angels) which have had a beginning but which have no substantial change and no ending.

6. People often speak of one time as different from another. They use expressions such as "our own times," "the golden age of literature," "grandfather's day," "the twentieth century." But these are only accidental divisions of time; time in itself is really one thing. Similarly, eviternity is one in itself, although it may be accidentally multiplied by referring it to this, and then to that eviternal being.

11. THE UNITY OF GOD

1. Unity means oneness, and oneness is the same as being. For every being is that one thing. A being cannot be multiplied or divided into a plurality of itself. To divide a thing into parts is to destroy its unity and also to destroy its being as that one thing. And yet each part is that one part, that one thing; still the truth holds that *being* and *the one* are really the same, although there is a logical distinction between them.

2. *The one* and *the many* are contrasted as opposites. The many (that is, plurality, multitude, more-than-one) is countable or measurable by the unit, that is by the one. And multitude (that is, two or more) when measured by the unit is called number. Thus number is contrasted with the unit which measures and determines it.

3. When we speak of the unity of God, we speak of the fact that there is one God and cannot be more than one God. God is infinite, and a plurality of infinities cannot be. If, by an impossible supposition, there were two infinite beings, "X" and "Y," then: either (a) "X" and "Y" would have identical perfections, and thus would actually be one being and not two; or (b) "X" would have its own perfections which "Y" would lack, and "Y" would have its own perfections which "X" would lack; thus neither being would be infinite, for what lacks any perfection is, by that fact, finite or imperfect. Thus it is inconceivable that there should be more than one infinite being. That is to say, it is inconceivable that there should be more than one God.

4. Since being and oneness are really the same, it follows that the

more perfect being is the more perfect unity. God is absolute being; therefore God is absolute unity.

[*Note:* The unity of God's being does not conflict in any way with the trinity of Persons in God. This fact will be discussed later.]

12. HOW WE CAN KNOW GOD

1. A thing is knowable in so far as it is actual. Since God is supremely actual, God is supremely knowable. God indeed is not well known by every mind, although a normal mind cannot come to maturity without at least some vague knowledge of God as a universal power or world-control. Those who say that man cannot truly know God are mistaken. Their teaching conflicts with the natural drive of the mind to grasp truth and to know the causes of things, including the First Cause. Besides, we know by faith that the blessed in heaven actually behold God's essence.

2. To see God in heaven, the created intellect requires a special added power which elevates and strengthens it.

3. The bodily eye cannot behold the nonbodily essence of God. Nor can the inner sense of imagination form an image of God; the infinite is not shown in a finite sense-image. Only the mind, the intellect, can behold God.

4. And the intellect needs more than its own natural power if it is to behold the divine essence itself. God must somehow elevate and join the intellect to himself that it may behold him: "In thy light we shall see light" (Ps. 35:10).

5. This union of God and intellect is effected in heaven by a supernatural gift or grace called the *lumen gloriae,* that is, the light of glory.

6. The more perfect a soul is in charity, that is, in the grace, love, and friendship of God, the more perfectly it beholds God in heaven. The degree of charity in the blessed soul determines the measure of the light of glory imparted to it.

7. By aid of the light of glory the soul in heaven sees God himself clearly and truly. This, to be sure, is no exhaustive viewing; the soul cannot understand all that is understandable in God; God is infinitely understandable, and the soul is finite.

8. Therefore the soul in heaven, seeing God by the light of glory, does not behold all that God does and can do; this would mean the actual encompassing of the infinite by a finite mind, a manifest contradiction and an impossibility.

9. By the light of glory the soul in heaven beholds God himself

13

and not merely a likeness or image of God. The soul beholds the divine essence directly, intuitively.

10. The knowledge of God enjoyed by the blessed soul in heaven is not piecemeal but complete and simultaneous. It is not a succession of viewings. The soul beholds God clearly and truly, and all that it beholds is seen at once.

11. The essence of God as seen in the light of glory constitutes the beatific vision. This is the essential reward of the blessed in heaven. Man cannot have the beatific vision here on earth. Here, although we can truly know God, we cannot have a direct and intuitive view of his very essence.

12. In the present life we use our natural power of reasoning, that is, the power of the thinking mind, to acquire true knowledge of the existence, nature, and attributes of God. This is essential knowledge of God, but it is not the direct beholding of the divine essence itself.

13. The knowledge of God which we can acquire by natural reasoning is richly enhanced by the faith and by divine revelation. Thus in the present earthly life we can know God by reason, by faith, by revelation.

13. THE NAMES OF GOD

1. We can justifiably name anything in so far as we know it. Now, we can know God naturally by reason, and supernaturally by faith and revelation. Therefore we can name God. And indeed we have many names for God; they are justified by the fact that we know what we are naming.

2. The names we apply to God express God himself so far as we know him. Even though our natural knowledge of God's perfection is acquired by considering the perfections of creatures, it justifies our names for God. We realize that creatural perfections are all in God, for it is God who bestows perfections on creatures, and he must have them in himself to bestow. Hence when we use a name expressing a perfection as a name for God, we apply this name to God himself, in his essence and substance.

3. Therefore our real names for God are not figurative or metaphorical; they are literal. The perfections these names express are actually in God and of God. Of course, these names do not perfectly express the *mode of eminence* by which the perfections named are identified with God's essence.

4. The names we give to God apply to the undivided divine essence. Yet they are not all synonyms. These names are distinct from one another by a logical distinction. They express various aspects of what is

not varied in itself. When we call God "the divine goodness," we express one true aspect of God; when we call him "the infinite " we express another; when we call God "the Almighty," we express still another. We do not thus imply that there are divisions in God; we only make various approaches to the one undivided divine essence.

5. Consider our use of names or terms. (a) When we apply a name or term to two or more things in exactly the same meaning, the term is, in that use, a univocal term. Thus the term being as applied to man, woman, and child, is a *univocal* term. (b) When, in the same context, we apply a term or name to two or more things in totally different meanings, the term is, in that use, an *equivocal* term. Thus the term bank used in the same context to indicate the side of a stream and also to indicate an institution for the care of money, is an equivocal term. (c) When, in the same context, we apply a term to two or more things in a different but related meaning, "a meaning partly the same, and partly different," the term is, in that use, an *analogous* term (or an analogical term, or a term used by analogy). Thus the term "healthy" applied to a man and also to his complexion is an analogical term. It means that the man *has* health, and that his color *shows* health. In each use the term refers to health, and this is its sameness; in one use, it means possession of health, and, in the other use, it means manifestation of health, and this is its difference. Now, when we apply to God and also to creatures a name which means a perfection, we use the name or term by analogy. For example we call God wise, and we also speak of wise men. What we mean is that God *is* wisdom as identified with his essence, and that men *have* wisdom as a quality, an accidental not identified with the human essence. Therefore, when in the same context (expressed or understood) a term or name is applied to God and to creatures, commonly, to express perfection, that term is an analogous term.

6. Terms or names which express perfections, such as life, knowledge, wise, good, apply primarily to God, and secondarily to creatures. But in our human use of such terms, they refer primarily to creatures. For our knowledge of perfection, and indeed all our knowledge, begins with knowledge of creatures. We rise from the knowledge of creatural perfections to the knowledge of infinite perfection.

7. Some names of God, such as *Creator, Preserver, Provider,* involve a relation between creatures and God. On the part of creatures, this is a *real* relation, for creatures depend essentially upon God. But God in no way whatever depends on creatures. Hence, on God's part, no reality exists by reason of his relationship with creatures. God's relation to creatures is not a real, but a *logical* relation. If God

did not create, preserve, and provide for creatures, they could not exist at all. But God would be God in complete and infinite perfection even if he never created anything to preserve and provide for; in which case, the names *Creator, Preserver,* and *Provider* would not actually apply to God. Therefore we say that the names or terms which express the relation of God to creatures do not apply to God eternally as indicating his essence, but temporally as expressing the time-marked dependence of creatures on God.

8. The name *God* means the supreme and infinite Being himself, in essence, substance, and nature.

9. Therefore, the name God is not accurately applied to any other being than God himself. It is an incommunicable name.

10. And when, as a fact, this name is used to indicate a creature, it is used by analogy only, inasmuch as creatures have limited perfection which is in God unlimitedly. As applied to an idol, the name God is simply misused.

11. The most perfect name for God is that which He applied to Himself. God said to Moses (Exod. 3:14), "Thus shalt thou say to the children of Israel: HE WHO IS hath sent me to you." The name HE WHO IS expresses the fact that it is God's very essence to exist, and it directly suggests God's infinity and eternity.

12. It has been said untruly that all our names for God are negative, and that we do not make affirmative statements about God. Some names for God are negative in form (such as *infinite* which is really *nonfinite*) but they negate negation, and are positive in meaning. Besides, we have many simply affirmative names for God, and we make true affirmative statements about him. Thus we say that God exists in unity and trinity; that God is all-good, all-knowing, all-wise, all-powerful, etc. We are careful to remember that various affirmative names for God, and various affirmative statements of truth about God, never indicate a division or a plurality of real elements in God, who is one undivided essence, one infinite and absolutely simple substance.

14. GOD'S KNOWLEDGE

1. Knowledge is a perfection. It is a pure or unmixed perfection, for it involves in its concept no necessary limitation. Now, since God is infinitely perfect, all pure perfections exist in him formally or as such, and also eminently as identified with his undivided essence. Therefore in God there is infinite knowledge. More accurately, God *is* infinite knowledge.

2. God knows himself perfectly. This is only saying that God is

himself. For God's knowledge is not something which God has; God's knowledge is what God is.

3. God's knowledge of himself is therefore comprehensive, that is, it perfectly embraces the complete knowability of the thing known. Thus, in our limited and imperfect mode of expression, we say that God knows himself to the infinite extent of his boundless knowability.

4. God's intellect or understanding is another name for God's essence and substance. In God, intellect, object of intellect, intelligible species (that is, the representation by which an intellect is aware of reality), and the operation of understanding, are all identified with the undivided essence and substance of God.

5. God knows all things other than himself, that is, all creatures, actual and possible; for infinite knowledge lacks nothing that can be known. In knowing himself, God knows his infinite power to create, and therefore knows all things creatable. And God knows his own will to create, and therefore knows all creatures that have existed, now exist, or are to exist. Thus in knowing himself, God knows all things other than himself. Our human knowledge is gained by learning; we know things not by knowing ourselves, but by becoming aware of things in themselves. God knows things eternally; man knows things only after the things are there, and are brought into the range of his knowing powers. God's knowledge is creative; man's knowledge is receptive.

6. God knows all things with perfect clarity, distinctness, and in fullest detail, and not in a mere general way. For infinite knowledge is comprehensive; it is identified with God's essence, and therefore is most perfect in all respects.

7. God does not need to reason, that is, to think things out. God does not know things by inferring one from another. Nor does God know things successively, one after another. Since God's knowledge of things is one with his essence, it is necessarily eternal, infinite, complete, comprehensive, and simultaneous.

8. Since God's knowledge of creatures is one with his will to create them (for intellect and will are one in the divine simplicity) this knowledge is truly the cause of creatures. And, since God's knowledge of creatures can be seen as the approval of his will to create, this creative knowledge is called "the knowledge of approbation."

9. God knows all things actual and possible. God beholds in eternal (and hence, present) vision all things that have been, are now, and will be. This is called God's "knowledge of vision." God also knows

all possible things that have never been, are not now, and never will be; this is God's "knowledge of simple intelligence."

10. God knows all things, all being. Therefore God knows all good. And God, by that fact, knows where good is lacking; therefore God knows evil. For evil is the lack or privation of good that should be present.

11. God's knowledge is most perfect because it is one with himself. There is in it no vagueness, no confusion; it is complete to the last detail of knowable reality. God knows all things in their being, their relations actual and possible, their classes, their individuality, their parts or elements. He knows all that things are, and all that they could be, and all that they would be in any circumstances and under any conditions.

12. By his knowledge of vision, God knows all the thoughts of men and angels which will go on unceasingly forever. In this sense, God knows "infinite things."

13. God knows by his knowledge of vision what are called *future contingencies,* that is, things that will exist or will happen in the future, dependently on the action of nonnecessitated causes. For instance, God knows what I shall say or do, or what persons I shall meet, at a given moment a year or ten years hence. These things are contingent (or dependent) upon the humanly unforeseeable action of free wills and upon fortuitous circumstances; they are future things, and they are contingent; hence they are rightly called future contingencies. These things are not merely what may happen; they are what *will* happen. Hence they are knowable as facts, and God knows them by his knowledge of vision.

14. God knows all the essences of things; therefore he knows all that can be truly said about all things. God knows all subjects and predicates that can be brought together in true statements or propositions about things, and he knows the propositions themselves.

15. God's knowledge is invariable or changeless for it is one with his changeless essence. God does not learn, nor need to learn; God does not forget. In God there is neither accession of knowledge, nor loss of knowledge.

16. Knowledge is called *speculative* when it is the awareness of what is so. Knowledge is called *practical* when it is the awareness of what to do. God's knowledge of himself is speculative. God's knowledge of things other than himself is both speculative and practical. God's knowledge of evil is practical inasmuch as God knows how to prevent evil, or to permit it and direct it so that good may come of it.

15. IDEAS IN GOD

1. An idea or concept is the mind's grasp of an essence. It is the understanding of what a definition means. Thus the idea *human being* is the mind's grasp of human being as such. It is the mind's grasp in one act of understanding of an essence that may be found in many individuals, and indeed is found in every man, woman, and child. Thus an idea or concept represents *in universal* an essence that may exist really *in individuals.* The idea or concept is called the species (or, more completely, the expressed intelligible species) in which things are understood. Now, since God perfectly understands all essences, we say that the ideas of all things are in God.

2. Yet the ideas of all things in God are not separate species in him; they do not bring complexity into the absolute simplicity of God. God's knowledge is not manifold in itself, but only in the creatural objects known. In knowing himself, God knows all things knowable, and hence God's essence is the single species in which he knows all things. This is what we must ever keep in mind as we use the imperfect human expression, "In God are the ideas of all things."

3. In so far as the divine ideas are concepts of things that can be created, they are called *exemplars.* In so far as these ideas are concepts of things simply knowable rather than creatable, they are called types or *archetypes.* Thus we say: in God are the exemplar-ideas and archetypal-ideas of all things.

16. TRUTH

1. Truth is the agreement or conformity of reality and the mind's judgment on reality. It is "the equation of thought and thing." Truth resides formally, or as such, in the mind which rightly judges a thing to be what it really is. Thus, formally, truth is truth of thought. There is also what is called truth of things; this is called ontological truth. It consists in the necessary conformity of things with the divine mind. For God knows all things perfectly, and upon this knowledge things depend for existence, and even for possibility of existence.

2. Formal or logical truth is in the mind's true judgment on reality. If the creatural mind judges wrongly, it is in the state of logical falsity or error. Truth is not, strictly speaking, in the ideas or concepts of the mind, but in the judgment by which the mind pronounces on the agreement or disagreement of its ideas and the reality which these ideas represent.

3. A thing is knowable, and can be conceived and pronounced upon by the mind, in so far as it is a thing at all, that is, in so far as it has being. And whatever has being is infallibly known for what it is by the divine mind; hence being and the true are really the same. Between them there exists only a logical distinction, not a real one.

4. In the human mind, being is prior to the true, for man adverts to the fact that a thing is a being before he notices that it stands in necessary conformity with the divine mind, and is therefore necessarily true.

5. As we have seen, God knows all things perfectly in knowing himself. Here we have absolute conformity of knower and object known; indeed, this conformity is identity. Hence we do not merely say that there is truth in the divine mind, or that God *has* truth. We say that God *is* Truth. God is Truth, eternal, absolute, sovereign, infinite, substantially existing as one with the undivided divine nature and substance.

6. All truths are in the divine mind. Many truths can be in creatural minds. Many truths can be in the same mind, and their number can increase as the mind makes more and more true judgments.

7. Truth is eternal in God alone. Man can know things that are eternally true, and these things are said to be true in themselves. But these truths are true in themselves only because God eternally knows them to be true.

8. And truth is changeless only in the changeless God. Creatures know many a changeless truth, but their knowing it is in no way the cause of its changelessness. And creatural knowing is not a changeless achievement. Creatural minds may disregard certainly known truths; human minds may forget truths once known. And there is a kind of change in a mind that learns new facts which make a known truth better known, or which reveal it in wider application.

17. FALSITY

1. There can be no falsity in things, for falsity is in judgment about things. Being and the true are really one. A thing is what it is, and is necessarily known as such by the infinite mind. Thus all things are true with real or ontological truth; there is no such thing as ontological falsity, that is, real falsity, falsity in things. Things, indeed, are often called false, but this is by reason of their use, or of their effect on the creatural mind. If one says, "Sentiment is a false basis for judgment," one is not saying that sentiment is not sentiment; the word false is loosely used in the statement, and means un-

safe or unsound, and not really false at all. And when a person speaks of false teeth or false whiskers, or says that a trunk has a false bottom, he merely means that these things resemble teeth or whiskers or the real bottom of the trunk; this resemblance in the things may lead a careless observer to judge that they are real teeth or whiskers or the real bottom of the trunk. Thus these things (which are what they are, and thus are true in themselves) may easily be the occasion for false judgment, that is for logical falsity, for falsity in a mistaken human mind. Thus the only falsity of what are called false things is falsity in judgment about the things, and not in the things themselves.

2. Is there falsity in our sense-knowledge? Do our senses ever deceive us? No, the senses themselves do not deceive us. Falsity in sensing may come from careless use of the senses, from disease or defect in a sense organ, from using a sense outside its normal and proper range of operation, or from using a sense in a medium or under conditions unsuitable for its functioning. If I glance at a drawing and judge that it is an eight-sided figure, whereas in fact it is nine-sided, I cannot justly say that my eyes have deceived me. The falsity is in my judgment which is made upon careless use of the eyes. Besides, the proper object of the sense of sight is light (that is, light diffused by refraction on a bodily surface, and thus appearing as color) and not the shape of what is seen. Falsity in sensing is always false judgment (of sense or mind) arising from misuse, defect, or unsuitable medium of operation. That is to say, falsity is not in the senses by their nature, but only as something accidental to their activity or use.

3. There can be no falsity in the divine mind, for God is truth, and God is all-knowing. But there can be falsity in human minds; we call such falsity *mistake* or *error*. The mind itself is never deceiving; there is nothing in the nature of the mind to cause false judgment about reality. Falsity of judgment comes from causes accidental to the use of the mind, such as hasty concluding without considering all the evidence; bias or prejudice or indifference which keeps the mind from looking at the evidence, and from other external factors in judging, such as disease or neuroses.

4. Truth and falsity are opposed as contraries, not as contradictories. For falsity is not merely the negation or denial of truth; falsity is the affirming of something in place of truth.

18. THE LIFE OF GOD

1. Things have life when they have the perfection of self-movement. In the world around us, this perfection is manifested by plants, ani-

mals, and human beings. Other bodily things (called, in general, minerals) have not this perfection. Therefore, not all things are alive; some things have life, some lack it.

2. Life is primarily the substantial principle or source of self-movement. Secondarily, it is the operation of self-movement.

3. Plants have vegetal life with the operations of nutrition, growth and development, and reproduction. Animals have vegetal life and also sentient life with is operations of sensing, appetizing, and local movement. Human beings have vegetal and sentient life and also rational life with its operations of understanding and will. Rational life is far superior to the other forms of life. Yet in earthly man, rational life is bound up with bodiliness. Even in angels it seeks a goal outside itself. Pure and perfect rational life is self-sufficient; its movement is not change; it tends to no goal outside itself; its activity is identified with its essence. Such rational life is all-perfect life, absolute life. It is pure perfection. Now, all pure perfection belongs to God eminently. Therefore, God is life.

4. God is life. God is knowledge. In the divine simplicity, the perfections of life and knowledge are one. Hence all things that are in God's knowledge are in God's life, and therefore we have the saying, "All things are life in God."

19. THE WILL OF GOD

1. Where there is intellect there is will. Now, God is absolute intellect. Therefore God is absolute will.

2. God wills (or loves) himself, the infinite goodness. In willing himself, God wills things other than himself to which his infinite goodness freely extends; that is, God wills creatures. Creatures are partakers of the divine goodness; they tend to the infinite good as to their ultimate end or goal.

3. God wills himself of necessity. This is not saying that some force compels God to will or love himself. It is only saying that God is God; for God's will is identified with himself, and he himself is necessary being. God wills creatures freely, and not by necessity; for God has no need of creatures.

4. God's will is the cause of creatures. But nothing is the cause of God's will to create. It is a mistake to say that God's goodness moves God to create, for God's goodness is actually God himself.

5. We seek no cause for God's creating, for God is not subject to the action of causes. Nor does God first set up an end for creatures to attain, and then create means by which creatures may attain their

end. If this were so the end would be a cause (final cause) for the creating of the means. End and means are all willed together in one eternal decree which is itself identified with God's essence.

6. God's will in creatures is unfailingly fulfilled. No creature can thwart it. A free creature can hurt himself, but cannot defeat the will of God. For God wills right order; thus he wills retribution due to responsible free conduct. A saint in heaven and a sinner in hell both fulfill this will.

7. God's will is changeless, for it is actually one with his essence. But a changeless will can changelessly decree changeable things. God's changelessness does not impose limitation on God, nor does it impose necessity on free creatures or on contingently operating causes. God changelessly decrees that free creatures shall exercise free activity, and that contingent causes shall operate contingently.

8. God alone is the primary cause. Creatures are true causes of their activity and its product, but they are all secondary causes. God wills that secondary causes should act according to their nature, some by necessity, some contingently.

9. Evil is the lack or privation of good. Evil is not a thing or essence or nature in itself; it is the hurtful absence of a thing; it is the lack of what should be present. Being is necessarily good, for being and the good are really the same. Evil is, in itself, nonbeing. Hence evil cannot be willed for its own sake; the will chooses being or good. Only when evil is masked with the appearance of good (rather, only when some good is bound up with deficiency, lack, privation of good), can it be chosen or willed. God never wills evil directly. God accidentally wills physical evil (such as pain or hardship) inasmuch as he wills a good with which such hardship is bound up, and which can be attained only by the enduring of such hardship. God never wills moral evil, or sin, in any way whatever, directly or indirectly. Moral evil is against God, and God is not against Himself.

10. As regards creatures, God's will is absolutely free. Freedom is a perfection and God is all-perfect.

11. God's will is made manifest to free creatures by their reason and by revelation. For instance, the Ten Commandments are an expression of God's will which is manifested by revelation; the same Commandments are manifested by reason, for a studious man could think them out.

12. The expression of God's will comes to free creatures in a variety of forms: precept, prohibition, counsel, permission, operation.

20. GOD'S LOVE

1. Where there is will there is love, for love is the fundamental act of will. Since God is will, God is love.

2. God loves all existing things, that is, things that have positive being. For these things exist by God's will, that is, by his love. To love a thing is to will the thing and to will good to it. God wills the existence, essence, and perfections of existing things; hence he loves these things. God's love is not like human love which is attracted to things by the good it finds in them; God's love causes the good in things.

3. God loves some things more than others inasmuch as he confers more perfection on some things than on others. A plant has more perfection than a lifeless body; an animal has more perfection than a plant; a human being has more perfection than an animal. In each case, greater perfection means greater love of God for that reality.

4. God wills or loves the better things more than others inasmuch as these better things have more good from the divine will.

21. THE MERCY AND JUSTICE OF GOD

1. Justice is the virtue which gives to every being all that belongs to it. There is a type of justice called commutative, which is the justice of give-and-take; it is exampled in a trade in which neither party cheats the other. There can be no commutative justice in God, for there is no exchange of goods between him and creatures; all good in creatures comes from God. There is another type of justice, called distributive, which consists in the bestowal of good according to the needs of the receiver. This type of justice is in God "who gives to all existing things whatever is proper to the condition of each one."

2. Sometimes God's justice is called truth inasmuch as it meets the known needs of creatures; for truth belongs to knowing.

3. In bestowing good on creatures, God manifests his goodness. In meeting the needs of creatures, he manifests his justice. In bestowing all that is useful, God manifests his liberality. And in giving what counteracts miseries and defects, God shows his mercy.

4. In all the works of God, justice and mercy are manifest. Justice and mercy are pure perfections; they are in God eminently as identified with his essence. In creating, God removes the misery of nonexistence; this is mercy. In supplying all that his creatures require,

God manifests justice. In making abundant supply of things required, God removes the misery of narrow circumstances; this again is mercy.

22. THE PROVIDENCE OF GOD

1. God, the all-knowing and all-wise, thoroughly understands his creation and directs it with wisest purpose. Creatures are made to tend to God as to their last end, their ultimate goal. God's plan for creatures to attain that purpose is called his providence. God acts to carry out the plan of providence by his divine government.

2. Since all positive being is from God, everything has a place in God's providence. And this in no mere general way, but in particular, in individual, down to the last and least detail of being and activity.

3. In applying his providence, God is the primary cause of government. God uses creatures as means or secondary causes in governing. But providence itself involves no means or medium. Providence itself is in God and of God and one with his essence.

4. Providence disposes that secondary causes should act according to the nature or working essence God gives them: some act by necessity (as a fire necessarily acts to consume dry paper that is cast into it) and some contingently (as a seed, to produce a plant, is contingent or dependent upon sufficient and suitable soil, proper depth, sufficient light, heat, and moisture). And man's free acts are contingent upon man's choice. Providence does not impose necessity upon contingently operating causes, nor does it defeat or hamper the action of man's free will.

23. PREDESTINATION

1. Providence disposing the supernatural means by which a man gets to heaven is called predestination.

2. On a person who is going to get to heaven, predestination sets no mark or character. For predestination is one phase of providence, and providence is in God and not in the things provided for.

3. As long as a free creature has not attained his goal, he may perversely turn aside and fail to attain it. Man in this life is a wayfarer; he is on the road; his journey is not finished. Man, by his own fault, may reject direction, and fail to reach his true goal. And, since man's goal is supernatural, he cannot reach it by his natural powers alone. He requires supernatural aid. Such aid is offered him, but he may refuse it. Now, inasmuch as God's providence permits a person to reject grace and to commit grave sin (and such permission is essential if the wayfarer is to be free), and so to refuse heaven and choose hell, we have what is called reprobation.

4. God loves, chooses, and predestines all who will use his grace and reach heaven. Hence love, election, and predestination are all within the scope of providence.

5. The whole effect of predestination has its cause in God, for all grace comes from him to dispose a man for salvation (that is, getting to heaven) and to support his efforts to attain it.

6. For those predestined, predestination is certain, for providence does not fail. Yet here we must be careful to avoid confused thought. We must not be misled by the "before and after" view which distorts our grasp of God's dealings with his free creatures. We recall that Scripture tells us that God wills all men to be saved; yet this does not negate God's will that men be free. St. John Damascene says, "God does not will evil, nor does He compel virtue." Man must cooperate with the saving will of God if he is to come to heaven. There is nothing mechanical or fatalistic about predestination, nor does it conflict with the exercise of free will.

7. Only God knows the number of those who will reach heaven.

8. Here on earth we cannot know whether we shall be among the elect in heaven. But we can know that we shall get to heaven if we choose to do so and use the grace of God to make our choice effective. St. Peter tells us (II Pet. 1:10), "Strive . . . by good works to make your calling and election sure."

24. THE BOOK OF LIFE

1. The Book of Life is a scriptural metaphor for predestination.

2. The life referred to in the phrase, Book of Life, is primarily the life of glory in heaven.

3. In one sense, however, anyone in the state of grace is in the Book of Life, inasmuch as he has, at the moment, a claim to be inscribed there. And a man who rejects the state of grace by committing mortal sin is, at least temporarily, "blotted from the Book of Life."

25. THE POWER OF GOD

1. Power is an ability for doing. It is, in itself, a pure perfection; therefore it is in God formally, or as such, and eminently, as identified with the divine essence. The passive capacity to be acted upon (called potentiality) is an imperfection, and is not in God at all.

2. The power of God is one with his infinite essence, and is therefore infinite itself. God is infinite power.

3. That is to say, God is omnipotent or almighty. God can do all things. Sometimes it is foolishly asked whether God can do what is

self-contradictory; for instance, it is asked whether God can make a square circle. Now, a contradictory thing is not a thing at all. It is a fiction in which two elements cancel each other and leave nothing. Thus a square circle is a circle that is not a circle; that is to say, it is nothing whatever. To ask whether God can make such a thing is to ask a meaningless question. To say that God cannot make a self-contradictory thing is not to limit God's power, but to declare his truth, for a self-contradictory thing is a self-annihilating lie. Similarly, to say that God cannot deceive is not to limit God's power, but to affirm his veracity.

4. Since there is no self-contradiction in God, and since objective self-contradiction is nothing at all, we see that God cannot make undone what is already done; that is, God cannot make the past not to have been.

5. God does all things with absolute freedom. God might make and do other things than those he actually makes and does. God's wisdom is manifest in all his works, but these works do not limit the divine wisdom itself, nor can their perfection exhaust the inexhaustible power of God. God's purpose in things could be achieved by some other plan and order of creation if God should so choose.

6. God might go on endlessly making better and better things, yet he is under no sort of compulsion to do so, for God is not subject to compulsion. What God makes is always admirably suited for the purpose it is meant to serve, and thus it is as worthy of infinite wisdom and power as a finite thing can be.

26. THE BEATITUDE OF GOD

1. Beatitude, or happiness, or blessedness, is the perfect good of an intellectual nature. It consists in the fact that an intellectual being (that is, being with understanding and free will) knows that it possesses its true good in sufficient measure, and that it is in control of its actions. Now, God is infinitely aware of himself as absolute good, and his perfect will is in absolute control. Hence God is infinitely happy. God is infinite beatitude.

2. In our human way of understanding, we attribute the divine happiness in a special way to the divine intellect. Yet we repeatedly remind ourselves that God's intellect is really God himself, for it is one with the divine essence.

3. Only God is infinitely happy; that is, only God is infinite beatitude. Rational creatures (men and angels) seek God as the object that will fulfill them, and make them perfectly happy: God is their objective happiness. And the possession of God in the beatific

vision constitutes their subjective happiness, that is, the happiness which is in them as its possessors or subjects. Inasmuch as all the blessed in heaven have not all the same degree of charity and its resultant measure of the light of glory, there are in heaven different subjective beatitudes.

4. The infinite beatitude of God perfectly embraces all beatitudes.

THE BLESSED TRINITY

(QUESTIONS 27 TO 43)

27. THE PROCEEDING OF THE DIVINE PERSONS

1. Scripture indicates a proceeding in God. This cannot be a creatural movement, nor an operation involving change. It must be in God and of God. And it must be in the order of intellect and will (that is, the intellective order), for this is the most perfect type of proceeding.

2. There is in God an eternal proceeding, likened to our human knowing, in which God (the Father) eternally begets the Word. The Word is God the Son. This proceeding is generation.

3. There is in God an eternal proceeding, likened to our willing or loving, in which Spirit proceeds from Father and Son. The Spirit is God the Holy Ghost. This proceeding is procession.

4. The two proceedings cannot both be called generation, for one is in the order of knowing, and the other is in the order of willing or loving. Speaking in terms of our creatural human processes, the mind begets reality by knowing; the mind generates the mental word or concept. Hence the divine proceeding which is likened to knowing is rightly called generation. And since, when we know a lovable being that can reciprocate our love, love proceeds from lover and beloved, the second divine proceeding is rightly called procession.

5. Proceedings of the intellective order which are *in* and *of* the agent, are two only: one in the likeness of knowing; one in the likeness of willing. Hence in God there are no other proceedings than generation and procession. There are other relations, as we shall see, but there are no other proceedings.

28. THE DIVINE RELATIONS

1. A relation is the standing of a thing with reference to something other. A relation, or relationship, exists between things that can be in some way referred to one another. If the basis of the relation is in things, the relation is called *real;* if the basis of the relation is in the mind's grasp and comparison of things, the relation is called *logical* or rational. Between sons of the same parents, the relation of brotherhood is a real relation. Between subject and predicate of a sentence, the relation is a logical relation. Now, in God there are real proceedings, and in consequence there are real relations in God.

2. A real relation in God cannot be an accidental, for there are no accidentals in God. As a thing, an entity, a real relation in God is one with the divine essence.

3. Now, a real relation involves contrast inasmuch as really related things must be really distinct from one another. Hence, real relations in God mean that in God there are real distinctions. These real distinctions cannot be in the simple and undivided essence of God. They must be really distinct respects which exist in God by reason of the divine proceedings. (It is to be remembered that distinction does not necessarily mean separation or separability. Things are distinct by a real distinction when they are distinguished one from another as thing and thing, even though they are completely inseparable. Thus, for example, the whiteness and the coldness of snow are really distinct from each other, and each is really distinct from the substance of the snow, although there is no separating these things.) The real respects in God which come from the divine proceedings are real relations and imply real distinction in their terminals (that is, in the divine Persons), but there is neither separation nor separability in God; the divine Persons are one in essence, nature, and substance; they are one and the same undivided God, eternally existing in absolute simplicity and unity of being.

4. There are four real relations in God: (a) The relation of the Father to the Son. This is paternity or fatherhood. (b) The relation of the Son to the Father. This is filiation or sonship. (c) The relation consequent upon the proceeding in which Father and Son are the principle whence proceeds the Holy Ghost. This is the spiration or breathing forth of the Holy Ghost. (d) The relation consequent upon the same proceeding as considered from the standpoint of the Person spirated. This is the procession of the Holy Ghost. These real relations in their essence and being as entities or things are one with the

simple and undivided divine essence; yet they are real relations and hence are really distinct in their terminals (that is, in the realities related), which are the three divine Persons.

29. THE DIVINE PERSONS

1. A person is a complete substance of the rational order.

2. A person is a substance, not an accidental. A person is a complete and subsistent substance, not a mere member or part of a greater substance. A person is of the rational order, or has a rational nature, that is, a person has (at least fundamentally) understanding and free will.

3. The name *person* indicates what is most perfect in nature. Hence it is a name rightly applied to God who is all-perfect. But in applying the term to God we exclude from its meaning all that is limited and imperfect in our concept of a creatural person.

4. Applied to God, the name *person* means a divine relation as subsisting, that is, as perfectly existing in the order of infinite substance. What actually subsists is, as we have said, the divine nature and essence itself. And this subsistence is actual in the terminals of the divine relations (that is, in the three Persons) without being merely shared among them. The undivided nature of God subsists perfectly in each of the three Persons, so that, while they are really distinct Persons, they are one and the same God.

30. PLURALITY OF PERSONS IN GOD

1. A divine Person is a real divine relation as subsisting in the divine nature or essence. Since there are several real relations in God, there are several Persons in God.

2. There are, in fact, three and only three Persons in God. The four real relations (paternity, filiation, relation consequent on spiration, relation consequent on procession) involve not four, but three, relatively opposed or contrasted terminals. These three are the Father, the Son, and the Holy Ghost.

3. When we call God "One," we indicate the undivided divine essence or nature. When we call the Persons "Three," we mean that each is really distinct from the others *as a Person,* but not *as God.*

4. The meaning of the term *person* is common to the three Persons in God. Whether applied to Father, Son, or Holy Ghost, the term *person* means a really distinct divine relation, in which subsists one and the same undivided divine nature or essence.

31. TERMS FOR UNITY AND PLURALITY IN GOD

1. The name *Trinity* as applied to God means the determinate number of three Persons in one and the same undivided God.

2. We rightly use the term *distinction* when we speak of the Persons of the Trinity. But we avoid the vagueness or the plain error of the terms *diversity* and *difference;* these words appear to suggest a cleavage in the undivided divine essence. We may, however, use the term *other* when we contrast the divine Persons, for this word stresses the distinction of Persons without implying a difference of essence or nature. Hence we may say, "The Son is other than the Father."

3. The terms *alone* and *only* are properly applied to God's name when we speak of God in comparison with creatures. Thus we say, "God alone is eternal," and "Only God is infinite." But we do not use the words *alone* and *only* in such a way as to suggest that God is solitary or lonely; such use would be an implied denial of the Trinity of Persons in God. Therefore, it is misleading to say, "Before there were creatures, God was alone."

4. The terms *alone* and *only* may be added to the name of one Person of the Trinity as distinct from the others when what is expressed is proper to that one Person. These words *alone* and *only* are not to be added to the name of any one divine Person if such expression would or could suggest the excluding of the other Persons from what is attributable to God in unity. Thus we may say, "The Son alone is begotten or generated." But we cannot rightly say, "The Holy Ghost alone gives us grace."

32. OUR KNOWLEDGE OF THE DIVINE PERSONS

1. We cannot come to the knowledge of the Trinity by reason alone, that is, by the natural and unaided efforts of the human mind. By our natural reason, we can know that God exists; that he is the First Cause of all; that he is one, infinite, simple, immutable, etc. But that the one God subsists in three really distinct Persons is a truth that can be known only by supernatural means. This is a truth beyond the reach of human reason to know, to prove, or to disprove. We know this truth by divine revelation, and accept it by supernatural faith; we take it upon the authority of God himself.

2. Once we know the truth, we naturally tend to discuss it. In our discussion we use such terms as we have, knowing that these are imperfect and inadequate. Some scholars think that we ought not name properties of the divine Persons, using abstract words. But this

is a mistaken view. We cannot discuss the divine Persons in concrete terms alone. And we are thoroughly justified in using abstract words, and, by their use, ascribing properties to the divine Persons, provided that we use terms that are neither mistaken nor misleading.

3. Five notable abstract terms are used with reference to the divine Persons: (a) *innascibility,* or unbegottenness, is proper to the First Person; (b) *paternity* is also proper to the Father; (c) *filiation* is proper to God the Son; (d) *spiration* is not proper to any one Person, but is common to the Father and the Son; (e) *procession* is proper to the Holy Ghost.

4. Disagreement about terms used with reference to God's unity and trinity may arise among scholars without involving any heresy, provided the Church has not spoken on the precise points at issue, and also provided that the terms employed are not plainly misleading or erroneous.

33. THE PERSON OF GOD THE FATHER

1. A principle is that from which anything takes its rise in any way whatever, or from which anything proceeds in any manner. A principle is not necessarily a cause; a cause is only one type of principle. The divine proceedings involve, in first instance, the Father begetting (but not causing) the Son. Hence the term *principle* is rightly applied to God the Father.

2. A name proper to the First Person of the Trinity is that which divine paternity (which is proper to the First Person) implies. This is the name *Father.*

3. The name Father is truly a personal name, that is, it applies to a divine person rather than to the divine essence in unity. But we often use the name Father as an essential name of God and not a personal name. When we say, for instance, "God is the Father of us all," we are not speaking of the First Person of the Trinity, but of the three Persons in undivided Godhead. Thus Father, strictly speaking, is a distinctive personal title of the First Person; less strictly, Father is one of our ordinary names for God in unity.

4. In the divine proceedings the Father is the principle whence proceeds the Son (by eternal begetting or generation); the Father and the Son together are the one principle whence proceeds the Holy Ghost (by spiration and procession). The Father himself does not proceed from any principle. It is the distinctive property of the Father to be unbegotten. This is the Father's innascibility.

34. THE PERSON OF GOD THE SON

1. The name *Son* is manifestly a personal name in God, not an essential name; that is, it refers to one of the three Persons, and not simply to God in unity. The name *Word* is also a personal name in God.

2. The name *Son* and the name *Word* are proper to the Second Person of the Trinity. The eternal generation or begetting of the Son is likened to the process by which the human intellect generates the concept or mental word. Hence the Word of God is the Person begotten by the Father. It is a personal name for God the Son.

3. God, in knowing himself by one eternal act of the divine intellect, that is, "by his only Word," knows his own essence, his operations, and all things. Hence he knows all creatures. And thus the name *Word* in God implies a relation with creatures.

35. THE SON AS IMAGE OF THE FATHER

1. The name *image* in God implies a relation, for an image refers to what is imaged. And this relation includes a contrast or relative opposition between image and thing imaged. Now, such a relation in God must be subsistent; that is, it must be a person. Hence, the name *image* in God refers to one of the three divine Persons. It is a personal, not an essential name.

2. The Person to whom the name image is proper is God the Son. Scripture (Col. 1:15) calls the Son, "the image of the invisible God," and (Heb. 1:3) "the figure of God's substance." Thus the Son is the image of the Father. We notice that while man is made *to* or *in* the image of God, the Son *is* the image of the Father. The image of a ruler is impressed on the coins of his country; his image is also found in his living child. This illustrates very imperfectly the difference between the image of God in man and the image of the Father in God the Son.

36. THE PERSON OF GOD THE HOLY GHOST

1. The Third Person of the Blessed Trinity is the *Holy Ghost* or the *Holy Spirit*. These two names mean the same thing. They are names proper to the Third Person; thus they are personal names, not essential names. Since the Holy Ghost proceeds from the Father and the Son as from a common principle, it is fitting that his name should be something that is common to Father and Son. St. Augustine says (*De Trin.* xv 17), "The Father is a spirit; the Son is a spirit. The Father is holy; the Son is holy." Therefore, Holy Spirit or Holy

Ghost is a name suitably applied to the Third Person of the Trinity.

2. The Holy Ghost proceeds from the Father and the Son, not from the Father alone. If the Holy Ghost were not from the Father and Son, there would be no relative opposition in the relation of Son and Holy Ghost, and these two would really be only one Person. Now, this is in conflict with the truth of the Trinity. Hence it is certain that the Holy Ghost proceeds from the Father *and* the Son.

3. The Son, eternally begotten of the Father, constitutes with the Father the principle whence proceeds the Holy Ghost. It is therefore permissible to say that the Holy Ghost proceeds from the Father through the Son.

4. The Father and the Son are one principle whence proceeds the Holy Ghost. The divine Persons are one in everything that is not relatively opposite (i.e., consisting in contrasted real relation). Now, in spirating the Holy Ghost, the Father and the Son act together as one and not as relatively opposed. Therefore Father and Son are one principle from which the Holy Ghost proceeds.

37. "LOVE" AS THE NAME OF THE HOLY GHOST

1. Although *love* is an essential name of God, as we have seen, the term is also used specifically as a personal name in God; as such it is proper to the Third Person of the Trinity. The Holy Ghost is love.

2. The Father and the Son love each other by the Holy Ghost, not, however, as though the Holy Ghost were the principle of this love; for God is love by His essence, and not by a Person.

38. "GIFT" AS THE NAME OF THE HOLY GHOST

1. The name *gift* in God is a personal name. A rational creature (man or angel) can possess God by or through a Person of the Trinity who is thus *given* to the creature.

2. This name *gift* in God is proper to the Third Person of the Trinity. A gift is the fruit of love. Love itself which dictates the giving is the first gift. Hence, as the Holy Ghost has the proper name of *love*, He is also properly called *gift*. St. Augustine (*De Trin.* vx) says, "By the gift which is the Holy Ghost, many particular gifts are bestowed on the members of Christ."

39. PERSONS AND ESSENCE IN GOD

1. Because God is absolutely simple in his being, the divine relations, as things or entities, are identified with God's essence. Essence in God is not really distinct from Person, and still the three Persons are really distinct from one another. They are real relations in God

which involve relative opposition in their terminals (the Persons) but none at all in their essence.

2. Therefore the three Persons in God, while really distinct from one another, are one and the same undivided and indivisible divine essence.

3. Hence when we use nouns or noun-expressions for the divine essence, we use them in the singular. We do not say, "Father, Son, and Holy Ghost are *Gods*"; we say, "Father, Son, and the Holy Ghost are *God*." Sometimes we may use adjective-expressions in the plural, for these often refer to the divine essence, not directly in itself, but as subsisting in the distinct Persons. Thus we may say that there are three eternal beings. But if the noun *beings* is stressed, rather than the adjective *eternal,* we should not use the expression, for it might be misunderstood as declaring the essence of God to be threefold, which is not the case.

4. Concrete names for the divine essence may sometimes be understood in a personal sense; whether such names are essential or personal depends on our use of them. Even the noun God can be used as a personal name: we may use it to indicate the Father only, as when we say, "God begets"; we may use it to indicate Father and Son, as when we say, "God spirates"; we may use it—and this is our ordinary use of the name—for the Trinity, as when we say, "God creates."

5. Abstract names for the divine essence cannot thus be used as personal names. While we can say, "God begets God," we cannot say, "Essence begets essence."

6. And names for the Persons may be applied to the divine essence, since, in entity or being, the Persons and divine essence are one and the same. Thus we may say, "The divine essence is the Father and the Son and the Holy Ghost"; or "The divine essence is the three Persons"; or "God is the three Persons."

7. Attributes of the divine essence (power, wisdom, knowledge, etc.) are sometimes *appropriated* to the Persons of the Trinity. Thus it is customary to appropriate power to the Father, wisdom to the Son, and goodness to the Holy Ghost. Or we may say that the Father creates, the Son redeems, and the Holy Ghost sanctifies. Yet all that God does proceeds from the undivided will of the undivided Trinity.

8. Such appropriation is justified inasmuch as it helps us better to understand and explain our faith. We derive all our knowledge from creatures, and thus we are led to consider God himself as we consider creatures, and to parcel out the divine attributes. We need constantly to remind ourselves, however, that these helpful appropriations

of essential divine attributes to distinct divine Persons are conveniences for us, and not accurate expressions of objective truth.

40. DIVINE RELATIONS AND DIVINE PERSONS

1. Boethius says that in God *what* is and *whereby* it is are the same. The Father is the Father by the divine relation of paternity; the *what* is the Father; the *whereby* is the relation of paternity; these are the same. In God, the subsistent real relations are the same as the Persons. Even the relation consequent upon spiration is identified with the Father and with the Son without involving the identity of these two divine Persons as persons.

2. But, though the divine relations are the same as the divine Persons, in our human way of understanding we distinguish the Persons one from another by the divine relations. It is the very notion of paternity in contrast with filiation that makes us aware of the distinct Persons of Father and Son.

3. We cannot think of Father except as one generating or begetting, nor of Son except as one generated or begotten. Therefore we cannot remove the divine relations from our idea or concept of the divine Persons without removing the Persons themselves and thus nullifying our idea of the Trinity.

4. It has been said that, in our human way of understanding, the thought of generating precedes the thought of paternity; that is, in technical words, "notional acts precede the relations." Generating as a "notional act" is our mental grasp of an operation; paternity is a relation. The saying, "notional acts precede relations," means that our grasp of the operation carries us on to the grasp of the operator. But this saying is not correct. It is not true that "generating precedes paternity in the order of human understanding." On the contrary, the human mind is aware of a person acting before it is aware of his action; or rather, the operator is there before we are aware of his operation. Hence, the Persons (that is, the subsistent relations which are the same as the Persons) precede the "notional acts" by which we conceive of the Persons as acting. Thus, the relation of paternity (which is the Father) precedes our notional act of generating. We reverse the saying that "notional acts precede the relations," and say, "the relations precede the notional acts."

41. OUR NOTIONS OF THE DIVINE PERSONS AS OPERATING

1. Our concepts or ideas of the divine operations of generating and spirating (that is our "notional acts") ascribe these operations to the

divine Persons. Only by thus ascribing "notional acts" to the proper Persons can we grasp and designate the distinction of Persons in the Trinity.

2. The divine operations are not in God by free choice but by the necessity of the divine nature itself. Just as God is necessary being, in the sense that he cannot be nonexistent, not by reason of any outside force, but by reason of his infinite excellence, so generating and spirating are in God by the necessity involved in the supreme excellence of the divine nature itself.

3. The divine operations do not proceed from nothing, as is the case in the external action of creating. The Son is generated, not from nothing, but from the Father.

4. The divine operations of generating and spirating are from God's almighty power, not, indeed from that power as creative, for the operations and relations are eternal and uncreated; they are from God's power as the principle of divine proceeding.

5. God's power to beget and his will to beget are one with his eternal essence. Hence the power of God means essence and not relation.

6. There is only one eternal generating in God and one spirating. There is only one Father, only one Son, only one Holy Ghost.

42. THE EQUALITY OF THE DIVINE PERSONS

1. The divine persons are coeternal and coequal, for they are, in undivided essence, one and the same God.

2. That the divine Persons are coeternal means that "whensoever the Father exists, the Son exists, and the Holy Ghost exists." There is no time in God, no succession of before-and-after. The eternal proceedings in God are one with his timeless essence and exist always in his changeless nature.

3. The standing or order of the Persons, as First, Second, Third, is not an order of priority, as though one Person should be in any way more excellent than another. It is an order of nature. Sometimes it is called an order of origin, taking the word origin in the sense of principle, not in the sense of a start or beginning, for there are no beginnings of the eternal Persons.

4. The Son is the Father's equal in greatness, as is the Holy Ghost. For greatness is a perfection of nature, and the divine nature is one and undivided in the three Persons.

5. By reason of the undivided divine essence, each Person is in each other Person of the Trinity. Our Lord says (John 14:10), "I am in the Father, and the Father is in me."

6. The divine Persons are equal in power, for power, like greatness,

is a perfection consequent upon nature, and the divine nature is one and the same in the three divine Persons.

43. THE "MISSION" OR "SENDING" OF THE DIVINE PERSONS

1. Our Lord says (John 8:16), that the Father *sent* him. God the Son is sent into the world. This sending or mission of a divine Person is not something done by command or even advice; this would seem to imply inferiority in the Person sent, and the divine Persons are coequal. For a divine Person to be sent means to begin to exist in a new way in the world or in the souls of human beings. God the Son is everywhere eternally; but when he became man, he began to be in the world in a new way, that is, as man. This is what is meant by his being sent.

2. If we should take the word *mission* to include the divine proceedings of generation and spiration, then the mission or sending of divine Persons is something eternal. But if we limit the word, as we usually do, to signify the coming of the Son into the world, and the coming of the Holy Ghost into men's souls by grace, then mission or sending means something temporal.

3. It is suitable that a divine Person should be sent, as newly existing in a rational creature. This sending is always by way of sanctifying grace.

4. The Person of God the Father is not sent. Sending or mission is *from* another, and the Father is not from another. The Son is *from* the Father, and the Holy Ghost is *from* the Father and the Son. Hence only the Son and the Holy Ghost are sent.

5. Thus it belongs to the Son and to the Holy Ghost to be sent to dwell in us by grace. The Father is in us too, but not *as sent*.

6. The invisible mission or sending of a divine Person by grace into men's souls is a fact in all who are in the state of grace and who are renewed or increased in grace.

7. The Holy Ghost came visibly on our Lord at His baptism by John; He also came visibly in the form of tongues of fire on Pentecost Day. And the Son came visibly when He was born of Mary. These visible missions or sendings are of greatest benefit, for man needs visible manifestations to help him understand invisible truths. Mission or sending of a divine Person is for man's sanctification. The Son is sent visibly as the author of sanctification; the Holy Ghost is sent visibly as the sign of sanctification.

8. When the Person sending is designated as the principle of the

Person sent, then the Son is sent by the Father only, and the Holy Ghost is sent by the Father and the Son only. But when the sender is considered as the principle, not of the Person sent, but of the effect of the mission, then the sender is the Trinity itself.

CREATION

(QUESTIONS 44 to 49)

44. GOD AS FIRST CAUSE OF ALL THINGS

1. Every actual reality, every existing thing, has its being either by necessity (and hence is necessary being, that is, God) or by participation, that is, by having its being given, imparted, or shared unto it. And that which has its being by participation must come, ultimately, from that which has its being by necessity. In other words, all creatures have their being, in ultimate analysis, from a direct act of God. God imparts or shares out being to creatures. God does not share or divide himself, for he is infinite and indivisible. God gives being directly by the act of creating. To create is to produce a thing in entirety out of nothing. All creatures have their first origin in creation.

2. Bodies are made up of two substantial elements, *primal matter* and *substantial form*. Primal matter has no proper existence of its own, but exists only in existing bodies; it cannot exist separately by itself, but only as *in*-formed by the substantial principle which makes a body an existing body of an essential kind; this constituting substantial principle is called substantial form. Primal matter is the common substrate of all existing bodies; it is that by which a body is bodily. Primal matter, though in all kinds of bodies and in each of every kind, has nothing *in itself* by which body is distinguished from body; for all bodies (mineral, vegetal, animal, human) are equally bodily things. Substantial form gives a body its existence in a specific or essential kind. Primal matter is the most imperfect of things, and yet it is a thing, it is a being, and, like all creatural things, it has being by participation. Hence primal matter has its first beginning in the act of God's creation. Primal matter is created by God. In creating bodies God creates their primal matter.

3. Things are of definite kinds; they are constituted according to some plan, model, or exemplar. As we have seen, all the exemplar ideas of creatable things are in God. Thus (since God's ideas or knowledge is identified with the divine essence) God himself is the exemplar of all things that have being by participation.

4. In creating things God does not act to acquire anything, for he is infinite and needs nothing, nor can he be in any way increased or made more excellent by acquiring anything. God creates to communicate his goodness. And creatures are made to manifest or acquire perfection in the likeness of God's goodness. Therefore the goodness of God is both the first effecting cause of things and the ultimate final cause (the end or goal) for which things are created.

45. HOW THINGS COME FROM GOD

1. The first beginning of things must be by total production out of nothing. All things, in final analysis, are created.

2. Things are coming into existence all the time; some, such as living things, come as the product of natural forces; some come as the products of man's activity and skill, that is, as products of art. But nature and art must have something to work upon; neither can give a completely first beginning. A living thing has something of itself, in germ or seed, derived from parent beings; nature develops this into the new living body. And a thing made by art (that is an artificial, as contrasted with a natural thing) is made of materials; thus a house is made of building materials; such materials are called the subject out of which the artificial thing is made. Thus nature and art require, for producing a new thing, either something of the thing itself, or some subject out of which the thing is to be made. But *first* beginning is absolute beginning; nothing of the thing to be produced exists; there is nothing either of itself or of a subject. Such first beginning is creation, which is defined as the producing of a thing out of nothing.

3. Creation, in God, is an act of infinite power. Creation, in the thing created, is a real relation to the Creator as the principle of creatural being.

4. God creates substances, and with them their accidentals. When God created the first man, Adam had a definite size, weight, shape, color, and so forth. These accidentals are said to have *in-being* rather than being, and they are cocreated with the substance in which they inhere. This explains their first beginning. Accidentals change according to what substances do or undergo, but their first origin must be in their *coming along with* the substance created.

5. Only absolute power can create; only the universal cause can produce the universal effect of being. Only infinite perfection can summon reality out of nothingness. Hence, only God can create. A creature cannot even serve as an instrument or ministering cause in the act of creating; for there is nothing, either of the creature to be produced or of any subject, upon which an instrument could be employed; there is nothing that a ministering cause could arrange or prepare or have at hand. Thus creation is an act proper to God alone.

6. Creation is not, strictly speaking, proper to any one Person of the Trinity; it is proper to the Trinity itself. Yet we may say that the creative act proceeds from the Father through his Word and through his Love, that is, from the Father through the Son and the Holy Ghost.

7. It is true that every maker leaves some sort of image of himself in what he makes, and in creatures there is a trace of the Trinity. In rational creatures (men and angels) there is the subsisting principle, the word of understanding, and the act of love proceeding from the will. In nonrational creatures as well as in rational creatures, there is that which exists, its kind by which it is distinct from other things, and its relationship to other things that sets and fits it in its order and place in the created world. Hence in every creature there is a trace, however imperfect and faint, of the Trinity.

8. Nature and art produce effects by using existing things. Creation is not mingled with nature and art, but is presupposed to them and to their activity. Creation gives *first* beginnings.

46. THE BEGINNING OF CREATURES

1. Only God is necessarily eternal. Now, absolutely speaking, God could create from eternity, so that creatures should exist without a beginning. But God does not need to create from eternity, nor, for that matter, does God need to create at all. And in creatures we discover no reason for supposing that God has created from eternity.

2. By revelation (Gen. 1:1) we know that God's eternal will and decree to create are a will and decree to create in time. For, "*In the beginning,* God created heaven and earth. . . .*" But apart from revelation and our faith, we cannot prove that the world did not always exist; that is, that God did not create from eternity. But we can prove that even a beginningless world is a created world, a caused world. For eternal matter, if it existed, would not be causeless matter; it would still have being by participation and not by necessity.

3. God created in the beginning of time. Time itself came into existence with the creation of things.

41

47. THE DISTINCTION OF THINGS

1. It is not true that God created the bodily world as a mass of matter which somehow has worked itself out into the many individual things and kinds of things which we find about us. Both distinction of things and multitude of things come from God. In creating, God communicates his goodness; creatures are to represent and manifest the divine goodness. And goodness, which in God is simple, in creatures is diversified; what phase of the divine goodness one creature fails to represent, may be represented by another. The whole multiple and varied universe manifests the divine goodness more perfectly than any single creature could do.

2. The variety of things in the created universe involves inequality in things. Mineral bodies, plant bodies, animal bodies, human bodies, are not on a level except in bodiliness. There is an arrangement in them, a series of degrees of excellence or perfection. The universe would not be so perfect if only one grade of being or goodness were found in creatures. Hence the inequality of things is from the Creator.

3. The world of creatures shows a marvelous unity and order. It is one world. A number of worlds, separate and wholly unrelated, would not be such a manifest work of divine Wisdom as one world, multiple and various, yet beautifully harmonious.

48. THE DISTINCTION OF GOOD AND EVIL

1. One opposite is known through the other, as, for instance, darkness is known through light. Evil is known through goodness, for evil is the privation of good. Evil is not a thing, an essence, a nature in itself; it exists by way of defect or failure in natures. Being as such is good; it is where being breaks off, or fails to be, that evil appears.

2. Evil is found in things in the world, just as inequality is found there. Inequality means that more perfect things should not lose their existence and less perfect things should lose their existence, and loss of existence is an evil. In a world in which there are things that can be broken up and changed and things that can die, it is manifest that there is evil.

3. The *subject* of evil is the thing in which evil exists. Now, evil is found in things, and things as such are good. Hence, the subject of evil is good. Not every absence of good is an evil, but only the absence of that good which the perfection of a thing demands. Thus the absence of life is not an evil in a stone, for the nature of a stone does not require life; absence of life is an evil for plant, animal, or man. Thus also blindness, or absence of the power to see, is an evil for a man,

but not for a plant. In a word, evil is an absence which deprives the thing in which it exists (its subject) of a perfection that *ought* to be there; evil is a *privation* of good. And its subject is good.

4. Evil which is failure, defect, or absence in the structure or processes of a thing, is called *physical* evil. Hunger, death, blindness, are examples of physical evil, as are lameness, deformity, injured members. Evil which is defect and failure of a free will to measure up to the standard of what its conduct should be, is *moral* evil; moral evil is sin and such imperfection as approximates to sin. Evil destroys good in the precise point in which it negates good, or deprives the subject of good, but otherwise it does not destroy good. The evil of sickness destroys health, but not the possibility of recovery by medical cure or by miracle. Mortal sin destroys the spiritual good of the soul, but does not destroy the aptitude of the soul for regaining grace.

5. In human experience evil takes the form of pain or fault. Evil is something that hampers and hurts, or it is a defection of the will by sin.

6. Man's greatest natural good is found in the proper use of his free will. Failure here is fault. Fault is failure in the greatest good; therefore, fault has more of the nature of evil than has pain or penalty.

49. THE CAUSE OF EVIL

1. Only good can be a cause, for only good has the positive being which is necessary in a cause. Therefore, the cause of evil is good; not, indeed, by the essence of natural bent of good, but accidentally. When a cause of itself tends to produce an effect, it is called the direct or the *per se* cause of that effect. And when a cause, acting *per se* to produce its effect, incidentally (or, in the old term, accidentally) produces another effect, this other effect is produced *per accidens* or accidentally, and the cause is called the *per accidens* or accidental cause of that effect. Thus a cow cropping grass is acting *per se* to nourish its own life; incidentally or *per accidens* it destroys the grass. Even sin is the defect, rather than the effect, of free will, which is good in itself, and which acts for apparent good even in sinning. The sinner is like a hungry person who bites into a piece of wax fruit; what he is after is good, but he fails to find the good he is after. Un like the man who bites wax fruit, the sinner is not merely the victim of a mistake, for the sinner knows better, if only he would consider; the sinner's judgment is perverse, and hence he is guilty of fault. But the point is that what he wants *per se* is good; he causes evil *per accidens* in his quest for good. Evil, therefore, has no direct or *per se*

cause, but only an accidental cause, a cause *per accidens.* And it is good which, acting *per accidens,* is the cause of evil.

2. In willing the order of the universe, God wills the existence of some things that endure and of other things that pass away. The evil of passing away, of losing existence, is accidental to the order of the universe, which is good. Thus God wills physical evils *per accidens* inasmuch as these are incidental to the working of good. But God wills no evil *per se.* And God does not will moral evil either *per se* or *per accidens.*

3. There is no supreme evil principle which is the source of all evil things. The old oriental doctrine of two supreme principles, one good and the other evil, is absurd. For first of all, there cannot be more than one supreme being. Secondly, as we have seen, the subject of evil is good; we have also seen that the cause of evil is good in itself and only accidentally the producer of evil. Besides, as Aristotle says, if there were a supreme evil, it would destroy itself, for, having destroyed all good (which it must do to be supreme evil), it would have destroyed all being, including its own being.

THE ANGELS

(QUESTIONS 50 TO 64)

50. THE SUBSTANCE OF THE ANGELS

1. Creatures exist in a series of grades. They participate and represent the goodness of God in various ways. In the world about us, there are three kinds of substances: mineral, vegetal, animal. These are all bodily substances. We find also in this world the human substance which is mineral, vegetal, and animal, and yet is something more; it is not *all* bodily; man has a spiritual soul. To round out the order of things, there must be some purely spiritual or nonbodily substances. Thus created substances are: the completely bodily substance, the substance that is a compound of body and spirit, and the completely spiritual substance. Completely spiritual substances are called angels.

2. A bodily substance is composed of two substantial elements, primal matter and substantial form. In angels there is no compounding

of matter and form. Matter does not exist in angels; they are pure substantial forms. That is to say, they are pure spirits; they are spirits with no admixture of matter in them.

3. Holy Scripture (Dan. 7:10) indicates the existence of a vast multitude of angels: "Thousands of thousands ministered to Him, and ten thousand times a hundred thousand stood before Him." Indeed, since the intention back of creation is the perfection of the universe as sharing and representing the divine goodness, it appears that the more perfect creatures should abound in largest multitude. It is, therefore, reasonable to suppose that angels exist in a multitude far exceeding the number of material things.

4. In bodily substances we distinguish their species or essential kind, and their status as individuals of that kind. For example, we distinguish in a man, (a) what makes him a human being, and (b) what make him this one human being. Now, that which constitutes a thing in its species or essential kind is called the principle of *specification*. And that which constitutes a thing as this one item or instance of its kind is called the principle of *individuation*. In all creatures, the principle of specification is the substantial form which makes the creature an existing thing of its essential kind. And the principle of individuation is matter or bodiliness inasmuch as it is marked by quantity. Since angels have in them no matter or bodiliness at all, for they are pure spirits, they are not individuated. This means that each angel is the only one of its kind. It means that *each angel is a species* or essential kind of substantial being. Hence each angel is essentially different from every other angel.

5. The angels are *incorruptible* substances. This means that they cannot die, decay, break up, or be substantially changed. For the root of corruptibility in a substance is matter, and in the angels there is no matter.

51. ANGELS AND BODIES

1. Angels have no bodies. An intellectual nature (that is, a substantial essence equipped for understanding and willing) does not require a body. In man, because the body is substantially united with the spiritual soul, intellectual activities (understanding and willing) presuppose the body and its senses. But an intellect in itself, or as such, requires nothing bodily for its activity. The angels are pure spirits without a body, and their intellectual operations of understanding and willing depend in no way at all upon material substance.

2. That the angels sometimes assume bodies is known from Holy Scripture. Angels appeared in bodily form to Abraham and his house-

hold; the angel Raphael came in the guise of a young man to be the companion of the younger Tobias.

3. In bodies thus assumed, angels do not actually exercise the functions of true bodily life. When an angel in human form walks and talks, he exercises angelic power and uses the bodily organs as instruments. But he does not make the body live, or make it his own body.

52. ANGELS AND PLACE

1. A body is naturally in a place according to its dimensions, that is, according to its measurable bodily quantity. A body is said to be in a place *circumscriptively*. But an angel has no bodily quantity or dimensions. Hence an angel is not in a place in the same way as a body is in a place. Still, an angel can be in a place, not as contained by the place, but rather, in a way, as containing the place. We might make a comparison (very distant and very imperfect) between angelic presence and the bodily presence of daylight in a room. The daylight is not contained by the room; we cannot suddenly close and shutter the room and imprison the daylight. It is more accurate to say that the room is in daylight than that daylight is in the room.

2. To be in a place means different things according to what is placed. God is in a place because He is everywhere. A body is in a place by its quantity or dimensions. An angel is in a place in so far as it exercises its powers there and not elsewhere. God is present *ubiquitously;* a body is located *circumscriptively;* an angel is in a place *definitively*. An angel cannot be in several places at once, since, as we have seen, definitive presence means presence here and not elsewhere.

3. Nor can more than one angel be in the same place at once. This is not because of the size of the place, for an angel is spiritual and has no size; size is a matter of quantity, and quantity is a property of bodies. An angel is the complete cause of the effect exercised in its place, and there cannot be more than one complete cause of the same effect. Just as it is impossible for more than one soul to be in the same human body, so it is impossible for more than one angel to be in the same place.

53. ANGELS AND LOCAL MOVEMENT

1. Since an angel can be in a place (by definitive presence), it can be first in this place and afterwards in that place. That is to say, an angel can move locally. But this local movement of an angel is not like the local movement of a body. An angel is in a place by exercising its powers there; it can cease to apply its powers there and begin to

apply them elsewhere; and this, equivalently at least, is a kind of local movement.

2. By this sort of local movement an angel may, at will, be present successively in several places and thus may be said to pass through the space between the first and the last place of the series. Or an angel may cease to apply its powers in the first place and begin to apply them in the last, not passing through the space between.

3. Since there is succession, that is, before-and-after, in the application of an angel's powers, now here and now there, it must be said that an angel's local movement occurs in time, and is not instantaneous. This time, however, is not measurable in our minutes or seconds; these units of time are applicable only to bodily movement.

54. THE KNOWLEDGE OF THE ANGELS

1. The act of an angel's understanding or intellect is not to be identified with the very substance of the angel. Only in God is operation one with the substance of the operator. An angel is a creature. Therefore, in an angel, to understand is not the same as to subsist.

2. Nor is an angel's operation of understanding the same as the angel's existence. It is in God alone that operation and existence are identified.

3. Nor is the angel's intellect the same as the angel's essence. The intellect as a faculty or power, and the exercise or operation of that power, are things which the angel *has,* not things which constitute the angel and make it what it is. In a creature, power, or the operation of power, is *not* identified with the creature's essence.

4. In the human intellect or understanding there is an active and a passive power: the active intellect (*intellectus agens*) works on sense-findings and renders them understandable; the passive intellect (*intellectus possibilis*) receives the understandable objects and expresses them within itself as ideas or concepts or expressed intelligible species. Now, an angel does not need to work out its knowledge in this way. It has its knowledge from God; its knowledge comes to it with its nature, that is, with its essence equipped for proper operation. An angel has no need to work out intellectual knowledge from sense-findings, an angel has no senses. An angel's intellect is not distinguished as an active and a passive faculty. An angel's knowledge is not acquired by effort of the knower; an angel's knowledge is imparted to it by its Creator at its creation.

5. An angel is a spirit, and hence has no sense-knowledge; it has only intellectual knowledge. But, an angel can have intellectual

knowledge of the material things which human beings know by use of the senses.

55. THE MEDIUM OF ANGELIC KNOWLEDGE

1. God gives the angels their knowledge of things when he brings them into existence. This knowledge is creatural knowledge, and hence is not comprehensive, as is the knowledge of God alone.

2. An angel's ideas or intelligible species are *directly imparted* by the Creator; hence an angel has no need to learn. God *gives* to angels that extent of knowledge that he chooses to give.

3. And the extent of knowledge is not the same in all the angels. There are higher and lower angels. Each receives what is fitting and necessary for its status and the service it is to render, and therefore some angels know more than others. As we shall see later, the imparting of knowledge to angels by the Creator is comparable to light that shines through a succession of panes of glass, one under the other, so that while the light pours out at once and penetrates the whole series of panes, it may be truly said that the lower panes receive their light from the upper panes. And so the lower angels (that is, the less perfectly endowed angelic natures) are illuminated or instructed by the higher angels. Nor, as we see, does this conflict with the fact that angels have their knowledge from God as soon as they come into existence.

56. ANGELIC KNOWLEDGE OF NONMATERIAL THINGS

1. An angel knows itself by being itself, for God creates it knowing. In knowing itself the angel knows a nonmaterial substance.

2. The knowledge of God, existing eternally in the divine Word, is imparted, according to God's will, to the angel; and thus the angel knows itself and other things. Each angel knows every other angel.

3. An angel knows that it is God's image, and thus far it knows God naturally. God also imparts to good angels the supernatural knowledge of himself which makes them happy or blessed in the beatific vision.

57. ANGELIC KNOWLEDGE OF MATERIAL THINGS

1. That an intellect (which is the spiritual faculty or power of understanding) can know material things is proved by our human experience. For we know material things by our intellect or understanding. We use our senses to know material things as singular or

individual things. But we render these intelligible by the process of abstraction, and can know things in their essences, and can define them. We know material things in a nonmaterial way, by essence and definition. Now, if the human intellect can know material things, it goes without saying that the angelic intellect can know such things, for it is more perfect than ours; what the less perfect mind or intellect can do, the more perfect can surely do.

2. In human intellectual knowledge the first and fundamental elements are ideas or concepts. We form these concepts by the process called abstraction. From our sense-knowledge of individual things the intellect draws out, or abstracts, a universal awareness of these things. For example, from our sense-knowledge of a tree (which is knowledge of an individual material thing) our mind can rise to a universal grasp of what any tree is, regardless of its size, location, botanical class, and so on. We can rise to the knowledge of tree as such. Hence we say that the senses deal with the individual or singular things, but the mind or intellect deals with things in universal. And after we have grasped a material thing in universal, the mind or intellect can also know it in the singular. The intellect asks, when a sense-object is presented, what kind of thing this is; after it has grasped the kind, the essence, it adverts, by a reflex action, to the individual thing and recognizes it as one of that kind. Now, knowledge of things in universal, and knowledge of singular things, are both perfections of the human intellect. These perfections cannot, therefore, be lacking in the superior angelic intellect. Hence angels know *singulars* as well as essences. But, as we have already noticed, angels do not have to work out any of their knowledge by abstraction or by studious attention. They have their knowledge with their nature, whereas man has, with his nature, not knowledge, but the *ability* to acquire knowledge.

3. Do the angels know the future? To know the future may mean one of several things: (a) to know, with physical certitude, what will happen by the operation of existing and necessitating causes; as, for example, to know that the sun will rise tomorrow; (b) to know conjecturally from present facts and circumstances what is very likely to occur in the future; thus, for example, a physician may know that his patient will be able to go back to work next week; (c) to know, with absolute certainty, future events themselves. This third type of knowing the future exists in God alone. Both angels and men have the first two types of knowledge of the future, angels more perfectly than men. But angels do not have direct and absolute knowledge of future events.

4. The secret thoughts of a man and his inner acts of free will are known only to himself and God. A man may unconsciously give some outward sign of his thoughts and will acts, so that these may be known conjecturally even by other observant men; angels can know thoughts and will acts thus revealed. But the angelic intellect cannot penetrate directly into minds and wills. An angel cannot know our secret thoughts and will acts themselves, neither can one angel know the thoughts of another angel which depend on that other angel's free will.

5. The mysteries of divine grace, which depend entirely on God's will, cannot be known *naturally* by angels. By the supernatural knowledge which beatifies an angel (that is, gives it the happiness of heaven in the vision of God), angels know such of the mysteries of grace as God chooses to reveal to them. And the higher angels, by their more perfect union with God, impart knowledge of such mysteries to the lower angels.

58. THE MODE OR MANNER OF ANGELIC KNOWING

1. An intellect is in potentiality in so far as it can know; it is in actuality in so far as it knows. An angelic intellect, in its natural knowing, has its full knowledge and there is nothing for it to learn. Yet it is not always considering everything that it knows. In regard to supernatural knowledge, the angelic intellect is always in actuality as to what it beholds in the divine Word; it may be in potentiality with reference to special divine revelations that may be made to it.

2. Angelic knowledge, arising from the vision of the divine Word (the beatific vision) is all possessed at once. In the realm of its natural knowledge, however, an angel may think of many things at once if these things are comprised under the same concept or species, but things comprised under various concepts or species cannot be all thought of at once by any creatural intellect.

3. Human intellectual knowledge is developed step by step; man advances from what he knows to what, at the start, is unknown. The process of human learning is exampled in the manner in which we prove a theorem in geometry. This way of thinking things out, step by step, is called *discursive* thinking or reasoning. Now, if, in the light of some master truth, we could see all that is implied in our thoughts, we should not need to work out knowledge by discursive thought. We should not, for example, need to work out the theorem in geometry, for we should instantly take in the whole demonstration and understand it thoroughly without effort. An angel actually has

this type of knowledge. An angel does not require discursive thinking. In whatever area of its natural knowledge the angelic intellect is employed, it sees the whole picture; it beholds the thing thought about together with its implications and consequences, and therefore has no need to move from point to point to round out knowledge.

4. The human intellect forms ideas or concepts, and then compares these and pronounces judgment on their agreement or disagreement. Two ideas in the human mind are, when brought into comparison for judgment, in the relation of subject and predicate. When the predicate idea is found in agreement with the subject idea, the mind affirms the predicate of the subject, thus, "A stone is a substance." The mind or intellect thus composes or compounds the two ideas into an affirmative judgment. And when the predicate and subject do not agree, the mind divides them by a negative judgment, thus, "A stone is not a spiritual substance." Thus the human intellect works out its knowledge "by composing and dividing"; and from its judgments (made by composing and dividing) it works out other judgments by reasoning or discursive thinking. Now, the angelic intellect, as we have seen, has no need of this knowing process (of composing, dividing, reasoning), for its knowledge is not built up by abstraction from the piecemeal findings of senses. The angelic mind is like a clear mirror that takes in the full meaning of what it turns upon. Yet an angel understands our way of thinking and knows how we go about the business of composing, dividing, and reasoning.

5. In the natural knowledge of an angel there can be no falsehood or error. An angel knows truly all that it knows, and all that can be said of the object of its knowledge. And it goes without saying that in its supernatural knowledge an angel knows all that God wills it to know, without error or falsehood. But the fallen angels (or demons) are totally divorced from divine wisdom, and hence, in things supernatural, there can be error or falsehood in their knowing.

6. Inasmuch as angels know creatures in the Word of God, the beatific vision, they have what St. Augustine calls "morning knowledge." And inasmuch as they know creatures in the creatures' own being and nature, they have "evening knowledge."

7. It seems that St. Augustine makes a real distinction between morning and evening knowledge in the angels, for he says (*Gen. ad lit.* IV 24): "There is a very great difference between knowing a thing as it is in the Word of God and as it is in its own nature."

59. THE WILL OF ANGELS

1. Where there is understanding of good, there is an understanding tendency to attain it. In other words, where there is intellect, there is will. There is intellect in angels; therefore there is will also.

2. In a creature, intellect and will are not identified. The angel's intellect is not the same faculty as the angel's will. These are two faculties, not one.

3. And will means free will. Will is an intellectual appetency; it is the faculty of tending to, or choosing, what is proposed by the intellect as good. Man, who is less perfect in the realm of intelligent creatures than angels, has free will; certainly, then, an angel possesses it. An angel exercises free will more perfectly than man does.

4. Man's will is subject to outside influence arising from the appetites of sense. The will is an appetency for good as such, good in its common aspects. But man's senses fix upon some particular good and tend towards it. These human sense-tendencies, when they are simple and uncomplicated tendencies, are called *concupiscible* appetites. And when these tendencies involve an awareness of difficulty in attaining the object (that is, the satisfying thing, the good, that they seek), they are called *irascible* appetites. Thus the sentient tendency or appetite called desire is a concupiscible appetite; whereas the sentient tendency of courage or daring, which tends to an object obtainable only by facing obstacle, threat, or danger, is an irascible appetite. These sentient appetites work into the intellective order in man and exercise an influence on the will and its choice. Now, since the angels have no sentient element, they are not subject to concupiscible and irascible appetites. Angels choose with a will uninfluenced by such nonspiritual tendencies.

60. LOVE IN THE ANGELS

1. Love is a natural inclination of a will towards its object. It is the fundamental operation of will. Where there is will, there is love. Hence there is love in the angels.

2. Love in an angel is not only a natural tendency, it is a knowing tendency of the intellectual order, and involves not only inclination but choice.

3. Every being loves itself inasmuch as it seeks its own good. Free creatures love themselves in this manner, and tend to, or desire, what will be a benefit to them. And in so far as free creatures exercise choice in striving for a beneficial object, they are said to love them-

selves by choice. Angels love themselves both by natural tendency and by choice.

4. Natural love of one creature for another is based upon some point of unity or sameness in lover and beloved. Since angels are all of the same spiritual nature, they naturally love one another. [*Note:* The angels are *generically* one; they are of the same genus or general essential class; we have already seen that they are *specifically* distinct, that each angel is the only one of its specific essential kind.]

5. By natural love, angels love God more than they love themselves. All creatures belong absolutely to God; they naturally tend to God as their ultimate end or goal. Freely loving creatures must recognize God as their end or goal and tend to him before all else. Hence love of God comes naturally (in free creatures) before love of self, and is the greater love. If this were not so, natural love would be a contradiction, for it would not be perfected by attaining its true object, but would be fruitless and self-destroying.

61. THE CREATION OF THE ANGELS

1. Angels are creatures. They exist, not by necessity, but by having existence given to them. That is, they have existence by participation. Now, what has existence by participation receives this existence from that which has existence by its own essence. Only God exists by his own essence. Therefore, angels have their existence from God; they are created.

2. God alone exists from eternity. He creates things by producing them from nothing. Creatures exist after they were nonexistent. Hence angels do not exist from eternity.

3. It seems most likely that angels and the bodily world were created at the same time, not angels first (as a kind of independent world of spirits) and the bodily world afterwards. Angels are part of the universe, and no part is perfect if it be entirely severed from the whole, the totality, to which it belongs.

4. The angels were created in heaven. And it is fitting that creatures of the most perfect nature should be created in the most noble place.

62. GRACE AND GLORY OF THE ANGELS

1. Although the angels were created in heaven, and with natural happiness or beatitude, they were not created in glory, that is, in the possession of the beatific vision.

2. To possess God in the beatific vision the angels require grace.

3. And, while the angels were created in the state of sanctifying

grace, this was not the grace which confirms the angels in glory. Had the angels been created with the confirming grace, none of them could have fallen, and some did fall.

4. Angels were created in grace, and by using this grace in their first act of charity (which is the friendship and love of God) they merited the beatific vision and heavenly beatitude.

5. Instantly upon meriting the beatitude of heaven, the angels possessed it. The angelic nature, being purely spiritual, is not suited for steps and degrees of progress to perfection, as is the case with man.

6. The higher angels, those of more perfect nature and keener intelligence, have greater gifts of grace than other angels; for their more perfect powers turn them more mightily and effectively to God than is the case with angels of lesser capacity.

7. The heavenly beatitude enjoyed by the angels does not destroy their nature or their natural operations; hence the natural knowledge and love of angels remain in them after they are beatified.

8. Beatified angels cannot sin. Their nature finds perfect fulfillment in the vision of God; it is disposed towards God exclusively. There is in beatified angels no possible tendency away from God, and therefore no possible sin.

9. Angels who possess God in beatific vision cannot be increased or advanced in beatitude. A capacity that is perfectly filled up cannot be made more full.

63. SIN OF THE FALLEN ANGELS

1. A rational creature (that is, a creature with intellect and will) can sin. If it be unable to sin, this is a gift of grace, not a condition of nature. While angels were yet unbeatified they could sin. And some of them did sin.

2. The sinning angels (or demons) are guilty of all sins in so far as they lead man to commit every kind of sin. But in the bad angels themselves there could be no tendency to fleshly sins, but only to such sins as can be committed by a purely spiritual being, and these sins are two only: *pride* and *envy*.

3. Lucifer who became Satan, leader of the fallen angels, wished to be as God. This prideful desire was not a wish to be equal to God, for Satan knew by his natural knowledge that equality of creature with creator is utterly impossible. Besides, no creature actually desires to destroy itself, even to become something greater. On this point man sometimes deceives himself by a trick of imagination; he imagines himself to be another and greater being, and yet it is himself that is somehow this other being. But an angel has no sense-faculty of

imagination to abuse in this fashion. The angelic intellect, with its clear knowledge, makes such self-deception impossible. Lucifer knew that to be equal with God, he would have to *be* God, and he knew perfectly that this could not be. What he wanted was to be *as* God; he wished to be like God in a way not suited to his nature, such as to create things by his own power, or to achieve final beatitude without God's help, or to have command over others in a way proper to God alone.

4. Every nature, that is every essence as operating, tends to some good. An intellectual nature tends to good in general, good under its common aspects, good as such. The fallen angels therefore are not naturally evil.

5. The devil did not sin in the very instant of his creation. When a perfect cause makes a nature, the first operation of that nature must be in line with the perfection of its cause. Hence the devil was not created in wickedness. He, like all the angels, was created in the state of sanctifying grace.

6. But the devil, with his companions, sinned *immediately* after creation. He rejected the grace in which he was created, and which he was meant to use, as the good angels used it, to merit beatitude. If, however, the angels were not created in grace (as some hold) but had grace available as soon as they were created, then it may be that some interval occurred between the creation and the sin of Lucifer and his companions.

7. Lucifer, chief of the sinning angels, was probably the highest of all the angels. But there are some who think that Lucifer was highest only among the rebel angels.

8. The sin of the highest angel was a bad example which attracted the other rebel angels, and, to this extent, was the cause of their sin.

9. The faithful angels are a greater multitude than the fallen angels. For sin is contrary to the natural order. Now, what is opposed to the natural order occurs less frequently, or in fewer instances, than what accords with the natural order.

64. STATE OF THE FALLEN ANGELS

1. The fallen angels did not lose their natural knowledge by their sin; nor did they lose their angelic intellect.

2. The fallen angels are obstinate in evil, unrepentant, inflexibly determined in their sin. This follows from their nature as pure spirits, for the choice of a pure spirit is necessarily final and unchanging.

3. Yet we must say that there is sorrow in the fallen angels, though not the sorrow of repentance. They have sorrow in the affliction of

knowing that they cannot attain beatitude; that there are curbs upon their wicked will; that men, despite their efforts, may get to heaven.

4. The fallen angels are engaged in battling against man's salvation and in torturing lost souls in hell. The fallen angels that beset man on earth, carry with them their own dark and punishing atmosphere, and wherever they are they endure the pains of hell. [*Note:* For further discussion of angels, see Qq. 106–114.]

THE DAYS OF CREATION

(QUESTIONS 65 TO 74)

65. THE CREATION OF BODIES

1. God is the source of being, bodily and spiritual, substantial and accidental. God is therefore the Creator of bodies as well as of spirits. And while some bodies can propagate and reproduce their kind, God had to give first beginnings and the power to propagate; God must also support the process of propagating in its being and effectiveness. Scripture says (Ps. 145) that God is the Creator "who made heaven and earth, the sea, and all things that are in them."

2. The entire universe, bodily and spiritual, is the work of God's goodness. All creatures manifest the divine goodness and tend to it as to their goal or final cause.

3. The theory that God made the angels, and then the angels made the bodily world, cannot stand. For, as we have seen elsewhere, only God can create. No secondary cause (that is, no creature) can produce anything without having something to work on. But creation is total production of a thing from nothing.

4. A body is made of primal matter and substantial form. Some have said that the substantial forms of bodies were taken from the angels. This is false doctrine. Bodies come in first instance from God the Creator; no bodily element is supplied by angels or other creatures.

66. THE ORDER OF BODILY CREATION

1. God did not make a supply of formless matter out of which bodily creatures were afterwards made. For existing formless matter is

a contradiction in terms; existence itself is a form, that is, a determinateness of being. The Scripture phrase about the earth being "void and empty," or, as some translators put it, "without form," does not indicate the utter absence of form, but the incompleteness of the work; for the earth was still covered with water, and was in darkness, and was unadorned with its finished beauty.

2. God created the matter and form of bodies together. Matter considered in itself is formless (the only contradiction in the concept of formless matter is found in the notion of *existing* formless matter). There can therefore be no interval of time between the creation of primal matter and the substantial forms which gave it existence in the first bodies created.

3. The heaven of the blessed was probably created at the same time as the bodily universe. It is suitable that the glorious heaven should be created with the lower world which looks to it as the hope and promise of its own ultimate renovation.

4. It is the opinion of many wise and holy writers that the first things created were created at the same instant: angels, heaven, the bodily world, and time.

67. LIGHT: WORK OF THE FIRST DAY OF CREATION

1. Light means what the eye requires so that it may see and also what the mind requires that it may understand. We constantly use the word *light* in both senses; we speak of the light of day, and we also say that an explanation of a problem or difficulty "throws light on the subject."

2. Light in its meaning as the illumination of the bodily universe is not a substance.

3. Bodily light is an active quality which pertains to a luminous bodily substance. The effect of light is different according to the different substances from which it comes.

4. It is suitable that the creation of light be the work of the first day, for in light other works may fittingly proceed.

68. WORK OF THE SECOND DAY OF CREATION

1. The firmament was made on the second day. Some say that the firmament means the starry heavens; others say it means the skyey mass of clouds and air.

2. At all events, the firmament lies between "the waters above and the waters below." And the term *waters* may mean bodily matter, or transparent bodies, or watery vapors.

3. Whatever the nature of these waters, the firmament is the divid-

ing element between the upper and lower kinds of them. Scripture says (Gen. 1:24–27), "And God said: 'Let there be a firmament made amidst the waters, and let it divide the waters from the waters.' And God made a firmament, and divided the waters that were under the firmament from those that were above the firmament."

4. Scripture speaks of a plurality of heavens. For instance, in Psalm 148, we read: "Praise Him, ye heaven of heavens." And St. Paul (II Cor. 12:2) "was caught up to the third heaven." The word *heaven* may mean the heaven of the blessed, or the starry firmament, or the space beyond the stars; it may mean any real or imaginary region in what we call outer space. And the word heaven may be used by metaphor for God himself, as in the expressions, "Heaven bless you," "Pray to heaven for guidance." St. Augustine says there are three types of supernatural visions—visions manifested to the eye, visions manifested to the imagination, visions manifested to the intellect—and these are three heavens. This is one explanation of the "third heaven" to which St. Paul was caught up.

69. WORK OF THE THIRD DAY OF CREATION

1. In the various *days* of creation some see an order of origin or of nature, and not of time. Others say that the days indicate an order of time. In any case, the work of the third day was suitably the forming of the ordered earth by the gathering together of waters and the appearing of land. For it seems logical and right that, after the creation of light and the heavens or firmament, the earth should be given perfected form.

2. And it appears suitable that on the same day there should come to the perfected earth the adornment of living plants.

70. WORK OF THE FOURTH DAY OF CREATION

1. The light that was created first was not the light of the luminous heavenly bodies, for these were not created until the fourth day. After the earth was formed and adorned with plants, it was fittingly furnished with the illumination that came with the creation of the luminous heavenly bodies.

2. These luminaries are accounted for in scripture which speaks of their usefulness to man, and they were provided for him before he was placed on the earth. They enable man to see with bodily sight; they support life in living bodies; they mark and occasion the changes of season; they are conveniences as signs and forecastings.

3. The luminous heavenly bodies are not living bodies.

71. WORK OF THE FIFTH DAY OF CREATION

1. The work of the fifth day was the production of fowls and fishes and things that creep in the waters. As the fourth day sees the firmament adorned with light-giving bodies, the fifth day sees the lower elements of air and water made fruitful with living things.

72. WORK OF THE SIXTH DAY OF CREATION

1. The sixth day sees the land furnished with living bodies, and its chief living creatures placed in charge. Scripture (Gen. 1:24,27) says, "Let the earth bring forth the living creature in its kind, cattle and creeping things, and beasts of the earth, according to their kinds. . . . And God created man to His own image."

73. THE SEVENTH DAY

1. The perfection of the universe is ascribed to the seventh day when the work of creation is seen completed. Perfection in a thing is either (a) its being completed as a thing, or (b) its doing what it was made to do. And the first perfection is the cause of the second. By the seventh day creation was *complete,* and, in this sense, perfect. But its purpose in existence, the salvation of men through Christ and his grace, will be fulfilled at the end of time, when it will have given all the help that bodily creatures can give to the serving and saving of mankind.

2. We read (Gen. 2:2) that "God ended his work which he had made, and he rested on the seventh day from all his work." God rested, not as one tired out by labor, but as one who ceases from his operation. And rest as referred to God means his complete blessedness or beatitude in himself which needs no creatures.

3. Scripture tells us (Gen. 2:2) that "God blessed the seventh day and sanctified it." God sanctified all creatures. And the special blessing and sanctification of creatures is their rest in God. The day itself is blessed and sanctified; it is properly a day of rest for creatures. Further, the blessing of creatures is expressed to them in God's word, "Increase and multiply."

74. MEANING OF THE SEVEN DAYS

1. There are different interpretations of the term *day* as used in the scriptural account of creation. Some say the six days of active creation are not periods of time but a listing of the order in which creatures were made. Others think these days have time significance, but hardly in the sense of our twenty-four hour day, for that day is

measured by the sun, and the sun was not created until the fourth day. In any case, the six days of creation and the seventh day of rest give an adequate account of the works of creation and their sanctification.

2. St. Augustine makes the days of creation into one period in which God manifests worldly creatures to the angels in seven ways.

3. It must be acknowledged that Scripture uses suitable words to express the works of creation, and to suggest or imply the operation of the three Persons of the divine Trinity in these works.

MAN

(QUESTIONS 75 TO 102)

75. MAN'S SOUL

1. A soul is the life-principle in a *living* body. The soul actualizes a body as living, and it is the substantial form which makes the living body the specific kind of living body it is: plant, animal, man. The soul of a plant and the soul of an animal are called material souls not as though they were made of bodily stuff, but to indicate their *dependence* upon the bodily organism which they determine and actualize.

2. The human soul is a nonbodily substance endowed with intellect and will. In this life the human soul has an extrinsic dependence on the body, but not an intrinsic dependence. It can exist and operate *per se* even if it be severed from the body. And this means that it is truly a *subsistent* substance.

3. The plant soul and the animal soul are not subsistent substances. They cannot exist and operate *per se* without the plant body and the animal body; indeed, it is the complete body, plant or animal, that exists and acts *per se*. Material souls are incomplete, *nonsubsistent* substances.

4. The human soul is subsistent, yet, while it is a complete soul, it is not a complete human being. The complete human being is a compound of body and soul. Plato mistakenly thought that the soul is the complete man, and that the body is a kind of container or prison. But this is not true. Man is a single compound substance made of

body and soul; the soul can exist and perform its proper operations even if severed from the body.

5. Therefore the human soul is a *spiritual* substance. It is an element of the human compound, but in itself it has no compounding or composition; there is no matter or material in it. It is a substantial spiritual form. It is a spirit.

6. The substantial and subsistent form cannot decay, break up, or cease to exist. For it has no material elements or parts to fall away; it has no intrinsic dependence on matter for existence and operation. Hence it is an incorruptible substance; it cannot perish or die.

7. The human soul is not of the same species (that is, definite and complete kind of essence) as the angels. Indeed, we have seen that each angel is a species in itself; angels are only of generic sameness. But a human soul is like an angel in the fact that it is a spiritual substance, and it is unlike an angel in the fact that it is a spiritual substance designed to be united with a body. Again, all human souls are of the *same* species, whereas each angel is itself the only member of its species.

76. UNION OF SOUL AND BODY IN MAN

1. The spiritual soul of a human being is the substantial form of the living man. It is this spiritual soul which, substantially joined with matter, sets up and constitutes an existing human being. Man's soul is not in his body as a hand is in a glove or as a rower is in a boat; it is not united with the body as an organist is united with the musical instrument in producing harmonies. All these examples are instances of *accidental* union. And the human soul is joined with its body in *substantial* union; with its body it constitutes one substance, the human substance.

2. Each human being has his own soul. Some ancient teachers mistakenly believed that there is one universal soul for all men, a general soul. There are as many human souls as there are individual human beings.

3. Each human being has his own soul and it constitutes him as an existing living substance of the human kind. And each man has *only* one soul. Although man has the three grades of life—vegetal, sentient or animal, and human—he is only one being, one substance. The human soul is, in itself or as such, a spiritual soul; this spiritual soul, inasmuch as, in the body, it can be the root-principle of bodily functions, is equivalently vegetal and sentient. We say, in technical words, the human soul is *formally* spiritual, and *virtually* vegetal and sentient.

4. The spiritual and intellectual soul of a man is his only substantial form. For a man is one substance; he is constituted as one substance of the human kind by one substantial form. But the human kind is the intellectual kind, not merely a plant or an animal. Hence a man is constituted in his kind by an intellectual or spiritual principle, and this is his *one* spiritual soul, his one substantial form.

5. The human soul does not receive its knowledge with its nature when it is created, as is the case with angels. It must acquire its knowledge. And it gains its knowledge through the ministering office of bodily senses. From sense-findings the soul arises, by use of its power or faculty of mind, understanding, intellect, to supra-sensible knowledge—to ideas, judgments, discursive thought.

6. The primal matter with which the human soul is joined as substantial form is not a specially prepared or "disposed" matter, with special or superior qualities. For primal matter is not of various kinds; primal matter has no qualities and can have none; primal matter does not even exist until existence is given it by substantial form.

7. A substantial form is united with primal matter to constitute an existing body. There is no medium, no connecting link, for this union of substantial form and primal matter. It is an immediate union. Therefore, the human soul (which is the substantial form of the living human body) is joined substantially and *immediately* with the body.

8. The substantial form of a body, living or lifeless, is in the body it constitutes, but not circumscriptively, not dimensionally, not part here and part there. The substantial form which makes a block of marble the kind of thing it is, is found in the block and in every part of the block. The whole block of marble is marble; so is any piece you break off from the block; and the unbroken block is marble in every part. And in a plant, one life is present throughout the living substance, in root and stem, in branch and twig, in flower and fruit; the life-principle or substantial form of the plant makes it this plant throughout. Now, a perfection found in lesser substantial forms is certainly not lacking in greater ones. What is true of bodies as such and of living bodies less than man, is true of man. Man's substantial form is whole in his living body and whole in every part of that unbroken living body. But the soul does not perform the same operations in every part of the body; there are different bodily parts or organs for different bodily operations. Hence we say: the human soul is present in its entirety of essence in the *body* and in *every part* of the body; but it is not thus wholly present in every part as to specific operations. The soul is primarily related to the body; it is secondarily related to the various parts of the body considered severally.

77. FACULTIES OF THE HUMAN SOUL: IN GENERAL

1. A faculty is the power of a living substance to exercise a specific life-operation. The faculties or powers of the human soul are not one with its substance. These faculties are powers which the soul *has;* they are not what the soul *is.* Only in God is power identified with substance.

2. There are various faculties of the human soul, for there are various life-operations in a man. Since man is composed of matter and spirit, powers material and powers spiritual meet in his soul, his substantial form.

3. The various human faculties are distinguished one from another by their respective operations and by the objects which these operations work on or seek to achieve. Thus, for instance, sight and hearing are not one faculty, but two distinct faculties, because they operate differently, and because sight is for perceiving color while hearing is for perceiving sound. However, accidental differences of operations do not require distinct faculties to explain them. Thus the power to walk, the power to run, the power to shuffle, the power to dance, and the power to kick, are not distinct faculties; they are only accidental variations of the one power of locomotion, that is, the power or faculty of moving from place to place.

4. The human faculties are not a haphazard collection of powers, unrelated and unco-ordinated. There is order in them and among them. In man, for example, the plant or vegetal operations serve the sentient operations, and these, in turn, serve the intellectual operations. The vegetal power of nutrition enables a man to exercise his senses, and from sense-findings the intellect gains concepts, and so the will is won to choose. Thus there is order and arrangement in and among the human faculties.

5. The *subject* of a faculty is the precise reality that exercises it. A man himself is the subject of all his faculties, but his human nature as such is not the immediate subject of them all. The soul is the subject of the intellective faculties of understanding and willing. Further, the soul-body compound is the subject of all other human faculties. The body alone is not the subject of any human faculty, for the body alone lacks life and all vital operation.

6. All the human vital operations, whether their subject is body-and-soul or soul alone, are rooted in the soul as in their basic principle.

7. Some human faculties operate through the medium of other faculties. It is, for example, through the operation of sense-faculties that the intellect operates to form its ideas or concepts.

63

8. When the soul is separated from the body by death, its own faculties remain in it. It is still *formally* an intellective operator; it still exercises intellect and will. But the soul is only *virtually* vegetal and sentient, and, when it is severed from the body, it has no need or ability actually to exercise the operations of vegetal and sensitive life.

78. FACULTIES OF THE HUMAN SOUL: IN PARTICULAR

1. A plant takes food and is nourished; it tends to grow to maturity, and to reproduce its kind. Thus the plant faculties are the nutritive faculty, the augmenting or growing faculty, and the generative faculty. An animal has all the plant faculties; in addition, it has the faculty or power of sensing (that is, knowing by the use of senses), the power of tending to go after what the senses grasp as good or desirable (and away from what the senses grasp as harmful), and the power of moving in accordance with that tendency. Thus an animal has, in addition to the vegetal powers or faculties, the faculties of sensing, appetizing, moving locally. Man has all the vegetal and the sentient (or animal) faculties; in addition, he has the specifically rational faculties of understanding and choosing in the light of understanding; that is, he has the faculties of intellect (or mind, or understanding) and will.

2. It is manifest that the *vegetal* functions or operations are three; for plants (and all living bodies inasmuch as they have vegetal life) tend to take food, grow to maturity, and reproduce their kind.

3. The *sensitive* faculties are the exterior and interior senses. The *exterior* senses have their organs, that is, the special body-parts that serve their operation, in the outer body. These exterior senses are five: sight, hearing, smell, taste, and feeling or touch. Sight is the noblest of these sense faculties, and hearing is next to it in excellence; these two senses are often called the superior senses. The other three, or inferior, senses are more sheerly material in their operation than sight and hearing.

4. In addition to the exterior senses, there are four *interior* senses: consciousness (often called the central sense, or the common sense), imagination, instinct (or the estimative sense), and memory.

79. THE INTELLECTIVE HUMAN FACULTIES

1. The intellective faculties of man are powers of the soul. They are the intellect and its appetency called the will.

2. The intellect (or mind, or understanding) is, first of all, a passive

power; that is, it *receives* its knowledge and does not make it up. But the intellect is not passive in a lifeless fashion as marble is passive under the chisel of the sculptor. It does not act to make knowledge, but it *re*-acts to the impression of knowledge. It receives knowledge and expresses it within itself in its own way.

3. Now, in this life all human knowledge begins with the senses. Man's intellect must therefore receive knowledge from the senses. But the sense order is the order of material and singular reality, whereas the intellect is a spiritual power to grasp things in universal. Hence there must be a power, belonging to the order of intellective faculties, which prepares sense-finding for the intellect proper; there must be an intellectual agency which renders sense-findings intelligible. This is the special intellectual faculty called the *intellectus agens* or active intellect. Therefore, man has these intellectual or intellective faculties: the *active* intellect, the intellect proper or *passive* intellect (called *intellectus possibilis*), and the *will*.

4. The active intellect is a faculty of the soul. It belongs to the intellective order, not the sentient order.

5. It is not true (as some have taught) that there is only one active intellect for all men, which renders things intelligible for everyone even as one sun renders things visible for everyone. The active intellect is a faculty of *each* soul.

6. The intellect proper, the *intellectus possibilis*, is the intellect which actually understands. Now, it retains what it understands, and in this function it is called the intellectual memory. Hence memory (in the intellective order) is not a faculty distinct from intellect; it is the intellect in a definite service or function. The recalling of things experienced in the past is rather the work of the sense-memory (one of the interior senses) than of the intellect.

7. Therefore the intellective memory is an act or operation of the intellect, and not a special faculty. It belongs to understanding to retain as well as to receive.

8. And the intellect often grasps or understands by a connected series of points or steps. It can think things out. In this operation the intellect (that is, the knowing intellect, the passive intellect) is called *reason*. The work of reasoning, of moving in connected steps of thought to reach a conclusion, is called discursive thought. The human reason is not, therefore, a special faculty; it is the act or operation of the faculty called intellect. [*Note:* Sometimes the term *reason* is used to signify man's rational nature, including both intellect and will. Thus we speak of a person's "coming to the use of reason," and of keeping the passions "subject to reason."]

9. St. Augustine draws a distinction between the higher reason which contemplates eternal truths, and the lower reason which thinks on temporal things. This is an accidental distinction of reason, not a multiplication of faculties. Reason itself is not a faculty really distinct from intellect; hence no types or varieties of reason can be distinct faculties.

10. In its actual operation of knowing, of understanding, of pronouncing true judgment, the intellect is called *intelligence*. Whether the judgment expresses a self-evident truth, or a truth known by immediate inference, or a truth reasoned out by discursive thinking, the very act of judging is called an act of intelligence. Hence intelligence is not a faculty distinct from intellect; it *is* intellect in a precise operation or action.

11. The intellect is called *speculative* inasmuch as it knows what is so; it is called *practical* inasmuch as is it knows what to do. Hence the speculative intellect and the practical intellect are not two faculties, but two functions of one faculty.

12. By his rational nature (that is, by his human essence equipped with understanding and will), a person comes early in life into possession of certain items of knowledge that enlighten and guide him in thinking and acting. These items of knowledge amount to first truths and first laws; we call them *first principles*. (a) First *intellectual* principles are: a person's direct awareness that he exists; that he can think straight; that what he thinks about cannot be what it is and, at the same time, something else. (b) First *moral* principles, or will-principles (that is, laws of conduct), are drawn from the direct awareness that there is such a thing as right and good, such a thing as wrong and evil, such a thing as obligation or duty. And thus first moral principles are, "Do good," "Avoid evil." And, since the knowledge of good and evil is not wholly abstract, it involves certain manifest objective instances of what is good and what is bad. This fundamental moral equipment of a human being, achieved as a person emerges from infancy to an age of responsible conduct, is called *synderesis*. Now, first principles, intellectual or moral, are habits, that is, enduring qualities, of intellect and will. Knowledge of first truths (that is, intellectual principles) is an intellectual habit; so is synderesis in so far as it is knowledge; synderesis in so far as it is a habitual guide and influence upon the will is a moral habit.

13. When a person reaches a reasoned conclusion about his own duty, the conclusion is a practical judgment. This judgment is called *conscience*. Hence conscience is not a special faculty; it is an act of the faculty of intellect as reason. Sometimes people confuse conscience

with synderesis, and call synderesis itself by the name conscience. This is an inaccurate use of terms. Synderesis is a *habit;* conscience is an *act;* neither is a faculty. Reason draws upon synderesis in forming the conscience-judgment.

80. THE APPETITIVE HUMAN FACULTIES

1. Everything has an inclination towards what accords with its nature; this inclination or tendency is called appetency or *appetite.* Things that lack knowledge have natural appetency only; this is exampled in the tendency of a plant to grow, of a body to cohere, of a stone to fall to the ground. Living bodies that have knowledge (animals and men) have, in addition to natural appetency, tendencies that are roused in them by their knowing, by their cognition; these are *cognitional* appetites. Cognitional appetency is of two orders: the order of sense, and the order of intellect. Sentient or sensitive appetency inclines animal or man towards what is sensed as good or desirable, and away from what is sensed as evil or harmful. Intellectual appetency inclines intelligent creatures (angels and men) towards what is intellectually understood as good, and away from what is understood as evil. The intellectual appetency or appetite is called the *will.*

2. The will is a faculty distinct from the sentient appetite, for it belongs to the intellective order, not the sensitive order. These two appetites sometimes conflict, as, for example, when a Catholic has hunger (i.e., sentient appetite) for meat on Friday, but wills not to eat it.

81. THE SENSITIVE APPETITE IN MAN

1. No appetite is a knowing power, but cognitional appetite is aroused by knowing. Knowledge *lays hold* of its object; appetite only *tends* to its object. Hence knowing is sometimes called rest, and appetizing is called movement.

2. Sentient or sensitive appetency is of two kinds. A concupiscible appetite is a simple tendency towards what is sensed as good and away from what is sensed as evil. An irascible appetite is a tendency to overcome difficulty or hindrance in attaining good and avoiding evil. Thus sentient desire is a concupiscible appetite; courage or daring is an irascible appetite. These two types of appetite or appetency in the sense-order are species of one genus. They cannot be reduced to one specific kind, for irascible appetency tends to grapple with difficulties from which concupiscible appetite tends away.

3. Reason, that is, the thinking mind, can exercise a controlling

influence upon the sentient appetency; by thinking, a person can stir up desire or courage; by fixing the mind on pacific things, a man can allay anger. The will controls the lower appetites by directing the mind's attention to objects other than those to which the appetites tend. Reason and will (and these two faculties together are most frequently called by the simple name of *reason*) have no absolute or despotic control over the lower appetites; they exercise a politic and persuasive influence.

82. THE INTELLECTIVE APPETITE IN MAN: THE WILL

1. The will is the intellective or rational appetency. The will tends of necessity to the end for which it is made; it tends towards what is intellectually grasped as desirable or good and towards its own happiness or repose in the possession of good. The will is necessitated in its tendency towards good *in general,* good in its common aspects. But the will is not necessitated with respect to *particular* things presented by the intellect as desirable.

2. The will, therefore, is not necessitated in its particular acts. Many of the things towards which the will tends have not a desirability of their own, but are understood as things by which good may be obtained. That is, many things are willed as means to the good desired, not as the good itself which is the end. Now, just as a person who is forced to seek a certain city but is free to choose the roads by which he hopes to reach it, so the will is necessitated and not free in its quest of the good, but is free to choose, wisely or unwisely, in the light of intellect, what particular means it shall use in its quest of the goal.

3. The intellect is, in itself, a more excellent faculty than the will; for the intellect attains its object by knowing it, and the will only tends toward its object. But, under certain aspects, the will is superior to the intellect. For when a good is greater or nobler than the soul itself, it is better to will it (that is, love it) than merely to know it; thus it is a better thing to love God than *simply* to know God. But when a good is less noble than the soul, intellect, with respect to this good, is superior to the will; thus to know material things is better than to love them.

4. The intellect moves the will by showing it what is attractive; thus intellect moves will in the manner of a final cause. The will, in turn, moves the intellect in the manner of an active or agent cause, an effecting cause. For the will can apply the intellect to the study of

this object or that; it can turn away the attention of the intellect from one thing and fix it on another. The will also exercises an active control over other natural faculties of a man, but it has no control over the vegetal powers in themselves.

5. The will is an appetency or appetite. But it has no departments of concupiscible and irascible tendencies. These belong to the sentient order, and the will belongs to the intellective order. The sentient appetites are in the body-and-soul compound; the will belongs to the soul.

83. FREE WILL

1. The will is free with the freedom of choice of *means*. If a man's will were not free, all counsels, exhortations, commands, rewards, and punishments would be meaningless things. Man does not always act from necessity. He weighs and considers a course of action; he seeks advice; he judges that *this* way is to be followed, then perhaps changes his judgment and decides on *that* way. Nor does a man act with the mere sense-judgment of an animal, an instinctive judgment; he works on understandable motives. Man acts with the unhampered judgment of an intellect which shows various courses open for choice and makes practical and nonnecessitated decision. In a word man has free will. In the fact that man is rational is involved the fact that he has free will.

2. The term *free will*, strictly understood, means the act of the will making a free *choice*. But the term free will is commonly used as a synonym for the will itself. And thus free will is the will in its character as a faculty for tending to or choosing, without being necessitated, goods upon which the intellect is capable of making various practical judgments.

3. Free will is an appetitive power, not a knowing power. It operates in the light of knowledge furnished by the intellect. Knowledge is, of course, necessary for the act of free will; choice cannot be made without knowledge of the field of choice. A traveler cannot choose a road in total darkness which prevents his seeing any roads at all. But the characteristic act of free will is the act of choosing, and therefore it is a faculty of the appetitive order, and not of the cognitional or knowing order.

4. Free will as an *act* is the will exercising its connatural tendency towards good and resultant beatitude by choosing, without being forced, some particular object apprehended by the intellect as good or desirable.

84. MAN'S KNOWLEDGE OF BODILY REALITY

1. Man's spiritual soul is the life-principle and the substantial form of the human living being. It is the root-principle of all vital activities in man. Its own proper faculties are the intellect and the will. But the soul is the substantial form of a body, and even its spiritual faculty of intellect must attain knowledge through the body and its senses. Therefore, in this present life, the *proper object* of the human intellect is the *essence* of material things which the senses lay hold of. The process by which the intellect gets its knowledge may be thus illustrated: A boy looks at five pictures of a triangle, drawn in different colors and in various sizes. The sense of sight takes in the pictures; the inner sense of imagination or phantasy expresses within itself these sight-images, and they are now called phantasms. The active intellect (the *intellectus agens*) focuses on the phantasms and, disregarding differences of size and color and location of the pictures themselves, reveals what it is that they represent; this action of the active intellect is called abstraction. By abstraction, then, the active intellect, throwing its light on phantasms, *de*-materializes them, *de*-individualizes them, and renders them intelligible. It does not matter, therefore, that there are five or fifty pictures of triangle, or that they are drawn here or drawn there, that they are in this color or that; by its operation of abstraction, the active intellect disregards all these individualizing things and thus shows up the essence of triangle itself, triangle as such. This abstracted essence is called the *intelligible species* (that is, the understandable essence) of triangle. Thus sense-findings are prepared for the grasp of the spiritual power of the intellect proper (the *intellectus possibilis*). The active intellect impresses the abstracted essence or species upon the intellect proper, and the intellect proper reacts to the impression by expressing the essence within itself as a concept or *idea*. The intellect now knows in idea what triangle is; it knows in universal, for it can now define triangle as such, and not merely this or that individual triangle. Thus does man rise from the individual findings of the senses to intellectual concepts and ideas which represent things in universal, or by definition of essence.

2. The intellect of man does not know things by its own essence, but must acquire its natural knowledge by its operation as just explained. Only God knows things by his own essence.

3. Nor has the human soul any knowledge born in it, or imparted to it with its nature as is the case with angels. All man's natural intellectual knowledge begins with the action of the senses. From sense-findings, intellectual knowledge is derived by abstraction. And the

intellect may rise from concepts or ideas, by a further abstraction, to higher concepts or ideas. But no ideas are naturally inborn in man; there are no innate ideas. All man's natural knowledge is *acquired*.

4. And, as we have seen, all ideas are, in last analysis, acquired by abstraction from phantasms, that is, imagination-images of sense-findings. Even ideas acquired from other ideas have to be traced back to the action of senses to start with. No ideas are impressed on man's mind from outside by "forms" that subsist, as Plato taught. No other process than that described above accounts for man's natural intellectual knowledge.

5. Man's intellect may be described as a kind of light given man by the Creator, a sort of participation of the divine understanding. Therefore it may be said that the human intellect has, in its imperfect creatural way, ideas that are in God eternally as archetypes and exemplars.

6. Sense-knowledge supplies what may be called the material from which the active intellect draws out or abstracts understandable forms. Hence, by metaphor, sense-knowledge may be called the material cause of intellectual knowledge.

7. Just as the intellect acquires ideas from phantasms, so it turns to *phantasms* when it uses knowledge already acquired. We know that this is so, for sometimes a bodily injury or disease may prevent a man from understanding what he previously understood. And when we wish to think a thing out, we use examples to help ourselves understand, and such examples are phantasms; we also explain things to others by use of examples. While the intellect is a spiritual power and understands in universal, it is never, in this earthly life, wholly divorced from material things and individual sense-grasp. The intellect of bodily man acquires knowledge through phantasms, and uses acquired knowledge by recurring to phantasms.

8. Therefore when the senses are impaired, the judgment of the mind or intellect is hampered. This does not mean that the intellect depends essentially on the senses, but that, in this earthly life, there is an *extrinsic* dependence of intellect on sense.

85. THE MANNER OR MODE OF MAN'S UNDERSTANDING

1. In this life, the human intellect rises from sense-findings to concepts. The human intellect is contrasted in this operation with the angelic intellect which descends from the knowledge of nonmaterial things to the knowledge of material things.

2. Man's intellect, by its concepts, knows reality. The ideas are that *by which* reality is known; they are not that *which* is known. For the intellect is not directly aware of its own ideas, but of what the ideas represent. The intellect, however, by reflecting upon itself, can become aware of its concepts as such, and aware of the way in which these concepts are formed. But by its direct operation the intellect knows *things,* not its own knowing of things.

3. Even though intellectual knowledge in man is acquired from individual and material phantasms, it is at first general and indefinite and afterwards more special and distinct. So at first a child might call all men father, but later learn to specify one.

4. The intellect cannot understand many things at one time except in so far as they are included in one concept or intelligible species. Our knowledge may include many things, but we understand and think of the items of knowledge one at a time. As the eye cannot see more than one view at a time, but can behold the many visible things that belong to that view, so the intellect cannot think of more than is contained in the one concept on which its attention is fixed, but it can understand many things that belong to that concept.

5. Intellect compares ideas, pronouncing upon them by affirming or denying their agreement as subject and predicate. In making an affirmative judgment, such as "A plant is a living body," the intellect puts together or *composes* subject-idea and predicate-idea. In making a negative judgment, such as "A plant is not a sentient body," the intellect *divides* subject-idea and predicate-idea by its denial. Thus the intellect knows things by composing and dividing. And the intellect proceeds from judgments to further judgments by reasoning or discursive thinking. The elements of intellectual knowledge in man are ideas or concepts which are formed upon sense-findings. The actual items of human intellectual knowledge are judgments, whether these be made directly by composing and dividing, or arrived at by inference from other judgments, that is, by reasoning.

6. The intellect cannot be false *in itself.* Error in intellectual knowledge comes from something *accidental* to the intellect, not from the intellect itself. For example, error may come from careless use of the intellect.

7. One human intellect cannot understand a thing *more* than another, but one intellect can understand *better* than another. Just so, two men, one with clear eyesight and the other with imperfect vision, look upon the same scene; one does not see more actually than the other sees, but one sees better or more clearly than the other.

8. Confused knowledge regularly precedes distinct knowledge. We

know things first in a general way, and later in a more detailed and distinct way. We first know a thing as undivided before we advert to its divisions; we know a whole object before we have knowledge of its various parts and their relation to one another.

86. WHAT THE INTELLECT KNOWS IN MATERIAL THINGS

1. In this life in which man's soul and body are substantially united, the object of the human intellect is the essences of material things. The intellect knows such essences *in universal* by acquiring ideas or concepts in the manner already described. By a second act which is a kind of reflex act or reflection, the intellect knows material things *in individual*. The intellect inquires, in this bodily world, "What *kind* of thing is that?" When it knows the kind or essence, it can advert to the individual things and say, "Yes, these are things of that kind." Primarily and directly, the intellect knows universals; secondarily and reflexly, the intellect knows singulars, that is, individual material things.

2. The human intellect is a created and finite power. Therefore it cannot perfectly know the infinite. The intellect can know *potential* infinity, which means unlimited possibility. The intellect itself has potential infinity inasmuch as it is never filled up, but can always know something more. But the intellect cannot know perfectly *actual* infinity.

3. Contingent things (that is, changeable things; things that have not in themselves a necessity for existing) are the direct object of sense-knowledge. The intellect, by its *secondary* and reflex act, can know singulars; hence the intellect can know contingent things. The intellect also knows the necessary and universal principles that are back of contingent things, such, for instance, as the truth that movement always requires a mover.

4. The human intellect cannot know the future except in cause. To know a thing in cause is to foresee the effects which will come from existing and necessitating causes. Thus astronomers know, even centuries before the event, the exact time at which an eclipse of the sun is to occur. To know the future, not merely in cause, but *in itself,* is beyond creatural power; such knowledge belongs to God alone. The human intellect has an abundance of conjectural knowledge of the future; such knowledge is a reasonable guess or supposition; it is usually founded upon experience of what has happened in the past.

87. MAN'S KNOWLEDGE OF HIMSELF

1. The more a thing is freed from the limitations of matter, the more knowable it is. And the more independent a knowing-power is, in its being and its operation, from the hamperings of matter, the more perfect a knowing-power it is. Therefore we say, "Nonmateriality is the root of knowledge and of knowing." Since God is infinite spirit, he is wholly nonmaterial; therefore God is supremely knowable, and supremely knowing. God knows himself by his essence, by being God. The angels are spirits, unhampered by matter; they know themselves *in* their essence, for God gives them knowledge as he creates them and gives them their essence. Man's intellect knows itself, not by or in its essence, but by its operation. The mind *directly* knows essences abstracted from phantasms (that is, it knows the essences of material things), and, by *reflection,* the mind can know that it knows; it can know itself by knowing. Of intellectual beings, God knows perfectly; angels less perfectly; man least perfectly.

2. Habits, in the intellectual order, are: (a) truths acquired, retained, and ready for use in our reasoning; and (b) the practiced facility to acquire knowledge by using these acquired and permanently retained truths as mental equipment. Our grasp of first principles (see above, 79, art. 12), whether intellectual or moral, is a habit; the intellectual first principles constitute a habit fundamental to our thinking; the moral first principles make a habit basic to all our responsible conduct. The mind or intellect is not directly aware of habits as such; it knows them by reflection.

3. The intellect, exercising its connatural operation of knowing the essences of material things, knows these essences in its own way, that is, in universal. And, as we have noted, the intellect can reflect, or turn its attention back upon itself; thus it can know things in singular, thus also it can know itself as operating, and can know its operation.

4. And the intellect can know the will. Knowing itself and its operations it knows the tendency of man to follow knowledge, to tend after what knowledge presents as desirable. Thus intellect knows will.

88. MAN'S KNOWLEDGE OF NONMATERIAL THINGS

1. Since the proper object of intellect, in the present earthly life of man, is the essences of material things, the intellect understands by using phantasms, that is, sense-images of material things presented in imagination. Now, there are no phantasms of nonmaterial things. Therefore, in this life, the human intellect cannot know

nonmaterial things directly or *per se.* It cannot know, for example, what nonmaterial substances, such as angels, are in themselves.

2. We know material things by turning the light of the agent intellect on phantasms; this is a sort of intellectual X-ray which penetrates what is individual in the phantasms and shows up their essence. We call this process abstraction. We say that the intellect abstracts its ideas from phantasms. This is a kind of process of *de*-materializing and *de*-individualizing material things. And we can continue this process, refining more and more, drawing ideas from ideas, and reaching more and more abstract ideas. But we can never attain by such a process to the perfect idea of spiritual substance as such. Spirit is an essence altogether different from matter; hence no process of *de*-materializing can reveal spirit as it is in itself.

3. We cannot, therefore, have a perfect knowledge of infinite spirit. By reasoning we can know God's existence, and many of the divine attributes. But to know God directly in his spiritual essence is something we cannot have this side of heaven with its light of glory. Therefore, here on earth and exercising natural powers, man cannot know God directly in himself, but indirectly by reasoning back to the First Cause of creatures. Therefore those teachers are much mistaken who hold that the *first* thing known by the human intellect is God.

89. KNOWLEDGE IN THE SEPARATED HUMAN SOUL

1. When the soul is separated from the body by death, it does not lose its faculties of intellect and will; nor does it lose its knowledge. But the intellect cannot, as it must in this life, turn to phantasms in using its acquired knowledge. For phantasms are sense-images, and the separated soul has 'no senses. Therefore, in the state of separation, there is a change of mode or manner in the operation of intellect.

2. The separated soul grasps things that are in themselves understandable by a direct grasp. For the soul, being separated from matter, is the more perfectly knowing and knowable; "nonmateriality is the root of knowing and of knowledge." Thus the soul knows other souls perfectly, and knows angels less perfectly.

3. The separated soul is suffused with light from God which gives it the intelligible species of things knowable, and thus it knows natural things. Angelic knowledge is more perfect than this knowledge of the separated soul, for angels are naturally constituted for knowing without using phantasms, and the separated soul is not naturally so constituted.

4. The separated soul knows individual things by its retained

knowledge, habits and affections, under the divinely imparted light which both supplies intelligible species and compensates for the lack of phantasms which the intellect naturally requires for its operation. A soul with no retained knowledge, such as the soul of an infant, has all its knowledge by divine ordinance and divine light. The separated soul does not know all individual things; it knows to the extent established by the divine order.

5. The habit of knowledge, such as the grasp of first principles, remains in the separated soul. Sentient knowing habits, of course, are not there, for the senses are not there. The soul cannot forget any longer, nor can it now be deceived by fallacious reasoning.

6. Thus the mode of intellectual operation in a separated soul is one in harmony with a spiritual being; it depends upon the help of God through the ministration of supernal light.

7. Distance from the object known cannot hinder knowledge in the separated soul, for it knows through species imparted or preserved by divinely bestowed light in which local distance makes no difference at all.

8. Separated souls are naturally ignorant of what takes place on earth. But it is likely that the souls of the blessed in heaven are aware of what goes on among people on earth. Angels have this knowledge, and the souls enjoying the beatific vision are on a par with angels.

90. THE FIRST PRODUCTION OF MAN'S SOUL

1. The human soul is not an outpouring or sharing of the substance of God. God is pure actuality and absolute simplicity. His substance, therefore, cannot be divided or parceled out. The human soul is not a thing eternally existing in God's being. It is a creature. It is a thing *made*.

2. The soul is made by God's creative act. It is created; it is made out of nothing. It is a spirit, having in itself no material element nor any essential dependence upon what is material. Now, such a spiritual being can have no possible origin but by the direct creative act of God.

3. Since creation is an act proper to God alone, in which no creature can serve as a medium (such as an instrumental cause or a ministering cause), the soul must be created immediately by almighty God.

4. The human soul is not created and held in readiness for union with its body. For every soul is the soul of one definite human being, and not just *a* soul, suitable for any one of a number of bodies. The

soul bears a definite real relation to its own body, that is, the body which it is to constitute as the living body of one individual human being. There is no pre-existence of human souls. Soul and body together make one substantial thing, one essence and nature; the soul begins to exist when this one nature begins to exist. Therefore, the human soul is not produced before the body.

91. THE PRODUCTION OF THE FIRST HUMAN BODY

1. Holy Scripture (Gen. 2:7) says: "God made man of the slime of the earth." Earth and water mingled make slime. Thus the first human body has elements that belong to lifeless things, and also to plants and animals. And man's soul is a spirit, like the angels. Hence man is called "a world in little," a microcosm, for he has in himself something of all creatures in the universe: mineral, vegetal, animal, spiritual.

2. The first human body was produced by creation. [*Note:* The slime of the earth was not really material for making a human being, and did not become human until the soul was joined to it. The human body did not exist as the human body until God's creative act produced and infused the spiritual soul.] Creation is an act which precludes any medium; hence the first human body was created *immediately* by almighty God.

3. Man's body is admirably suited for its connatural operations. God gives to every nature the best constitution and equipment for the purpose it is to serve. This is not absolutely the best, but relatively the best—that is, best in relation to its purpose and use.

4. Scripture fittingly describes the production of man, and indicates that other earthly creatures are made for man's use and benefit.

92. THE PRODUCTION OF WOMAN

1. Woman is necessary to man for purposes of generation according to God's plan for the propagation of the human race. When the first man had been created, God said (Gen. 2:18): "It is not good for man to be alone; let us make him a helper like to himself."

2. It is entirely fitting that woman should be made from man. This fact shows the likeness of man to God; for as one God is the principle of the whole universe, so one man is the principle of the whole human race. Further, the fact that woman is derived from man should make a man love his wife and cherish her as "bone of my bone, and flesh of my flesh." Again, this fact indicates the order of domestic life, with man as the natural head of the household. Finally, the origin of woman from man has a holy allegorical meaning, and foreshadows the origin of the Church from Christ.

3. The first woman was formed from a rib of the first man: "God built the rib which he took from Adam into a woman" (Gen. 2:22). Woman was suitably taken from man's side, to indicate social equality and companionship; she was not taken from man's head to rule him, nor from his feet to be his slave.

4. Only God can produce a man from the slime of the earth and a woman from the rib of a man. Therefore the woman, as well as the man, was formed immediately by almighty God.

93. MAN AS THE IMAGE OF GOD

1. Scripture (Gen. 1:26) tells us that God said, "Let us make man to our own image and likeness." An image is a kind of copy of its prototype. Unless the image is in every way perfect, it is not the equal of its prototype. Finite man cannot be a perfect image of the infinite God. Man is an imperfect image of God. This means that man is made to resemble God in some manner.

2. The image of God in man makes him superior to other earthly creatures. St. Augustine says (*Gen. ad lit.* vi 12), "Man's excellence consists in the fact that God made him to His own image by giving him an intellectual soul which raises him above the beasts of the field." It is true that all creatures have a likeness to God, some by the fact that they exist, some by the further fact that they live, some by the still further fact that they have knowledge. But only intellectual creatures (angels and men) have a close likeness to God; only such creatures have the spiritual operations of understanding and willing. Of earthly creatures, man has a true likeness to God; other creatures have a trace or vestige of God rather than an image.

3. The angels are pure spirits, that is, they are unmingled with matter, and they are not intended for substantial union with matter. Therefore they are more perfect in their intellectual nature than man is, and, in consequence, they bear a more perfect image of God than man does. In some respects, however, man is more like to God than angels are. For man proceeds from man, as God (in the mysterious proceeding of the divine Persons) proceeds from God; whereas angels do not proceed from angels. And again, man's soul is entirely in the whole body and entirely in every part of the body; thus it images the mode of God's presence in the universe.

4. The image of God is in every individual human being. It shows in this: that God perfectly knows and loves himself, and the individual human being has a natural aptitude for knowing and loving God. Man, by grace, can love God on earth, although imperfectly; in heaven, by grace and glory, man can love God perfectly. Hence

the image of God is in the individual man. [*Note:* It is important to ponder the fact here presented in a day when more and more importance and value is ascribed to society as such.]

5. The divine image in man reflects God in Unity and also in Trinity. In creating man, God said (Gen. 1:26): "Let *us* make man to *our* own image and likeness."

6. The image of God in Trinity appears in man's intellect and will and their interaction. In God, the Father begets the Word; the Father and the Word spirate the Holy Ghost. In man, the intellect begets the word or concept; the intellect with its word wins the recognition or love of the will.

7. Thus the image of the Trinity is found in the acts of the soul. In a secondary way, this image is found in the faculties of the soul, and in the habits which render the faculties apt and facile in operation.

8. The image of God is in the soul, not because the soul can know and love, but because it can know and love God. And the divine image is found in the soul because the soul turns to God, or, at any rate, has a nature that enables it to turn to God.

9. Man is created to the image and likeness of God. The image of God is discerned in the acts and faculties and habits of the soul. The likeness of God is either a quality of this image, or it is the state of the soul as spiritual, not subject to decay or dissolution.

94. THE INTELLECT OF THE FIRST MAN

1. The first man in the state of innocence had a perfect human intellect. It was unclouded and unhampered by any disorder in the lower faculties. Yet this perfect intellect did not enable the first man to see God in his essence. Had the first man seen God so, he would have instantly adhered changelessly to the divine will, and could never have sinned. The first man's knowledge of God was vastly superior to our own, both because of his unimpaired natural faculties, and because of God's gifts and graces. Yet this splendid knowledge was not the knowledge of vision.

2. Nor could the first man directly and perfectly understand the essence of angels. For man, even in the perfection of his sinless nature, was still man; his intellect operated by turning to phantasms (sense-images in imagination). But angels cannot be perceived by means of sense-images. Angels cannot be perfectly known, as they are in themselves, by the human intellect even in its state of pristine perfection.

3. Man was created in the state of natural perfection; he was supplied with all knowledge necessary for the proper conduct of his life,

for the instructing and ruling of offspring. The first man was supplied *divinely* with knowledge of all things that man has an aptitude
to know. Further, since man is made for a supernatural end, the
first man was endowed with supernatural faith, and with knowledge
of supernatural truths necessary for the supernatural direction of his
life and his efforts. But the first man was not given knowledge of
things needless to know, which he could not know naturally, such as
the secret thoughts of others, or knowledge of events to occur contingently in future time.

4. The good of the intellect is truth; its evil is falsity. The perfect
human intellect of the first man had no tendency whatever to admit
its evil. Hence the first man, so long as he retained the state of innocence, could not be deceived. He might lack knowledge of particular truths that he had no need to know, but he could not possibly
accept a false statement as true. When Eve was deceived by the
serpent, she must have already sinned inwardly by pride, and so lost
the first innocence which is immune to deception.

95. THE WILL OF THE FIRST MAN

1. Man was created in grace. The subjection of his reason to God,
and of his lower appetites to his reason, were gifts of grace, not
merely natural perfections.

2. The lower appetites of man are the tendencies of his bodily
nature. Now, that which experiences appetency or tendency undergoes something. The Latin word for an undergoing is *passio*. Hence
the experience, the kick-back, of sentient appetites (concupiscible
and irascible) is called *passion*. We distinguish the passions, according to the appetites which they follow upon, as concupiscible and
irascible passions. And, although the passions belong to the sentient
order, we call them the passions of the soul because they exercise an
influence which rises into the intellective order and affects the faculties
of the soul, especially the will. The passions of the soul are: (a) the
concupiscible passions: love-hatred, desire-aversion, joy-grief; (b) the
irascible passions: hope-despair, courage-fear, anger. Our first parents,
in the state of innocence, were not subject to the passions that have
reference to evil, for they had to face no evil, present or threatening;
hence they were not subject to fear, grief, despair, anger, or inordinate desire. They had only such passions as refer to present and
future good: joy, love, hope, orderly desire. And these passions of our
first parents were, before the fall, perfectly subject to their reason,
that is, to their intellectually enlightened will.

3. Virtues are habits (that is, stable qualities) which steadily dis-

pose the soul to act in accordance with reason and God's law. The
first man had all the virtues that suited his state, and he had the
habitual aptitude for those virtues which had no place in the state of
innocence, such, for instance, as the virtue of penance.

4. Considering the full and unimpeded flow of grace to the sinless soul, we find that the actions of man in the state of innocence
were of greater merit than those performed after the fall. But
considering the difficulty which fallen man experiences in performing good works, we may discern a greater merit in good actions performed after the fall. A small thing done *with difficulty* may mean
more than a great thing done with ease. Our Lord said that the poor
widow who gave only two small coins in charity, which were all
she had, gave more than the rich people who, out of their abundance,
made large contributions.

96. THE RULING POWER OF MAN IN THE STATE OF INNOCENCE

1. The first man had absolute rule and command over the animate
creatures of the earth. For God said (Gen. 1:26): "Let him [man]
have dominion over the fishes of the sea, and the birds of the air, and
the beasts of the earth." Now dominion means lordship, mastership,
even ownership. All sentient creatures obeyed innocent man and
none disobeyed him. When, however, man disobeyed God, these
sentient creatures were no longer subject to man's absolute control or
mastership.

2. Man was created as master of all earthly creatures. And he was
master of his own powers and tendencies, finding in them no rebellion
against his reason, that is, against his intellectually enlightened free
will.

3. Human beings are all equal as images and children of God. But,
as we plainly see, there are otherwise many inequalities among human beings. They differ in sex, size, age, tastes, manners, abilities,
health, strength, skills, and in countless other ways. Now, in the state
of innocence there would have been some of these inequalities, but
none that involved defect or fault, whether of soul or of body.

4. In the state of innocence, man could not have been master of
other men in the sense of holding them in thrall or slavery. But there
would still have been need of a social order; there would have been
rulers and subjects. Parents, too, would have ruled and guided their
children. But there would have been no harshness of rule, no injustice,
no resentment in those ruled against their rulers.

97. THE PRESERVATION OF MAN IN THE STATE OF INNOCENCE

1. Man, in the state of innocence, was immortal; he was not to die. But immortality was a supernaturally bestowed gift; it was not merely a perfection of man's nature. And man lost this supernatural gift by his rebellion against God. It was by sin that death came into the world.

2. In view of the supernatural gift of immortality or deathlessness, man was to be free from the ravages of age, sickness, injury, breakdown, decay. To this extent, man was to be impassible, that is, not subject to suffering or harmful influence. Man could have undergone normal and nonharming experiences, such as appetite for food and the tendency to sleep. Man's impassibility was lost, with his immortality, by the original sin.

3. In the state of innocence, man needed food; God told our first parents (Gen. 2:16) to eat of the fruits of all the trees of Paradise except that of one certain tree. Food will always be a requirement of living man until the body is spiritualized at the general resurrection; then there will be no need whatever of bodily sustenance.

4. Scripture indicates that fallen man might have gained immortality again by eating of the "tree of life" (Gen. 3:22). But this would not have been an absolute immortality such as man had lost. The "tree of life" could have rejuvenated man, but it would not have given man permanent youth and unaging perfection; it would have had to be eaten again and again; it would save man from age, but age would come on anew.

98. THE PRESERVING OF THE HUMAN RACE IN THE STATE OF INNOCENCE

1. The human race is preserved by propagation. When there were only two human beings, they received God's command (Gen. 1:28), "Increase and multiply and fill the earth." Hence, in the state of innocence, there would have been generation.

2. And this generation would have been accomplished as it is now accomplished, but with orderly tendency, and with full subjection to reason, without any unruly passion.

99. THE BODILY LIFE OF OFFSPRING IN THE STATE OF INNOCENCE

1. There is no reason to suppose that children born in the state of innocence would have been perfectly strong and able to use their members (to walk, for instance) right from the moment of their birth. The tender weakness of infancy is not a defect of nature consequent upon sin; it is a normal and natural condition; for nature tends to develop its perfections, moving from a less perfect to a more perfect state. Children born in the state of innocence would have possessed strength and power suitable to their age, and advancing with their age.

2. Nor should we suppose, as some have done, that, in the state of innocence, there would have been no distinction of sex. Distinction of sex was present in our first parents in their innocence; it belongs to the rounded completeness of human nature; it is a requirement for the propagation of the race according to the Creator's plan; it manifests, in its order, the graded variety and perfection of the universe.

100. THE RIGHTEOUSNESS OF OFFSPRING IN THE STATE OF INNOCENCE

1. In the state of innocence, children would have been born in righteousness or grace. Just as the children of fallen first parents inherit the original sin, so the children of sinless first parents would have inherited the original righteousness.

2. But children born in the state of innocence would not have been confirmed in grace. They would have been capable of committing sin. Man is never confirmed in grace until he beholds the beatific vision.

101. THE KNOWLEDGE OF OFFSPRING IN THE STATE OF INNOCENCE

1. It is in accord with human nature to acquire knowledge, not to be born with knowledge already in the mind. The fact that man, at birth, is unequipped with knowledge, is not a defect; it is a normal condition of nature. In the state of innocence, children would doubtless have had a perfect aptitude for learning without difficulty, and would have acquired knowledge readily as they advanced in age and experience. But they would not have possessed knowledge from birth.

2. And therefore children in the state of innocence would not have

had the use of reason from earliest infancy. They would have come to the use of reason more readily and perfectly than do children in the fallen state of mankind.

102. PARADISE

1. The name *paradise* means a garden. Some have thought that the Paradise in which our first parents were placed was their spiritual state, enriched as it was with supernatural graces and gifts. Others maintain that Paradise was a place. St. Augustine thinks that Paradise means both the spiritual condition and the local habitation of our first parents.

2. Paradise must have been a place perfectly suitable for man, a dwelling place in exquisite accord with his state of innocence. It is reasonable to suppose that Paradise was a place of great beauty, a bright place, temperate in climate, and with purest atmosphere.

3. Man was placed in Paradise to work therein and to keep it (Gen. 2:15). Man's labor there would have been a most pleasing activity, not burdensome nor fatiguing. This task was given to man as a blessing. It was to engage his attention, to keep him from idleness which might engender pride and sin. Laboring in Paradise, man would have been increasingly aware of its beauty and precious character; he would have been moved to love and thank God for it, and would thus have tended to continual watchfulness lest by sin he should lose so great a treasure.

4. Adam was placed in Paradise after he had been created (Gen. 2:15). But Eve was created in Paradise itself. Had these two remained faithful and innocent, their children would have been born in Paradise.

THE DIVINE GOVERNMENT

(QUESTIONS 103 TO 119)

103. GOD'S GOVERNING OF THINGS

1. We observe an unfailing order in the world. Order involves an orderer, a governor. In an earlier part of our study we saw that things in the world have existence and direction to their end or purpose by the divine goodness. Therefore, divine goodness governs the world.

2. The universe is not an end unto itself. It is contingent being, not necessary being; it has being or goodness by participation. Hence it comes from a cause other than itself, and is directed to an end other than itself. It is directed or governed by the necessary being, the necessary goodness, the divine goodness. That is, the universe is made to express and manifest the divine goodness.

3. Ultimately, the world has one governor, not many governors. The harmony of the universe manifests this fact. Besides, there is only one divine goodness.

4. The effects of government in the world may be variously considered. In so far as all creatures are to manifest the divine goodness, the effect of government is one. In so far as creatures are divinely governed so as to *be* good and to *do* good, the effect of government is twofold. In so far as the effects of government are discerned in a vast multitude of individual creatures, the effect of government is manifold.

5. All things are subject to the divine government, since this is the divine goodness of God himself. The divine goodness is both the first effecting cause and the ultimate final cause (or ultimate goal) of everything. No positive being can exist without the divine goodness, and therefore everything, in particular and in singular as well as in general, is governed by the same divine goodness.

6. God alone designs the government of the universe, and this is his *providence*. The design is carried into execution or actual governing operation through use of secondary causes (creatures) as media or means of governing.

7. Since God is the first and universal cause, nothing in the universe can lie outside the order of his government. When something seems to evade divine government, the very cause of the seeming evasion will be found in the divine government itself. As we saw in our study of divine providence, nothing whatever is outside the divine rule.

8. Nothing can resist the general order of divine government. Even a sinner in his act of sin aims at apparent good; it is good that the sinner is after, although he perversely seeks it in the wrong place. Sin is against God's law and will, but it cannot upset the general order of divine government. And, out of evil God draws good, "ordering all things pleasingly," as he "moves from end to end mightily."

104. SPECIAL EFFECTS OF DIVINE GOVERNMENT

1. God creates things out of nothing. He must also preserve things created or they would fall back into nothingness. Preservation or *conservation* as it is often called, is a fundamental effect of divine govern-

ment. Now, things may be preserved indirectly by putting them out of the way of danger; thus a mother preserves a precious vase by setting it out of reach of her romping children. And things may be preserved directly by positive conserving action; thus one who catches a fragile vase as it is falling preserves it directly. God preserves *all* things directly. He also preserves some bodily things indirectly. Spirits need no indirect preserving, for nothing can threaten or destroy them. The same divine power which gives existence to creatures (their cause *in fieri,* their cause in becoming) is exercised to preserve creatures in existence (their cause *in esse,* their cause in being). Therefore it is justly said that "conservation is a continuous creation."

2. God preserves all creatures, as we have just seen, by positive sustaining power; that is, God conserves all creatures directly. But he does not conserve all things *immediately,* that is, without using any creatural means or medium. In some cases God uses creatures to preserve creatures; thus by air, light, warmth, and the fruits of the earth, God sustains and preserves living bodies. Yet God is himself present *in* and *to* these media.

3. God creates and preserves. The direct opposite of creation is annihilation. Conservation keeps creation from being followed by annihilation, that is, complete reduction to nothing. God has the power to annihilate creatures. For he who has power to produce by his free choice has ability to withdraw that power by free choice. And if God were to withdraw his creative power from creatures, they would simply not exist; they would be annihilated.

4. But, as a fact, God does not annihilate anything. In creating, God establishes an order of things which manifests the divine goodness; this order is maintained by preserving things, not by utterly destroying them. Divine wisdom would not be expressed in creating a thing merely to annihilate it.

105. GOD'S MOVING OR CHANGING OF CREATURES

1. We speak first of bodily creatures. A body is made of matter and form. Matter is common to all bodies; it has no existence of its own apart from existing bodies. Form, joined substantially with matter, constitutes a body as an existing material substance of an essential kind. We speak here of matter and form, and we mean primal matter and substantial form. An *existing* body is not primal matter, but secondary matter. And the variable determinations of a body (size, shape, color, temperature, rest or motion, resemblance to other things, etc.) are accidental forms, not substantial forms. Now, God, in cre-

ating bodies, joins substantial form to primal matter in each case, and so produces actual bodily substances.

2. God can move or effect bodily substance in any way he wills, for he is the universal cause and is also infinite power. Nor is there anything unworthy in the notion of God moving matter. Though matter is the least of creatures, it *is* a creature, and not unworthy of the operation of the Creator.

3. Speaking now of God's moving of nonbodily creatures, we say that God moves the intellect of men and angels by giving them power to understand, and by impressing and preserving in them (directly, or through connatural operation designed by God) the intelligible species by which they understand.

4. God alone is the supreme and universal good which is the necessary object of the will of intellectual creatures. God moves the will by giving it power to act, by making it tend to the good in universal, and, without destroying its liberty, moving it in its individual choices.

5. God works in all things in such a way as suits the operation natural to each thing. For it is God who gives creatures existence and nature, and works in them to preserve both.

6. God can do things that are not in the established course of nature so long as such action would not mean a contradiction in God himself. For God as First Cause gives things their determinate essence, and to be such things they must have that essence. God cannot give an essence and not give it. Since, for example, God has chosen to make man a rational animal, he cannot make a man who is not a rational animal. Thus in the immediate reference of things to their First Cause, there can be no divinely imparted movement or change outside the divinely determined order. But God can act outside the ordinary course in which divine government is exercised through secondary causes. God can produce the effects of secondary causes even when such causes are absent, and he can have them produce effects which are altogether beyond their natural powers, or even in conflict with their natural action. Our Lord used clay, spittle, and the waters of a certain pool to cure blindness; he used the flames of the fiery furnace rather to preserve than to destroy the three young men.

7. An effect produced by God in the bodily universe, outside the order of created nature, is called a *miracle*.

8. Miracles differ in greatness, not with reference to God's power which is infinite and therefore has no greater or less, but with reference to the extent by which miracles surpass the powers of creatures. There are three grades or orders of miracles: (a) The first and greatest

order of miracles is that of miracles in the very *substance* of the deed
or fact. A miracle of this type is altogether outside the reach of any created power. Such would be the miracle of glorifying a human body, or
the miracle of two bodies simultaneously occupying one place. (b) The
second order of miracles is that of miracles in the *subject* in which
they occur. Such, for example, would be the miracle of raising a dead
person to life. Now, nature actually can give life; hence, in raising the
dead, there is no miracle of substance of the fact. But nature cannot
give life to a corpse. It is utterly beyond the powers of creatures to
give life to such a subject. (c) The third order of miracles is that of
miracles of manner or *mode*. Such a miracle, for example, would be
the *instantaneous* healing of a grievous wound or sore. Nature can
heal; nature can heal in such a subject (that is, the person afflicted);
but nature cannot heal in this way, that is, instantaneously. Nature
heals in a gradual and successive manner which requires much time.

106. HOW ONE CREATURE MOVES ANOTHER:
ANGELS

1. One angel can enlighten another, the superior angel manifesting
truths which it grasps perfectly to inferior angels whose grasp is less
perfect. It agrees with the nature of intellectual creatures to move or
effect others of their kind in this fashion of one teaching and others
being taught.

2. Thus, by affording enlightenment, one angel may move another
angel's intellect. But one angel cannot change another's will. Only God
can effect such a change.

3. An inferior angel cannot enlighten a superior angel any more than
a candle can bring illumination to the sun. Among human beings, who
learn by degrees, because their knowing is bound up with material
things, it can happen that one who knows much may be enlightened
by one who knows little. This cannot be so among pure spirits who do
not achieve knowledge ploddingly and piecemeal as human beings do.

4. The higher an angel is, the more it participates the divine goodness; consequently, the more it tends to impart its gifts to lesser angels.
The superior angel tends to give all that it knows to inferior angels,
but these cannot perfectly receive all that is given. Hence the superior
angels remain superior even though they impart all their knowledge.
Somewhat similarly, the human teacher who does all he can to impart
his own complete knowledge to his young pupils, remains superior in
knowledge even after he has taught the lesson; for the pupils take in
by a lesser capacity than that of the giver.

107. THE SPEECH OF ANGELS

1. Angels manifest knowledge to one another, and to this extent they "speak" to one another. But the speech of angels is not a matter of sounds or of uttered words. The speech of angels is a direct communication of knowledge from spirit to spirit.

2. An inferior angel can speak to a superior angel, even though, as we have seen, it cannot enlighten the superior angel; a candle cannot enlighten the sun, but it can burn visibly in the sunlight. An angel speaks by directing its thought in such wise that it is made known to another angel, superior or inferior. Such directing is done according to the free will of the angel speaking.

3. Certainly the angels "speak" to God by consulting his divine will and by contemplating with admiration his infinite excellence.

4. Neither time nor place has any influence on angelic speech or its effect. Local distance cannot impede the communication of angels.

5. Angelic speech is the ordering of angelic mind to angelic mind by the *will* of the angel speaking. Now, it belongs to the perfection of intellectual communication that it can be private; even a human being can speak to another person alone. Therefore, the angels who are superior to human beings, must be capable of communicating thoughts, angel to angel, without making their communication known to all the other angels. The scope of angelic communication depends on the will of the angel speaking; this will determines the communication for one other angel, or for several, or for all.

108. THE HIERARCHIES AND ORDERS OF ANGELS

1. A hierarchy is a sacred principality. And a principality means ruler and subjects. If we speak of the hierarchy of God and creatures, there is only one hierarchy. But if we consider only creatures who are dowered with God's gifts, there are many hierarchies. There is, for example, a human hierarchy; there is an angelic hierarchy. Indeed, among the angels themselves, there are three hierarchies according to three grades of angelic knowledge. But in God himself, that is, in the Blessed Trinity, there is no hierarchy. For there is no greater or lesser among the three Persons in God. All three Persons are one and the same God. The trinity is an order of distinct Persons, but it is not a hierarchical order.

2. The nature of a hierarchy requires a classifying of orders within it; these may be loosely described as upper, middle, and lower orders. In human social and political groups we have such a classification: the nobility or aristocracy; the middle classes; the common people.

Among angels there are three orders in each hierarchy (upper, middle, and lower orders), and, since there are three angelic hierarchies, there are, in all, nine orders of angels.

3. As we have noticed, our human knowledge of angels is not direct and perfect; we cannot know angels as they are in themselves. In our imperfect way, we assign many angels to each order, even while we realize that, since each angel is a complete species, it has its own specific office, and, to that extent, its own order. We cannot discern what these specific offices and orders are. If star differ from star in glory, much more does angel differ from angel. Our classification of angelic orders is, therefore, a kind of general classification.

4. Among human beings, who are all of one species and nature, a hierarchy, in the true sense of sacred principality, is a hierarchy of holiness, that is, of God's grace. But, as we have just recalled, angels are distinguished from one another, not only by the gifts of grace, but by their very nature; for each angel is the *only* being of its specific kind. Each angel is essentially different from every other angel, whereas each human being is essentially the same as every other human being. Moreover, the gifts of grace are given to angels to the full of their natural capacity to receive them; this is not the case with human beings.

5. There are three angelic hierarchies. Each hierarchy has three orders. All the heavenly spirits of all hierarchies and orders are called angels. Thus the term angel is common and generic. The same name, usually with a capital letter, is the proper and collective name for the lowest order of the lowest hierarchy of heavenly spirits. We must therefore distinguish *angel*, which means any heavenly spirit from highest to lowest, from *Angel* which means a member of the lowest order of all.

6. The following hierarchies and orders exist among the angels: (a) The highest hierarchy includes the orders of (in descending order of rank) Seraphim, Cherubim, Thrones. (b) The middle hierarchy includes (in descending order of rank) the orders of Dominations, Virtues, Powers. (c) The lowest hierarchy includes (in descending order of rank) Principalities, Archangels, Angels. This classification is commonly, but not unanimously, accepted by learned doctors.

7. After the end of this bodily world, the angelic orders will continue to exist, but their offices will not be altogether the same as they now are, for they will then no longer need to help human beings to save their souls.

8. By the gifts of grace, human beings can merit glory in a degree that makes them equal to the angels in each of the orders. Therefore,

human beings who get to heaven are taken into the angelic orders. But these human beings remain human beings; they are not turned into angels.

109. ORDERS AMONG THE FALLEN ANGELS

1. The angels that rebelled and became demons did not lose their nature or their connatural gifts. They cast away, by their sin, the grace in which they were created. They did not cast away the beatific vision, for they never had it. Now, if we think of angelic orders as orders of angels in glory, then, of course, there are no orders of bad angels. But if we consider angelic orders as orders of angelic nature simply, there are orders among the demons.

2. Certainly, there is a precedence among bad angels; there is a subjection of some to others.

3. Demons of superior nature do not enlighten inferior demons; enlightenment here could only mean the manifestation of truth with reference to God, and the fallen angels have perversely and permanently turned away from God. But demons can speak to one another, that is, they can make known their thoughts to one another, for this ability belongs to the angelic nature which the demons retain.

4. The nearer creatures are to God the greater is their rule over other creatures. Therefore, the good angels rule and control the demons.

110. THE ACTION OF ANGELS ON BODIES

1. Superior rules inferior; hence angels rule the bodily world. St. Gregory says that in this visible world nothing occurs without the agency of invisible creatures.

2. Angels, however, have not power to produce or transform bodies at will. God alone gives first existence to things; after first creation, bodies come from bodies. But angels can stir bodily agencies to produce change in bodies.

3. Angels can directly control the local movement of bodies, for this is an accidental change in bodies, not a substantial production of bodies nor a substantial change.

4. Angels cannot, *of themselves,* work miracles. A miracle, by definition, is a work proper to God alone. Of course, angels can serve, even as holy men may serve, as ministers or instruments in the performing of miracles. Angels, good or bad, can do wonderful things, but only such as lie within the power of angelic nature, and a miracle surpasses the powers of all created natures.

111. THE ACTION OF ANGELS ON MEN

1. Since angels are superior to man, they can enlighten man. They can strengthen the understanding of human beings and make men aware, in some sensible manner, of the truths to be imparted. Thus angels can act upon the human intellect.

2. But angels cannot act directly upon the human will; God alone can do this.

3. Nevertheless, angels, good or bad, can exercise an *indirect* influence on human wills by stirring up images in the human imagination. And angels, good or bad, can, by their natural power, arouse sentient appetites and passions in the same way, that is, by producing images in the human imagination.

4. Equally, an angel can work upon the human senses, either outwardly, as, for example, by assuming some visible form, or inwardly, by disturbing the sense-functions themselves, as, for example, making a man see what is not really there.

112. THE MISSION OR MINISTRY OF ANGELS

1. God sends angels to minister to his purposes among bodily creatures. This sending or mission is not the dispatching of angels upon a journey. To be sent means to be present in a new place in which one was not present before, or to be present where one was but in a *new way*. An angel is present where it exercises or applies its powers, and not elsewhere. When God has an angel apply its powers to a creature, the angel is *sent* to that creature. God is the sender and the first principle of the effect produced by the angel sent; God is also the ultimate goal or final cause of the work so produced. The angel is God's minister or intelligent instrument; by its being sent it renders ministry to God.

2. It seems that, of the nine orders of angels, only five orders are sent for the external ministry, and that the superior angels are never sent.

3. Angels are said to assist before the throne of God. All angels assist inasmuch as all permanently possess the beatific vision. But, in a special sense, only the superior angels assist before God's throne. These superior angels, beholding mysteries in God, communicate what they behold to the inferior angels. All good angels see God in the beatific vision, but the superior angels behold deeper and wider mysteries in God than do the lesser angels. By their deeper and wider knowledge of divine mysteries, the superior angels are said to assist.

4. Angels sent in the external ministry are those whose names indicate some kind of administrative or executive office. These are, in descending rank, Virtues, Powers, Principalities, Archangels, Angels.

113. ANGEL GUARDIANS

1. It is fitting that changeable and fallible human beings should be guarded by angels, and thus steadily moved and regulated to good.

2. St. Jerome, in his commentary on Matthew 8:10, says, "The dignity of human souls is great, for each has an angel appointed to guard it." God's providence extends, not only to mankind as a whole, but to individual human beings. Each human being has, by God's loving providence, his own guardian angel.

3. It seems that the office of being guardians to men belongs to the lowest order of heavenly spirits, that is, the ninth order, the order of Angels.

4. Each human being, without exception, has a guardian angel as long as he is a wayfarer, that is, during his whole earthly life. In heaven a man will have an angel companion to reign with him, but not a guardian; no guardian is needed when the guarded journey has been successfully completed. In hell, each man will have a fallen angel to punish him.

5. Each human being has his guardian angel from the moment of his birth, and not, as some have taught, only from the moment of baptism.

6. The guardian angel is a gift of divine providence. He never fails or forsakes his charge. Sometimes, in the workings of providence, a man must suffer trouble; this is not prevented by the guardian angel.

7. Guardian angels do not grieve over the ills that befall their wards. For all angels uninterruptedly enjoy the beatific vision and are forever filled with joy and happiness. Guardian angels do not will the sin which their wards commit, nor do they directly will the punishment of this sin; they do will the fulfillment of divine justice which requires that a man be allowed to have his way, to commit sin if he so choose, to endure trials and troubles, and to suffer punishment.

8. All angels are in perfect agreement with the divine will in so far as it is revealed to them. But it may happen that not all angels have the same revelations of the divine will for their several ministries, and thus, among angels, there may arise a conflict, discord, or strife. This explains what is said in Daniel 10:13 about the guardian angel of the Persians resisting "for one and twenty days" the prayer of Daniel offered by the Archangel Gabriel.

114. ASSAULTS OF BAD ANGELS ON MAN

1. To tempt means one of two things: (a) to make a test or trial; thus "God tempted Abraham" (Gen. 22:1); (b) to invite, incite, or allure someone to sin. It is in the second sense of the word that the fallen angels tempt human beings. God permits this assault of the demons upon men, and turns it into a human opportunity and benefit; God gives to men all requisite aid to repulse the assaults of demons, and to advance in grace and merit by resisting temptation.

2. To the devil (who is the fallen Lucifer, now Satan) belong exclusively the plan and campaign of the demons' assaults upon mankind.

3. In one way the devil is the cause of every human sin; he tempted Adam and thus contributed to the fall which renders men prone to sin. But, in a strict sense, diabolical influence does not enter into every sin of man. Some sins come of the weakness of human nature and from inordinateness of appetites which the sinner freely allows to prevail.

4. Angels cannot perform miracles; therefore demons cannot. But demons can do astonishing things, and can occasion real havoc.

5. When the assault of demons is repulsed, the devil is not rendered incapable of further attack. But it seems that he cannot return immediately to the assault, but only after the lapse of a definite time. God's mercy as well as the shrewdness of the tempter, seems to promise so much.

115. HOW ONE CREATURE MOVES ANOTHER: BODIES

1. Bodies act upon other bodies. Fire burns wood; food supports living substance; a horse pulls a wagon; wind erodes a mountain; water moistens earth. Every bodily substance, by its being what it is, by its actuality, has an activity by which it affects other bodies, and is in potentiality to be affected by other bodies.

2. Living bodies bear the germs or seeds of offspring which they tend to move into existence. Nonliving bodies have aptitude to be moved or affected by other bodies. In a word, all bodies exhibit a basic fitness or aptitude for the movement of body by body.

3. The heavenly bodies, and notably the sun, produce effects in inferior bodies. Each inferior body receives, according to its nature, the action of a superior body. The movement of earthly bodies is referred to movements of the heavenly bodies.

4. The heavenly bodies cannot directly affect the higher powers of

man, that is, the intellect and the will. They may, however, exercise an indirect influence on the intellective powers through the senses of the human body. It is impossible that the heavenly bodies should be the direct cause of human actions.

5. The heavenly bodies can have no effect at all upon the demons or bad angels; these angels are spirits, and no influence of extraneous bodies on spirits is possible.

6. Nor is the direct influence of heavenly bodies on matter always and necessarily effective.

116. FATE

1. *Fate* in the sense of a rigid controlling power over human actions, with its focus or seat in the stars, is not only nonexistent, but impossible.

2. But sometimes the word *fate* is used for divine providence.

3. Fate as divine providence is a changeless rule, but this does not mean fixity and mechanical necessity of events. As we have noted elsewhere, providence does not interfere with free will itself, nor does it render meaningless the notion of contingent happenings.

4. Fate as providence has reference to creatures and creatural effects; it has no reference to the divine operations in themselves.

117. MAN'S ACTION UPON THINGS

1. Man acts upon his fellow man. In special, man can enlighten or teach others.

2. Man cannot teach or enlighten angels, but by his speech or prayer he can make known to angels what they could not otherwise know, that is, his own secret thoughts and intentions.

3. Man cannot move or affect bodies directly by acts of free will. Indirectly his will can move or change bodies by its decision which makes a man take hold on bodies and change them. And indirectly, by holding the mind and imagination to a certain train of thought or fancy, the will can work a change in a man's own body. Thus may a man move himself to resolution, to calmness in trial, to anger; and concomitant changes result in the body itself. Of course, by natural action, man's will commands the normal movements of the body exercised in such acts as stretching out the hands, or walking.

4. When the human soul is separated from its body by death, it has no further control over the members of that body, or of any other body, unless God, by a miracle, should give it that power.

118. THE PRODUCTION OF MAN'S SOUL

1. Plant-souls and animal-souls, after first creation, come into existence by generation; they are propagated with the living bodies they animate.

2. The human soul, being rational, is a spirit; it cannot be generated; it cannot come from matter, which is a thing inferior to itself. It cannot originate except by the direct creative act of God in each instance.

3. The human soul does not exist before its body. By one single act of creation God produces the soul and joins it with matter, and the soul constitutes this matter as a living human being. The human body is generated by parents, but it is made a living human being by the soul which God creates, and, by an act indivisible from creation, joins to matter within the body of the human mother.

119. THE PRODUCTION OF MAN'S BODY

1. Man preserves life and grows to maturity by taking nutriment or food. By the process called nutrition, man changes food into his own living substance.

2. Nutriment or food, assimilated by the body and made one with its living essence and nature, enables man to continue life and to exercise his connatural operations. It thus enables man to propagate his kind.

[Ia IIae]

The FIRST PART *of* THE SECOND PART

[*Questions 1-114*]

⌢⌣⌢

MAN'S LAST END

(QUESTIONS 1 TO 5)

1. THE END MAN SEEKS

1. Alone among earthly creatures, man is master of his acts. The distinctively *human* characteristic is the exercise of free will. Hence free will acts are human acts. A free will act is any thought, word, deed, desire, or omission which comes from a man acting with full knowledge of what he is doing, who is free to act or to refrain from action, and who gives the full assent of his will to the act. Only such an act is a *human act* in full perfection. Other acts performed by a man, but inadvertently, or without full knowledge, freedom, and choice, are indeed acts of a man, but they are not human acts. Since human acts are free will acts, and since free will acts are acts chosen and performed in view of an end or purpose or goal, it is evident that human acts are *acts for an end,* that is, acts done for the purpose of attaining an end. The common phrase for such acts is, "acts to an end," the word *to* meaning *towards* or *in view of.*

2. Now, it is true that all acts of every being are acts to an end. Every agent (doer, actor, performer) acts to an end. There is purpose in every activity. But only man, among earthly creatures, chooses or moves himself to an end by exercising free will.

3. That which gives a thing its essential character is said to *specify* the thing. Now, what gives human acts their essential character is the fact that they are freely chosen for a purpose—an end to be attained. That which specifies any single human act is the end or purpose it seeks to achieve. Hence we say that a human act is specified by its end.

4. There is one ultimate end and purpose to be attained by human beings, and to this end all human acts tend.

5. The ultimate end towards which man tends in all his human acts is his crowning good, his ultimate and perfect *fulfillment.* This is a single end; man cannot possibly tend to several last ends.

6. Back of all his free will acts is man's drive towards supreme and universal good, wholly complete, perfectly satisfying. Even in his sinful acts, a man is seeking good, that is, satisfaction, although he is

perversely seeking it in the wrong place. All individual choices, all separate human acts, are as steps (real or apparent) towards the supreme good, just as every step in every stairway is a step *upwards*. Whatever man freely wills, he wills to the last end.

7. All human beings have the same nature, that is, the same human essence equipped for normal human operations. Therefore all men have the same last end, the same ultimate goal. This last end is complete and enduring satisfaction or fulfillment; such fulfillment is called *beatitude* or happiness. But all men do not agree about the precise things in which their fulfillment and consequent happiness are to be found. Some think to attain the end by becoming rich, some by enjoying pleasures, some by exercising power, some by being praised and honored, and so on. It is as though all men were determinately set to reach a certain city, but were not all in agreement about the right road they must take to get there. In this case, surely, prudence suggests that the men of soundest and most studious judgment should be permitted to indicate the way.

8. All men seek fulfillment or satisfaction, that is, all seek beatitude or happiness. This is the *subjective* last end of man; it is to be *in* man as in its *subject;* for the subject of anything is that reality in which the thing resides or takes place. Now, the *objective* last end of man is the object which, when possessed, will give him happiness. The objective last end of man, the object he seeks to attain so that he may have perfect satisfaction in it, is the infinite good. The infinite good is God. Man seeks God in all his human acts inasmuch as in all these acts he seeks what will please, and satisfy, and fill up needs and desires, and crown his human quest with enduring joy. In this, man differs from all other earthly substances, minerals, plants, animals. For, while all these things are the products of divine goodness and exist to reflect and manifest that goodness, they do not seek to attain the infinite good *subjectively;* only man does that. Hence man does not have the active concurrence of earthly creatures in his own ultimate quest of God and eternal happiness.

2. WHERE HAPPINESS IS FOUND

1. Man's happiness is not to be found in wealth, whether this be natural wealth which serves his normal needs (such as food, clothing, housing), or artificial wealth which can provide the items of natural wealth, that is, money. Wealth of any kind is a *means* for acquiring something else; it is a thing that serves; it does not fulfill. Hence it cannot be the true last end of man and the object that will render him enduringly and completely happy.

2. Nor can man's full happiness consist in honors bestowed because of some excellence in him. Any excellence in a man is in him by reason of some good already possessed; it means that he already has some degree of happiness. Honors come to him *because of* this happiness, and therefore honors cannot themselves be the constituting elements of perfect happiness.

3. Nor can man's happiness be found in fame and glory. These, like honors bestowed, presuppose some degree of happiness already attained, and this they publicize and praise. Fame and glory are *consequent* upon an imperfect happiness, and are, in some sense, the product of it. They cannot, therefore, be the essential elements of perfect happiness.

4. Man's perfect happiness cannot consist in the possession of power, for power is not a complete end, but a means; power is valuable according to the use to which it may be put. In a word, power looks on to something further; it cannot itself be the ultimate goal.

5. Man's ultimate happiness does not consist in goods of the body—life, health, strength, beauty, agility, etc.—for these goods preserve the body and its perfections. Merely to preserve life cannot be the end of life. Goods of the body are to be used by reason (intellect and will) somewhat as a ship is used by its master; the master does not use the ship merely to preserve the ship, but to carry profitable cargoes to desired ports. Thus it appears that the goods of the body are *means*, not complete ends. Besides, man is a rational being as well as a bodily being; he can never be completely fulfilled and satisfied by bodily goods.

6. Pleasures, whether bodily or intellectual, cannot bring a man ultimate happiness. We have just seen that bodily things cannot be man's perfect fulfillment. And mental enjoyments presuppose the end already attained; enjoyment follows upon possession of some good or end; what is consequent upon the end cannot itself be the end.

7. The goods of the soul—its essence, faculties, acts, habits, perfections—cannot constitute man's ultimate end. Happiness is *for* the soul, and to be attained *by* the soul. The objective ultimate happiness is something *outside* the soul, which the soul seeks to bring into itself and possess subjectively. Hence this ultimate end is not the soul itself, nor the goods belonging to the soul.

8. Indeed, no created good can give man perfect happiness. Only the essential, universal, and boundless good can bring man complete and unfading fulfillment. No created good is universal, essential, and boundless; only the *uncreated good* can be the ultimate end of man. And this uncreated good is God.

3. WHAT HAPPINESS IS

1. Ultimate *subjective* happiness is the state of fulfillment and satisfaction in a person who has obtained the end for which he is made. Ultimate *objective* happiness is the reality which, when possessed, will render the possessor subjectively happy by completely fulfilling and satisfying his entire nature. God is man's objective happiness. Possession of God in the beatific vision is man's ultimate subjective happiness.

2. Man's subjective happiness is a state and an operation. As a *state*, it is the permanent possession of fulfillment. As an *operation*, it is an act by which man lays hold of, and possesses, the object which renders him happy.

3. As an operation, man's ultimate subjective happiness is an operation of the intellective faculties, not of the senses. The senses cannot behold God in the beatific vision. Yet, as St. Augustine says, after the general resurrection, when souls and their bodies have been reunited, the happiness of the soul will overflow into the senses and make their operation perfect.

4. Man's ultimate subjective happiness, as an operation, is an act of intellect rather than an act of will. St. John (17:3) says, "This is eternal life, to know thee. . . ." Yet the delight or enjoyment consequent upon the attainment of happiness belongs to the will. The intellect possesses the object which gives happiness; the will rests delighted in its possession.

5. The intellect is *speculative* inasmuch as it knows and contemplates truth; it is *practical* inasmuch as it knows how to go after and possess good. Man's ultimate happiness is possessed in heaven; it is no longer sought after. Hence the act of ultimate happiness is an act of the speculative intellect.

6. The knowledge which a man acquires during earthly life, such as scientific and philosophical knowledge, will be, in heaven, an accidental item in his perfect happiness, but not an essential element of that happiness.

7. In heaven a man will have some happiness from contemplating the angels, but his pure and perfect happiness must come from contemplating God in the *beatific vision*. Man's intellect, which possesses the vision with the aid of the light of glory, is made for truth, and God alone is essential truth. God alone is the boundless fulfillment of the human intellect, as he is of the entire human nature.

8. Only in the beatific vision will the human intellect find its perfect

object. Possessing this object, the intellect will have nothing further to desire or to seek.

4. REQUISITES FOR HAPPINESS

1. The perfect happiness which man will have by the operation of the speculative intellect as it beholds God in the beatific vision, will be accompanied by rest and enjoyment of the will; in this consists the joy and delight of heaven.

2. In the act of happiness, the operation of the intellect ranks above the delight of the will, for the will's *fruition* or enjoyment depends upon the intellect's beholding of God in vision.

3. During earthly life man is a wayfarer, a traveler on the road, one whose journey is not yet completed; he is a *viator*. In heaven, the journey is over, and man beholds God; he is a *comprehensor*. This name does not indicate that man actually comprehends God in the full sense of the word comprehend; for, as we saw early in our studies, to comprehend means to know all that is knowable about an object known, and such knowledge can be found only in the infinite mind of God. Man in heaven is a comprehensor in the sense that he has now a direct and intuitive knowledge of the divine essence itself. The happiness of man in heaven involves three things: *vision* or direct and intuitive knowledge of God, man's last end; *comprehension* or the present possession of God, the last end; and *fruition* or delight of the will in the last end possessed.

4. Happiness cannot be perfectly attained without rightness or rectitude in the will, for this sets the will in proper alignment with the supreme good, and makes the will love what it loves in perfect subordination to God. In such subordination consists the perfection of the human will, and without this perfection man cannot be perfectly happy.

5. Man's ultimate happiness is essentially an operation of the intellect which is a faculty of the soul. Therefore the body is not *essential* to man's ultimate happiness. But there is a connatural tendency in each soul to *in*-form its own body, and if this tendency is defeated, there is a certain imperfection in the soul.

6. In the present life, a well-disposed body is required for earthly happiness. And, while the body, as we have seen, is not essential to the soul's happiness in heaven, it will be supplied to the soul at the general resurrection. Then the body itself will attain full perfection, and will contribute as an accidental factor to the happiness of the complete man in glory.

7. External goods, such as food, drink, and property, which are required in due measure for earthly happiness, will not be required at all in heaven. When souls and bodies are reunited at the general resurrection, human bodies will be spiritualized and will no longer have material or animal needs.

8. In heaven, the fellowship of friends is not essential to man's happiness, for God is all-sufficing. Yet doubtless friends will be loved and their fellowship will be enjoyed *in God*.

5. THE ATTAINMENT OF HAPPINESS

1. Man is manifestly made for happiness or fulfillment. His mind or intellect grasps the notion of universal good; his will tends to it. And the all-good God who made man has not given him *deceiving* gifts of mind and will. Happiness must be attainable.

2. In heaven, the objective happiness of man is God, and hence the happiness of heaven is objectively *one*. But subjectively one man can be happier than another in heaven, for one man may have a greater capacity (because of greater charity and a consequently larger endowment of the light of glory) for the happiness of heaven. Capacities will vary, but all capacities will be completely filled up.

3. In the present earthly life man may attain a degree of happiness, but cannot have perfect happiness. On earth limitations and drawbacks are associated with happiness. Only God possessed in beatific vision can make man perfectly happy, and this vision cannot be had in earthly life.

4. Once perfect happiness has been attained, it cannot be lost. For perfect happiness fills up man's capacity and all his appetites for good; there is no tendency left in man which might lead him astray and cause him to reject his happy state.

5. Man's natural powers can bring him happiness, but not perfect happiness, for man's nature tends to what it cannot itself achieve; it tends to, needs, and desires the supernatural. Man's true end is *super*natural, and is to be attained only by the aid of grace in this life, and the elevating and enlightening light of glory in heaven.

6. Only God can confer upon the soul in heaven the supernatural gift and grace called the light of glory which raises and illumines the intellect to enable it to behold God in his divine essence as the beatific vision. No angel or other creature can serve as intermediary in the bestowal of this gift of the light of glory; it is bestowed directly and immediately (that is, without intermediary) by God himself.

7. From a man who spends a period of responsible life on earth,

good works are required for the attaining of heaven. The will must choose the good it wishes to attain, and the will expresses its choice by its acts. To attain heaven, the will must choose and exercise works of virtue. Each meritorious work represents a step towards the supreme good.

8. All men have a connatural and inescapable desire for their own fulfillment, for their crowning good and what it will give them; that is, all men necessarily crave happiness, complete and unending. Although all men do not have the *right notion* of what true happiness is, and of how it is to be attained, all men, without exception, *crave* it.

HUMAN ACTS

(QUESTIONS 6 TO 21)

6. VOLUNTARINESS

1. We have seen that a human act is a free will act. It is any thought, word, deed, desire, or omission which comes from a man by his free, knowing, and deliberate choice. The Latin noun *voluntas* means the will, and the adjective which means pertaining to the will is *voluntarius*. From these Latin words we have the terms voluntary and voluntariness. A voluntary act is an act which proceeds from free will acting in the light of knowledge; such an act has voluntariness. Since every human act is a free will act, every human act is voluntary; every human act is performed with voluntariness.

2. Animals less than man are incapable of acting with true voluntariness, for they lack intellect and free will. Animals have sense knowledge, and can make sense judgment a guide for their action. But their acts never have a free and responsible voluntariness.

3. Voluntariness appears in every human act, even in human acts of omission, that is, in man's willful failure to act when he should act, or at least could act.

4. Violence, or force applied from outside, cannot *directly* affect the human will. The will has two kinds of acts: *elicited* acts which it completes within itself, such as loving, desiring, intending; and *commanded* acts which are completed, on command of the will, by other powers of human nature, such as studying, deliberate walking,

speaking. Now, violence cannot directly affect elicited acts, but it can hamper or prevent commanded acts. A man securely tied may will to walk, but he cannot walk. Or a man may choose to read or study and have his will hampered by fading light, or thwarted by a person who takes away his book.

5. An act which is opposed to the will is *involuntary*. Acts done from violence are therefore involuntary acts; they are not human acts because they are not chosen, but are opposed, by the will.

6. When *fear* is the motive of an act, the act remains a human act, and is voluntary. But, since such an act would not be done were it not for the stress of fear, there is something involuntary about it. The captain of a vessel who throws valuable cargo overboard to lighten ship in a storm does what he chooses to do; his act is, *in itself* or *simply*, a voluntary act. But the same act is *in a way* an involuntary act inasmuch as it would not be done were it not for fear of disaster; there is in the act an element of involuntariness. Hence we say that an act done out of fear (not merely done *in* fear or *with* fear) is *simply* voluntary, and, *in some respects*, involuntary.

7. *Concupiscence* is strong tendency or desire in the sensitive appetites. When the will permits the influence of concupiscence to rise out of the sentient order into the intellective order, this influence can strongly affect the will and its acts. Inasmuch as concupiscence makes the will act more intense, it is said to increase voluntariness; inasmuch as it hurries and hampers free and deliberate choice, concupiscence lessens voluntariness.

8. *Ignorance* affects the voluntariness of human acts. (a) *Antecedent* ignorance, which is ignorance blamelessly present before the will-act, destroys voluntariness. (b) *Consequent* ignorance, which is present by the will's choice or deliberate fault, does not destroy voluntariness, but regularly lessens it. (c) *Concomitant* ignorance, which accompanies the will-act without influencing it, renders the will-act non-voluntary.

7. CIRCUMSTANCES OF HUMAN ACTS

1. Conditions which are outside the essence of a human act and yet touch it or bear upon it, are called *circumstances* of the human act. Circumstances are accidentals of a human act.

2. Circumstances influence human acts (a) in point of their measuring up to their end; (b) in point of morality; (c) in point of merit and demerit. Therefore, theologians who study human conduct in its reference to God, cannot ignore circumstances, but must discuss, weigh, and judge them, to establish prudent rules for human living.

3. A convenient list of the circumstances of human acts is given by Aristotle (*Ethic.* III), and is slightly emended by Cicero. This listing is a series of seven questions to be asked by one who wishes to know all the circumstances of a human act. The questions are: who, what, where, by what aids, why, how, when? Following the suggestion of these questions, we may list circumstances in this manner: (1) circumstance of *person,* (2) circumstance of *quality* of the act, (3) circumstance of *place,* (4) circumstance of helps or *influences,* (5) circumstance of *intention,* (6) circumstance of mode or *manner,* (7) circumstance of *time.*

4. The most notable of the circumstances are those of *intention* and *quality of the act.* The intention of the agent (doer, performer of the act) touches the essential character of a free will-act; quality of the act respects the act itself as a deed done. No other circumstances are so intimately bound up with human acts as these two.

8. VOLITION AND ITS OBJECT

1. The will is the intellective or rational appetite. It is the tendency of the soul to go after and possess what the intellect proposes as good or desirable. The will always and necessarily tends towards what is intellectually apprehended as good, even if this should not be truly good in itself.

2. Volition is the actual exercise of the act of willing. Volition is the willing of an end or a good. It is primarily a willing of an end; secondarily it is the willing of means to gain an end. An *end* (or good) is desirable for its own sake; a *means* is desirable inasmuch as it leads to an end or makes possible the attaining of an end.

3. The will is not moved to volition by *means* as such, but only inasmuch as they lead on to an end desired. To act effectively, the will must consent to the use of means necessary to attain the end desired. Hence it is said: "He who wills the end, wills the means."

9. WHAT MOVES THE WILL

1. The will goes after what the intellect, by its practical judgment, presents to the will as a good, as an end, as something to be gone after. By its practical judgment the intellect moves the will.

2. When the sensitive appetites are permitted by the will to rise out of their proper bodily order and to exercise an influence on reason (intellect and will), they serve to move the will. The urgency of sensitive appetency invades the intellective order and tends to warp the practical judgment of the intellect and through its warped judgment to influence or move the will. Thus a man who acts under

stress of anger may deem fitting (that is, good, desirable) words and deeds that would not be judged fitting if he were calm.

3. But, in last analysis, it is the *will* which *moves itself* to its act. For any influence that moves the will has to be accepted by the will before it is effective.

4. Among things that can be admitted by the will as influences or movers are exterior things. Exterior objects may exercise an appeal through the senses and then through the intellect; the intellect may ponder and take counsel with itself, and finally reach the practical judgment (to do or not do to) which it presents to the will. A person who has seen articles displayed for sale, and has felt their appeal, knows that their attractiveness (in themselves or in view of use, pleasure, or profit they will bring) is a factor in the will's decision to purchase them. Thus is the will moved by exterior objects.

5. Those who think the will is necessitated in its acts by the stars, and that man is thus the plaything of fate, are quite mistaken. The will is a spiritual power and cannot be *directly* influenced by exterior objects, but only *indirectly* inasmuch as their appeal is accepted by the will from the intellect judging on sense findings. A man, looking at the stars, may be impressed by the beauty and power which they manifest, and may be led to a will-act of adoration of the stars' creator. But the stars have no direct influence on the will; much less have they power to control the will.

6. The will moves itself because God made it so. And only God can directly move the will as an exterior principle of its movement. God moves the free will directly and naturally, *without destroying its freedom.*

10. HOW THE WILL IS MOVED

1. The will is the intellective appetite for good, and its natural and necessary drive is towards what is intellectually grasped as good. The will tends towards good *in universal,* and, in its individual acts, it tends towards good *in particular.*

2. The good is always the object of the will. But, in particular choices, the particular good envisioned as object does not compel or force the will's act. To say that, in general, the will necessarily chooses good, is merely to say that the will is the will; that is its definition: the intellective power which appetizes good. But to say that the will must necessarily choose this good or that good is never true. Somewhat similarly, we say that a man, to sustain life, must eat food; but to say that a man must eat *this* or *that* item of food placed

before him, is not true. The will is free and not necessitated in its *particular* choices, yet each choice is a choice of something as good, that is, as satisfying, as desirable. Now, the will is not a knowing power; the intellect must show it its object and make practical judgment that this object is to be gone after. The will necessarily follows the *ultimate* practical judgment of intellect in its particular choices, but it is the will which decides in each case whether the judgment shall be ultimate. Thus, though the will necessarily follows the intellect, it is not necessitated by the intellect. In following the ultimate practical judgment of intellect, the will is like the driver of a car who necessarily follows his headlights, but is not necessitated by his headlights. The driver decides upon which precise road the headlights are to shine, and yet he cannot take that freely chosen road except by following the headlights into it. The will must follow the ultimate practical judgment of intellect, but the *will decides* which judgment shall be ultimate.

3. We have seen that the lower or sensitive appetites may send their influence up into the intellective area, and, when this influence is admitted there, it may work upon the mind's practical judgment and so affect the act of the will. But as long as a man remains sane, this influence is never a compelling influence. For example, no matter how angry a man may be (short of a frenzy that robs him of responsibility and makes him momentarily insane), he can turn the intellect upon motives for restraint and self-control, and so may banish the anger, refusing to be led by it into violence of word or deed.

4. Nor does God move the will to act of necessity in particular choices. God moves all things that move; he moves them to act *according to the nature* that he gave them. God moves contingent things to act contingently; God moves man's free will to act freely. Under God's movement the will necessarily acts, but it does not act necessarily in the sense that it has no true choice of its object.

11. FRUITION OR ENJOYMENT

1. The will tends to attain good, and to repose in it with delight or enjoyment when it is attained. This delight or enjoyment of the will in good attained is called *fruition*.

2. Every cognitional appetite (that is, appetency stirred by *knowing*) can find fulfillment and fruition. Among earthly creatures, only men and animals have cognitional appetency. Men have sentient appetency and intellectual appetency; animals have sentient appetency. Nonliving things have only *natural* and nonsentient appetency, that

is, a nonknowing tendency to hold on to their being and their proper activities. Natural appetency leads to no fruition or enjoyment.

3. Just as every particular choice of good is made, consciously or not, as an expression of man's necessary quest of his ultimate good, so all human fruition or enjoyment has a reference to the supreme and perfectly enjoyable good. During life on earth a person may have many joys, but none of these can perfectly fill up the appetite for enjoyment. Man wants *full* enjoyment, endlessly possessed. Only in heaven, in possession of his ultimate good, can man have this fruition.

4. Fruition or enjoyment is found in the good possessed. But even in the intention to lay hold of good, and in the quest for good, there is an imperfect fruition.

12. INTENTION

1. Intention is an elicited act of the will, by which the will purposes to go after an object.

2. Thus intention is the determining of an end; it is the setting up of a choice. The end intended may be the object of immediate choice, or it may be something that is to be attained by the use of means; effective intention must take in necessary means as well as the end which is to be attained by them. A means to an end is itself an end until it is attained.

3. Intention can therefore be directed to one object in itself directly, or as the goal of a series of means. And an intention may be singular, having only one thing in view, or it may be plural, having several nonconflicting things in view. Thus a man may, in giving alms, intend simply to relieve poverty. Or he may have several intentions in his almsgiving: to relieve the poor; to practice self-denial; to do penance; to please God; to show good example; to win grace for his soul.

4. There is a difference between the will-acts of wish and intention. A man may wish for something without intending to make use of means to achieve it. Thus a man who is much overweight may *wish* to be thinner without *intending* to endure the hardship of a reducing diet.

5. Man alone, among earthly creatures, can form a true intention. Animals, plants, and minerals, and man in his bodily being, act with "the intention of nature," whether the activity be exercised with or without sentient knowledge. Intention in its true meaning is a free will-act, and belongs only to a being of the rational order.

13. ELECTION OR CHOICE OF MEANS

1. The will chooses the end and the means to the end in its particular acts. The intellect judges means as to suitability, but the choice or *election* of means is an act of the will.

2. Since choice or election is an operation of the rational appetite called the will, it cannot be exercised by nonrational animals. Animals make sense judgments and act on them by *instinct,* which is an interior sensing power, an inner sense. But animals cannot know means as such, nor choose means in the light of understanding, for they do not possess understanding.

3. Man's last end or ultimate good is not subject to choice; man tends to it by necessity. Man's choice is limited to the field of *means.* Yet each means is chosen as a good or an end, but not as *ultimate* end. In choosing a particular end or good, the human will is actually choosing a means to the ultimate end.

4. The field of choice of means, the arena of human freedom, is the field of human acts. No man, according to Aristotle, chooses anything but what he can do himself.

5. And thus choice is limited to the realm of things humanly possible. Aristotle says (*Ethic.* III): "There is no choice among impossibilities."

6. Choice, by its very nature, is free. A necessitated choice is not a choice at all. The compelling attraction of the last end of man, that is, the supreme good, removes it from the field of choice; man *must* will the last end for he cannot will unfulfillment. But no particular good or end is so perfect as to *compel* the will to tend to it. In every particular thing, the intellect can discern points or phases of attractiveness and of unattractiveness. Sin is evil, but it offers the sinner an apparent and ready satisfaction, that is, it is seen in the light of something good or desirable. And virtue is entirely attractive, yet it can be regarded as undesirable in so far as it exacts effort and is to be attained only by sustained and tedious labor. Thus in a particular choice, the will may go either way. This is what is meant by freedom of choice.

14. COUNSEL

1. Counsel is the studious inquiry of the mind into the object proposed for choice. The mind thinks things over, and offers its recommendations to the will. The mind or intellect thus takes counsel within itself, and offers its advice or counsel to the will. To illustrate: a man suffering a malady ponders his suitable course of action; he

asks himself whether he had not better go at once to a hospital for surgery; he considers expense, and dependents, and his job and whether he could retain it through a long absence; he considers the possibility of deferring radical treatment and of getting on for a time with palliative medicines; he considers danger both in the surgery and in delay in undergoing surgery. These and other matters are pondered by the mind before the will decides. And this pondering and judging is *counsel*.

2. Counsel, like choice, has to do with *means*. It is the mind's judgment on the suitability of means to an end.

3. St. Gregory of Nyssa says that we take counsel about things that are within the range of what we can do. Counsel looks on to the act of free choice. It concerns *doing*, not *being*; it looks to action, not to facts or truths; it weighs facts and truths with a view to action.

4. Counsel is not concerned with trifles; man does not truly take counsel about slight or insignificant action, but about things of weight and importance. Nor is there any place for counsel about a thing to be done if the thing belongs to the established order of science or art, for science and art have their changeless principles. Counsel has place in the more notable instances of free human conduct, and seeks to know the best mode of procedure.

5. Counsel is a kind of analysis of a situation. It takes into view an end intended, and judges what is here and now to be done as steps or means to that end.

6. And counsel does not result in a diffuse or general recommendation, nor a recommendation of countless steps towards an end. Counsel is definite and precise in its judgments and recommendations.

15. CONSENT

1. Consent is the will-act of accepting the means (chosen under counsel) to attain an end.

2. Consent, like all will-acts, is found in man alone among earthly creatures.

3. Like choice, consent is a will-act that concerns the means to an end, not the end itself.

4. Consent is the final decision of the enlightened and counseled will to take up the means required for attaining an end. Sometimes consent is called an act of *reason*. Now, reason is, strictly speaking, the thinking mind, the intellect using discursive thought. But reason is a term often used for the whole intellective equipment of man, that is for intellect and will. Consent is, in itself, an act proper to the will.

But since the will gives consent to the judgment of the thinking mind which counsels it, consent is often called an act of reason. Here reason means the intellectually enlightened and counseled will.

16. USE

1. Use is an act by which the will applies itself and other powers to the carrying out of an intention by means chosen and consented to. First of all, use is the will's applying of itself to its operation. When the will uses subordinate powers to carry out its commanded acts, these powers are employed as instruments for the will's use; the will remains the principal cause of the act. Use, primarily, is *use of will*.

2. Since use presupposes intention, counsel, consent, and election, it is an act that belongs to the rational or intellectual order, and therefore it is not found in nonrational animals.

3. Use applies the will to means for achieving an end. Hence use refers to means. When the last end is attained, use will have no further service to render.

4. In the sequence of will-acts, use regularly follows choice; means are chosen, and then the will uses them. There is one exception to this sequence, for use precedes choice in the applying of the intellect to study and counsel before choice of means is made.

17. COMMANDED ACTS OF THE WILL

1. Will acts such as intention, consent, and election, are acts *elicited* by the will; these acts are begun and completed in the will itself. Other acts, carried out by the intellect or the sentient and bodily powers, are *commanded* by the will. Thus, in considering will-acts, we distinguish elicited acts and commanded acts. Command is an order of reason (the counseled will) for the carrying out of an intention.

2. Command is a product of reason, and therefore it is not found in animals less perfect than man.

3. Command as direction or advice belongs to the counseling intellect; as an executive order, command is in the will; it precedes *use*.

4. In the will, the commanded act and the command are really one; the human act here considered is that of the *commanding will*, and is one act.

5. Intellect may be said to command will in so far as it counsels the will, and also in so far as the will-act always follows upon the

ultimate practical judgment of the intellect. And the will commands the intellect by applying it to its operation, by fixing its attention now on this, and now on that, object.

6. Therefore we may say that will commands reason, understanding reason to mean the thinking mind, the intellect using discursive thought. But when by reason we mean the intellect and will working together, we rather say that reason commands itself.

7. Reason (intellect and will together) governs the sensitive appetites, not by a direct and *despotic* rule, but by a *politic* influence. Sometimes, however, sensitive appetites are aroused by conditions of the body which are not subject to reason. And sometimes the sensitive appetites are so suddenly aroused that they elude, at least momentarily, the control of reason. But, in the main, reason can control the sensitive appetites, both concupiscible and irascible.

8. But reason has no control over the vegetal or plant functions of a man: "No man, by taking thought, can add to his stature one cubit."

9. Movements of bodily members which exercise sentient life are normally (barring injury or crippling disease) under control of reason. Movements of external members which exercise vegetal action, such as growth, are not subject to reason.

18. MORAL GOOD AND EVIL IN HUMAN ACTS

1. Human acts that measure up to what sound reason sees they ought to be, are good acts. Human acts that fall short of what they ought to be are, to the extent of their failure to measure up, evil acts.

2. The *object*, when we speak of human acts, is the human act itself and whatever it necessarily involves. Now, the object is the primary determinant of the moral good or evil of a human act.

3. If the object, the act itself considered as a deed done, does not manifest the good or evil of the act, then we look to the secondary determinants of morality, that is, to the circumstances of the human act as performed. To be morally good, a human act must be what it ought to be in itself and in its circumstances. Hence *object* and *circumstances* are determinants of the morality of a human act.

4. In determining the moral character of a human act by circumstances, the circumstance of *end of the agent* is most important. This circumstance most often ceases to be merely a circumstance, and enters into the object itself. The end intended by the author of a human act is so important a determinant of the morality of his act that we give it special mention; therefore we usually list the determinants of the morality of human acts in this way: object, end, circumstances.

5. Good acts are specifically different from evil acts. Acts are specified by their objects, that is, by what they are in themselves, and there is an essential difference between an act in accord with right reason and an act not in such accord. Hence, by their objects, good acts and evil acts are specifically different.

6. Acts are also specified by their ends. On this score also good acts are specifically different from evil acts.

7. The specific difference between a good act and an evil act on the basis of end or intention is a more general or diffuse difference than that which is based on the objects of the acts. For an act which is one in itself may be done for several nonconflicting purposes; that is, it may have several ends.

8. Some human acts, considered in themselves abstractly, as in their definitions, are neither morally good nor morally bad; they are *indifferent* acts. Thus talking, singing, reading, pondering a subject, are (not as humanly done, but as defined in a dictionary) indifferent acts. Such acts have *in themselves* no necessary agreement, and no necessary disagreement with right reason.

9. But every *individual* human act as performed, as humanly done, is necessarily either in accord with right reason or out of line with it. Individual human acts are not acts in abstract definition, but acts in concrete performance. And such acts must be considered, not in themselves only or as objects; they must be considered in the purpose for which they are done, and in the circumstances in which they are performed. And they will thus be seen to be either morally good or morally evil, but never indifferent. To illustrate: Talking is, in itself, an indifferent act. But talking which is done in moderation to make oneself agreeable, to console, to give good advice, to impart truth prudently, to encourage virtue, to divert people from unfriendly argument, or for other good purpose, *is a morally good act*. And talking which is done immoderately, or to irritate, to deceive, to prod people into a quarrel, in the wrong place or at the wrong time, in the wrong fashion, or to the wrong persons, *is a morally evil act*. Hence we have a true saying: Human acts are sometimes morally indifferent in their *kind,* but they are never morally indifferent as *individual acts performed.* If human acts do not have definite moral character in their objects, they have it in their end or their circumstances.

10. Thus it appears that circumstances sometimes specify an act in its moral character. Now, circumstances as such are accidentals of a human act, and accidentals cannot specify an essence. Only when a circumstance is taken into the essence of an act as a principal con-

dition can it specify the act. Circumstances are really *more* than circumstances when they are absorbed, so to speak, into the act itself to give it moral character.

11. A circumstance may affect a human act in two ways. For (a) either it leaves the act unchanged in its kind, and merely intensifies it, that is, makes it better or worse; or (b) it changes the nature of the act, or, more precisely, it introduces a new element into the act. A man who is deliberately angry for an hour does something worse than if he were deliberately angry for five minutes; here the circumstance of manner makes the more enduring act worse than the less enduring, but does not make it different. But a man who steals money from a church is guilty of theft and also of sacrilege; the circumstance of place changes the nature of simple theft into sacrilegious theft. The two types of circumstances which affect the moral character of human acts are called, respectively, (a) *aggravating* circumstances, and (b) circumstances *which change the nature* of the act.

19. MORALITY IN ACTS OF THE WILL

1. A human act takes its morality (its character as good or evil) primarily from the act itself as object, and secondarily from those circumstances that enter the act and affect it essentially.

2. As we have seen, circumstances that affect the moral character of an act have to be more than mere circumstances or accidentals; they must somehow amalgamate essentially with the act itself. Hence, in last analysis, the act itself as object is the only determinant or specifier of morality in will-acts.

3. The intellect by its counsel and practical judgment proposes the object to the will, not only as a simple act to be done, but with its moral implications. Hence there is a dependence of will on intellect respecting the moral character of a human act.

4. Human reason (the thinking mind) becomes aware, early in life, of an order in the world. The order which reason recognizes in things is the order put there by God as eternal law. Inasmuch as this order requires right moral conduct, and is known naturally (without revelation) by sound human reason, it is called the *natural law*. The natural law is the eternal law as knowable in this world by right reason. When the will conforms to the natural law, it conforms to the eternal law, and thus conforms to God, and its acts are morally good. Hence the morality of will-acts depends on God, the eternal law.

5. Reason—the thinking mind—is man's only natural guide in moral matters. The judgment of reason on the morality of a proposed act is *conscience*. When the will acts in conformity with this conscience-

judgment the act is morally good; when the will acts in contradiction to conscience the act is morally evil. Man is obliged to act in conformity with his conscience, even when reason is mistaken and the conscience judgment is false.

6. However, if error in the conscience-judgment is a man's own fault—as the result of culpable ignorance, willful negligence to learn what should be learned—the will which follows the erroneous conscience is an evil will, and the act of that will is an evil act to the extent of the fault involved in judgment.

7. We have already seen that the end of the agent, that is, the intention of the doer, enters into the essence of a human act, becoming part and parcel with the act as object, and so bears directly on the goodness or evil of the act.

8. But the degree of good or evil in the intention is not a measure of good or evil in the will itself. For an evil will may sometimes act with good intention, as, for example, when a person tells a deliberate lie to prevent friction or quarreling. And sometimes a good will is less good or noble than its intention, as, for instance, when a person prays carelessly for a great and holy purpose. Intention, therefore, while it is a determinant of morality in an act, is not a *measure* of the moral quality of the will which elicits the intention.

9. For a human act to be good, it must be in conformity with the sovereign good—it must conform to the will of God.

10. To be in conformity with the divine will, a human will must, in all its acts, will what God wills—it must will the accomplishment of universal good.

20. GOOD AND EVIL IN EXTERNAL ACTS

1. Moral good and moral evil are primarily in the will. Human acts performed externally under command of the will, take their morality, first and foremost, from the will itself.

2. Yet there are some external acts which are evil in themselves because, by their very nature, they are out of line with right reason; the will cannot make these acts good. Such external acts are, for example, murders, injuries inflicted, impure conduct. The moral character of an external human act is not, therefore, wholly determined by the will of the person who performs the act.

3. When an external act takes its moral character from the will of the person who performs it, the goodness or evil of the act is one with the goodness or evil of the will. But when the act has *intrinsic* goodness or evil, there is a difference between the moral quality of the act and the moral quality of the will which commands it. True,

these moralities coalesce, but they are not the same thing. A group of people praying vocally are all performing the same intrinsically good act. But each member of the group brings his own degree of devotion to the act of praying vocally. The external act is the same for all, but it is not equally good in all by that goodness which the act has from individual wills.

4. The external act adds something to the internal act of will. For the external act is the perfecting of the internal act. A man who intends to do a good deed, but fails to carry out the intention, has less good in his conduct than another who has the same good intention and fulfills it by performing the external good deed.

5. The consequences of an external act do not of themselves affect the goodness or evil of the act. Of course, such consequences as are foreseen, or should be foreseen because they follow naturally from the act, are part and parcel of the act itself, and are willed by the fact that the act is willed. But consequences unforeseen, and unconnected with the act by any natural or necessary bond, cannot work back upon the act and make it better or worse after it has been performed.

6. One and the same external act cannot be both morally good and morally evil. In the physical order an action may be good and also bad, as, for example, the taking of a medicine which is a relief for pain but harmful to the heart. In the moral order this cannot be. If a person steps out to commit a crime, and, on the way, decides not to commit it, we have one physical act of walking, but two acts of the will. The walking, as a *human* act, is morally bad up to the point of the person's change of intention; then it becomes another walking altogether, and is a morally good act. Here we have two acts, not one.

21. CONSEQUENCES OF GOOD AND EVIL ACTS

1. Since the eternal law is the ultimate norm of good or evil in human acts, it follows that moral evil is *sinful,* and moral goodness is *righteous.*

2. It also follows that morally good acts are *praiseworthy,* and morally evil acts are *blameworthy.*

3. The praise or blame due to human acts by reason of their moral goodness or badness is not a mere matter of words or opinions, but of retribution according to the demands of justice. That is, human acts have *merit* or *demerit* according to their goodness or evil.

4. The merit and demerit of human acts are not a matter of human justice merely, but of divine justice; human acts have merit or demerit in the sight of God.

THE PASSIONS

(QUESTIONS 22 TO 48)

22. THE SUBJECT OF THE PASSIONS OF THE SOUL

1. The *subject* of a thing is that in which the thing resides or occurs. We inquire here about the subject of the passions of the soul. We ask whether these passions really reside in the soul itself. Now, since the soul is the substantial form of a man and so makes him exist as a human being, the soul can be called, fundamentally, the subject of all that pertains to human nature. Since man is the subject of the passions, the soul is the subject of the passions. In another aspect of the matter, we may say that whatever exercises an influence upon the powers or faculties of the soul, belongs to the soul as to its subject. In this sense, too, the soul is the subject of the passions.

2. The passions of the soul belong to the realm of tendency and desire rather than to the realm of knowledge. Passions presuppose knowledge and follow upon it; but they are in the appetitive order, not the knowing order.

3. And, strictly speaking, the passions of the soul belong to the sensitive order, the order of the bodily faculties. Yet the influence of these passions is so readily admitted by the will into the intellective order (the order of the spiritual faculties of the soul), that there is justification for the name of "passions of the soul." Strictly then, the *proper* subject of the passions of the soul is the sensitive part of man; by justified extension of the phrase *of the soul*, these same passions are ascribed to the soul itself as their subject, though not their *proper* subject.

23. DISTINCTION OF THE PASSIONS

1. The word passion means an *undergoing*. When sensitive appetite operates, the body undergoes some modification, some change. Sometimes such change is manifested outwardly, as, for instance, in the bright eye and animated manner of a person speaking of what he loves; or in the flushed face and stammering tongue of a man who is very angry. Passion is a kind of recoil or kick-back of the operation

of sentient appetite; it is what a sentient being *undergoes* because of the functioning of such appetite. There are two kinds of passions, and they take their general names from the appetites they follow; thus we distinguish the *concupiscible* passions which follow the concupiscible appetites, and the *irascible* passions which follow the irascible appetites. The concupiscible passions are: love and hatred; desire and aversion; joy or delight, and sorrow or grief or pain. The irascible passions are: hope and despair; fear (timidity) and courage (daring), and anger.

2. The concupiscible passions stand related to good and evil *simply*. Love is for good, hatred for evil; desire is for good, aversion for evil; joy is for good, sorrow for evil. But the irascible passions are related to good and evil *under the aspect of difficulty*. Hope is for a good in some degree difficult to achieve; despair is for an evil too difficult to avoid; fear is for an evil hard to escape; courage is for a good difficult to attain; anger is resentment of an evil difficult to throw off. As they work out, all irascible passions turn into concupiscible passions: hope and courage, once successful, are turned into love and joy; anger, fear, and despair, when their force is spent, end in sorrow, and sometimes, when they have been mistaken or groundless, they end in joy.

3. Anger is the only passion of the soul which is not paired off with a contrary passion. For anger stands alone among the passions in having no natural contrary. Serenity might be called a contrary state, but serenity is not a passion.

4. Some passions are specifically distinct (within their genus as concupiscible or irascible) without being opposed. Thus love and joy are specifically different passions, but they can exist together with reference to the same object. Nay, one may cause the other, as love for a good thing attained causes joy in possessing it.

24. MORAL GOOD AND EVIL IN THE PASSIONS

1. The passions of the soul as movements of man's sensitive part are outside the scope of moral classification; they are neither morally good nor morally bad. But in so far as these passions are truly *of the soul* because the will accepts them and renders them *voluntary*, they have moral goodness or moral evil.

2. When the will permits a disorder, an inordinateness, in the passions they are evil. But passions rightly controlled by reason (that is, the intellectually illuminated will) are the occasions of virtue, not of vice. Thus, for example, love, hope, and desire enhance, and do not defile, the will's drive for good.

3. Therefore passions controlled by reason are morally good. A good act performed with feeling as well as with intention is all the better for thus coming more completely from the whole man. But when passions rise suddenly or strongly before the will can choose its act (and they are then called *antecedent* passions), they obscure the mind's judgment and the will's ready control, and thus they tend to diminish or destroy the goodness of a human act. When passion follows the will-act (and this is *consequent* passion) it does so either (a) because of the reaction of lower to higher appetites in man, or (b) because the will directly arouses the sentient appetites so as to have their prompt cooperation. In good acts, consequent passion indicates the will's intensity in good; when directly stirred up by the will, consequent passion increases the goodness of the good act. Thus, for instance, a man may directly rouse up courage to help him perform some difficult duty. Here the good act is all the better for having courage joined to good purpose.

4. Passions take their own specific good or evil quality from that of the act to which they incline a man.

25. THE ORDER OF OCCURRENCE AMONG THE PASSIONS OF THE SOUL

1. Concupiscible passion, which tends simply to an end, precedes irascible passion, which is aroused by difficulty in achieving the end. Thus desire for a thing precedes the courage with which one faces difficulty in obtaining the thing. But concupiscible passion, which rests or is quiet in an end attained or lost (joy; sorrow) follows the irascible passion which overcame difficulty or succumbed to it. Hence, in passions of *movement* concupiscible precedes irascible; in passions of *repose* irascible precedes concupiscible.

2. In the *order of execution,* that is, in the carrying out of the drive of passion, love of the end sought comes first, then follows desire, then comes joy in the end attained or sorrow in its loss. But in the *order of intention,* the thing first wanted is joy in the object attained; by this anticipated joy, love and desire are aroused.

3. The first of the irascible passions is hope. Hope looks for a good to come, but involves knowledge that difficulty may lie in the way, and that the end hoped for may not, as a fact, be achieved. A person does not have hope for what is certainly to come; thus no one *hopes* that tomorrow will come, although he may *desire* its coming.

4. The four principal passions after love are joy, sorrow, hope, and fear; love is the fundamental passion. Joy and sorrow mark the subsid-

ing of the passions; hope and fear direct their movement. Joy and sorrow are in things present; hope and fear are for things to come.

26. LOVE

1. Love is the simple appetite or appetency for good. There are three types of appetite and therefore there are three kinds of love. (a) First, there is the *natural appetite* implanted in all creatures by their Creator. This is the tendency of things to maintain their existence, their being, their connatural activities. By this appetite or tendency, things are said to have a natural love of themselves. Natural appetite and natural love involve no knowledge, no awareness, in the beings that have it. (b) In sentient creatures (men and animals) there is, in addition to natural appetency, an appetite for things which *sense* knowledge presents as desirable; that is, as good, as things to be gone after. By sentient appetency, for example, a dog tends to come at his master's call, to go after food which is known pleasingly by the sense of smell, and so on. Now, the quest of good is the expression of love of good; sentient appetency means sentient love. (c) In man alone among earthly creatures there is a spiritual, an *intellectual* appetency. It is the tendency to follow and obtain what the intellect—the mind, the understanding—presents as good, as desirable. And this intellectual appetency is called the will. Man, to be sure, has natural appetency and sentient appetency; he has, in consequence, natural love of himself, and he is stirred by the sentient love which is a concupiscible passion. But man's spiritual and intellectual appetency is, as we have seen, in control of the sentient appetency; yet this is no despotic control, and the sentient appetites with their resultant passions are always trying, so to speak, to swing the will their way. The sentient passions are frequently permitted by the will to enter and influence the intellective soul-faculties; when so permitted, they become truly passions of the soul. The fundamental passion of the soul is sentient love which is permitted to rise into the intellective order and influence mind and will. To sum up: the three types of love are: natural love, sentient love, intellectual or rational love. Love is a simple appetency and passion; it involves in itself no element of difficulty or of freedom from difficulty in attaining its end; it is a concupiscible appetite in the sentient order; in the will, as we have seen, there is no distinction of concupiscible and irascible tendencies.

2. Love as a passion is the undergoing, the kick-back, of the movement of appetite to good.

3. The words love, dilection, charity, and friendship are not com-

pletely synonymous, but they have a common core of meaning; dilection, charity, and friendship, are types or phases of love.

4. Love as a tendency to have or possess good is called *love of desire* (the ancient name is love of concupiscence); love as a tendency to do good is *love of benevolence* or love of well-wishing, and sometimes this is love of *friendship*.

27. THE CAUSE OF LOVE

1. Since love is the tendency experienced by its subject to have or to do good, and since good thus stirs love to action, it is manifest that good or *the good* is the proper cause of love.

2. Good, which is the goal as well as the cause of love, must, in sentient and rational beings, be *known* before it can exercise its appeal. Hence knowledge is a cause of love.

3. Likeness or similarity is a cause of love between and among creatures, for like attracts like. A creature necessarily loves itself; hence it has a natural tendency to love what is like itself.

4. None of the other passions, singly or together, can be regarded as the universal cause of love. A particular passion, such as desire, may cause a particular act of love, for one good can cause another good. But in general it must be said that the other passions presuppose love; they are products, rather than causes, of love.

28. THE EFFECTS OF LOVE

1. Love seeks either to possess what is loved or to bestow benefit upon it. In either case, love seeks to be united with its object, in fact or in affection. Hence *union* with the beloved thing is an effect of love.

2. Another effect of love is that lover and beloved dwell in each other in some manner. The lover says, "I have you in my heart," or "This project is close to my heart." And, speaking of the love of God, scripture says (I John 4:16): "He that abideth in charity, abideth in God, and God in him." Thus a kind of mutual indwelling of lover and beloved is an effect of love.

3. Sometimes love is so intense that the lover is said to be "carried away" or "raised out of himself." This effect of love is called *ecstasy*.

4. Another effect of love is *zeal*. In its good meaning, zeal is steady ardor in loving. In one evil meaning, zeal is an unreasonable and intemperate ardor for making other people love something; this zeal is called zealotry. In another evil meaning, zeal is an inordinate ardor for exclusive possession of the object of love, and an unreasonable effort to block out others from loving it; this zeal is called jealousy.

Zealous and jealous are, in root, the same word. Zealotry and jealousy are effects of misdirected and disordered love.

5. Love in itself is a perfecting and preserving force. But in its material aspects and elements, love may sometimes induce excessive and hurtful change in the lover.

6. Love is appetite for good; good defines end; all things act to an end. Therefore, all things act from love of one kind or another.

29. HATRED

1. The opposite of love is hatred. If love is "heads," hatred is "tails." To love a thing is to hate its opposite; to hate a thing is to love its opposite. Now, love is caused by *good;* hence hatred is caused by that which is a deprivation of good; hatred is caused by *evil.*

2. Hatred is caused by what hinders us from attaining good. Such hindrance not only deprives us of the good object, but deprives the object of its availability. Now, if we did not love a thing, we should not be aware of any block or hindrance in our way to it. If we did not love, we should not hate. Hence love is a cause of hatred.

3. Love is stronger than hatred. Sometimes hatred is more keenly felt than love, and so seems stronger.

4. Strictly speaking, a man cannot hate himself. In practice, a man may harm himself by sin or evil habit; we may say of a man that he is his own worst enemy. And a man may live like the beasts of the field, directing his love to things that cannot bring him to his true end. Yet such mistaken lives are not lives of self-hatred in the strict sense, but of self-love that is misdirected.

5. A man can actually hate the truth, not in general, but in particular instances in which truth proves embarrassing, or hampering, or otherwise contrary to his desires.

6. Hatred can be universal only in the sense that everything of a certain kind can be hated. The sheep hates all wolves. The good Christian hates all sin.

30. CONCUPISCENCE

1. Concupiscence is a strong tendency or appetite arising in the sensitive part of man. As we have seen, concupiscence can be admitted by the will to the intellective part of man, and thus may sway the judgment of intellect and the decision of will. Therefore we say that concupiscence can influence reason.

2. Concupiscence is caused by love, and it tends to pleasure or joy.

It is a passion specifically distinct from its cause (love) and from its end (joy); it is the specific passion called *desire*.

3. Men and animals have certain strong and necessary desires—for life, for food, for drink, for propagation; these are forms of *natural* concupiscence. Only man, among earthly creatures, may have desire for things beyond natural needs—for fame, wealth, promotion, entertainment, modish attire, etc. Such desires are forms of nonnatural concupiscence; this is sometimes called *rational* concupiscence, since it is proper to man who is the only rational animal. When strong or disordered, nonnatural concupiscence (especially with reference to wealth) is called *cupidity*.

4. Natural concupiscence is finite; nonnatural concupiscence can be indefinite or potentially infinite. Thus a man may aspire to unlimited fame or power. But no man desires limitless supplies of food and drink; he desires merely ample supplies.

31. DELIGHT OR JOY OR PLEASURE

1. Delight (pleasure, joy, enjoyment) is a passion of the sensitive order, and comes from awareness of possessing what is suitable and pleasing. It is, like other passions of sentient origin, a *passion of the soul* because it is readily permitted by the will to arise from the sensitive order to the intellective order.

2. Delight or pleasure does not involve *in itself* any reference to time, although it is aroused by possession of present good; conceivably it could go on without end.

3. The words delight, pleasure, joy, and enjoyment are not perfect synonyms. Both animals and men can be stirred by pleasure or delight, but only man can experience joy; joy comes of achieving the object of rational ('nonnatural) concupiscence or desire.

4. Delight rises from sentient to intellective order if reason permits; and, indeed, in reason itself, apart from sense movements, there is joy of fruition in the activity of the intellect and will. There are intellectual or rational pleasures as well as pleasures of sense appropriated or approved by reason.

5. Bodily pleasures are often more intense than intellectual pleasures, but they are not so great or so lasting. The objects of bodily pleasure quickly pass away; spiritual goods are incorruptible.

6. In the sensitive order, pleasures arising from the tactile sense (touch; feeling) are greater than the pleasures of the other senses. Indeed, the sense of touch must serve the other senses by giving their sense organs contact with their respective objects. However, if

we speak of the sense pleasures of *knowing,* omitting those of *using,* we find that the sense of sight is the source of the greatest pleasures.

7. There are pleasures in accord with nature, and there are also nonnatural pleasures which exist because of some defect or disorder in the one who experiences them.

8. Pleasures as emotions or passions are sometimes incompatible and are in conflict with one another.

32. THE CAUSE OF PLEASURE

1. Pleasure is the result of attaining a suitable thing, a thing which satisfies, and is therefore *a good.* It is the attaining of a good, together with awareness of the fact that the good is attained.

2. As we have said, pleasure in itself is not subject to time, and yet it is not incompatible with movement, and hence with time which is movement. A man enjoying an interesting story takes pleasure in moving on from chapter to chapter in the prospect of finally knowing the whole story. And there is pleasure in moving from aspect to aspect of a pleasing thing, and even in going over and over the details of a delightful event which is cherished in memory, or in looking again and again at the minutest features of a prized possession. Hence movement itself can be a cause of pleasure. One's own movement locally can cause pleasure, and people enjoy walking, riding, and sailing.

3. Things hoped for can stir pleasure, as can remembered joys. Thus hope and memory are causes of pleasure.

4. Even sadness or sorrow can be a cause of pleasure. Sorrow over a loss calls to mind the beloved object with which remembered joys are associated. Sorrow over an evil once sustained is accompanied by knowledge of escape or deliverance, and this knowledge is pleasurable.

5. The actions of others may cause us pleasure, (a) because they are the actions of one we love; thus parents take keen pleasure in beholding the meaningless movements of their baby; or (b) because these actions confer a benefit on us; or (c) because these actions make us appreciate the good we ourselves possess. Thus the slow and careful gait of an old man may make us rejoice in our youth and agility.

6. Doing good to others causes us pleasure, for it makes us aware of a pleasing ability in ourselves, and also pleasurably aware of an abundance of good that we can share. Further, to do good is in accordance with our nature, and there is pleasure in orderly natural action. Finally, in doing good to others we show our love for them, and love is the principal cause of pleasure.

7. Because like has a tendency to love like, likeness itself is a cause of pleasure. Creatures normally take pleasure in associating with their kind. Youth enjoys being with youth. People of like interests have pleasure in one another's company and conversation. Yet, accidentally, likeness which should cause pleasure sometimes occasions displeasure. A man may be displeased with another who is in the same line of business, not because of likeness of occupation, but because of something accidental to that likeness in this particular case, such as the fact that the other man is a competitor, a limiting factor in financial gain, and perhaps a challenger for a place of social prominence in a community.

8. Things that excite wonder are pleasurable. They give pleasing knowledge of striking facts or events, together with a desire for further knowledge (that is, the explanation of the wondrous things), and this desire itself is pleasing. And sometimes there is pleasure in studying and comparing things which, in themselves, are not pleasing; thus a medical student may find pleasure in working with specimens of deteriorating tissue.

33. THE EFFECTS OF PLEASURE

1. One of the effects of pleasure is a certain expansion of feeling; thus a person may say that his heart swells with delight. We read in scripture (Isa. 40:5): "Thou shalt see and abound, and thy heart shall wonder and be enlarged."

2. Another effect of pleasure is the thirst or desire for its continuance or its recurrence. Yet sometimes, when a pleasure has been enjoyed too completely, there is no immediate pleasure in the thought of it, and no actual desire for continuance. Thus a person who has eaten overmuch is displeased rather than pleased at the thought of food which recently gave him pleasure. Pleasures of the intellectual order are less likely to cloy than those of the sentient order. Spiritual pleasure is always enjoyed with a thirst for more.

3. In the realm of reason, pleasure lends impetus to the mind. The enjoyment of study or thinking keeps us at the work and makes us do the work better. But bodily pleasures hinder the use of the mind by distracting it, occasionally conflicting with it, and sometimes (as in the pleasure of drinking intoxicants) by fettering it.

4. In general, orderly pleasure within the proper field of an operation gives some perfection to the operation itself. What is done with pleasure is usually done with care and attention.

34. MORAL GOOD AND EVIL OF PLEASURE

1. Just as desires for good acts are morally good, and desires for evil acts are morally evil, so the pleasures arising from good acts are morally good, and those from evil acts are morally bad.

2. Scripture speaks (Prov. 2:14) of those "who are glad when they have done evil, and rejoice in most wicked things." Not all pleasures are morally good. Yet every appetite is for good, and pleasure comes from satisfied appetite. Now, it must be remembered that the good which an appetite craves is good taken *simply*. But a man, in a particular choice, may approve and appetize what is merely a good aspect of what is not good simply. And a man may allow this good aspect to mask the whole evil object. Thus evil can be chosen under the guise of good. Evil so chosen can be enjoyed. Such enjoyment is morally evil pleasure. It is bad or sinful pleasure.

3. Man's happiness in heaven, in the vision of God, will include perfect pleasures, and these, of course, will be morally good pleasures.

4. A good will enjoys the work of virtue; an evil will takes pleasure in sinful works. Thus the pleasure of the will in its human acts is a measure of the moral quality of these acts. But sense pleasures are no measure at all of the moral quality of human acts, for a man may have sense pleasure in wrongdoing, and may find good deeds difficult and distasteful to sense.

35. SORROW OR PAIN

1. Sorrow or pain is a passion of the soul which is burdened by present evil. Pain, as a synonym for sorrow or sadness or grief, is not merely bodily pain from ache, or sore, or wound; it is rather the pain of distress, of worry, of concern.

2. Pain is, first of all, in the sentient order and in the exterior senses. It passes to the interior sense of imagination, whence it is readily admitted into the intellective order and becomes truly a passion of the soul.

3. Pain or sorrow is a passion directly opposed to the passion of pleasure or delight. Pain labors under present evil; pleasure delights in present good. For, while pleasure has no time limits, as we have noted earlier in our study, it is enjoyed as of the present. Even remembered joys or anticipated pleasures, are brought under present consideration in imagination and memory before they are experienced as pleasurable.

4. Not every sorrow or pain is contrary to every pleasure, and pleasure and pain may be associated; thus a man may have sorrow at

the loss of a friend, but rejoice in the fact that his friend died a holy death. Pain and sorrow stand opposed in a contrary object; thus the pain of the loss of a friend is opposed to the pleasure of having him alive.

5. The mind is at its best in *contemplation,* in confronting and dwelling with wisdom. Pain cannot enter here. Pain is not contrary to the pleasure of contemplation, except in what is accidental to contemplation.

6. Pleasure is desired for the sake of good, of satisfaction; pain or sorrow is shunned because of evil. Since good is stronger than evil, the desire for pleasure is stronger than the desire to avoid pain. Accidentally, however, the desire to avoid pain my be the stronger desire.

7. Pain felt in heart or mind is greater and keener than pain felt in the body.

8. St. John Damascene classifies pain or sorrow as torpor (stupefaction), distress or anxiety, pity, and envy.

36. CAUSES OF SORROW OR PAIN

1. Present evil is a cause of sorrow. Evil, which is the privation, and hence the absence, of good that should be present, is a negative thing. Yet the evil which causes pain or sorrow is sensed and understood as a positive thing; it is experienced as something present, not as something absent.

2. Desire and love can be causes of pain inasmuch as these passions are thwarted in their longing for, or grasp of a good that is withheld or removed.

3. The natural craving of a creature for the integrity of its being and nature is the cause of pain when the creature is wounded, diseased, hampered in action, or in any way made deficient.

4. St. Augustine says that sorrow in the soul is caused by the will resisting a stronger power; that pain in the body is caused when the sentient body resists a stronger body. Hence resistance to an oppressing and conquering force is a cause of pain or sorrow.

37. EFFECTS OF SORROW OR PAIN

1. Bodily pain is a hindrance to the mind in its efforts to study, whether to learn new things or to attend to what is already learned. Pain may be so intense as to draw the whole attention of the mind to itself, and this makes learning impossible. Yet a man deeply devoted to learning may continue to use his mind despite a considerable degree of bodily pain. As for mental distress, a mild sorrow may actually incline the mind to study, especially to study the things of

God through whom man hopes to be freed from pain and sorrow.

2. Pain is a burden upon the soul; it is a cause of depression.

3. Therefore, sorrow weakens the activity of the soul. What is done in sorrow or pain is ordinarily not so well done as it would be done without a burdening influence upon the soul. But, unless sorrow be overwhelming, it may sometimes, indirectly, improve the work of the soul inasmuch as the soul is determined to shake it off and banish it by strict and careful attention to the work in hand.

4. Of all the passions, sorrow or pain is the most harmful to man's bodily being. It is a depressing and contractive influence, repugnant to the normal movements of life.

38. REMEDIES FOR SORROW OR PAIN

1. The weariness of sorrow or pain is relieved by pleasure, just as bodily fatigue is relieved by rest.

2. Tears and other outward expressions of sorrow give some relief to the afflicted person; these are natural manifestations; they seem to disperse sorrow, letting it escape outwardly, rather than keeping it pent up in the sufferer.

3. Pain is assuaged and sorrow is abated by the consolation of kindly words and deeds, the sympathy of friends.

4. The contemplation of truth, which is the noblest employment of the mind, gives the greatest pleasure, and therefore is a powerful relief for pain or sorrow. The greater is one's love of wisdom, the more powerfully does contemplation of truth counteract pain.

5. Bodily remedies, such as sleep and baths, are valuable remedies for sorrow or pain in so far as they quiet the disturbance of nature caused by pain.

39. THE MORAL GOOD AND EVIL OF SORROW
OR PAIN

1. Sorrow or pain is not in itself a matter of free human activity, and hence has no moral aspects. But it can be the occasion of moral acts. St. Augustine says that it is good to sorrow for the good that is lost; that is, it is morally right and good to show appreciation of a valuable thing of which one is deprived. Similarly, sorrow for evil, as for our own sins, is morally good.

2. Nay, sorrow may be a *virtue*, that is, a stable habit of rightly judging an oppressive evil and of steadfastly rejecting it by the will. "Blessed are they that mourn," says scripture (Matt. 5:5). Mourning or sorrow can, therefore, be a virtuous good.

3. Sorrow can be a useful good, too. It can make man alert and careful to avoid what causes it, and what leads to it. In this way, sorrow for sin is very useful to man.

4. Bodily pain is not the greatest evil that a man can suffer, nor can interior sorrow as such be the ultimate evil. Greater than sorrow or pain is the evil of *failing to judge* evil rightly, and greater still is the evil of *not willing to reject* evil.

40. HOPE AND DESPAIR

1. Hope is an irascible passion. It is the looking forward to a good to come, not simply but with awareness that the good thing may not be attained, or at least that it will take *effort* to attain it. Now, all irascible passion presupposes concupiscible passion. Hope presupposes desire; we wish or long for a thing before we hope to attain it; and desire and hope are passions specifically distinct.

2. Hope is an appetite; it is not a knowing power. It is a power for tending towards, or striving after, what is known as good, in the face of delay or difficulty.

3. In man alone, of earthly creatures, does true hope exist. Animals, indeed, have a kind of hope, a sensitive tendency towards "future good to be attained with effort or by overcoming difficulty." The dog chasing a rabbit, hopes to catch it. Even plants and lifeless things, by striving to fulfill their natural tendencies in spite of what would repress or defeat them, manifest a kind of hope. We may say that a plant, growing in unsuitable soil and with insufficient sunlight, is hopefully striving to survive. But the tendency of quasi hope, implanted naturally in things by their Creator, is not hope in the sense of an understanding tendency consciously exercised in the effort to achieve a possible (future) good. Hope, in this meaning of the word, is found in man only among earthly creatures.

4. Despair is the opposite of hope; it is the *contrary* of hope. Despair is not the mere absence of hope; it is the *surrender* or withdrawal of hope in a situation in which a desired good is considered unattainable.

5. Hope looks to a future good, difficult but possible to attain. Hope is caused by whatever makes a difficult goal really or apparently accessible. *Experience* can be such a cause of hope, for experience may make a man realize that he can do what he once thought impossible. On the other hand, experience may make a man realize that he cannot do what he once believed he could do. Thus experience can be the cause either of hope or of despair.

6. Whatever stirs up confidence and lends assurance in the face of

difficulties, may be called a cause of hope. *Youth* is such a cause. Even *drunkenness* is such a cause, for a man who has had too much to drink is likely to be expansive, self-confident, and hopeful of doing what, in sober moments, he would not even attempt. Similarly, *foolhardiness* and *thoughtlessness* may be causes of hope.

7. *Love* can cause hope. We hope only for what we desire and love. Our hope for good to come to us through another person makes us love that person. Thus love begets hope, and hope begets love.

8. Hope is a notable help to action; it gives to action intensity and earnestness. And hope causes pleasure; and we have already seen that pleasure is an aid to operation.

41. FEAR

1. Fear is an irascible passion. Like all passions it is fundamentally in the sensitive order, but may rise into the intellective order, and influence intellect and will; thus we say it influences *reason*. Fear, thus admitted to the intellective order, is a trepidation of mind and a troublesome indecision of will in the face of impending evil, that is, of danger. Fear is a kind of shrinking back from an evil which seems difficult, *yet possible,* to avoid or overcome. In a word, fear is agitation caused by impending evil.

2. Fear is not a general condition affecting all the passions; it is a special passion. The object of fear is an evil that is future, threatening, and apparently hard and even well-nigh impossible to avoid or overcome.

3. Fear is found in human beings and in animals; it can in no wise affect plants and lifeless things. Fear is called *natural* when it is a shrinking from what conflicts with normal tendencies; such is the fear of death, or the fear of pain. Fear is *nonnatural* or *rationalized* if it is a shrinking from an evil that only the mind can grasp; such is the fear, for example, of failing in an examination, or the fear of loss of good name when one is the victim of compromising circumstances.

4. Fear has various forms. *Laziness* fears the trouble of toil. *Shamefacedness* dreads the doing of a disgraceful thing. *Shame* fears the disgrace of a thing already done. *Amazement* shrinks from the enormity of impending evil. *Stupefaction* dreads great and altogether unusual evils impending. *Anxiety* dreads possible evils, not distinctly foreseen.

42. THE OBJECT OF FEAR

1. The proper object of fear is something oppressive, unwanted, harmful, which is imminent, and which one longs to avoid. This object

may be the loss of a good which is possessed but threatened. Or it may be something good in itself (such as justice) which may operate to one's hurt.

2. Fear arises from the *imagination* of a future evil, and of evil envisioned as close at hand. What is feared is not yet actually present, but imagination makes it seem present, or nearly so. On the other hand, imagination may remove a fearsome thing to a distance, making it seem far off despite the fact that it is close at hand. Even a very old person, afflicted with disease and near to death, may think of death as far off, and so may have no fear of it. For, distant evils are not really feared. Even natural evils, such as death and bodily pain, are not feared until imagination presents them as imminent.

3. The evil of sin is the product of man's free choice, and hence is not properly the object of fear. Yet a man may fear external things, not subject to choice, which may lead him to sin. And, considering his own weakness as he imagines possible future trials, he may fear that he will sin.

4. Fear itself can be feared. A person can fear things that will cause fear, even if such things are not fearsome in themselves. Thus a legislator may fear to promote legislation, not extreme or frightening in itself, which might be used by unfriendly nations as the excuse or occasion for war.

5. Sometimes the suddenness with which a fearsome situation arises lends force and intensity to fear. Thus the very unexpectedness of menacing evil is an object of fear.

6. The threat of *irremediable* evils makes them peculiarly the object of fear. A military leader fears to lose any battle, even a skirmish. But he is doubly and trebly afraid of losing a decisive battle. A person fears the threat of injury or pain, but he fears much more the threat of death.

43. THE CAUSE OF FEAR

1. The cause of fear is the threatened loss of what we love, or the impending failure to gain what we desire and love. Hence love is a cause of fear.

2. Another cause of fear is a realized want of power to repel impending evil. The realization of power existing in the impending evil is also a cause of fear.

44. THE EFFECT OF FEAR

1. Fear makes a person shrink into himself; it is a kind of contracting of the appetites.

2. Fear drives a man to seek advice and direction, for the dread of impending evil takes away self-confidence and self-reliance.

3. In the body, fear manifests itself by trembling, pallor, nervousness, and other types of agitation.

4. Unless fear be so great as to deprive a person, momentarily, of the use of reason, it does not remove the person's responsibility for his acts. Fear indeed may have effects which interfere with bodily action; trembling hands may be ineffective, quaking knees may not support the body. But fear, short of that which takes away reason, cannot directly affect the intellect and will. Indeed, a *moderate* fear is a stimulus to the mind.

45. DARING OR COURAGE

1. The contrary of fear is daring or courage. Fear shrinks from an evil; daring faces up to the evil and *strives to overcome it*.

2. Courage or daring springs from hope that the impending evil can be overcome. Yet fear, which is the opposite of courage, does not spring from the opposite of hope, that is, fear does not come from despair. On the contrary, despair comes from overwhelming fear, from fear that the impending evil cannot be escaped, that the difficulty confronting one cannot be overcome.

3. The hope that begets courage is a *positive* hope; it arises from the conviction, and the imagination, that means of safety are at hand, and that, in consequence, the fearsome thing is not so fearsome after all. Courage involves nothing negative, no lack, no deficiency. Hence it is wrong to suppose, as some have done, that courage is caused by some defect or lack in the courageous being.

4. True courage or daring is not a mere impulsive surge of valor, not a mere burst of boldness that is quickly spent when the impending evil is actually encountered. True courage, as a passion of the soul, faces up to danger and carries through its effort perseveringly. Courage stands up; it endures.

46. ANGER

1. Anger is a passion which tends to strike back at evil, to inflict punishment or to have revenge upon the cause of the evil.

2. Anger can be aroused by other passions, and even by passions that stand opposed to one another, as, for instance, by sorrow and by hope. Anger has thus a kind of contrariety in itself, and has no contrary passion outside itself; anger is the only passion that is not paired off with an opposite. Anger wants satisfaction (a good) by striking back at what afflicts or disturbs or deters (that is, at an evil). Thus anger has a sort of dual object, including both good and evil.

3. Anger belongs to the irascible appetites; indeed it gives its name to the whole irascible order, for *ira* is Latin for anger, and *irasci* means to be angry. All the other irascible passions tend to turn into anger; hope, despair; fear, daring.

4. When anger rises from the sensitive part of man into the intellective part, it becomes an actual passion of the soul. Such a passion is aroused when the intellect judges that something is to be resented, or that a person inflicting an injury is to be punished. The will backs up this judgment of intellect. And this type of anger is therefore said to require an act of *reason* (intellect and will).

5. Indeed, in man, anger more consistently follows an act of reason than does desire. Therefore anger may be called more natural to man than desire is.

6. Anger may be more intense than hatred, but it is not so enduring, nor is it so grievous a thing in a person. St. Augustine views anger as the mote and hatred as the beam in the passionate conduct of a man.

7. Anger in man involves some aspect of justice and injustice. The harmful thing which arouses anger is understood as an injustice to the person who suffers it; the person suffering is stirred to mete out justice.

8. Anger is of three types: wrath, ill will, and rancor. *Wrath* is the angry outburst. *Ill will* is the continuing effect of the outburst. *Rancor* is the determination of the angry person to have revenge or to inflict deserved punishment.

47. THE CAUSE OF ANGER

1. Anger is always caused by something done to oneself. If we are angered by what is done to others, this is because we imaginatively put ourselves in their place, and consider what is done to them as done to ourselves.

2. The cause of anger is some slight or insult involved in what is done to us. This insult may be one of three kinds: *contempt, frustration of our will,* and *insolence.*

3. Thus anger is provoked by what we deem derogatory to our own excellence. If a person actually excels in something—strength, riches, learning, beauty, grace of speech, etc.—he is "touchy" on these subjects, and is easily angered by what slights or contemns them. And if a person is aware of a defect or deficiency in himself, he is already hurt by this realization; his defect is a sore spot in him, and he is easily angered by what touches it unkindly.

4. Unmerited contempt, more than any other slight or insult, arouses anger. Hence deficiency or littleness in the author of an insult

increases anger, for we feel that a slight from such a source is doubly unmerited. Thus an accomplished speaker or singer is more quickly and bitterly incensed against an ignoramus offering insult than against an educated and experienced man whose opinion of good speaking or singing has presumably a claim to hearing. But, on the other hand, the littleness of the offender who repents and asks pardon dispels anger more quickly than the formal apology of an offender whose abilities are superior.

48. THE EFFECTS OF ANGER

1. One of the effects of anger is certainly pleasure. An angry person has pleasure in thinking of vengeance. And the active wreaking of vengeance gives pleasure, for it is judged to be the righting of an injustice.

2. More than other passions, anger affects the body, stirring it to force, impetuosity, and vehemence in action; anger is therefore said to "influence the heart" more than the other passions.

3. Because anger is so markedly upsetting, its effect on reason is the more notable. More than any other passion, anger obstructs sound and sane judgment.

4. Another effect of anger is the enraged silence which is called *taciturnity*. An angry man may control anger in so far as fiery words are concerned, and remain silent although he burns inwardly. This is taciturnity. Again, anger may so suddenly or powerfully overwhelm a man that he cannot say a word; he stands speechless, though seething. This also is a type of taciturnity.

HABITS IN GENERAL

(QUESTIONS 49 TO 54)

49. HABITS

1. A habit is a stable quality, a quality not readily changed, which disposes its possessor with respect to well-being or ill-being in himself or in his relation to things other than himself. For example, health is a habit; so is knowledge.

2. Habit is a distinct kind or species of quality.

3. Inasmuch as habit directly affects its possessor in well-being or ill-being, it extends to his operations. A habit which affects its possessor in himself (such as health, or fatness) is called an *entitative* habit; a habit which affects its possessor in his operation (such as the acquired skill of playing a musical instrument) is called an *operative* habit.

4. Now, whatever has reference to an operation has reference also to the end towards which that operation tends. Hence good habits are useful, and even necessary, to man for the attaining of the ends of his normal operations.

50. THE SUBJECT OF HABITS

1. The subject of anything is the precise reality in which the thing resides or has place. The subject of habits is that precise reality to which habits are properly ascribed. The body has habits, such as health, beauty, fatness, leanness, etc., and therefore the body is the subject of habits. But body-habits are not perfect habits, for they have not a high degree of stability; they are to some extent readily changeable. Hence body-habits are more properly called *habitual dispositions* than habits simply. The principle and primary subject of habits is the soul. Even operative habits which are exercised by bodily members have their root in the life principle or soul.

2. Human habits are rooted in the soul. They are not, indeed, in the essence of the soul, but in its powers and operations. An operative habit can exist where a variety of operations is possible; it disposes the operator to exercise one rather than any other of these possible operations. Where there is only one way of doing a thing (as, for example, in digesting food), there can be no operative habit.

3. The sensitive powers of a man can be called subjects of habits in so far as these powers are under the control of reason. Animals, which have no higher powers than sentient powers, are not properly the subjects of habits. Wild animals that are domesticated may appear to have changed their habits, but this is only seeming. Animals are instinctively inclined to act in a manner that is good for them; the same instinct that guides them in the wild state, guides them, with different outer effects, in the tame state. Besides, animals have no free choice among possible modes of action, and such choice appears to belong to the very essence of operative habit.

4. Knowledge in the human mind or intellect is a habit; it disposes a man to act in accordance with it. Science (that is, evidenced knowledge) and wisdom (that is, deep, valuable, and appreciated knowledge) are also habits of the mind or intellect. Therefore the intellect is the subject of habits.

5. The will likewise is the subject of habits. Indeed, habit is specially referred to will. It is said of human action that "habit is what one uses when one wills." The moral virtues, for example, are habits of the will.

6. In the angels, too, there are habits, for angels have intellect and will. Yet habits are in angels in a manner suited to their superior nature, and not precisely as habits are in the human soul.

51. THE CAUSE OF HABITS

1. Human nature itself, that is, the operating essence of man, may be said to form certain habits inasmuch as it is disposed for them and needs them for smooth and prompt operation. Likewise, an individual man's temperament or disposition may tend to develop habits in him; these may be called natural habits. Thus we speak of one man as naturally self-possessed and of another man as naturally quick tempered.

2. Certain operative habits are formed in a man by repeated acts. In this way, for instance, a man develops a virtue or contracts a vice. Thus, too, a mechanical skill can be developed, even to such a degree as to be called "almost a second nature."

3. Habits are regularly the product of repeated acts, not of one or two acts but of very many. A man has not the habit (or virtue) of generosity because he has made a few gifts to the poor; nor is a man said to have the habit (or vice) of drunkenness because of a single act of overindulgence in drink.

4. Some habits are not acquired by repeated acts, but are infused by almighty God. These are supernatural habits or virtues. Scripture mentions such habits, as, for example, in the statement (Ecclus. 15:5), "God filled him with the spirit of wisdom and understanding."

52. THE INCREASE OF HABITS

1. A habit is said to increase inasmuch as its influence on its subject (the person who has it) grows fuller, wider, or more intense.

2. Increase in habit is usually a matter of *greater* influence, rather than of *more instances* of the habitual act. Habit does not increase merely by addition of act to act. Sometimes, indeed, more frequently repeated acts come from increased habit, and they may be said, in a sense, to further the increase. But the increase itself is somewhat like that of the growing body which is not *measured* by mere additional items of food added to the diet, even though the intake of food accompanies growth and furthers it.

3. Hence not every act which springs from habit is an increase of the habit. Indeed, an act which accords with a habit, but is less intense

than the habit itself, actually tends to decrease the habit rather than to increase it. Thus the habit of studiousness is not increased, but rather harmed and diminished, by an hour's careless or halfhearted study. Acts give increase to habit when considered cumulatively, not individually. Similarly, it is the cumulative effect of drops of steadily falling water that hollows out a stone, not the individual action of each drop.

53. THE WEAKENING OR BREAKING OF HABITS

1. Some habits cannot be directly destroyed. The intellectual habit of *first principles,* for instance, cannot be directly overcome or banished; as long as a man is normal and conscious, he knows that he exists, and that he can think, and that an existing thing cannot be at the same time nonexistent. But many habits can be destroyed. The habit of a science (that is, evidenced knowledge in a definite field) can be forgotten, or may be spoiled by deception entering into it. And a moral virtue (which is a habit) can be destroyed by perversity and sin.

2. Habits can be increased, and some of them can be decreased or weakened. Not every habit that increases can be decreased, for some habits grow like a growing body which increases to maturity but cannot decrease to immaturity again.

3. Some habits may be weakened or destroyed by neglect, that is, by continued failure to perform acts which accord with them. A musician may lose his skill by neglecting practice. A friendship may perish through failure of friends to meet or communicate.

54. THE DISTINCTION OF HABITS

1. In the same subject there may be a variety of habits which are specifically (that is, essentially) distinct from one another.

2. Habits are distinguished one from another on three scores: (a) their respective active principles; thus, for example, habits of intellect are distinguished from habits of will; (b) their own nature; thus knowledge differs from moral virtue; (c) their respective ends or objects; thus knowledge which aims at truth is distinguished from moral virtue which aims at moral goodness.

3. Habits affect their subjects with respect to well-being or ill-being. Thus habits are distinguished as good habits and bad habits. This distinction of habits holds in the physical order (health; infirmity), in the intellectual order (knowledge; ignorance), and in the moral order (virtue; vice).

4. A habit is a simple thing, and hence a single thing. No habit is

a collection or coalescence of other habits. Many habits may, indeed, be found together in one subject, but they do not fuse into general or compound habits in the subject. A man is sometimes said to be "a bundle of habits." The phrase is often used as a description of what we call a man's "character." But no habit is a bundle of other habits.

VIRTUES

(QUESTIONS 55 TO 70)

55. THE VIRTUES

1. Virtue is a word formed from the Latin *virtus* which means power or strength or valor or manliness. In man, a virtue is a habit that accords with human nature, lending power, smoothness, promptitude to the operation of that nature. Virtue is a good habit either in the intellectual or the moral order; hence we distinguish *intellectual* virtues and *moral* virtues.

2. Virtue is an operative habit; it has to do with *doing*, not *being*. Hence we do not call physical habits such as health or leanness by the name of virtue, for these are habits of being (entitative habits) rather than habits of doing (operative habits).

3. Virtue is a good habit. Aristotle says (*Ethic.* II), "Virtue makes its subject good, and makes the subject's work good." For virtue implies perfection of power.

4. Virtue may be called "a good habit of reason by which we live rightly, and which cannot be put to bad use." When we speak of "divinely infused supernatural virtue," we add to this description of virtue the words, "which God puts into us without our contributing anything to the gift."

56. THE SUBJECT OF VIRTUE

1. Virtue belongs to the soul; it is a perfection of a *power* of the soul, whether intellect or will. Virtue is a true habit, and we have already seen that the proper subject of habits in a living being is the life principle.

2. One and the same virtue cannot be in a plurality of powers. For creatural virtue is, like every habit, a quality, an accidental, and

no accidental can be individually and identically in a plurality of subjects. Thus a moral virtue, such as obedience, is in the will and not in any other power. The intellect indeed has knowledge of the duty of obedience and of how to exercise it; this knowledge is not the virtue of obedience, but a condition required for the exercise of obedience.

3. Virtue is called a habit of *reason*. Reason is, primarily, the thinking mind; yet it includes the will when there is question of practical reasoning. To say that virtue is a habit of reason is merely to say that it is a habit that belongs to a power of the soul. The mind, the intellect, has its virtues; so has the will.

4. Since the concupiscible and irascible appetites are essentially of the sentient order, they are not subjects of virtue. Yet in man these appetites rise quickly into the intellective order, being admitted there by the will. Inasmuch as the appetites participate the order of reason, they may constitute virtues. Thus fortitude, which stands up to extremes of pain and danger, is a virtue of the irascible order, although it comes to full perfection as a will-virtue, a moral virtue. And temperance, as tendency to use material goods in due measure, is of the concupiscible order, although in full perfection as a virtue, it belongs to the will.

5. All virtues are either *intellectual* (that is, of the order of understanding) or *moral* (that is, of the order of will). As we have just noted, the virtues of the appetites are reduced to moral virtues. The sentient knowing powers are not subjects of virtues; although they may be used in aid of moral or intellectual virtues; thus a person may preserve the virtue of purity by habitually imagining, in moments of temptation, the actual presence of our Lord or the Blessed Virgin.

6. Habit perfects an acting power. The will is an acting power. Hence the will has habits. In so far as these are good habits and perfect the power by which a man directs his responsible life, they are virtues. Thus the will has virtues. They are known as moral virtues.

57. INTELLECTUAL VIRTUES

1. The intellect, mind, or understanding is *speculative* inasmuch as it simply knows, or contemplates what is known. The intellect is *practical* inasmuch as its knowing guides the will's choice. As we have said previously, the speculative intellect knows what is so; the practical intellect knows what to do. Now, even the speculative intellect has virtues.

2. Virtues of the speculative intellect are wisdom, science, understanding. *Understanding* is the habit of first principles. It is the mind's habitual awareness of fundamental and self-evident truths (one's existence; one's ability to think straight; the fact that a thing cannot be, at the same time, existent and nonexistent). *Science* is the mind's habitual possession (or virtue) of truth that has been thought out and evidenced or proved. *Wisdom* is the habit or virtue of the deepest and most valuable knowledge. There are many sciences, and these may be severally in the same mind as virtues. But there is only one wisdom. Still, the *characteristics* of wisdom can appear in various departments of human activity; we say that a man is wise in one particular, and unwise in another. But wisdom, in its perfection, is the deepest and most valuable knowledge the mind can possess and it centers in the supreme truth; the truly wise man contemplates ultimates, and guides his life by that knowledge.

3. *Art*, as a virtue of the intellect, is the acquired and habitual knowledge of how to make things rightly. Art is of the practical, rather than the speculative, order, but it is regularly aligned with the virtues of the speculative intellect. For the practical intellect is concerned with moral conduct; the intellect is specifically practical when it shows the will the way to righteous action, or even unrighteous action. But such guiding knowledge as refers to things other than moral conduct is simply ascribed to the speculative intellect.

4. *Prudence* is an intellectual virtue of the practical order. It is not the same as art. For art is the habitual knowledge—the habit, the intellectual virtue—of how to *make* things rightly; prudence is the virtue of knowing how *to act* rightly. Art looks to perfection in things, in its fruits; prudence looks to perfection in its subject, that is, in the person who possesses it. The one perfects the act, the other perfects the agent.

5. Prudence is a virtue most necessary to man, and is listed with the cardinal virtues. Life is made up of human acts; right knowledge of how these human acts should be performed is of first necessity for the living of a good life.

6. Annexed to prudence, but distinct from it and subordinate to it, are certain habits of the practical intellect. These are practical *counsel* upon proposed action, and practical *judgment* to perform or omit proposed action. Prudence, after counsel and judgment, presents the action to the will (to be undertaken or avoided) with recommendation, and even some semblance of command.

58. MORAL VIRTUES AND INTELLECTUAL VIRTUES

1. A moral virtue is a will-virtue. It does not belong to the order of speculative or practical intellect, but to the will, the appetitive part of reason. Moral virtue has to do, not with knowing, but with *acting* or *choosing* in the light of knowledge.

2. An intellectual virtue belongs to the order of *knowing*. Even the virtues of the practical intellect, which regard action, are truly intellectual virtues; they are not appetites or tendencies to action; they merely show the way to action. And when, through prudence, they recommend or command action, they cannot enforce the command. They give knowledge of what ought to be done. But the tendency, desire, and decision in the matter belong to the will.

3. The distinction of virtues as intellectual virtues and moral virtues is complete. This classification covers the whole field. In last analysis every virtue is either an intellectual virtue or a moral virtue.

4. The intellectual virtues of understanding and prudence are required for every moral virtue.

5. And, on the other hand, the intellectual virtue of prudence cannot exist unless moral virtue accompany it. Hence prudence is often listed as a moral virtue.

59. MORAL VIRTUES AND THE PASSIONS

1. Although moral virtue is an appetitive habit, it is not a passion. Passion is properly of the sentient order; moral virtue belongs to the intellective order and specifically to the will. Besides, passions in themselves are neither good nor bad in a moral sense, and moral virtues are necessarily good.

2. The passions (called "passions of the soul" because they rise readily to the intellective order through the will's permission, and exercise influence there) are compatible with moral virtues as long as they remain in line with reason. Indeed, when rightly ordered, the passions enhance moral virtue, as is manifest in the man who exercises the works of justice with love and joy.

3. Even the passion of sorrow is compatible with moral virtue if it be sorrow for what thwarts or opposes that virtue.

4. Moral virtues serve the will by giving right direction to all that comes under the rule of reason; this includes the passions of the soul and the intellectual operations.

5. Moral virtues bring the passions along with them or overflow into the passions. Thus perfect justice is not a thing coldly aloof, but joyous; and joy is a passion.

60. THE DISTINCTION OF MORAL VIRTUES

1. The moral virtues are habits of the intellective appetency called the will. Like all habits they are distinguished by their respective objects.

2. First, moral virtues may be classified as those that control operations (for instance, justice) and those that control the passions (temperance). There is an overlapping in the exercise of these two classes of moral virtues, as, for example, when a man acts justly with pleasure or joy, or performs his duty (justice) with courage.

3. In reference to operations there are various moral virtues, such as religion and piety; yet all these are rooted in the virtue of justice.

4. And likewise there are various moral virtues which control passions. Fortitude touches fear and courage; meekness moderates anger; temperance controls desire.

5. The moral virtues which regulate passions are distinguished from one another by the distinct objects of the passions involved inasmuch as these are subject to reason. Thus, we distinguish fortitude, liberality, temperance, friendship, truthfulness, etc.

61. THE CARDINAL VIRTUES

1. There are four principal moral virtues. On these the other virtues depend as a door depends on its hinges. And indeed the name *cardinal* virtues means hinge virtues; for the Latin *cardines* means hinges. The cardinal moral virtues are prudence, justice, fortitude, and temperance. Prudence, indeed, is really an intellectual virtue, for it is the habitual knowledge of how to act rightly. But prudence is so intimately bound up with will-action that all moral virtues require its direction. Therefore, by reason of association and service, prudence is commonly listed with the moral virtues.

2. St. Gregory (*Moral.* II) says that the whole structure of good works is built upon the four cardinal virtues. Virtues direct good deeds and good lives. Now good is in the reason by the virtue of *prudence;* it is carried into operation by the virtue of *justice;* it directs the passions of the soul by *fortitude,* and curbs them from excess by *temperance.*

3. The four cardinal virtues cover the ground of moral virtue. All other moral virtues are subordinate to these four.

4. The cardinal virtues are distinct habits, each with its own determinate area of application. These virtues are not merely four phases of one master virtue.

5. The cardinal virtues may be called *social* virtues inasmuch as man requires them for living rightly in human society. They may be

called *perfecting* virtues inasmuch as they help man to perfect his character and attain his end. They may be called *perfect* virtues since they are always found in perfected human nature. Finally, they may be called *exemplar* virtues, for they are the model or exemplar upon which human conduct is to be patterned; besides, the perfection which they involve is found eminently in God, man's divine exemplar.

62. THE THEOLOGICAL VIRTUES

1. The supernatural virtues which guide and direct us to God are called theological virtues. These are faith, hope, charity.

2. These theological virtues are not acquired by any act or effort of man. They are supernaturally *infused;* they are poured into the soul by almighty God. The existence and nature of these virtues are made known to us by divine revelation. Hence these virtues are essentially distinct from the moral and intellectual virtues. The theological virtues are supernaturally infused; the moral and intellectual virtues are acquired. And we must be careful to distinguish the supernatural theological virtues of faith, hope, and charity, from the natural virtues which are known by the same names.

3. St. Paul says (I Cor. 13:13), "Now, there remain faith, hope, charity, these three." *Faith* enlightens the intellect by imparting knowledge of supernatural truths. *Hope* directs the will to its supernatural last end as to something that requires effort and cooperation with grace, but as something attainable. *Charity* unites the will with God, its end and object; charity sets the soul into the love and friendship of God.

4. The three supernatural virtues called theological virtues are all infused into the soul as habits; they are infused by almighty God; they are infused together at one and the same instant. Yet in the operation of these virtues we discern priority: faith gives knowledge which arouses hope, and hope tends to set up union with the end desired. Thus faith precedes hope, and hope precedes charity. But on the score of perfection, charity comes first, for it is more noble and valuable to embrace the desired object than merely to know it or hope for it. Says St. Paul (*loc. cit.*), "Now, there remain faith, hope, charity, these three; but the greatest of these is charity."

63. THE CAUSE OF VIRTUES

1. Virtues, even those called natural because they can be acquired by man's natural powers and efforts, are not in man by his nature. For whatever belongs to the nature of man is found in all men, and is not lost by man's defection or sin.

2. Virtues of the natural order are acquired by repeated good acts.

But virtues of the supernatural order are, by their name and definition, beyond the reach of nature, and therefore cannot be acquired by repeated natural acts, however good these may be.

3. God infuses the supernatural virtues of faith, hope, and charity; He also infuses such other virtues as correspond to these three and renders them effective.

4. Acquired virtues are essentially distinct from infused virtues. Of the infused virtues, St. Augustine says that "God works them in us without us." But we have to work to possess the acquired virtues.

64. THE MEAN OR MEASURE OF VIRTUE

1. By the *mean* or *measure* we do not understand something to estimate the extent of virtue; we indicate that which makes virtue show a sane balance, having neither excess nor deficiency. The measure of virtue does not reduce virtue to an average. Nor does it signify that every virtue is in itself something that, as the ancients said, "stands in the middle"; something requiring only a moderate exercise. The mean or measure of virtue is what determines its perfect practice. Thus, for example, justice, by the mean or measure, demands the exact rendering to everyone of what is due him. A debtor who omits part of what is due, offends against the measure by defect; a debtor who pays in full but with vainglory and boastfulness, offends against the measure of justice by excess. Justice itself cannot, of course, be in excess; but there can be excess (as illustrated in our example) in the manifestation or exercise of justice. Now, with respect to the moral virtues, the mean or measure is conformity with right reason.

2. The virtue of justice conforms to reason, and thus manifests the measure or mean, when human actions are in accord with the requirements of reality, of things. Hence we call the mean or measure of justice a *real* mean or measure. Other moral virtues which regulate the passions, cannot be applied with the exactness of justice, but are in conformity with the mean or measure according to the judgment of reason in the circumstances in which they operate; hence we call their mean or measure a *rational* mean or measure. If a man owes five dollars, justice (by the very facts of the case) requires the payment of that exact amount. But to observe temperance, a man does not have to weigh out a precise number of ounces of food and drink; nor would a determinate amount be called temperate for every person in every circumstance.

3. The mean or measure for the intellectual virtues of the speculative order is *truth*. The mean or measure for the intellectual virtues of the practical order is *prudence*.

4. The theological virtues are not subject to measure or mean except accidentally, in so far as they are humanly manifested. No excess is possible in the theological virtues themselves. Scripture (Ecclus. 43:33) says, "Blessing the Lord, exalt him as much as you can, for he is above all praise."

65. THE CONNECTION OF VIRTUES WITH ONE ANOTHER

1. Moral virtues are connected with one another. St. Ambrose (*In Luc.* vi 20) says that the virtues are linked together "so that whoever has one is seen to have several." All the moral virtues have their mean or measure in conformity with right reason, and virtue shines through virtue in the human conduct which is regulated by right reason. However, when we consider the moral virtues, not in themselves essentially or in reference to reason which is consistently right, but as practiced by imperfect man, we find them disconnected. Thus a man may have the virtue of liberality and lack the virtue of temperance.

2. There can be no supernatural moral virtue without supernatural charity which is the infused moral virtue of love and friendship with God.

3. With the infusion of supernatural charity, all supernatural moral virtues are given to man, for these are so many means of executing the mandates of charity. Charity directs man to his last end; it is the principle of all good works directed to that end. Hence charity must bring the supernatural moral virtues along with it, since one cannot have charity without these moral virtues.

4. Nor can supernatural faith be perfectly possessed without charity.

5. Charity, which is supernatural love and friendship with God, brings supernatural faith and supernatural hope along with it to the soul of man. Unless a responsible person supernaturally believe in God and hope to attain him, he cannot be in God's love and friendship. No one can love a being which he does not believe, nor can a person have true friendship for a being whose presence and favor he does not hope to share.

66. EQUALITY AMONG VIRTUES

1. A virtue *in itself* is not capable of being greater or lesser. But in its *subject* (that is, in the person who has it) a virtue can be greater or lesser at different times; it can be greater or lesser in different persons at the same time.

2. And virtues, *by comparison* with one another, can be greater or lesser. St. Paul says that charity is greater than faith or hope. But different virtues in the one subject are not properly to be compared and called greater or lesser. The fingers of a perfectly formed hand are of different sizes, yet they are proportionally equal inasmuch as each finger is fitted to its own proper use. So it is with virtues in a person.

3. Considered in themselves, the intellectual virtues are more excellent than the moral virtues, for they pertain to the intellective part of man, while the moral virtues regulate the passions which are essentially of the sensitive part. But considered in the service which they render to man, the moral virtues are more excellent than the intellectual virtues; they do more to get a man on towards his last end.

4. The chief moral virtue is justice. Justice regulates operation, so that everyone shall have what is exactly right and due. Thus justice is most closely allied with reason itself, which is the mean or measure of all the moral virtues. Other moral virtues are subordinate to justice. In the descending order of excellence, we have justice, fortitude, temperance; and all of these are suffused with prudence.

5. Among the intellectual virtues, wisdom is the greatest. Wisdom exercises judgment over the other intellectual virtues, directs them, and, as a master architect, builds with them.

6. We have the testimony of Sacred Scripture (I Cor. 13:13) that charity is the greatest of the theological virtues. Of course, all the theological virtues have God as their object, and on this score there is no greater or lesser among them. But charity is closer to that common object than are faith and hope. Faith pertains to what is not yet seen; hope, to what is not yet possessed; charity, albeit imperfectly, possesses its object in the present clasp of love.

67. DURATION OF VIRTUES AFTER THIS LIFE

1. When a good man dies, do moral virtues remain in the separated soul? Justice remains, for (Wisd. 1:15), "Justice is perpetual and immortal." The moral virtues which regulate the passions remain in the separated soul in their essence as perfections of the soul, but they no longer regulate irregularities of appetite; in the future life of the virtuous soul there are no irregularities of any kind.

2. The intellectual virtues remain in the separated soul, but in a manner which renders their use more perfect than it was during earthly life. In the present life, man must recur to sense images (in phantasy or imagination) as he uses acquired knowledge. But the separated soul will not have the service of the senses or their images, nor will the soul require that service.

3. Faith which pertains to "things that appear not," cannot continue after the things actually appear. In the next life, faith will be fulfilled in the more perfect habit of vision, and will be supplanted by vision.

4. And hope, which looks on to a good not yet possessed, can have no place in the soul which possesses all that it once hoped for. In heaven, hope will be crowned with fulfillment, and will cease to exist as a specific habit or virtue of the soul.

5. Not even remnants or elements of faith and hope can remain in the soul in heaven, for these virtues are simple habits, and they are either present entirely or absent entirely.

6. But charity will remain in the separated soul in glory. St. Paul says (I Cor. 13:8), "Charity never falleth away." Charity will be fulfilled in heaven, not as faith is filled and supplanted by vision, not as hope is fulfilled and supplanted by possession: charity will be fulfilled by being perfected in its own nature; that is, imperfect charity will become perfect charity.

68. THE GIFTS OF THE HOLY GHOST

1. The gifts of the Holy Ghost are distinguished from the theological virtues. The gifts dispose us to obey divine influence and inspiration, whereas the virtues enable us to carry out the works of this obedience.

2. The gifts render a man amenable to the promptings of grace. Where there is need of such prompting, there is need of a gift. Man, working to attain his supernatural end, often needs the prompting of grace as well as the actual use of grace; hence the gifts are necessary to man.

3. The gifts are not merely acts, nor are they passions; they are habits that abide in a man and make him tend to obey God.

4. The gifts of the Holy Ghost are: wisdom and understanding, which perfect the speculative reason; counsel and knowledge, which perfect the practical reason; piety, which perfects the appetitive powers with reference to other persons; fortitude, which perfects the appetitive powers with reference to danger threatening oneself; fear of the Lord, which perfects the appetitive powers by keeping them from inordinateness in their tendency to pleasures.

5. Just as moral virtues are united and focused in prudence, so the gifts are focused in charity. Without charity—the love and friendship of God in the soul—no one can enjoy the active presence of the gifts.

6. In the soul in heaven the gifts will remain as perfections, but they

will not render the service which they rendered on earth. For the soul which has the beatific vision and is confirmed in grace has no longer any need of habits to dispose it to obey God. When the end is attained, helps to attain the end have completed their service.

7. The gifts of the Holy Ghost are adequately listed by Isaias in their order of dignity (11:2–3): wisdom, understanding, counsel, fortitude, knowledge, piety (or godliness), and fear of the Lord.

8. When we compare the theological virtues and the gifts (and both come directly to the soul from God), it seems that the theological virtues are in themselves more excellent than the gifts, for they regulate the gifts. But the gifts are more excellent than all virtues other than the theological virtues.

69. BEATITUDES

1. The beatitudes pronounced by our Lord in his sermon on the Mount are acts rather than habits of the soul. Hence the beatitudes differ from the virtues and from the gifts, all of which are habits.

2. The rewards (the blessedness) promised in the beatitudes are not exclusively for enjoyment in heaven; some of them at least may have a beginning in this present life. For rewards that can be perfectly enjoyed in the perfect state of man in heaven, may, in some measure, be partially enjoyed in the present and imperfect state of man on earth.

3. The beatitudes are suitably enumerated in scripture. They seem to carry man from the things of sense, through the active life, to contemplation. First, man is taught not to seek happiness in the things of sense—riches, honors, self-indulgence; he is to be poor in spirit, meek, mourning. Next, man is directed towards happiness in his activity with reference to his neighbor; he is to thirst after justice, he is to be merciful. Finally, man is to prepare for contemplation, for seeing God; he is to be clean of heart, he is to be a peacemaker.

4. The rewards promised in the beatitudes—kingdom of heaven, land (of the living), fullness of justice, mercy obtained, sight of God, full status as children of God—all these rewards are to be obtained *perfectly* in heaven; they are included in the perfect happiness of heaven. It is suitable that these phases of the perfect heavenly reward should be enumerated in the beatitudes for our better understanding.

70. THE FRUITS OF THE HOLY GHOST

1. What proceeds from man's reason is a *fruit* of reason. What proceeds from man by the working in him of a higher power is the *fruit* of that higher power. Hence, the action of a man which proceeds

from him as the product of what is implanted in him, like a seed, by the Holy Ghost, is the fruit of the Holy Ghost.

2. The beatitudes are perfect works; the fruits of the Holy Ghost are virtuous and delightful works. The beatitudes are fruits; but not all fruits are beatitudes.

3. The fruits of the Holy Ghost are enumerated by St. Paul (Gal. 5:22–23): charity, joy, peace, patience, benignity, goodness, long-suffering, mildness, faith, modesty, continency, chastity.

4. In general, the sensitive appetites tend to draw man to goods less than himself; the fruits tend to lift man to what is greater than himself, not only as lying beyond the reach of sense, but beyond the reach of natural reason. Hence there is contrast and opposition between the works of the flesh and the fruits.

VICES AND SINS

(QUESTIONS 71 TO 89)

71. VICE AND SIN

1. A sin is a human act (that is, a deliberate thought, word, deed, desire, omission) contrary to right reason, and therefore contrary to God. A vice is a habit of sin. Vice is a morally bad habit; it stands contrasted with virtue which is a morally good habit. And sin, which is a vicious act, is contrasted with a virtuous act, that is, a morally good act.

2. Vice is contrary to order and reason; it is opposed to the rational nature of man.

3. In itself, a bad act is worse than a bad habit; for a bad act is a deed done, whereas a bad habit is only a stable disposition to commit bad deeds. Even human law punishes a criminal act, but not a criminal disposition.

4. One sin does not destroy the opposed virtue as a habit. Just as one good act does not establish a virtue, so neither does one bad act establish a vice. But one mortal sin destroys all infused virtues as virtues (as living and active virtues), but not as habits. A mortal sin destroys charity and thus renders faith and hope inoperative for getting a man on towards heaven. Mortal sin robs faith and hope of

their power as virtues, but it does not expel them as habits. Venial sin neither destroys nor expels charity or other virtues.

5. A person who sins by omission must, of course, be doing something at the time, but, for the sin of omission no determinate act is required to take the place of the omitted duty. The sin of omission is not in what a person is doing but in what he is failing to do.

6. Sin is sometimes defined as "word, deed, or desire contrary to the eternal law." The definition is adequate, for sinful "words, deeds, desires," involve thoughts and imaginings. And a sin of omission is actually a deed; it is the deed of omitting what one should do.

72. THE DISTINCTION OF SINS

1. Sins are essentially distinguished one from another by their objective reality as things out of line with reason and God's law. That is, sins are distinguished from one another as objects. Thus we distinguish sinful words from sinful deeds, and both of these from sinful desires.

2. A sin comes from inordinate desire for some creatural good or from inordinate pleasure in a creatural good. This inordinateness may be in things of the mind (as, for instance, prideful thoughts or undue love of praise) or in things of sense (as, for example, food or sex). Thus there is a distinction of sins (still on the score of their objective reality) as *spiritual* sins and *carnal* sins.

3. Sins are not specifically distinguished on the score of their causes except in the case of the final cause, that is, the intention or end-in-view of the sinner.

4. Sins are distinguished as: (a) sins against God, such as blasphemy, heresy, and sacrilege; (b) sins against self, such as intemperance; and (c) sins against others, such as theft, murder, or slander. Of course, all sins are against God, but those that have this specific name are *directly* against God or the things of God.

5. Sins are not specifically distinct on the score of the punishment due to them. All mortal sins are at one in deserving eternal punishment, although there are essential distinctions among mortal sins, as, for example, between blasphemy and murder. And while mortal sins (which deserve eternal punishment) are essentially distinct from venial sins (which deserve temporal punishment only) this distinction does not find its cause in the punishment due.

6. Neither are sins specifically distinct on the score of commission or omission. A man who steals ten dollars, and the thief who omits to restore ten dollars he has stolen, are guilty of the same kind of sin against injustice.

7. In each species or essential kind of sin we distinguish sins of

thought (involving imaginings and even desires), word, and deed (involving the deed of omission). Thought precedes word, and word may lead on to action. Sin may be in thought alone, or in thought and desire, or in thought and word, or in all three—thought, word, deed.

8. Sins are distinguished specifically as sins of excess and sins of defect or deficiency. One sins by excess in inordinately loving a creatural good; one sins by defect in being insensible to good. Inordinate love and sinful indifference are not the same species of sin.

9. In sins that spring from a single motive, circumstances may change the degree of sin but not its species or essential kind. Sins that spring from a manifold motive have *circumstances* which really enter into the essence of the act and introduce new species. Thus a man who steals money from a church to bribe a politician to enact unjust legislation, really commits three distinct sins against justice and one against religion.

73. THE STANDING OF SINS TOWARDS ONE ANOTHER

1. Sins are sometimes contrary to one another, as, for instance, sinful love and sinful hatred. It is therefore not true to say that all sins are connected.

2. Nor are all grave sins equal in gravity. Their gravity is measured by the extent in which they depart from the rule of right reason. Our Lord said to Pilate (John 19:11): "He that hath delivered me to thee hath the greater sin." Yet Pilate's sin was certainly great.

3. The gravity of mortal sin varies according to its species, and this species is determined by the objective character of the sin. Thus, murder is more grave than great theft.

4. The gravity of any sin is discerned in its opposition to a virtue. The more excellent a virtue, the graver the sin that opposes it. Venial sins may stand opposed to great virtues, but not directly so. An analogy illustrates all this: the most serious illness is that which directly opposes health and tends to destroy it utterly; yet minor ailments also oppose health, but not in direct and totally destructive fashion: conversely, the more perfect is health, the more free it is from destructive disease, and the more readily it overcomes minor ailments. Thus also, the more excellent a virtue is, the more remote it is from its full opposite, and the more readily it withdraws a man from the minor faults that could lead to that full opposite.

5. Carnal sins are, in general, less grave than spiritual sins; yet they bring greater shame on the sinner, and tend more to brutalize him.

Carnal sins usually spring from a stronger impulse than spiritual sins; they are a turning *to* inordinate pleasure, while spiritual sins are a direct turning *from* God and right reason.

6. The more intense the will is in choosing and cleaving to sin, the more grievous is the sin. For the will is the cause of sin, and the greater the cause, the greater is the effect. Yet when the will is made more intense in sin by things external to itself and contrary to its nature, the sin is diminished in gravity. Thus ignorance (which weakens the judgment of reason and therefore hampers the will's choice) reduces the gravity of sin; so also does concupiscence, which hampers free action.

7. Circumstances, as we have seen, can introduce new elements into sin and thus change its specific nature, or rather, add to one sin another specifically different sin. The circumstance of *person* may thus add a sin of filial impiety to a sin of injustice, as, for example, when a man injures his own father. And circumstances can turn a sin through different areas so that the sinner commits the same sin in more than one way; as, for instance, when a wasteful man gives when he ought not, and to whom he ought not. Again, circumstances may make a sin more grave without changing its nature or species, as, for example, when grave anger is nursed and made more lasting.

8. A sin is made more grave by the graver harm it does, unless this harm is accidental to the sin and is neither foreseen nor intended by the sinner.

9. In sins against others, the status of the person offended may make the sin greater; thus disrespect for parents is more grave than disrespect towards respectable strangers. So too, a sin is greater for being committed against a person who, by holiness, or by his official station, is closer to God than others.

10. The more excellent the person or status of the sinner, the greater is his sin. For such a person has resources for more easily avoiding sin. Besides, in sinning, such a person shows a greater ingratitude to God who has bestowed more excellent gifts on him. Finally, sin in such a person is especially inconsistent with his gifts and his station, and so gives the greater scandal.

74. THE SUBJECT OF SIN

1. The principle of human acts is the will, and sins are human acts; hence the will is the principle of sin. Now, the principle of sin is called the *subject* of sin. Hence the will is the subject of sin. St. Augustine says (*Retract.* 1): "It is by the will that we sin, and by the will that we live righteously."

2. The will *elicits* some of its acts (completing them within itself) and *commands* others (which are carried out by subordinate powers

of mind or body or both). Hence the total subject of sin includes, with the will itself, all the powers which can be put into operation, or restrained from operation, by the will.

3. Therefore, even sensitive or sensual powers may be the subject of sin inasmuch as their exercise is voluntary, that is, willed.

4. Yet mortal sin is never, properly speaking, in the sensitive part of man, but in reason which disposes the order of human acts in accordance with sensual bent or tendency.

5. Sin is in the reason (that is, the intellectually enlightened and counseled will) when the sin results from ignorance of what the sinner could and should know and has neglected to know, and also when reason commands inordinate movement in the lower powers, or fails to check such movement.

6. When reason permits the lower powers or appetites to move inordinately, and dwells upon the pleasure of their avoidable movement, without, however, carrying into action what is thus dwelt upon, it is guilty of the sin of *morose delectation*. One commits the sin of morose delectation by dwelling pleasurably or consentingly upon unlawful movements or imaginings of lust, revenge, envy, covetousness, or other vice.

7. St. Augustine draws a distinction between the *higher* reason which contemplates eternal truths, and the *lower* reason which deals with temporal things. Now, the consent which sinful reason gives to a sinful act is of the higher reason, for it is the higher reason which knows the divine and eternal law against which the sin offends.

8. Delight in the thought of what is gravely sinful is itself a grave sin when reason consents to this delight, envisioning and tending towards the sin itself. In a word, it is gravely sinful to consent to the inclination to grave sin.

9. Consent to the sinful act is a sin of the higher reason. It is mortally or venially sinful, according as the act consented to is mortally or venially sinful.

10. In its own domain, the higher reason may be guilty of venial sin as well as of mortal sin. We say "in its own domain," to indicate the excluding of the pull of lower appetites. For example, a sudden movement of unbelief might be a venial sin if it came from a momentary carelessness of the higher reason itself.

75. THE CAUSES OF SIN

1. The direct cause of sin is the will inasmuch as it culpably lacks the direction of right reason (the truly enlightening and counseling intellect) and God's law, and is intent upon some creatural good.

2. Thus the interior and *proximate* cause of sin is found in the will.

We usually say that this interior and proximate cause of sin is in the reason, meaning by the word reason the whole intellective element or part of man, that is, his intellect and will together. The *remote*, as contrasted with the proximate, interior cause of sin is the influence of the sentient appetites and the imagination. This remote interior cause of sin is never the complete cause; it must be admitted into the intellective part of man by free will before it can become thoroughly effective.

3. *Exterior* things can be, in some sense, the cause of sin, but only partially and incompletely in so far as external objects can stir the senses and, through the senses, exercise an influence on reason. Thus a precious gem may stir a person to desire it, to dwell imaginatively upon the joy of possessing it, and so lead him to steal it. But, in the last analysis, the theft is not truly caused by the gem itself; the theft is caused by the thief's will, acting without the right ordering of reason.

4. One sin may be said to cause another, since a human act may dispose a person to perform its like. One breakthrough of the restraints that keep a person from sin may invite, so to speak, other sins to follow in the wake of the first. But, in each case, the complete cause of the sin is the will, the reason, of the sinner.

76. IGNORANCE AS A CAUSE OF SIN

1. The active cause of sin is the will under the light and judgment of intellect; that is, the cause of sin is the reason. Now, ignorance may deprive reason of guiding knowledge that it ought to have, and therefore may bear upon the committing of sin. Thus, in some sense, ignorance may be the cause of sin.

2. Ignorance is itself a sin when it is a man's own fault and pertains to things that he is under obligation to know.

3. Ignorance which is not one's own fault, and which deprives one of knowledge which would have prevented a sinful act, excuses from the guilt of sin.

4. Ignorance that is not directly willed tends to diminish the guilt of sin that comes as a result of it.

77. THE SENSITIVE APPETITES AS THE CAUSE OF SIN

1. Sense-passion or appetite cannot directly move the will to sin, but it can work indirectly upon the will. For the judgment of reason sometimes follows sense-tendency, and the will's choice follows this judgment.

2. When passion is so intense that a person loses the use of reason,

the consequent act is not a human act at all, and the person who performs the act is guilty only in so far as he knowingly permitted the wild passion to take hold on him. But, short of this insane excess, a person is responsible for his act, although this responsibility is lessened by high passion. It is possible for a person, in responsible acts performed under stress of passion, to allow reason to be so strongly swayed that he acts against his knowledge of what is right and sane. Thus a man, in an outburst of wild temper, will say and do things that he knows "at the very moment" are futile and foolish. And a man, well aware of a truth, may, through passion, fail to recognize or apply it in a particular case, and thus may deny what he really knows to be true.

3. Therefore, a sin committed through passion is a sin of weakness. As the body is weak because of disorder in its parts, so the soul is weak when passion disorders the right rule of reason.

4. Sin comes from loving or willing a temporal good as though it were the eternal good. And back of the desire for such a good lies the inordinate love of self. For the sinner wants to have his own way; he wants to please himself. Hence, every sin is truly the fruit of inordinate self-love.

5. The influences which bear upon reason to induce it to sin are rightly set forth in Sacred Scripture (I John 2:16) as follows: (a) the concupiscence of the flesh, that is, passionate desire for bodily delights; (b) the concupiscence of the eyes, that is, inordinate desire for wealth and temporal goods; (c) pride of life, that is, the soul's hunger for honors, praise, and power to rule.

6. Passion that precedes sin (that is, *antecedent* passion) not only brings urgency upon the will, but also obscures the judgment of the thinking mind that guides the will; hence, antecedent passion diminishes sin. But *consequent* passion, that is, passion stirred up by the will itself (as in one who deliberately works himself into a rage, or nerves himself to do an evil thing) rather increases a sin than diminishes it, for such passion shows the intensity of the will's determination to sin.

7. Passion so great as to destroy free choice excuses from sin. But if this great passion comes from the will's faulty neglect to prevent it, it does not wholly excuse from sin.

8. In serious matters sins committed through passion, even through passion that diminishes responsibility, are mortal sins. For as long as passion does not render a man temporarily insane, it can be allayed. A man can work to banish the passionate urge, and can prevent it from having its sinful effect. If he fails to do this, he sins, and, in serious matters, he sins mortally.

78. MALICE AS THE CAUSE OF SIN

1. Malice is badly disposed reason. It is commonly called bad will. A sin committed through malice or bad will is a kind of cold-blooded sin. From the standpoint of the disposition of reason towards sin, there are three types of sin: (a) sins of negligence; for example, sins that come from culpable ignorance; (b) sins of passion; (c) sins of malice.

2. There is malice in a sin committed through habit. For a habit is not compelling; the victim of habit is free to reject its influence. So long as a person knowingly allows a sinful habit to continue, and does not take effective measures to banish it, he shows malice or bad will.

3. Yet a man may sin, and sin with malice, without having the habit of such a sin.

4. Malice makes a sin more grievous than it would be if it were committed under the stress of passion. For malice shows a coldly purposive will to sin, despite the clear judgment of reason which is at the will's service. But passion surges hotly upon a person and blurs the judgment that precedes the act of will.

79. EXTERNAL CAUSES OF SIN

1. In no way whatever, directly or indirectly, is God the cause of any sin.

2. God supports his creatures in being and existence. God therefore supports man's free will, even while man is abusing free will by sinning. God causes the man who sins, and causes his will, and enables or causes it to act. But, though God is the cause of *the act* which free will makes sinful, he is in no way the cause of *the sin* as such.

3. God is called the cause of spiritual blindness and of hardness of heart, in the sense that he withdraws or withholds his grace from those in whom he finds an obstacle or block to the entry and effectiveness of such grace.

4. Spiritual blindness and hardness of heart indicate a man's determined abandonment of God, and, consequently, his abandonment of the hope of heaven. Sometimes, however, a *temporary* spiritual blindness may work towards a man's good by warning him; just so a temporary blindness of the bodily eyes may warn a man to avoid strain and unsuitable light which could permanently injure or destroy his vision.

80. THE DEVIL AS THE CAUSE OF SIN

1. The devil cannot be the direct cause of human sin, for he cannot directly move man's will. God is the only external cause that can

directly move the will, and God never moves the will to sin. The will moves itself to its object. The devil may induce man to sin by persuasion, by presenting attractive objects to human appetites. Only thus can the devil cause man to sin.

2. The devil exercises his powers of persuasion by stirring a man's imagination and by cooperating with whatever moves the sensitive appetites. Thus does the devil *inwardly* instigate a man to sin.

3. In a man who is possessed, the devil may compel acts of sin, but these are not human acts of the man himself, for he is not free. For the rest, the devil can in no wise compel a man to sin.

4. In one sense the devil is the cause of every human sin, for he induced the first man to commit the sin that has infected human nature with the tendency to sin. But apart from this, the devil is not the cause of all human sins. Origen (*Peri Archon.* III) says that even if the devil were to cease to exist, man would still be subject to inordinate desires and to the abuse of free will by sin.

81. HUMAN BEINGS AS THE CAUSE OF SIN

1. The first sin of the first man is transmitted to his descendants by way of origin, and therefore is called original sin. In a sense, all men are one; they are one in nature; they are one in origin. In Adam's sin, human nature sinned; that nature sinned in which all men are one. As a murder committed by the hand would not be the hand's fault, yet would be imputed to the hand as part of the murderer's person, so Adam's sin appears in his descendants *as members of the human nature* that sinned. Adam's sin is imputed to his descendants as the murder is imputed to the "guilty hand" of the murderer.

2. As the original justice of Adam was to be transmitted to his descendants, so was the disordering of that justice to be transmitted. Original sin is transmitted, but no other actual sin of the first parent, or of any parent, is transmitted to descendants.

3. The original sin is transmitted to all men except to Christ, who is God-made-man, and to those whom God, through Christ, exempts from the common human heritage of sin. [*Note:* The Immaculate Mother of God was never infected with original sin. This doctrine of the faith had not been defined in the day of St. Thomas Aquinas; it was defined in 1854.]

4. If God were to make a man miraculously from human flesh, but not by the normal process of generation, that man would not contract the original sin. For original sin is "the sin of nature," and is transmitted only by way of nature, that is, by generation.

5. If Eve alone had sinned, her sin would not have been transmitted to descendants. For in the order of nature the active principle of prop-

agation is the male principle. Hence, it is Adam's sin, not Eve's, that is transmitted.

82. THE ESSENCE OF ORIGINAL SIN

1. A habit is a steady or enduring quality which inclines a power to act. In this sense, original sin is not a habit in us who inherit it. But, in a second sense, a habit is a lasting disposition in a complex nature which makes for the well-being or ill-being of that nature; this type of habit is sometimes called "almost a second nature." Original sin is this latter type of habit in all who inherit it. It is an ill disposition of fallen human nature. St. Augustine (*In Ps. 118, serm.* 3) calls it "the languor of nature."

2. Original sin is specifically one sin. It is not a complexity or plurality of sins in each human individual. It is one sin in each individual.

3. In its own essence, original sin is the "deprivation of the original justice." In consequence of this deprivation, man's normal drive and desire for God are changed into a drive and desire for temporary and changeable good. Since drive and desire are called concupiscence, it is accurate to call original sin (as it works out in human beings) by the name of concupiscence.

4. Original sin is not more in one person than in another; it is equally in all, and is equal in each one.

83. THE SUBJECT OF ORIGINAL SIN

1. Sin is in the soul, not the body; hence original sin is in the soul. The defects, weaknesses, and tendencies of the flesh which come from original sin are punishments, not guilt. When actual sin occurs because of bodily tendencies, it is really committed by man through his will. The flesh of itself does not sin, nor has it the guilt of sin.

2. Original sin primarily affects the very nature of man. It is in the essence of the soul rather than in the powers of the soul.

3. Through the soul's essence original sin infects the soul's powers. It strikes first at the will. The will is the seat of appetency, and it is the source of man's first inclination to sin.

4. In the subordinate powers, the infection of original sin is most apparent in the generative power, the appetites, and the sense of touch.

84. ONE SIN AS CAUSE OF ANOTHER

1. Covetousness, not as a general inordinateness of desire or as a general tendency to such inordinateness, but *as a special sin,* is the root of all actual sins. This special covetousness is the inordinate desire for riches. Riches (that is, money) open a ready avenue to all excesses and sins, and are longed for by sinners. Not money itself, but the love

of money, the desire for it, is the root of all evil, as St. Paul says (I Tim. 6:10).

2. Pride as an inordinate desire to excel (not the pride which is an actual contempt of God or an inclination to this contempt), is back of the primal covetousness. Pride is therefore the beginning of all sins. Man wants goods or riches to have some perfection by possessing them, or some excellence, or some outstanding quality, or some notable enjoyment. Thus, while covetousness is the root of evil, pride is the beginning of sins.

3. Therefore covetousness and pride are fundamental or *capital* sins. These sins are like generals in an evil army; all the action of the evil warfare stems from them. And there are also colonels and majors in the evil army; these too are listed with the capital sins.

4. There are five sins in addition to pride and covetousness that are rightly reckoned as capital sins. Hence, the count of capital sins is seven: pride, covetousness, lust, anger, gluttony, envy, sloth.

85. THE EFFECTS OF SIN

1. The *good of human nature* means one or all of three things: (a) the constitution and properties of human nature itself; (b) the inclination to virtue; (c) the original justice. Now, sin does not diminish or destroy the constitution of human nature. Nor does sin take away the original justice, for this was taken away in the beginning by Adam's sin. Sin diminishes the good of human nature inasmuch as this good is the inclination to virtue.

2. Thus sin can never destroy the entire good of human nature, although it may go on diminishing a man's inclination to virtue.

3. The wounds which sin inflicts on human nature may be listed as four: weakness, ignorance, malice, and concupiscence. The concupiscence mentioned here is an expression or stressing of the concupiscence which is often used as a name for original sin itself.

4. A thing has *good* in its species, its mode, its order (cf. Ia, q. 5). Its species is a thing's complete essential kind. Its mode is discerned in both essential and accidental qualities that it has. Its order is its purpose or direction to an end or goal. Now, sin destroys or diminishes all three types of goodness *in the soul's inclinations, virtues, and actions.* But sin does not diminish or destroy the good of species, mode, and order in the soul's *essence and substance.*

5. By the sin of the first man, the original justice was forfeited. In consequence, human nature was stricken with disorder in the soul, and, through this disorder, with corruption in the body. Hence, death came by sin; bodily disorders and defects came by sin.

6. Human nature, like every existing nature, tends to preserve itself

and to hold on to its perfections. In view of this fact, death and defects are not natural to man. Yet, despite the inclination of bodily natures to preserve and perfect themselves, the matter or bodiliness of their constitution cannot support them in endless existence. For matter as such is subject to corruption, that is, to essential breakup. Therefore, in this view, death and defects *are* natural to man. In our first parents, God supplied for the deficiency of matter, and bestowed on human nature the supernatural gift of incorruptibility or immortality. This gift was rejected, together with the original justice, by human nature in Adam's sin. Hence, death came through sin, and is a penalty consequent upon sin.

86. THE STAIN OF SIN

1. Sin is called, by metaphor, "a stain on the soul." A stain is a blot or ugly mark which destroys what is bright and comely. A stain is caused by contact with soiling and unsuitable things. Sin dims or blots out the brightness of perfected human nature; it blots out the wisdom and grace of God in the soul. It is therefore a stain upon the soul. We speak here of grave sin, not of the actual sin which is called venial.

2. A stain remains after the contact that caused it has ceased. So also the stain of serious sin remains in the soul after the act of sin has been completed. This stain is not removed except by a new act of returning by recovered grace to the unsmirched beauty of the soul.

87. THE DEBT OF PUNISHMENT FOR SIN

1. What offends against an order is punished by that order. If a man offends against the order of reason (as he offends in sinning), he is punished by reason through remorse of conscience. If a man offends against human law he is fined or imprisoned by human law. If a man rebels against the divine law, he deserves punishment by that same law. Hence, sin incurs punishment; it lays the debt of punishment upon the sinner. Sin by its very nature incurs the debt of due punishment.

2. Sin can be (not essentially, but accidentally) the punishment for sin. For by sin man loses grace, and so leaves himself open to further sins; these, if they occur, may be regarded in the light of punishment for the first offense. For these sins plunge the sinner more deeply into his weakness and they lay upon him an increasing debt of punishment due. Sometimes the effect of sin is actual pain or even disease; here the punishment is not only for preceding sins, but for the sin which causes the pain. In this sense a sin can sometimes be called its own punishment.

3. Sins which destroy charity by turning man entirely away from

God cause a complete disruption of the order which aligns a man with his true good. This destruction of charity is, in itself, irreparable; it is as irreparable as the destruction of human life by murder is irreparable. Yet God's power can repair the total destruction of charity, even as God's power can restore a murdered man to life. But unless and until God's power restores the soul to its true order of charity, the soul remains disrupted forever. Hence, serious sin merits eternal punishment.

4. But sin does not incur infinite punishment. It inflicts infinite loss, since it causes the loss of the infinite God. But it cannot incur infinite pain, for the senses are finite.

5. Not all sins are completely destructive of charity. Some sins are only a partial turning from God. These sins deserve punishment, but not eternal punishment. Such sins are called venial sins. They deserve temporal punishment.

6. When the act of sin is over, guilt remains in the sinner's soul, and the debt of due punishment remains. And when the stain of serious sin is removed by repentance and grace, there may still be need of some punishment as satisfaction, but not as simple penalty. To this extent, the *debt* of punishment can remain after forgiven sin.

7. Punishment taken simply as penalty always has reference to sin, original or actual. But we must not suppose that all the trials and hardships of life are punishments. Many of these are tonics for the soul, and remedies for its deficiencies. The physician who requires his patient to swallow bitter medicine or to undertake painful exercise, is not punishing the patient, but assisting him to health. The physician is not inflicting penalty, but conferring benefit. So it is with many of the pains and distresses which we endure in life; these are medicines prescribed by God for our eternal welfare.

8. Punishment as penalty for sin is never imposed on anyone but the sinner. Except in the medicinal sense explained in the preceding paragraph, the sins of parents are not visited on the children who are in no sense partakers of their parents' sins. In spiritual matters, no one suffers loss without some fault of his own. Therefore, penalties, whether material or spiritual, are not inflicted on one person for another's sin.

88. VENIAL AND MORTAL SIN

1. Mortal sin utterly destroys the order which directs the soul by reason and God's law; it inflicts on the soul damage that is naturally irreparable. Venial sin is a disorder, but not a destructive one.

2. By their genus, or general essential class, some sins are mortal and some are venial.

3. Venial sin may dispose the sinner to commit mortal sin, not by its nature (for it is generically different from mortal sin) but by its consequences in the soul. For venial sin may accustom the soul to disorder. Or, by its own disorder, venial sin may remove from the soul some special barrier which kept out mortal sin.

4. A venial sin cannot grow into a mortal sin. But, inasmuch as it can dispose to mortal sin, it may be followed by mortal sin, and by mortal sin in its own field. Thus a person who pilfers a trifling sum may, when opportunity offers, be ready to steal a great amount. But this is not a case of a little sin becoming a big sin. The big sin is an entirely new act of the sinner's will. Both the big and the little sin offend against justice, but they are not in the same essential class of sins against justice, for one is mortal and the other venial sin. These sins may look the same, and one may be inclined to think that they differ, not in generic kind, but only in degree. This is an error. Jabbing a man with a pin, even repeatedly, is never the same thing as running a sword through the man's heart. The sword thrust is not merely an enlarged pin puncture. Between annoying a man with a pin and killing a man with a sword, there is more than a difference of degree. There is an essential difference in the kind of deed done.

5. Therefore, no circumstance can turn a venial sin into a mortal sin. For when a circumstance "changes the nature of a sin," it is *more* than a circumstance; it is a new sin added to, or amalgamated with, the sin of which it is called a circumstance. A theft from a church is said to be a sin of injustice with a circumstance of place which changes its nature and makes it a sacrilege. But the theft is still a theft; that fact is not changed when it becomes a sacrilegious theft. We have not here the case of a theft being turned into a sacrilege, but of a theft having the nature of sacrilege added to its own nature as theft. The "change" induced by a circumstance is the change of something simple into something complex because of the addition or annexation of an entirely new sin to the unchanged old sin.

6. Nor can a mortal sin become a venial sin. Of course, a sin which is mortal in its kind may be venial in its performance. This happens when the sinner does not fully advert to the grievous character of his act, or when he does not give his full consent to the sin. But such a sin, as committed, is simply a venial sin. It is not a mortal sin reduced to venial status.

89. VENIAL SIN

1. Venial sin does not leave a stain on the soul, as mortal sin does. Venial sin is like a passing cloud which puts the soul into shadow, but

leaves no mark on the soul itself. Mortal sin is like an ink-dripping cloth which leaves a stain on what it has touched.

2. St. Paul (I Cor. 3:12) speaks of venial sins under the names of wood, hay, stubble. These are such things as may be found in a man's house, and may be burned up without burning the house itself. And venial sins may be multiplied in a person, even as wood, hay, and stubble may be stored up in quantity in a house. Such venial sins are capable of being "burned up" by the penance of temporal punishment in this life or in purgatory, while the house of the soul still stands.

3. Man in his primal innocence could not have committed a venial sin. The first sin of man had to be a mortal sin. For venial sin comes of disorder in the sensitive appetites or in reason itself. But man in the state of innocence had "an unerring stability of order." Until mortal sin brought disorder, the irregularities and imperfections which occasion venial sin did not exist. Therefore, the first human sin was a mortal sin.

4. The angels could not have sinned venially. The angels have not parts or elements; they have no sentient appetites, no passions to become inordinate. They are pure spirits. No inordinateness is possible in an angel except complete, total, entire inordinateness. And such inordinateness is mortal sin. Hence the fallen angels sinned mortally. The good angels are now in glory and cannot commit sin. The fallen angels are in the essential disorder of mortal sin; this they reiterate or emphasize in all their acts; hence all these acts are mortal sins.

5. The sins of persons not of the faith are less grievous than sins of Catholics. For unbelievers do not know the malice of sin as believers do. When believers sin, they "sin against the light"; unbelievers are always in at least partial darkness. In anyone, believer or unbeliever, the *beginning* or first movement of sensuality is not a mortal sin, for this beginning-movement has not yet the approval of the will which is required to make a sin mortal.

6. When an unbaptized person comes to the use of reason, he will, according to this capacity, begin to direct his life to its true end. If he knowingly fails to do this, he is guilty of mortal sin. Before he comes to responsible life (that is, to the use of reason), an unbaptized person is in the state of original sin, but is incapable of committing actual sin. When he becomes capable of actual sin, and commits it, his first sin is necessarily mortal sin. It is impossible for a person to be guilty of venial sin with original sin alone.

LAW

(QUESTIONS 90 to 108)

90. THE ESSENCE OF LAW

1. Law is an ordinance of reason. The word *law* derives from a Latin word which means *to bind*. Now, the rule or measure of human acts is reason; what binds a man in reference to human acts pertains to reason.

2. Law is an ordinance of reason for the common good of persons in a society. Law is not directly for the benefit of individual persons as such, although it binds individual persons. Law is primarily for the benefit of individuals in a group, in a society.

3. A law is thus an ordinance of reason for the common good. A law is made either by the society which it binds, or it is imposed on that society by the public personage who has charge of the society and authority to rule it.

4. A law must be promulgated. That is, it must be sufficiently announced and made known to those upon whom it lays obligation. Without knowledge of a law, a person cannot be guided by it in his human acts. The full definition of law is: an ordinance of reason, made and promulgated for the common good by one who has charge of a community or society.

91. KINDS OF LAW

1. The community of all things in the universe is governed by divine reason. This government is law. Since divine reason is eternal, being identified with God himself, this law is the eternal law.

2. All things are subject to the eternal law; it directs all things to their proper ends. But it is, in a special way, the law which governs rational creatures. Human beings share the divine reason by becoming aware of an order in things according to which man is to attain his last end, his true purpose in existing. The eternal law, thus manifest to human reason, is called the *natural law*. The natural law is the eternal moral law as knowable by sound human reason without the aid of supernatural revelation.

166

3. From the precepts of the natural law, human reason derives details of direction and order for conducting the affairs of life. Human reason interprets or applies the natural law in particular cases. Each enactment and application of the natural law for particular cases is a *human law*.

4. Over and above the natural law, and human laws derived from it, man needs to have the eternal and divine law *revealed* to him supernaturally. For man has a supernatural end to attain; merely natural means are inadequate to attain this end. Besides, human judgment about particular acts and situations is variable and uncertain, so that human laws are sometimes contrary to one another. Nothing short of an unmistakable declaration of divine and eternal law can adequately direct and curb the interior acts of a man. Such declaration is made only by supernatural revelation. Human laws cannot forbid and punish all evils; when human laws attempt to do this, they invariably destroy much that is good. Only the divine law, supernaturally manifested, can forbid and punish all evils, and at the same time perfectly serve the common good of human society.

5. The divine and revealed law is manifested in the Old and the New Testaments of Holy Scripture. We call these the *Old Law* and the *New Law*. These two laws are distinct, as the imperfect state of a thing is distinct from its fully developed and perfect state; as the baby is distinct from the adult into which it is developing; as the sapling is distinct from the tree that it is to become. For the New Law is the perfection of the Old Law. The Old Law worked for the good of mankind through material things; the New Law works for the good of mankind through spiritual things. The Old Law was enforced by fear; the New Law is enforced by love.

6. By sin, man turned away from God and fell under the influence of strong sensual impulses. These impulses are always ready to flame up instantly; they are called *fomes* of sin. *Fomes* is the Latin word for touchwood or tinder that catches fire from the smallest spark. Now, while *fomes* is a deviation from the rule of reason, it is a constant directive force, and therefore it is called (though not with strict propriety) a *law*. St. Paul speaks of it so when he says (Rom. 7:23): "I see another law in my members fighting against the law of my mind."

92. EFFECTS OF LAW

1. The effect of law is to make men good. For law is an ordinance of reason; it is the function of such ordinance to direct men, through virtue, to their true end. If, however, the intention of the lawgiver is not to direct men to their true goal, the law does not tend to make men

good *simply;* it tends to make men good only in the sense that they conform well with the intention of the law. Hence, a tyrannous law that aims at herding men into servile obedience, tends to make men *good slaves.* But after all, a tyrannous law is not a true law, for it is not in line with reason; it is not truly an ordinance of reason.

2. Law seeks to obtain its effect by directing those bound by it, and its requirements are expressed in four ways: permission, command, prohibition, penalty.

93. THE ETERNAL LAW

1. A governor has in mind the type of order he desires among his subjects. God is the infinite and all-perfect governor. God therefore has in himself the "type" of what creatures are to do to attain their end and purpose. This "type" is divine wisdom viewed as eternal law. Hence, we say, "The eternal law is the type of divine wisdom directing all acts and movements."

2. Normal human beings, as they emerge from infancy into responsible life (the use of reason), begin to have a grasp of the requirements of eternal law. They are increasingly aware of the meaning of *duty* and *obligation;* that is, they recognize the requirement of *doing good* and *avoiding evil.* Thus does human reason reflect the eternal law. As we have seen, this human awareness of the eternal law is called the natural law.

3. Since God is the first and perfect governor, the true plans and laws of lesser governors must be in line with God's plan and law. Therefore, all right and true laws are, in last analysis, derived from the eternal law.

4. God is not subject to his own eternal law, for God himself is the eternal law.

5. All actions and movements in the universe are subject to the eternal law working through divine providence and divine government.

6. Therefore, all human affairs fall under the direction of eternal law. Good men are perfectly subject to the eternal law; bad men are imperfectly subject. Ultimately, order and triumphant justice must prevail; good men and evil men will ultimately be in harmony with justice, whether in glory or in punishment.

94. THE NATURAL LAW

1. As we have seen, the natural law is the eternal law as knowable by sound human reason without the aid of supernatural revelation. The natural law becomes naturally known (and is thus *promulgated*) to normal human beings as they advance from infancy to fuller and fuller

use of reason. The natural law is not, in itself, a *habit* in the human mind, but it tends to become a habit. The habitual knowledge of first moral principles (summed up in: "Do good—avoid evil") becomes a true habit in the human mind; it is a habit called by the name *synderesis.*

2. The basic precept of the natural law, "Do good—avoid evil," is the root out of which definite precepts and prohibitions grow as a person advances in awareness of things and recognizes their good or their evil. The natural law embraces all these directives.

3. The natural law indicates and directs man's inclination to act in accordance with reason. Hence, since all virtues accord with reason, we may say that all virtues are prescribed by the natural law.

4. The natural law is one and the same for all men. Yet, in certain persons, it may be perverted by passion, habit, or evil disposition, as, for instance, in ancient Sparta where lies and thefts and successful trickery were not considered wrong. Now, such exceptions only prove the rule. Such exceptions do not destroy the universality of the natural law anymore than the prevalence of malaria among a certain people destroys the universal understanding of what is meant by human health.

5. The natural law is changeless in the sense that its precepts cannot be upset or destroyed. It can change by extension, by new applications, as experience brings new situations and circumstances. Such a change is not in the natural law itself; it is extrinsic to the natural law; it is merely a new use of the natural law. For instance, the question may arise as to the use of atom bombs in warfare; we may inquire whether the use of such weapons is in conflict with the natural law. Such a question is new; it could not arise in the days when atom bombs were entirely unknown. The question seeks to apply the unchanging natural law in a changing world.

6. The basic and general principles of the natural law cannot be eradicated from human nature. St. Augustine (*Conf.* ii) says, "The law is written in the hearts of men; iniquity itself does not efface it."

95. HUMAN LAW

1. Man has an aptitude for virtue, but, since the fall, he has also a strong inclination to inordinate pleasure and a proneness to evil. Man requires training, especially when he is young, so that he may avoid evil. And men who are evil need to be restrained. Both helpful training and suitable restraints must deal in some detail with human actions. Hence, to promote the application and fulfillment of the natural law, human laws are framed.

2. True human laws are rooted in the natural law, for they are derived from it, and they seek to apply it in special situations.

3. St. Isidore lists the qualities of human positive laws (that is, laws set forth in positive enactments of government) as follows: "Law shall be virtuous, just, possible to nature, according to the customs of a country, suitable in place and time, necessary, useful, clearly expressed, framed for no private benefit but for the common good of the people."

4. Human law as a reasoned general conclusion or derivation from the natural law appears in "the law of nations" or *international law*. As applied in various situations within each nation, human law is called *civil law*.

96. THE POWER OF HUMAN LAW

1. Human law, according to the Pandects of Justinian, "should be made to suit the majority of instances, not for what may possibly happen in individual cases." As St. Isidore says (*Etym.* ɪɪ): "Law should be framed for the common good of all citizens, and not for any private benefit." It is apparent then that human laws are primarily for the community rather than for any individual member of the community.

2. In *prohibiting*, human laws cannot refer specifically to all human vices, but only to the more grievous ones, and chiefly those that are hurtful to fellowmen (such as theft or murder) and which must be prohibited if the necessary order of life in human society is to be maintained.

3. Nor can human laws, in *commanding*, prescribe every act of every virtue by special enactment. Human law must prescribe all virtues that serve the common good, but not in full detail.

4. Just human laws derive, through the natural law, from the eternal law. Hence such laws bind a man in conscience. Unjust human laws do not bind in conscience, except to the extent that a man must endure some hardship rather than upset an established system of harmonious rule. But laws which are unjust because they directly contravene God's law are not only not binding, but a man is bound in conscience to disregard them, to oppose them, and to do what he can to have them revoked.

5. Human law binds all its subjects equally, and without exception.

6. The letter of the law is to be observed except where such observance would be harmful to the general welfare. Sometimes necessity dispenses from law. When pressure of necessity is not so sudden

or strong as to demand instant decision, a dispensation from the law is to be obtained from those in authority.

97. CHANGE IN LAW

1. Human laws are made by fallible man. They are therefore subject to change as men gain more experience and are thus enabled to frame laws that more and more consistently serve the general welfare. Further, there may arise in a society conditions which require new laws or alterations in existing laws.

2. Yet frequent or sudden changes in human laws are to be avoided. To serve its purpose, law requires a certain permanence; a change is, in itself, usually prejudicial to the general welfare. Therefore, unless the good to be achieved by change is great enough to warrant the upheaval occasioned by the change itself, law is not to be altered.

3. Human reason which puts laws into *words* of enactment may also express itself in *deeds*. And thus *customs* arise to serve the common good. Customs can come to have the force of law itself. Indeed, it is possible for custom to become so firmly and widely established that it supplants existing statute law. For the rest, custom is regularly the standard by which existing law is interpreted.

4. It may be that a law which works generally for the common welfare is found, in certain cases, to inflict damage upon individuals. The person in charge of the society concerned may, in such instances, excuse the individuals from observing the law. The authoritative decree of excuse is called a *dispensation* from the law.

98. THE OLD LAW

1. The Old Law is the law of God as expressed in the Old Testament of the Holy Scriptures. The Old Law was meant to repress passion and prevent sin. It could not confer the grace that man needs to reach his true end and goal. Such grace came with New Law of charity, which is the law of Christ. Hence the Old Law was good, but not perfect.

2. The Old Law came from God; it was a divine law. It disposed and prepared men for the coming of Christ with his perfect law of charity. The imperfect serves to bring on the perfect, even in the dealings of God with men. No art is learned except by progressing from imperfect to more perfect and still more perfect, until perfection itself is achieved. And the same master who guides a beginner, may guide him still as his work grows better; may, indeed, guide him until his work is roundedly perfect. So, by the Old Law, God guides man to-

wards perfection, and continues to guide him in the perfection of the New Law.

3. God gave the Old Law to man by his ministering angels. St. Paul (Gal. 3:19) says: "The old law was given by angels in the hand of a mediator." But the New Law was given by God himself who became man to rule and save us.

4. It is fitting that the special people through whom the Redeemer was to come should, in the choice of providence, be made the recipient of the Old Law.

5. In so far as the Old Law expressed precepts of the natural law, it was binding on all peoples, Jew and Gentile. But the special prescriptions of the Old Law which were to sanctify the Jews for the coming of Christ through their nation, were binding upon the Jews alone.

6. The Old Law was suitably given at the time of Moses. By that time man had realized his great fault in rebelling against God; human pride had been humbled by crushing experience. And, lest the fall of pride lead to despairing abandonment of efforts to serve God, the chastisement could not be too long continued. At the time of Moses pride had been humbled, and, while vice was rampant, it had not yet thrown men into despair. The Old Law came in most timely manner to repress evil and to encourage good.

99. THE PRECEPTS OF THE OLD LAW

1. The precepts of the Old Law have a single purpose, but they concern various things.

2. In the Old Law we find *moral precepts,* for the law that is to bring man back to God must make man morally good.

3. Besides moral precepts the Old Law contains *ceremonial prescriptions* for giving expression to man's turning to God, by a common and fitting ceremonial worship.

4. Further, the Old Law contains certain *judicial directives* or precepts which regulate the conduct of the Chosen People towards one another, towards strangers in their midst, and among those occupying different stations in life.

5. These three items make up the whole prescription of the Old Law: moral precepts, ceremonial laws, and judicial directives.

6. The Old Law disposed man for the Christian dispensation, that is, for the New Law, as the imperfect disposes for the perfect. Hence, it was fitting that temporal rewards and punishments were used to enforce the Old Law; such incentives suit man in his imperfect state.

100. MORAL PRECEPTS OF THE OLD LAW

1. All the moral precepts of the Old Law belong to the natural law, that is the eternal law as recognized, in moral matters, by sound human reason. But the moral precepts of the Old Law do not all belong to the natural law in the same way. Some are manifest expressions of the natural law; others are derived from the natural law, either by human reason or by supernatural illumination.

2. The moral precepts of the Old Law cover the ground adequately to put human reason into its right order towards God. These precepts, with their associated counsels, touch upon all the virtues.

3. All the moral precepts of the Old Law are summed up in the Decalogue, that is, in the Ten Commandments.

4. The precepts of the Decalogue are specifically distinct commands and prohibitions. Three of the Ten Commandments regulate human conduct as directly referring to God; the other seven regulate man's conduct, under God, towards his fellowman.

5. The Decalogue directs man to God by way of reverence, fidelity, and service. It regulates man's conduct towards his fellows by requiring special reverence for parents, and forbidding evil and harmful *deeds* (killing, stealing, adultery), *words* (false witness), and *thoughts and desires* (covetousness).

6. The Decalogue presents its precepts of command and prohibition in an admirable order.

7. The Commandments are clearly, plainly, and suitably formulated.

8. The Decalogue expresses the will of God. If man does not fulfill its precepts, he cannot conform to the will of God and attain his true end. Hence, the precepts of the Decalogue are *essential* precepts which never admit of a dispensation.

9. To fulfill a law *perfectly,* a human act must be performed knowingly, freely, and from a settled habit of virtue. Yet a law is fulfilled *sufficiently* by the human act which observes it knowingly and freely. A man ought to have the virtue from which obedience to law flows readily. This is a requirement of the natural law, but it is not included in the prescription of any individual law. Thus, the man who honors his parents now, fulfills the law now, whether he has the fixed habit of honoring his parents or not.

10. Moral virtues are exercised perfectly only when they are exercised in, with, or through charity. Charity is thus the *mode* of every moral virtue. Now, strictly speaking, the mode of a virtue does not fall under the prescription or law of a virtue. Thus, if a person have the habit or virtue of obedience, and act obediently in a certain matter,

he observes the law of obedience, even though his obedience in this instance is from policy and not from charity. He has a fault, of course, but his fault is not disobedience; he fulfills the law of obedience.

11. All the moral precepts of the Old Law are summed up, but not fully expressed, in the Ten Commandments. There are special commandments, given by Moses and Aaron for the guidance of the Chosen People in special circumstances and under particular conditions; these are all implied in the Decalogue; they are corollaries to it.

12. The moral precepts of the Old Law were to guide men to good and to prepare them for Christ. But the fulfilling of these precepts could not, of itself, confer grace, in which is justification.

101. CEREMONIAL PRECEPTS OF THE OLD LAW

1. The ceremonial precepts of the Old Law were divinely determined ways of giving God proper external worship. Now, the duty of worshiping God, outwardly as well as interiorly, rests on man as a moral obligation. Hence, the ceremonial precepts were determinate applications of the moral law.

2. The fullness of revelation had not been made when the Old Law was promulgated. Hence, it was fitting that the ceremonies prescribed in the Old Law should look forward to that fullness: they should have a figurative and prophetic meaning; they should prophetically refer to Christ and His Church and the way to heaven opened by the Christian dispensation. And so indeed they do.

3. The Old Law had many ceremonial precepts to instruct and guide the people, and to counteract their tendency to idolatry.

4. The ceremonies of the Old Law may be classified under four heads: sacrifices; sacred things (tabernacles, vessels, instruments of worship); purifying preparations for divine worship (sometimes called consecrations or sacraments); and observances with reference to special food, vestments, actions, etc.

102. REASONS FOR THE CEREMONIAL PRECEPTS
OF THE OLD LAW

1. Since the ceremonial precepts were instituted by divine wisdom, they were most reasonable means to a necessary end.

2. Worship conducted according to the ceremonial precepts was partly direct worship of God and partly a prefiguring of Christ and his Church.

3. Sacrifice is the highest act of religion. It directs men's minds to God, to recognize him as creator and lord of all. It withdraws men from the worship of false gods. According to its importance, sacrifice

in the Old Law was the most vivid of all ceremonial proceedings in prefiguring the New Law; it forecast in a striking way the coming of the perfect sacrifice, that of the cross.

4. The very instruments and vestments used in the ceremonial service of the Old Law were treated with ceremonious reverence. Thus were men's minds impressed with the truth that the formal worship of God is no routine action of ordinary life.

5. The sacred things and the purifying preparations (such as washings, sprinkling with ashes, prescribed anointings, and so forth) were significant both as contributing to the formal worship of God and to the foreshadowing of Christ.

6. And the observances (clean and unclean foods, special garments, planting of divers seeds, etc.) helped to keep the minds of an easily distracted people employed with truly religious thoughts, making them aware in all things of their duty to God. The observances also prefigured the perfect food of the Eucharist, the perfect garment of grace, and the fruitful works of Christian penance.

103. DURATION OF THE CEREMONIAL PRECEPTS

1. When the Old Law was given to men, it made obligatory some ceremonies that were already practiced by good men of prophetic gifts. Other ceremonies were newly set up by the Law.

2. The cleansing ceremonies of the Old Law were to remove irregularities of a material nature which unfitted a man for ceremonial worship. But they could not take away sin from the soul. They expressed faith in the Redeemer to come, and signified the purifying of the soul to be achieved through the merits of Christ. But they could not confer grace.

3. The ceremonial law ceased with the coming of Christ. For, as we have seen, the ceremonies prescribed by the Old Law were also prophecies. And when a prophecy has been fulfilled, it ceases to exist; it has reached its term; it no longer has meaning. Even such Old Law ceremonies as prefigured heaven gave way to the more perfect prophecies and prefigurings of the New Law.

4. It would be seriously sinful to observe the ceremonies of the Old Law as though they still had significance and binding force. This would be a practical denial that the prophecies expressed in the ceremonies had been fulfilled. It would be a practical denial of Christ, and of the necessity and sufficiency of the Christian order.

104. JUDICIAL DIRECTIVES OF THE OLD LAW

1. Man has the moral obligation of loving God and neighbor. The ceremonial precepts of the Old Law regulated man's moral obligation

to God. The judicial precepts or directives regulated man's moral obligation towards his neighbor. Thus both ceremonies and judicial precepts were rooted in the moral law.

2. The judicial directives were to regulate the conduct of the people according to justice and equity. Yet even these directives had a prophetic aspect inasmuch as they were to prepare the way for the coming of the sun of justice and the daylight of his divinely equitable dealings with mankind.

3. The judicial precepts had the character of the Old Law itself as "our pedagogue in Christ," that is, a teacher leading men to Christ. When the teacher has led men to Christ, he retires; his work is finished. Hence the judicial precepts of the Old Law were no longer in force after Christ came and founded his Church. All that remains of the Old Law is what it had of the eternal law and the natural law.

4. Judicial precepts of the Old Law were of four classes: precepts for rulers; precepts for citizens with respect to other citizens; precepts for the treatment of strangers and foreigners; precepts for home life.

105. REASONS FOR THE JUDICIAL PRECEPTS

1. The form of government established by divine law for the Chosen People was partly monarchy, partly aristocracy, and partly democracy. Moses and his successors governed as kings; there were seventy elders to assist in the rule; these elders were raised to their aristocratic status from the ranks of the people and by the votes of the people.

2. The judicial precepts of the Old Law were admirably suited to the people; they regulated acts and holdings in a just and effective way; they guarded the rights of individuals and of society.

3. The judicial precepts of the Old Law made kind and just provision for foreigners passing through the country or coming to dwell in it. As regards hostile foreigners, the precepts required that war be undertaken only after offers of peace and efforts to maintain it; that once in war the people should persevere bravely, trusting in God; that after victory the people should be moderate in conduct, not vengeful or destructive.

4. As for home life, the precepts of the Old Law gave fitting directions to husband and wife, to parents and children, to masters and servants, and to young couples about to marry.

106. THE NEW LAW

1. The New Law is the law of the New Testament. In essence, it is the law of grace given through faith in Christ. In a secondary way, the New Law is a written law prescribing directives for the receiving and using of grace.

2. The New Law *as grace,* justifies; that is, it takes away sin from a man's soul. The New Law as *teaching* or as *doctrine,* does not justify; it shows the way to justification.

3. It was notably fitting that the New Law came when it did, not earlier. The promise of the New Law was, indeed, given immediately after Adam's sin. But the fulfillment of the promise was rightly deferred for a long time, and this for two reasons: first, that man might properly prepare himself for its wondrous benefits; second, that man might have a thorough realization of his own inadequacy, his weakness, his need of redemption and grace.

4. The New Law is, by its nature, the proximate preparation for heaven. It is not a promise or prophecy of some more perfect state to be attained in this world. The New Law is a fulfillment; nothing further, nothing more perfect, can be conceived for this present life. Therefore, the New Law will not give way to another Law, but will last to the end of the world.

107. THE NEW LAW AND THE OLD LAW COMPARED

1. The New Law and the Old Law are at one in their effort to bring man into proper order with God. But the Laws are otherwise distinct. The Old Law stands to the New Law as imperfect to perfect, as promise to fulfillment, as childhood to perfect manhood.

2. The Old Law could not move man to righteousness (justification, grace), but it could prepare man for righteousness, could foreshadow it, and promise it. The New Law fulfills the promise by making men righteous in the grace of Christ. The New Law brings the substance of Christ to take the place of the shadow of prophecy and prefiguring set forth in the Old Law. Even the moral precepts of the Old Law, though eternal in value, were perfected in the New; these precepts were made more definite and clear by our Lord's teaching, and had the counsels of perfection added to them.

3. The New Law is the flowering and fruitage of what was, in the Old Law, the seed. Thus, the New Law was contained in the Old, not *formally* or as such, but *virtually* as a plant is contained in the seed from which it springs.

4. The New Law imposes a lighter burden than the Old Law, in the sense that it has not so many ceremonies to be performed with painful accuracy and bothersome frequency. Yet the New Law imposes a heavier burden than the Old, inasmuch as it demands the unceasing practice of virtue in the spirit of promptitude and joy. And hence St. Augustine (*In John* v 3) says that Christ's commandments "are not heavy to the man that loveth, but they are a burden to him that loveth not."

108. CONTENT OF THE NEW LAW

1. One who lives by the New Law of grace must show a life of worthy deeds. Hence the New Law legislates for external acts as well as for internal acts and virtues. Grace is imparted by certain external and sensible signs, and grace in the soul shows forth in suitable external conduct.

2. The external signs and producers of grace are the seven sacraments: baptism, confirmation, penance, Holy Eucharist, extreme unction, order, matrimony. The sacraments are, in their order, necessary and sufficient for the sanctifying and saving of men. The proper use of grace gained by the sacraments is indicated in the eternal moral precepts.

3. The New Law directs man's interior acts by prohibiting evil thoughts and desires, and by directing man's intention towards his external good; it forbids rash judgments; it teaches prayer and watchfulness.

4. The New Law also proposes the *counsels* by which a man may the more speedily attain perfection. These are the counsels of poverty, chastity, obedience. By following the counsels, man surrenders lawful but distracting things, and is wholly concerned with the things of God and his eternal salvation. The counsels enable a man to counteract, powerfully and directly, the evil influences found in the world: poverty counteracts the concupiscence of the eyes, chastity counteracts the concupiscence of the flesh, obedience counteracts the pride of life.

GRACE

(QUESTIONS 109 TO 114)

109. THE NECESSITY OF GRACE

1. A creature depends upon God for its existence and its ability to act, and also for the exercise of its ability to act. Man's intellect therefore needs God to know anything whatever. But man's intellect needs God in a special way to know truths that lie beyond its natural range. To grasp such truths, the mind of man requires supernatural

light in addition to its own natural light. This supernatural light is the light of *grace*.

2. Man's will also needs supernatural aid to choose and accomplish supernatural good. This aid is a strength added to the natural strength of the will, and bestowed on the will as a gift of God. The name of this gift is *grace*.

3. Speaking absolutely, man can love God above all things without grace, for this is the very drive and purpose of his nature. But man is fallen; sin has hurt his nature; he can no longer achieve what ought to be naturally attainable. Therefore, even to love God *naturally* above all things, man requires supernatural grace. Certainly, to love God *supernaturally* above all things, man requires grace, and would require it even if he had retained his primal innocence.

4. Man cannot fulfill the Commandments of the Law without the help of grace. Before the fall, innocent man could, without grace, perform the works required by the Commandments, but could not perform them out of supernatural charity as their perfection demands. Therefore, man, innocent as well as fallen, needs the grace of God to fulfill the law of God.

5. Hence it is clear that man cannot merit heaven by his unaided efforts. Man labors for a supernatural end, and such an end is, by the very force of ideas and words, outside the range and grasp of natural powers: the natural cannot compass the supernatural. To win heaven, man must have divine grace.

6. Indeed, man cannot, without grace, even prepare himself to receive grace. To prepare himself for grace, man must be turned to God in a supernatural way; for this supernatural turning to God, supernatural aid is required; grace is required.

7. Man cannot rise from sin without grace. By serious sin, man stains his soul, brings disorder into his natural powers, and incurs the debt of everlasting punishment. And man cannot, without grace, remove these evil consequences of grave sin.

8. Nor, without grace, can a man avoid sin. For the fall of Adam has left man prone to sin, and has dulled his natural powers of alertness and ready opposition to its attacks. Without supernatural aid, man must certainly succumb to some of the assaults of temptation. Hence, man needs grace to avoid sin.

9. Once he has attained grace, man is not thereby permanently equipped for doing good and avoiding evil. He needs new graces, constantly supplied. True, once grace is attained, man's nature is healed and made capable of meritorious acts; his soul has the state or habit of sanctifying grace. But, in addition to this habitual grace, man needs

special helps to meet continual emergencies, unruly tendencies and urges in his nature, darkness of mind and weakness of will in particular cases where he needs to know what to do and needs prompt strength to do it valorously. Man in the state of *sanctifying* grace needs an unfailing supply of *actual* graces. Just so, a man in robust health needs an unfailing supply of food and the other things that will keep him in health.

10. Perseverance in God's grace to the end of life requires the sustained giving of graces by almighty God, and is itself a special grace. The fact that a man has obtained grace is not a guarantee that he will never lose it, nor is it guarantee that, if lost, grace will be recovered and possessed at the time of death. Yet it is of paramount importance that man have grace at the moment of death. He is required to "persevere unto the end," if he is to be saved. Hence man needs the special gift and grace of God which is called "the grace of final perseverance," and for this gift and grace he must ever pray.

110. THE ESSENCE OF GRACE

1. The grace of God is a gift bestowed on man's soul to enlighten and strengthen it above the measure of its natural light and strength.

2. Grace is received into the soul as a quality of the soul. It is a supernatural quality which disposes the soul to supernatural well-being and supernatural well-doing.

3. Grace is not identical with supernatural virtue; it is prior to such virtue, and is its root. Supernatural virtue is a habit which works by, through, and with grace.

4. Grace is not, as virtue is, primarily in the powers of the soul; it is received into the essence of the soul, and flows from the soul's essence into the soul's powers.

111. CLASSIFICATION OF GRACES

1. Grace given to make the receiver holy is *sanctifying* grace. Grace given to one person for the benefit and holiness of others is *gratuitous* grace; such, for example, is the grace of miracles, or the grace of prophecy.

2. Grace which directly moves the mind or will to act is *operating* grace; grace which disposes mind and will to receive and use operating grace is *cooperating* grace.

3. Grace which precedes an operation or state of the soul is *prevenient* grace; grace which follows a prior effect of grace is *subsequent* grace. Grace has five effects: (a) it heals the soul; (b) it awakens the desire for good; (c) it helps carry the desire for good to the actual

achievement of good; (d) it gives perseverance; (e) it conducts the soul to glory. The same grace may be subsequent to one of these effects and prevenient to another.

4. Gratuitous graces are thus listed by St. Paul (I Cor. 12:8–10): wisdom, knowledge, miracles, prophecy, discerning of spirits, tongues, interpretation of speeches.

5. Sanctifying grace sets man directly in line with God, his last end. Gratuitous grace stirs man and prepares him to get in line with his last end. Thus a man observing a miracle (wrought by the gratuitous grace of miracles in the person God uses as instrument to perform the miracle) may be stirred to repentance or to deeper piety, and so be moved to obtain sanctifying grace. It is clear, therefore, that sanctifying grace is, in itself, more noble and excellent than gratuitous grace; it is better to be in the state of sanctifying grace than to have the grace of miracles.

112. THE CAUSE OF GRACE

1. Only God can make a man a sharer in the divine nature. Only God can bestow the gift of God. Now, grace is "a participation in the divine nature"; grace is a gift of God. Hence, God alone is the true cause of grace.

2. Grace which helps move us to good, in being or action, is all from God, and not in any way from ourselves. Even the preparation or disposition for grace is entirely from God. By accepting cooperating grace, we enter into the disposition which prepares us for the receiving of sanctifying or habitual grace.

3. In so far as the human will can thus (by accepting cooperating grace and using it) make preparation for grace, it can set up no necessity or demand that grace should actually follow upon the preparation. For no merely human preparation can adequately and compellingly dispose the soul for supernatural gifts. But in so far as man's preparation is from God, grace follows it infallibly.

4. Sanctifying grace is a greater or lesser gift (not in itself, for in itself it admits of no degrees), according to the capacity and readiness of the receiver. Yet, since God alone can effectively dispose the soul to receive grace, it is God who is truly "the measure of grace." St. Paul (Eph. 4:7) says, "To every one of us is given grace according to the measure of the giving of Christ."

5. Man cannot know for certain that he has the grace of God unless God reveal the fact to him. Merely natural knowledge cannot give certitude of a supernatural fact or experience. But man may have an imperfect knowledge of the fact that he has grace; that is, he may have

justified conjectural knowledge, based on signs, such as delight in the thought of God, a contempt for merely material and worldly goods, and the fact that he is not conscious of mortal sin.

113. THE EFFECTS OF GRACE

1. A man is *justified* by the remission or removal of the guilt of sin.

2. This removal or remission of sins is effected in man by the in-pouring of supernatural grace.

3. God gives the grace which justifies; he also gives to free will the grace to accept justification. God moves all things according to the nature he gave them in creating them; to man's nature he gave free will; hence, by grace he moves man's will to accept *freely* the justifying or sanctifying grace which removes the guilt of sin from the soul.

4. To move the will to accept grace, the mind or intellect is moved; for free will follows in its choice the ultimate practical judgment of the intellect. Now, the intellect is here moved by being turned to God by faith. Hence, a movement of faith is required for the justifying of a sinner.

5. Since free will cannot choose to turn to God unless it also chooses to turn away from sin, there are two will-acts required for justification: the repudiating of sin, and the embracing of God's justice.

6. Four things are required for the justification of a sinner: (a) the infusion of grace; (b) the movement of the free will towards God; (c) the movement of the free will to reject sin; (d) the remission of sins.

7. The justification of a sinner, which is the change from the state of sin to the state of grace, is not a gradual change but an instantaneous one. The effective factor in this change is the infusion of grace, and this is an instantaneous act. Sometimes, indeed, the soul is gradually disposed, by successive influences, to receive justification. But the actual justification does not consume time, or admit of successive degrees or steps.

8. In the actual justification of a sinner, all four requisites—grace, faith, hatred of sin, remission—concur in the same instant. But in their own nature there is priority among these requisites for justification. Thus considered, first comes the infusion of grace; then, the will's movement towards God by faith and love; then, the will's rejection of sin; finally, the remission of guilt.

9. The justifying of sinners by grace can be called the greatest work of God. Not only is this work great in itself; it is great in the fact that it is done for those unworthy of it. Psalm 144 says that God's tender

mercies are over all his works. And the work of justifying a sinner is a work of most tender mercy.

10. Apart from wondrous and unusual manifestations, as in the conversion of St. Paul, the justifying of a sinner is not called a miracle. For a miracle, taken in its widest meaning as a wondrous work divinely wrought, is always something outside the usual course of God's proceeding with men. Now, justification regularly proceeds by the same course: grace, faith, rejection of sin, remission.

114. MERIT

1. Merit, taken objectively, is something earned, something owed to a person. Taken subjectively, merit is the right of a person to his earnings, to what is owed him. Now, man cannot by his own nature set up a *right* towards God, and demand by the law of justice that he be paid for anything he has done. Yet God has been pleased to allow man what creatural nature cannot achieve of itself. God has provided that man can have merit, and can establish a just claim for supernatural reward. The basis of this blessed situation lies in the fact that human free will, although moved by unmerited grace, actually does cooperate with God's will in accepting and using grace.

2. Eternal life (that is, the enjoyment of the beatific vision forever in heaven) is something beyond the power of any created nature to achieve unaided. Even in his primal state of innocence, man could not merit eternal life by his natural powers. For meriting eternal life, supernatural grace is absolutely necessary.

3. There are two types of merit, *condign* merit and *congruous* merit. Condign merit is the right in strict justice to a reward. Congruous merit is not so much a right as a claim; it rests upon what is suitable or fitting in a situation; it is a kind of deserving rather than an earning. Now, in so far as a man's meritorious work is human, although performed in and by grace, it can merit only congruously. But in so far as the meritorious work is God's work in man, it can merit condignly, and thus establish a right to eternal life. By his grace, God makes us participators in the divine nature; he makes us his adopted children; he makes us "sons of God." And St. Paul says (Rom. 7:17): "If sons, heirs also." And thus we can merit our inheritance as God's children; we can merit eternal life.

4. The meriting of eternal life by grace comes first by charity; and under charity, by the other virtues.

5. Man cannot merit the first grace which justifies him. For to have merit, man must have grace; merit is the fruit of grace. Hence the

first grace, the grace which removes the guilt of sin and establishes the soul in the state of grace, is imparted to the soul by God, with no right or claim on man's part to demand or deserve it.

6. No one but Christ can condignly merit the first grace for another. But a man in the state of grace, praying and offering good works for the justification of another person, may set up a claim for God's mercy towards that person. Thus one may merit *congruously*, but never *condignly*, the first grace for another.

7. A man who sins mortally cuts himself off from God and from all claims on God. He cannot merit his own restoration to grace, either condignly or congruously. Nor can a man in the state of grace merit his own restoration in case he should commit mortal sin at some future time. For mortal sin, if it comes, will destroy all existing merits.

8. But a man in grace can, by using present grace, condignly merit further grace; that is, a man in grace can condignly merit increase in grace.

9. The special grace of final perseverance cannot be merited. It is the free gift of God to those who will receive it.

10. Man cannot merit temporal goods except in so far as these are needed for virtuous works that lead to heaven.

[IIa IIae]

The SECOND PART *of* THE SECOND PART

[*Questions 1-189*]

FAITH

(QUESTIONS 1 TO 16)

1. THE OBJECT OF FAITH

1. The faith of which we speak here is not the mere human faith by which we accept the testimony of men, but the faith by which we accept the revealed word of God. The object of this faith is truth about God and the things that pertain to God.

2. To human understanding, the truth about God and divine things is not simple, but complex. For though God is infinite simplicity, the finite human mind cannot grasp his being, and truths related to his being, with simplicity. The finite mind does the best it can, in its limited way, with the infinite. Therefore, the truths which constitute the object of faith are involved, for the human understanding, in some complexity.

3. Since faith has for its object the truth about God, nothing false can enter into its content.

4. The object of faith is not something seen or sensed; nor, in itself, is this object grasped by the intellect. Faith, says St. Paul (Heb. 11:1), "is the evidence of things that appear not."

5. The object of faith cannot be, at the same time, the object of scientific knowledge. St. Gregory says (*Hom.* xxi *in Ev.*): "When a thing is manifest, it is the object, not of faith, but of perceiving."

6. It is a convenient and useful practice, in studying the object of faith, to arrange its truths as logically connected heads or topics. These heads or topics are then called the *articles* of faith.

7. The articles of faith are never increased in their substantial content, as time goes on. But, since the study of anything tends to reveal in detail what is implicitly contained in it, the study of the object of faith may result in an increased number of articles inasmuch as these are explicit statements of what is implicitly contained in the original articles.

8. The articles of faith are adequately expressed in the Apostles' Creed.

9. A *creed* or *symbolum* is a compact statement, or series of formulas which express the articles of faith. There are several of such creeds

or *symbola* in general use in the Church: the Apostles' Creed, the Nicene Creed, the Athanasian Creed. Such creeds differ only as to fullness of expression; all are identical in substance. A creed is useful, both as an approved expression of the whole object of faith, and as a means of instruction and guidance for the faithful.

10. It is essential that a creed have the approval of the sovereign pontiff to whom is committed the infallible teaching office in what pertains to the whole Church.

2. THE INTERNAL ACT OF FAITH

1. What we hold by faith, we *believe*. St. Augustine (*De Praedest. Sanct.* II) says that the verb *to believe* means "to think with assent." In this definition the verb *to think* means to inquire mentally and consider what the truth is. Having found, by such consideration, sufficient motive for accepting what is proposed as true, the mind, under command of the will, accepts it without hesitation. And this is belief or faith; rather, it is the internal act of faith. Hence, the internal act of faith is the unhesitant assent of the mind or intellect, under the direction of the will, to truth that is proposed for belief upon sufficient authority. In the case of religious faith, the authority is God, who is truth itself.

2. One and the same act of faith in divine truths involves three things: (a) belief in a God—that is, belief that God exists; (b) believing God—that is, recognizing his word as the truth; (c) belief in God—that is, accepting his word as the rule of life and the way to salvation.

3. For a man to reach heaven, he must accept, and live by, the word of God even as a pupil accepts the word and direction of a good and trusted teacher. And though human reason—the thinking mind—can prove many of the truths that man must know about God, there are other necessary truths beyond the reach of reason which a man must hold by faith in the word of his infallible Teacher.

4. And even the truths that reason can prove in its study of God and divine things are a part of the object of faith. For a man needs to know these truths from his early youth before he has opportunity or ability to think them out. Besides, many men have neither talent nor training for the sustained reasoning needed to think these truths out. And many men are lazy in mind, or are preoccupied with other things, and these men would never study out these necessary truths at all. Moreover, in a long and involved process of reasoning, mistakes are likely to creep in, as is evident from the disputes of scholars. Hence, it is needful that man should have the certitude of God's infallible word for all divine

truths, even those naturally knowable, which must be known quickly, clearly, and without error. Now, all truths to be held on God's authority belong to the object of faith.

5. Faith is not a foggy or general acceptance of truth in bulk. It is explicit and definite in its essential articles. Other points of faith, involved in these articles in an implicit manner, may, in time, be worked out explicitly. Meanwhile, these truths are accepted implicitly by the believer.

6. The simplest man and the most learned scholar hold the same faith. Each person, according to his state and capacity, holds explicit knowledge of the truths of faith. But the explicitness of the scholar's grasp of essential truths is far more detailed than that of the simple-minded man, the young, and less gifted persons. In God's plan, the more learned and enlightened are to teach others; upon these teachers rests the obligation of having a more detailed knowledge than others of the truths of faith which all hold in common.

7. Everyone who is capable of explicit faith must have such faith in Christ as God made man for our salvation, who died, and rose again, and ascended into heaven, opening the way thither for mankind.

8. And all must believe explicitly in the Blessed Trinity, one God in three divine Persons, who are really distinct and equal.

9. Since the act of faith is an act of intellect moved by the will, under influence of grace, to assent fully to divine truths, it can be a meritorious act. For merit can be gained by any will-act freely performed with God's grace.

10. Although we accept the truths of faith on God's authority, it is right for us to study these truths, to think seriously upon them, and to notice how they are in accord with human reason. Such study is not a doubting or skeptical inquiry; nor is it a presumptuous summoning of God to the bar of our poor judgment. Rather, such study is an effort to appreciate the truths of faith; it indicates our interest in divine truth, and our devotion to it. Hence, such study does not decrease, but rather increases, the merit of the act of faith.

3. THE EXTERNAL ACT OF FAITH

1. The external declaration, in words or deeds, of what we believe, is a true act of faith. Though faith itself is in the soul, and its act is primarily internal, it can be outwardly expressed without losing its essential character. Hence, if internal thought and assent make an act of faith, the external expression of that thought and assent makes an act of faith.

2. A man is obliged to declare his faith outwardly (that is, he is

obliged to make an external act of faith) whenever the honor of God or his neighbor's good requires that he should do so.

4. THE VIRTUE OF FAITH

1. St. Paul (Heb. 11:1) defines faith as "the substance of things to be hoped for, the evidence of things that appear not."

2. The act of believing, the act of faith, is the assent of the intellect under the motion of the will; both intellect and will are involved in the act of faith. But the *virtue* of faith is a habit of the *intellect*. Faith thus resides in the intellect which assents to truth and holds onto it possessingly. This fact is in no wise affected by the further fact that the intellect was moved to its assent by the will.

3. Whatever gives a thing a determinateness of being is called, in the language of philosophy, a *form* of that thing. What gives a thing its essential being in itself, is its *intrinsic* form; what comes to a thing from outside, lending perfection or effectiveness, is an *extrinsic* form. Now, the virtue of faith has its intrinsic form in being the habitual assent of the intellect to truth. But for the virtue of faith to be operative, to be living and active, it must be suffused with charity. Hence, it is often said that "charity is the form of faith." Charity is here an *extrinsic* form.

4. And when charity (which is the grace, love, and friendship of God) is not in the soul, faith is not operative; it is lifeless; it is without its activating extrinsic form. Such faith is called *formless*. Thus, when a person commits a mortal sin, and thereby deprives his soul of charity, he does not lose the faith, but he renders it powerless to get him on to heaven; he renders the faith in him "formless."

5. Faith with its extrinsic form of charity is living faith. This is the *virtue* of faith, that is a habit in a man that serves as the principle of good acts. Lifeless or formless faith is not a virtue.

6. Faith in itself is one virtue, and it is also one in its content of truths, that is, in its object. Of course, there is a subjective distinction between John's faith and Richard's faith, inasmuch as these are two individual persons, each with his own faith. But the faith itself is one and the same, whether it be in John or Richard. Says St. Paul (Eph. 4:5): "One Lord, one faith, one baptism."

7. Living faith is the first of virtues, preceding all others. As St. Augustine says (*Contra Julian.* iv), there are no real virtues unless faith be presupposed. He speaks, of course, of supernatural virtues.

8. Faith gives absolute certitude of the truths believed, because it is a virtue directly infused into the soul by God who is truth itself.

5. THOSE WHO HAVE FAITH

1. Man in the state of innocence before the fall, and angels before their confirmation in grace and glory, had faith. Some of the truths which for us are in the object of *faith* were doubtless in their *knowledge*, but they could not have known all the divine truths thus; they held some by faith.

2. The fallen angels have faith. St. James (2:19) says: "The devils . . . believe and tremble." Yet their faith is not a living faith, not a virtue. It is formless or lifeless faith, and consists, not in the infused virtue, but in the fact that the fallen angels see many signs by which they understand that the teaching of the Church is from God and is therefore true.

3. To reject any article of the faith is to reject the faith itself. This is like pulling one stone out of an arch; it is like putting one hole in the hull of a ship. The whole arch tumbles down; the whole ship sinks. A man who has the faith, accepts God's word. Now, God's word has set up the Church as man's infallible teacher and guide. If a man, therefore, rejects one article of the faith, and says that he believes all the other articles, he believes these by his own choice and opinion, not by faith. Rejecting one article of the faith, he rejects the whole authority of the Church, and he rejects the authority of God which has set up and authorized the Church to teach truth. Hence, it is entirely incorrect to say that a man may have lifeless or formless faith in some articles of the Creed while he rejects others; such a man has not the faith at all, living or lifeless.

4. One man's faith can be greater than that of another in the sense that one man can have a fuller and more explicit knowledge of the truths of faith than another has. And one man's faith may be called greater than the faith of another in the sense that he has a greater confidence and devotion in the practice of faith than another has. But the faith, considered in itself, is one thing, not capable of being lesser or greater.

6. CAUSE OF FAITH

1. What is proposed for man's belief as the object of supernatural faith, is revealed by God. The truths of supernatural faith surpass the power of human reason to discover. Man is moved inwardly by grace to accept what is divinely proposed for belief. Therefore, faith is *infused* into the soul by almighty God. God is the cause of faith.

2. Thus, faith is a gift of God. Even lifeless or formless faith, which

is not the virtue of faith, is God's gift. For a gift is a gift, even when it is mistreated and spoiled by the receiver.

7. EFFECTS OF FAITH

1. Faith makes us aware of God's judgment, and thus arouses fear of incurring penalties for sin. This is *servile* fear. And faith also makes the soul fear to be separated from God by sin, and to *deserve* the penalties of sin. This is *filial* fear. Servile fear is an effect of lifeless faith; filial fear is an effect of living faith.

2. Faith raises the heart and reason to the love of God, and so takes away or lessens our tendency to cling to creatural goods. Thus, an effect of faith is the purifying of the heart.

8. THE GIFT OF UNDERSTANDING

1. Man has by nature a power to penetrate into the meaning of things and to grasp reality in its essence. This is the natural power of mind, intellect, understanding. But man needs more than natural intellect to understand the end for which he exists and the means of attaining it. For this, man requires the light of the gift of supernatural understanding.

2. The light of supernatural understanding does not impart scientific knowledge of divine things, so that man ceases to know them by faith. By the gift of supernatural understanding man knows the mysteries of the faith surely, but imperfectly. He sees that these mysteries involve no contradiction, and he assents to their truth on God's word; thus he holds these truths by faith.

3. The gift of understanding gives knowledge of the truths of faith and also of things subordinate to faith, such as human action which springs from faith. Hence this gift is not purely *speculative* or theoretical; it is also *practical* or directive.

4. Just as the gift of charity, which is the love, grace, and friendship of God, is found in all who are in the state of sanctifying grace, so also is the gift of supernatural understanding found in them.

5. And, without sanctifying grace, no one has the gift of supernatural understanding.

6. The gift of supernatural understanding gives to the mind of man the light of faith. In this light, the gift of wisdom enables a person to judge rightly of divine things; the gift of knowledge makes him capable of right judgment about created things; the gift of counsel equips him to apply the judgments of wisdom and knowledge in individual human acts.

7. The sixth beatitude, "Blessed are the clean of heart, for they

shall see God," corresponds to the gift of supernatural understanding. For there is a special cleanness in the mind and heart which, purged of evil phantasms, understands the truths of faith. Such an understanding sees God in his creatures on earth, and will behold him hereafter in the heavenly vision.

8. The fruit of the Holy Ghost called faith, that is, the certitude of faith, also corresponds to the gift of spiritual understanding.

9. THE GIFT OF KNOWLEDGE

1. Man needs a sound grasp of the truths of faith, and he has it by the gift of understanding. And man also needs to make sure and right judgments, in the light of faith, in all the affairs and situations of life; he is equipped to do this by the gift of knowledge.

2. The gift of knowledge is concerned with human and created things inasmuch as these pertain to the faith in any way.

3. The gift of knowledge is primarily of speculative knowledge, for it deals with certitude in judging what things are in the light of faith. But all knowledge of creatures that refers to God and the faith must indicate, in some manner, what a person is to do as he strives to walk in the way of such knowledge. Therefore, the gift of knowledge is not entirely speculative; it is also practical.

4. The third beatitude, "Blessed are they that mourn, for they shall be comforted," corresponds to the gift of knowledge. For knowledge of creatures in reference to God, and in the light of faith, is knowledge of how man fails through creatures, and loses his true good by putting his trust in them. Hence, knowledge involves sorrow for sin—that is, fruitful *mourning*.

10. UNBELIEF

1. The unbelief of a person who refuses to hear the truths of faith, or who despises these truths, is a sin.

2. Unbelief, like faith, is in the intellect as its proper subject. It is also in the will, inasmuch as every human act is in the will as its principle. Unbelief in the intellect, accepted or at least unrejected by the will, is sinful unbelief.

3. Apart from the sins directly opposed to the other theological virtues (that is, hope and charity), unbelief is the greatest of sins, because it severs a man completely from God and falsifies his very notion of God. Unbelief is the greatest of sins against faith.

4. Great as the sin of unbelief is, it does not make sinful every human act of the unbeliever, but only such human acts as proceed from it as from their principle.

5. There are three main types of unbelief: that of pagans who resist the faith; that of the chosen people; that of heretics.

6. The unbelief of pagans who *resist* the true faith is not so great a sin as the unbelief of heretics or Jews who *reject* the faith.

7. Arguing or disputing about the faith is sometimes justified; indeed, it is sometimes necessary. Such disputation must never be a manifestation of doubt or weakness in the faith. And it must never be of a nature unsuited to the capacity of those who hear it.

8. A person who has not the faith cannot be compelled by human means or authority to accept it. Yet such a person should be compelled by human means not to interfere with the faithful, not to scandalize them by blasphemy, not to bring persecution upon them. Those who have lapsed from the faith, as apostates and heretics, might justly be compelled to consider their error and their breaking of their promises.

9. We should not be on familiar terms with those who sinfully reject the faith. Nor can we have any part in the false worship of apostates or heretics. Those who are strong in the faith, and are equipped for solid discussion, should try to win back unbelievers who have rejected the faith, but never in such a way as to scandalize the more simple-minded among the faithful.

10. Unbelievers are not to be permitted to set up authority over the faithful. But in governments already established, unbelievers in office have authority over the faithful, apart from matters of divine law.

11. The religious rites of unbelievers are to be tolerated, since these are lesser evils than those that would arise by reason of an effort to forbid or eradicate such rites. In themselves, the rites of unbelievers are sinful, for they are not of divine origin, but are in conflict with divine ordinance. Yet these rites are not recognized as evil by those who honestly use them; hence, they are not formally sinful, but only materially so. To tolerate such rites seems to be the best way of winning the good will of the user of them, and so obtaining opportunity to instruct him in the true faith.

12. Children of Jews and unbelievers are not to be baptized against the will of their parents.

11. HERESY

1. A heresy is false doctrine held by a person who intends to assent to Christ's teaching, but who actually assents to his own choice and opinion. The word *heresy* means picking and choosing. A heretic is one who picks and chooses what he wishes to believe.

2. Heresy is a corruption of Christian faith. It has no reference to

secular doctrines and opinions, but only to those that have a bearing on the faith itself.

3. Heresy is error, and hence cannot be tolerated by the mind. It is against God, and hence cannot be tolerated by faith. Heresy is therefore not to be tolerated, but heretics are to be tolerated, except in so far as they are a menace to the faith of believers.

4. The Church receives to penance and reconciliation those who return after a lapse into heresy.

12. APOSTASY

1. Apostasy, in the simple sense of the word, is the renouncing of the faith. Hence, apostasy is a sin of unbelief.

2. In Catholic countries a ruler who proves apostate is, upon excommunication, justly deprived of the allegiance of his subjects.

13. BLASPHEMY

1. Blasphemy is a direct disparging of the divine goodness. It is therefore a sin in conflict with the faith. For he who has the faith confesses to the divine goodness.

2. Blasphemy, by its *genus* or the general essential class of sins to which it belongs, is always a mortal sin.

3. We have seen that unbelief is the greatest of sins against faith. Blasphemy is an emphatic form of unbelief. Hence, in speaking of sins against faith, blasphemy is often called the worst of sins.

4. The wicked in hell detest the divine goodness and justice, and thus they blaspheme. It is believable that, after the resurrection of the body at general judgment, human beings in hell will utter their blasphemies audibly.

14. THE SIN AGAINST THE HOLY GHOST

1. St. Augustine says that the sin against the Holy Ghost mentioned specifically in scripture (Matt. 12:31) is the sin of *final impenitence* by which a man rejects grace and pardon, up to and including the moment of his death. Others, speaking of sins against the Holy Ghost, say that a sin of weakness is a sin against God the Father; a sin of ignorance is a sin against God the Son; a sin of malice is a sin against God the Holy Ghost.

2. There are, in fact, six kinds of sins against the Holy Ghost, and all are sins of malice. These are: despair, presumption, impenitence, obstinacy, resisting the known truth, and envy of another's spiritual good.

3. In Matthew (12:31) we read, "He that shall speak against the

Holy Ghost, it shall not be forgiven him, neither in this world, nor in the world to come." We may take the phrase, "speak against the Holy Ghost," for "sin against the Holy Ghost," since a sin of speech expresses the internal state of mind and will. If final impenitence is "the sin against the Holy Ghost," it is clear that this sin cannot be forgiven, because the sinner goes to his death and judgment unrepentant and resisting the grace of pardon. If "the sin against the Holy Ghost" is any sin of malice, it is unforgivable in itself, although God may forgive it none the less. It may be incurable as a disease is incurable; yet God can cure an incurable disease.

4. It is possible for a person to commit his very first sin by sinning against the Holy Ghost. Yet it is so unlikely as to be practically impossible. For the sin against the Holy Ghost is regularly the outcome of many previous sins, and comes of a gradual turning of the mind and will to contempt for the means of salvation.

15. VICES OPPOSED TO KNOWLEDGE AND UNDERSTANDING

1. A person who turns away his mind from all consideration of God, or who so busies himself with creatural things that he has no time to think of God and of his own soul's needs, is subject to mental and spiritual blindness; in so far as this is a person's own fault, it is a sin.

2. *Blindness of mind* is a complete privation of the consideration of spiritual goods. *Dullness of sense* is a partial privation; it is a weakness, not a total absence, of mental vision which beholds spiritual goods. Thus dullness, in so far as it is voluntary, is also sinful.

3. It appears that both dullness of sense and blindness of mind arise primarily from sins of the flesh; the former from gluttony, and the latter from lust.

16. PRECEPTS OF FAITH, KNOWLEDGE, AND UNDERSTANDING

1. The precept of faith—the command to believe in the articles of faith—is given perfectly in the New Law. In the Old Law, the precept of faith is presupposed; it is understood in general, and not expressed in specific and detailed terms.

2. The Old Law contains precepts of knowledge and understanding with reference to man's end. These precepts are more clearly and perfectly set forth in the New Law.

HOPE

(QUESTIONS 17 TO 22)

17. THE VIRTUE OF HOPE

1. Hope is the theological virtue by which we aspire with confidence to grace and heaven, trusting God, and being resolved to use his help.

2. Hope looks directly to our eternal happiness. It is the reaching after good, and, in last analysis, after the supreme good, that is, God. Now, in reaching after God, we also reach for what the possession of God will give us, that is, eternal happiness.

3. Hope, in the strict sense of the word, is in a person and for himself. Hope is for a good not to come automatically, and indeed not easy to attain, which the person hoping seeks, if possible, to achieve for himself. Hence, properly speaking, we cannot hope for another; we can only wish others well. But, since love unites those who have it, a person may be said to hope for his beloved as for himself; in this sense it is possible for one person to hope on behalf of another.

4. We pin our hope on God, not man. We may indeed have hope in a creature as the instrument of divine providence in our behalf. In this way, for example, we hope in the saints.

5. Hope directs the efforts of man *to God* and eternal happiness *in God*. Hence, hope is a *theological* virtue. (The Greek word *theos* means God; from *theos* we have the word theological for whatever directly pertains or has reference to God.)

6. Faith makes us adhere to God as the source of truth; hope makes us adhere to God as the source of good; charity makes us adhere to God for his own sake. Hence, it appears that hope is a virtue distinct from the other two theological virtues.

7. Hope comes after faith inasmuch as faith gives knowledge of what is to be hoped for.

8. Hope precedes charity inasmuch as the hope of good engenders love of it. Yet when love is stirred for what was hoped for—perhaps, up to that point, out of fear or self-interest—it gives hope a perfection; hope from then on is newly perfect; in this sense charity precedes perfected hope.

18. THE SUBJECT OF HOPE

1. Hope belongs to the order of appetency, not merely to the order of knowing. It is a striving for something. Now, it cannot be in the sense appetites, for hope as a theological virtue strives for the divine good, and the senses know nothing of this. Hence, hope belongs to the order of intellectual appetency, that is, it belongs to the will. Therefore, the proper subject of hope is the will. We recall, as we have done many times, that the *subject* of anything is that in which the thing is properly said to reside, or by which the thing is possessed.

2. As we noticed elsewhere in our study, the virtue of hope is fulfilled in heaven. It is supplanted by the vision of God. When that which is hoped for is attained, the hope for it no longer exists. Hence, in heaven, hope does not exist.

3. The angels and the blessed souls in heaven have nothing further to hope for. But what of the damned? Do they hope for pardon and release? By no means. The damned know perfectly that they have actually and willfully rejected happiness, and they continue to reject it; hence, they do not hope for it. Hope exists only on earth and in purgatory. Man on earth hopes for heaven and the means to get there; souls in purgatory are sure of heaven, but they hope for their moment of being ready to enter it.

4. Our hope for God and heaven gives us assurance—nay, it gives us certainty—that we shall attain what we hope for if we do our part. The certainty of this hope rests on the unfailing goodness and mercy of God, and on his absolute fidelity to his promises.

19. FEAR

1. Fear is a shrinking back from evil. Hence, we cannot fear God in himself, for God is infinite goodness. But one is said *to fear God* in the sense of fearing the evil of being separated from God by sin, and in the sense of fearing to incur his punishments for sin.

2. Fear is called *servile* fear when it is the dread of punishment alone. It is called *filial* fear or chaste fear when it is primarily the dread of offending God, our loving father. Between these two types of fear is *initial* fear, which is properly the beginning of filial fear, and differs from it only as imperfect differs from perfect. There is another type of fear called *worldly* fear which is the dread of losing temporal things to which the heart clings as to the ultimate good.

3. Worldly fear is always evil, for it discounts God and eternity, and dreads only the loss of creatural goods.

4. Servile fear is not good in point of its servility, but it is good in-

asmuch as it recognizes and dreads the evil that attends upon sin. From such a dread a person may readily rise to the higher and noble type of fear, and through this, to charity and repentance.

5. However, servile fear is essentially different from filial fear. Servile fear dreads punishment; filial fear dreads offending God. These two types of fear differ in their specific objects, and therefore differ essentially from each other.

6. Yet servile fear, as we have seen, has a good aspect, and, in this respect it comes from the Holy Ghost; but it is not the gift of the Holy Ghost that we call fear. Hence, servile fear, in so far as it is good, can remain in the soul which has charity, that is, which is in the state of sanctifying or habitual grace, and therefore in the friendship and love of God.

7. Wisdom is knowledge of God together with the will to serve him and possess him. Now, the beginning of wisdom itself is faith, for by faith we know God and are directed to him. But the beginning of wisdom, in the sense of what arouses one and stirs one to be wise, is fear. This beginning of wisdom is both servile fear and filial fear; such fear puts spurs to a man, so to speak, and makes him cultivate wisdom. In this sense, "the fear of the Lord is the beginning of wisdom" (Psalm 110).

8. Initial fear is, as we have said, *beginning* fear. Both servile fear and filial fear may be, in some way, the start of fearing the Lord. Yet initial fear is closer to filial fear than to servile fear; indeed, it is, properly speaking, an imperfect form of filial fear.

9. Filial or chaste fear of the Lord is one of the seven gifts of the Holy Ghost. By it we revere God and avoid what separates us from him.

10. Filial fear increases with charity, for the more one loves God, the more one fears to offend him. Servile fear loses its servility as charity increases, and then, as the nonservile dread of deserved punishments, it decreases in the glow of charity. For charity fixes the soul more and more on God, and thus the thought of self, and even of deserved punishment of oneself, becomes less and less. Besides, the greater one's charity is, the more confident is one's soul of escape from punishment. And thus, finally, the only fear in the charity-filled soul is filial fear.

11. Filial fear will exist in a perfected state in heaven. It cannot be the same as it is during earthly life, for in heaven all possibility of losing or offending God will be taken away. Servile fear will not exist at all in heaven.

12. The first beatitude, "Blessed are the poor in spirit," corresponds

to the gift of fear. For if a man fears God perfectly, as he may do by the gift, he does not pridefully seek to be rich or honored, but is humble and poor in spirit.

20. DESPAIR

1. Despair, which is the loss or abandonment of hope, is a sin, and it leads to other sins. St. Paul says (Eph. 4:19): "Who, despairing, have given themselves up to lasciviousness, unto the working of all uncleanness, and unto covetousness."

2. Not everyone who despairs has lost or rejected the faith. A person may know by faith that all sin is pardonable, and yet, by a corrupted judgment on his own particular case, may abandon all hope of pardon for himself.

3. Despair is a most grievous sin. It turns a person completely away from God. In itself, despair is not so grievous as unbelief or hatred of God. Yet for man it is more dangerous than these sins. For despair leads a person to fling himself headlong into all manner of sins.

4. Despair arises from disorders in the soul, such as lust. But in a special way, it comes from the sin of sloth, from spiritual laziness which will not let the soul grapple with difficulties, and overcome them in the strength and grace of supernatural hope.

21. PRESUMPTION

1. Presumption as a sin against hope is the wholly unreasonable expectation that God will save us despite the bad will in us which makes that saving impossible. Under the name and guise of reliance on God, presumption insults God and dishonors our own intelligence. It is presumption, for example, to expect forgiveness for sins without repentance. It is presumption to expect heaven without working to get there by merit.

2. Presumption is a sin, and can be a very grave sin, but it is not so grave a sin as despair. For, though it is inordinate and unreasonable in its expectation, presumption does recognize (however insultingly and distortedly) the divine mercy and goodness which despair utterly rejects and denies.

3. Presumption seems, at first glance, to be contrary to fear rather than to hope. For the presumptuous man seems to fear nothing, whether by servile fear or by filial fear. But this is mere seeming. The virtue to which presumption stands directly opposed is hope. Hope and presumption deal with the same object; hope, in an orderly manner; presumption, inordinately.

4. Presumption arises from vainglory, that is, from a prideful trust

that a person has in himself as powerful enough to cope with anything, and as a being so excellent that God could not allow him to be punished.

22. PRECEPTS REGARDING HOPE AND FEAR

1. Every scriptural promise of reward is an implied precept of hope. Besides, Holy Writ has warnings and commands which tell us to have hope. For instance, in Psalm 61 we read: "Hope in Him, all ye congregation of the people."

2. The precept of fear is found in every scriptural promise; for promised reward is not only something to stir hope of attainment, but to stir fear of failure to attain. And fear is directly inculcated by both the Old Law and the New; for instance, in Deuteronomy (10:12) we read: "And now, Israel, what doth the Lord thy God require of thee, but that thou fear the Lord thy God?"

CHARITY

(QUESTIONS 23 TO 46)

23. THE VIRTUE OF CHARITY

1. Charity as a supernatural virtue is the friendship of man and God. On God's part, it is love, benevolence, and communication of benefits and graces; on man's part charity involves devotion and service to God. It was in charity that our Lord said to his apostles (John 15:15): "I will not now call you servants . . . but friends."

2. Charity is in a person as a determinate, supernatural, habitual power, added to the natural power of the soul, which inclines the will to act with ease and delight in the exercise of loving friendship with God.

3. St. Augustine says (*De Morib. Eccl.*, xi): "Charity is a virtue which, when our affections are perfectly ordered, unites us to God; for it is by charity that we love him."

4. Charity is not a general virtue, nor an overlapping of virtues; it is a special virtue in its own nature; it is on a level with the other theological virtues (faith and hope), and is distinct from these virtues.

5. And charity is *one* virtue; it is not divided into different species or essential kinds.

6. Charity is the most excellent of all virtues. Faith knows truth about God; hope aspires to good in God; charity attains God himself simply, and not as having something to gain from him.

7. All true virtue directs a man to God, his ultimate good, his last end. Hence, charity, which embraces the ultimate good simply, must be in the soul that has any true and living virtue. No true supernatural virtue is possible without charity.

8. Charity therefore directs the acts of all the other virtues, making these serve to get man onward to his last end. And thus charity gives to these virtues their determinate being as effective instruments. Thus charity is said to be the "form" of the other virtues.

24. THE SUBJECT OF CHARITY

1. Charity as a supernatural virtue resides in man's soul; specifically, it resides in the appetitive part of man's soul, that is, in man's will. For the object towards which the will tends is *the good,* and charity is the virtue which, above all others, tends to and actually embraces the ultimate good of man. Charity lays hold on God himself.

2. This charity is not in us by our nature; it is *supernatural.* Hence, we cannot acquire charity by our natural powers. Charity is in us *by divine infusion,* by *in*-pouring. St. Paul (Rom. 5:5) says: "The charity of God is poured forth in our hearts by the Holy Ghost who is given to us."

3. Our natural gifts and capacities have no part in determining the quantity, so to speak, of charity in us. For (John 3:8), "the Spirit breatheth where he will"; and (I Cor. 12:11), "all these things one and the same Spirit worketh, dividing to everyone according as he will." Thus the measure of charity is not our capacity, but the will of God.

4. Charity can increase in us while we are in this life, on the way to God; that is, while we are *wayfarers.* If charity did not increase, we could make no progress along the way to God.

5. Charity increases not by having new elements added to it, but by growing more intense.

6. Not every act of charity increases the virtue of charity. It is possible that an act of charity, done imperfectly, should mean no increase at all in the person who performs the act. But each act of charity, rightly performed, leads to another, and ultimately to a favor of action which increases charity.

7. Charity may go on increasing and increasing; it is not possible to fix limits to this increase while earthly life endures.

8. A perfection of charity (which in no way marks a stay or limit

to its increase) is found in those who give their whole hearts habitually to God, not thinking or desiring anything contrary to his love.

9. We may distinguish three steps or degrees in charity; it has its beginning, its progress, and its (nonlimiting) perfection.

10. Charity cannot decrease. It is altogether lost by mortal sin, but it cannot be merely lessened in the soul. Human friendship may grow weak and be diminished through the negligence of friends and their forgetfulness. But charity is divine friendship; it depends on God, the infinitely perfect friend, who never grows negligent or forgetful; hence, charity does not decrease. However, to neglect acts of charity and to commit venial sins, may be to dispose ourselves to lose charity entirely through mortal sin; only in this extrinsic way may charity be said to suffer decrease.

11. Once we have charity, we have with it no guarantee that, during this life, we shall not lose it. The charity of the blessed in heaven (comprehensors) cannot be lost; the charity of men on earth (wayfarers) can be lost.

12. Charity is lost by mortal sin. For whoever has charity is deserving of eternal life; a man who commits mortal sin is deserving of eternal death, that is, of everlasting punishment. It is therefore impossible for a person to have charity and, at the same time, to be in the state of mortal sin. One mortal sin drives out charity.

25. THE OBJECT OF CHARITY

1. The object of charity, that towards which the act of charity is directed, is *God*, and our *fellowmen in God*. Says St. John (I John 4:21): "This commandment we have from God, that he who loveth God love also his brother."

2. Charity is love and friendship. We have charity when we love God and neighbor, and wish for our neighbor the good of God's friendship. Thus, out of charity, we love charity itself.

3. We cannot wish to creatures less than man, that is, to irrational creatures, the "fellowship of everlasting happiness." Therefore we cannot love such creatures out of charity.

4. We are to love ourselves out of true charity. For our love of ourselves is the standard of the sort of love we must have for others. Says Holy Scripture (Levit. 19:18): "Love thy neighbor as thyself."

5. Even our body is to be loved out of charity, for it is God's creature to be used by reason in man's service of God. St. Paul says (Rom. 6:13): "Present . . . your members as instruments of justice unto God." We are not, however, to love the disorder of bodily tendencies which are the result in us of the primal fall.

6. We are to love our neighbor out of charity, even if he be a sinner. We must hate sin, yet we must love the person who sins, wishing him repentance, pardon, and eternal life, for God's sake.

7. Sinners do not love themselves truly. They love only an apparent good in themselves, and they love external and creatural goods as things worth having for their own sake. And thus sinners miss the goal of charity which is endless happiness in God. Sinners, therefore, do not love themselves, for, as Holy Writ tells us (Psalm 10): "He that loveth iniquity, hateth his own soul."

8. We have the direct command of our Lord that we are to love our enemies. In St. Matthew (5:44) we read: "Love your enemies: do good to them that hate you: pray for them that persecute and calumniate you."

9. We must, therefore, love our enemies in general, and we must also be ready, if God wills to put opportunity in our way, to show them, as individuals, the signs and offices of love.

10. We are to love God's angels out of charity, for we hope to share with them "the fellowship of everlasting happiness"; this expectation is an element in the friendship called charity.

11. The fallen angels, that is, the demons in hell, cannot share the "fellowship of everlasting happiness," and therefore they are outside the scope of charity.

12. St. Augustine (*De Doct. Christ.* i) says: "There are four things to be loved: one is above us, God; another is ourselves; a third is near us, our neighbor; a fourth is below us, our body."

26. THE ORDER OF CHARITY

1. There is an order in charity, and God is the principle of that order. God is to be loved out of charity, before all others. The other beings that are to be loved out of charity are, so to speak, lined up in their proper places, subordinate to God.

2. God is to be loved for himself and as the cause of happiness. Hence, God is to be loved more than our neighbor, who is loved, not for himself, but for God.

3. And we are to love God more than we love ourselves. What we love in ourselves is from God, and is lovable only on account of God.

4. A person rightly loves himself by charity when he seeks to be united with God and to partake of God's eternal happiness. And a person loves his neighbor as one to whom he wishes this union and happiness. Now, since seeking to obtain something for oneself is a more intense act than wishing well to one's neighbor, a person manifestly loves himself more than he loves his neighbor. As evidence of this

fact, consider this: a man would rightly refuse to sin if, by sinning, he could free his neighbor from sin.

5. While we love ourselves more than we love our neighbor, we are required to love our neighbor more than we love our body.

6. And we rightly love one neighbor more than another—our parents, for instance, or our children. In this we violate no law so long as we do not withhold requisite love from any neighbor.

7. Our dearest objects of charity among neighbors are those who are closest to us by some tie—relationship, common country, and so on.

8. The tie that is strongest of all is the tie of blood. Hence it is natural that we should love our kindred more than others.

9. And in those related to us by blood there is an order. St. Ambrose says that we ought to love God first, then our parents, then our children, then the others of our household.

10. We are to love father and mother. Strictly speaking, the love of father precedes the love of mother.

11. A man loves his wife more intensely than he loves his parents. Yet he loves his parents with greater reverence.

12. It seems that we love those on whom we confer benefits more than those who confer benefits on us.

13. The order of charity, since it is right and reasonable, will endure in heaven.

27. LOVE, CHIEF ACT OF CHARITY

1. Charity consists in loving rather than in being loved.

2. Charity is *active* friendship and love. It is therefore something more than good will, which is the condition and the beginning of friendship.

3. God is loved out of charity for his own sake, not on account of anything other than himself. Yet in one way we can love God out of charity, and still have something else in view, as when we love God for the favors we receive or expect, but in such a way that these very favors are loved because they dispose us to love God the more.

4. Even in this life, in which we are wayfarers, we can have an *immediate* love of God, that is, love without a medium between lover and beloved. We know God through the medium of created things; love moves the other way, for we love God first and then love created things for the love of God.

5. We can love God *wholly* according to our own creatural whole-ness, but not according to the infinite wholeness of God. For we are finite, and cannot compass infinity.

6. We need no test or mode or measure in our love for God. St. Augustine says we need only go on measurelessly loving God.

7. It is, in itself, more meritorious to love a friend than to love an enemy, just as it is worse to hate a friend than to hate an enemy. But, considering that the love of a friend is likely to be less purely the effect of love of God, and also considering the distaste and difficulty that one must overcome to love an enemy, we see that it can be more meritorious to love an enemy than to love a friend.

8. To love God is more meritorious than to love one's neighbor. Indeed, to love one's neighbor is a meritorious act only when we love him for the sake of God.

28. JOY

1. Spiritual joy, often called joy in God, is an effect of charity.

2. Spiritual joy admits no admixture of sorrow, for it is joy in the divine wisdom of which Scripture says (Wisd. 8:16), "Her conversation hath no bitterness."

3. Spiritual joy is full and perfect when God is possessed by the soul, and nothing remains to be desired. It is manifest, therefore, that we cannot achieve the fullness of spiritual joy until we reach heaven.

4. Joy is not a virtue in itself; it is an act and an effect of the virtue of charity, and it is numbered among the fruits of the Holy Ghost.

29. PEACE

1. Peace is not merely quiet agreement among men. Peace means harmony and satisfaction in all the tendencies and desires of a man's heart. Peace, therefore, is more than outer concord; it is inner repose in the attainment of all that can be desired.

2. Peace is the end of all desiring. Wherever there is tendency, there is the drive for repose in the attaining of the object of tendency. Peace is fulfillment, with tendency at rest. All things, inasmuch as they tend to their connatural or supernatural end, tend to peace; we may even say that everything desires peace.

3. Peace in a man's soul, spiritual peace, results from charity. When a person focuses his harmonious inner tendencies on God, he exercises charity, and he has peace. When men exercise charity one towards another as true neighbors, they tend together unto God, and they have peace.

4. Peace, like joy, is not a virtue on its own account or in itself; it is the exercise of a virtue; it is an act and an effect of the virtue of charity. Like joy, it is one of the twelve fruits of the Holy Ghost.

30. MERCY

1. St. Augustine (*De Civ. Dei*, IX) says: "Mercy is heartfelt sympathy for another's distress, impelling us to help him if we can." Hence, the distress of another, that is, the evil suffered by another, is the motive of mercy.

2. Pity is a kind of sorrow for some defect. We feel pity for others in so far as we look upon their defect or deficiency as though it were our own. And pity stirs us to deeds of mercy. The terms mercy and pity are frequently used interchangeably.

3. *Mercy* is a name sometimes applied to a feeling or sentiment; so also is *pity*. But when mercy or pity is more than a sentiment; when it is the habitual and regulated movement of the soul, acting in the light of reason, it is a virtue.

4. Indeed, mercy is *in itself* the greatest of virtues, and it is said of God that "his mercies are above all his works." But *among creatures* mercy is not so great a virtue as charity, and, without charity, would be wholly ineffective. However, mercy ranks next to charity itself, and, of the purely social virtues, mercy is the greatest.

31. BENEFICENCE

1. Beneficence is doing good to another. It is an act of charity or friendship.

2. We are bound to exercise beneficence, for we are obligated to "do good to all men." St. Paul (Gal. 6:10) indicates this fact when he points out beneficence as our lifelong duty: "While we have time, let us do good to all men."

3. The opportunity of actually exercising beneficence for the benefit of all mankind is not given to many. We have the duty, then, of exercising beneficence towards those who are about us, to those who are more closely united to us.

4. Beneficence, like good will, is an act of charity; it is not a special virtue in itself.

32. ALMSDEEDS

1. An alms is "something given to the needy, out of compassion, and for the sake of God." Almsdeeds are works of compassion or mercy; mercy itself is suffused with charity; hence, almsgiving can be called an act of charity.

2. The different almsdeeds are well enumerated as *corporal* alms and *spiritual* alms. These are commonly called the corporal and spiritual works of mercy. The corporal works of mercy are seven: (a) to feed

the hungry; (b) to give drink to the thirsty; (c) to clothe the naked; (d) to harbor the harborless; (e) to visit the sick; (f) to ransom the captive; (g) to bury the dead. The spiritual works of mercy are also seven: (a) to instruct the ignorant; (b) to counsel the doubtful; (c) to comfort the sorrowing; (d) to reprove sinners; (e) to forgive injuries; (f) to bear wrongs patiently; (g) to pray for the living and the dead.

3. By their nature, spiritual almsdeeds are more excellent than corporal almsdeeds. Yet in particular cases, the corporal deeds may be of greater value. It is, for instance, more valuable to feed a hungry man than to instruct him.

4. Corporal almsdeeds may have a spiritual effect; they may, for example, lead a man to pray for his benefactor.

5. Almsgiving is a matter of precept; it is involved in the precept of loving one's neighbor. We are therefore obliged to give alms out of what we possess as surplus, that is, out of goods remaining to us after we have taken care of our own needs and the needs of those who are under our charge. The precept of almsgiving binds us to help those who are in need. We cannot help all who are in need, of course, but we can, and must, help those needy persons whose need would not be relieved unless we relieved it. Thus the precept of almsgiving binds when two conditions are fulfilled: (a) our having available means; and (b) a case of need dependent on us for relief. In other cases, in which these two conditions are not both fulfilled, almsgiving is not of precept, but of counsel.

6. A man may sometimes sacrifice what is commonly considered necessary to his position, so that he can relieve the needy. So long as he does not act inordinately, or do an injustice to others (such as wife, children, dependent parents), such a sacrifice is noble, and may even be heroic. Ordinarily, however, there is no obligation on a person to make such a sacrifice.

7. Alms are to be given out of the donor's own property. To use the surplus of a rich neighbor to relieve the needy, is to be guilty of theft. The goods of others are not ours to dispose of without their direction or permission.

8. Therefore, a person who is under the direction or rule of another as to the disposal of goods, must have that other's permission before he bestows alms.

9. The claims of those more closely united to us are to be considered in giving alms, when otherwise the conditions among claimants are fairly equal.

10. We are to give alms according to the means available. Scripture says (Tob. 4:9): "If thou have much, give abundantly: if thou have little, take care . . . willingly to bestow a little." And the abundance of our almsgiving should rather appear in the relief of many needy persons or causes than in an oversupply bestowed on one.

33. FRATERNAL CORRECTION

1. Fraternal correction is the spiritual almsdeed of reproving a sinner; it is an act of charity.

2. Sometimes we are under obligation of giving fraternal correction. This is always so when a discreet word of ours could lead a grievous sinner to amend his ways.

3. Correction as an act of *justice* is the duty of those whose place and station require them to direct others spiritually. Correction as an act of *charity* is a warning properly given on due occasion by anyone who can prudently prevent sin or cause a sinner to repent and amend.

4. Fraternal correction can be given by anyone to any other person, be that person's place high or low. Indeed, sometimes conditions make it the *duty* of a subject to correct his superior. Yet correction must always be given with prudence and discretion, and never with insolence.

5. One sinner cannot justly rebuke another in such a way that his own sin seems less to be condemned than that of the person he rebukes. Yet, if the thing be done humbly, one sinner may correct another, even though he condemns himself at the same time. The good thief at the Crucifixion humbly acknowledged his own sin as he rebuked the bad thief for upbraiding Christ.

6. Fraternal correction, to deserve the name, must be an act of charity, not of officiousness, or meddling, or pride, or hyprocrisy. It is to be given in the spirit of loving friendship in God. And when such correction is necessary, those bound to administer it, by reason either of justice or of charity, are not to refrain from it for fear that the person corrected may be angry or resentful, or may be worse in conduct because of what is said to him in correction.

7. Certainly, fraternal correction is always to be given in a manner befitting the exercise of charity. It is to be given *privately*—at least, at first. Some evils may call for public denunciation, but private admonition should be given first. Sacred Scripture directs that this course be taken. (See Matt. 18:15.)

8. After private admonition has proved fruitless, the sinner should be corrected before "one or two more" prudent witnesses, and thus

every opportunity should be given him to amend without suffering public dishonor.

34. HATRED

1. It is possible for a debased human will to hate God. God is altogether lovable, but to the sinner who incurs the necessary penalties of sin, hatred of the divine justice, which imposes the penalties, is possible.

2. Hatred of God is manifestly the worst of sins. For the evil of sin consists in the fact that it turns the soul away from God. And there can be no more complete and dreadful turning from God than by hatred of God.

3. It is always a sin to hate one's neighbor. For, as St. John says (I John 2:9): "He that hateth his brother is in darkness." We are to hate sin in our brother, but we are to love our brother.

4. Our hatred of our neighbor is a sin less hurtful to him than other sins, such as theft, or murder, or adultery. Therefore, it is not true to say that hatred is the most grievous of sins against a neighbor.

5. Hatred is not listed with the capital sins. For, though other sins may arise from hatred as from their capital source, hatred itself is not promptly present to fallen nature, but comes as the result of the gradual deterioration and destruction of love.

6. Hatred grows out of the capital sin of envy, which is sorrow over a neighbor's good. Envy makes a neighbor's good hateful to the envious man, and thus, as St. Augustine says in his Rule: "Out of envy cometh hatred."

35. SLOTH

1. Sloth is sluggishness of mind which neglects to begin good. It is a kind of oppressive sorrow (for what is, in itself, good) which so weighs on a person's mind that he chooses to do nothing. Sloth is spiritual laziness. It is a sin, and a capital sin.

2. Sloth is sorrow for spiritual good. It is a special vice opposed to charity. For charity rejoices in the good which sloth finds the occasion for sadness.

3. Sloth is, therefore, by its nature, contrary to charity, and, by that fact, it is a mortal sin in its genus or general essential kind. Yet, like all sins that are mortal in their genus, sloth is not mortal in fact, unless it be fully accepted by the deliberate will.

4. Sloth is rightly listed among the capital (or source) sins—from which many other sins flow.

36. ENVY

1. Envy is sorrow or sadness over another's good, because that good is regarded as something withheld or taken away from the envious person's excellence or reputation.

2. Envy is a sin; it grieves over what charity finds capable of causing joy; it is a spiritual disorder.

3. Envy in its kind (or genus) is a mortal sin, for it is in conflict with the precept of charity. But in the envious person the sin of envy is mortal only when it is committed with full knowledge and full consent.

4. Envy is a fruitful source of other sins, and therefore it is listed with the capital sins.

37. DISCORD

1. Discord or dissension is a conflict of wills to the offense of charity and the destruction of peace. Being contrary to charity, it is sinful.

2. Discord arises from vainglory which makes a man cling inordinately to his own will, and leads him to despise the way and the opinions of others. Hence, discord is rightly known as "the daughter of vainglory."

38. CONTENTION

1. Contention is discord that finds expression in words. It is bickering, unreasonable arguing, without regard to charity, and often without regard to truth. Contention is sinful, and it is possible for it to be mortally sinful.

2. Contention, like discord, is a daughter of vainglory. For the contentious man clings pridefully to his own way and his own opinion, arguing stubbornly even in the face of evidence and the manifestation of truth.

39. SCHISM

1. Schism is a breaking away, a division which disrupts unity. As a sin, it is the disruption of unity born of charity. In special, it is the sin of cutting away from the unity of the faithful under the rule of the Vicar of Christ; it is the refusal to submit to the rule and jurisdiction of the sovereign pontiff.

2. Schism is a grave sin, but it is not so grave as heresy and unbelief. Heresy cuts a person off from the unity of the faithful just as schism does; but heresy adds to this the evil of embracing false doctrine. [*Note:* When papal infallibility and the primacy and jurisdiction of

the sovereign pontiff were solemnly defined, schism became a practical denial of truths of the faith, and hence is itself heretical.]

3. Schismatics lose the right to exercise spiritual powers; they lose jurisdiction itself, and not merely its licit use.

4. It is right and just that schismatics, who sever themselves from the unity of the Church, should be punished by the Church with the penalty their action invites, namely, excommunication.

40. WAR

1. War, which is armed conflict between countries or nations, may be sometimes lawful and without sin. Three conditions are necessary for a justified war: (a) it must be waged by lawful public authority in defense of the common good; (b) it must be waged for a just cause; (c) it must be waged with the right intention, not vengefully nor to inflict harm.

2. It is not lawful for bishops and other clerics to fight in a war; such action is not in harmony with their place and their duties.

3. Ambushes are strategems of war; they are part of the normal conduct of war, and are not considered to be unfair tricks. Hence, if the war be just, strategems, including ambushes, are not wrong in themselves.

4. For the safeguarding of the common welfare, it is lawful to carry on the acts of a just war, and to wage fights, if need be even on Sundays and holy days.

41. STRIFE OR QUARRELING

1. Strife or quarreling means fighting among individuals, even as war means fighting among peoples or nations. Strife comes from inordinate or perverse wills. It is therefore contrary to reason; it is a sin; it can be a mortal sin.

2. Strife, as here understood, is not a mere affair of words as contention is; it includes deeds intended to hurt or harm another. Strife is rightly called "the daughter of anger."

42. SEDITION

1. Sedition, strictly understood, is the uprising of part of a people against another; it is also the stir and effort of individuals and groups to make one part of a people rise against another. Sedition is opposed to the unity and peace of a people, which is a special good; hence, sedition is a special sin. It is, therefore, a sin distinct from war, fighting, discord, contention.

2. In its genus or essential kind, sedition is a mortal sin, for it involves a grievous offense against law and the common good. The leaders of a sedition are the most guilty, and, after them, with a lesser degree of guilt, come the people who are led to the disturbing of the common good.

43. SCANDAL

1. Scandal is a needless word or deed which does spiritual harm to those who hear or observe it. Scandal is word or deed that occasions sin in another; it is bad example.

2. In the person scandalized (that is, led to sin) the scandal is *passive;* in the person doing or saying the scandalous thing, the scandal is *active.* Active scandal is a sin against charity, which bids us seek our neighbor's good. Active scandal is not only what actually leads a person to sin, but it is also what is intended to lead him to sin (or, *by its nature* is calculated to lead him to sin), even if, as a fact, he does not commit sin. Passive scandal is sometimes taken, by mistake or by perversity, from what is not, in itself, calculated to lead a person to sin.

3. Scandal is a special kind of sin, because it is opposed to a special kind of good work, which is called fraternal correction.

4. Scandal, in the person who actively gives it, is either a mortal or a venial sin, according to the gravity of the scandalous word or deed, and also according to the awareness and the intention of the scandalizer.

5. Scandal is taken by (that is, affects) persons of a mind unsettled in adherence to good. Those who adhere perfectly to God by charity are not scandalized; passive scandal is not found in them.

6. Nor can those perfectly united to God by charity be the cause of scandal; they cannot be active scandalizers. For scandal is inordinate, and solidly virtuous persons direct their lives with order; they live according to the direction of St. Paul (I Cor. 14:40): "Let all things be done decently, and according to order." The slight weaknesses of thoroughly good people never amount to an occasion of sin in others.

7. There is a type of passive scandal, called *pharisaical,* or "scandal of the Pharisees," which tries to make evil out of what is good, just as the Pharisees tried to make our Lord's words and deeds seem seditious and even diabolical. There is another type of passive scandal, called "scandal of the little ones" or scandal of the weak, which sees evil where there is none, not by reason of malice, but by want of understanding and lack of instruction. We should never forego a spiritual good because of pharisaical scandal, for this type of scandal is born of hypocrisy and malice, and is to be treated with contempt. But

we ought to do all we can, without being guilty of sinful remissness, to avoid what occasions the scandal of the weak.

8. We are not always obliged to forego all claim, even on temporal goods, because of scandal of the weak. But the scandal should be removed by explanation or instruction. If this cannot be done, there are occasions on which we must forego temporal goods to avoid giving scandal. St. Paul (I Cor. 8:13) says that if his eating meat will scandalize his brother, he will not eat meat.

44. THE PRECEPTS OF CHARITY

1. Whatever God requires of us is a matter of precept. Now, God requires us to love him, and to love our neighbor for his sake. Hence, there are precepts of charity, which is the love of God and friendship with God in his holy grace. We have such precepts in scripture: (Deut. 10:12), "Fear the Lord thy God, and walk in His ways and love Him"; (Matt. 22:37, 39), "Thou shalt love the Lord thy God with thy whole heart, and with thy whole soul, and with thy whole mind"; "Thou shalt love thy neighbor as thyself."

2. The love of God involves love of neighbor for God. For who can really love God and not love what God loves? And God loves all men. Yet, since many would not notice that love of neighbor is included in the love of God, it is fitting that the great law of charity should have expression in two precepts: love of God, and love of neighbor.

3. These two precepts of charity suffice. Our Lord himself says (Matt. 22:40): "On these two commandments dependeth the whole law, and the prophets."

4. God is to be loved as the last end, the ultimate goal, the eternal purpose to which all things are to be referred. This *totality* of order and direction of creatures to God is indicated to mankind in the precept requiring all men to love God with the whole heart . . . whole soul . . . whole mind.

5. Other expressions of scripture emphasize the same totality of tendency to God; we are told to love God with our whole might, and with all our strength.

6. Perfect fulfillment of the great precept of charity, that is, total love of God, cannot be attained in this earthly life; it will come in heaven. St. Augustine says (*De Perfect. Justit.*), in the "fullness of heavenly charity, this precept will be fulfilled. . . . As long as carnal concupiscence remains to be restrained by continence, man cannot love God with his whole heart." Yet it is man's duty on earth to come nearer and nearer to the fulfilling of the precept of perfect charity.

7. We are to love our neighbor *as* ourselves; not, indeed, as *much* as we love ourselves, but in the same manner, and with desire for the

same good that we seek for ourselves. We seek to attain God, and, loving our neighbor as ourselves, we seek to have our neighbor attain God.

8. The order of charity is expressed in the precept of charity: love of God first, and love of neighbor second. And yet the second love is in the first.

45. THE GIFT OF WISDOM

1. To be wise is to know the deepest causes in that department of knowledge and conduct in which one is said to be wise. A wise physician must know the fundamental principles of medicine. The term *wisdom*, taken simply, means the knowledge of the highest cause of all, that is, God. Out of this knowledge comes clear judgment about all things, judgment made in the divine light of the knowledge. Now, man attains this judgment through the Holy Ghost. Wisdom is, therefore, a gift of the Holy Ghost.

2. Wisdom, notwithstanding it has the power to direct man's life according to the charity which resides in his will, is itself in the intellect as in its proper subject.

3. Wisdom is in the practical intellect as well as in the speculative intellect. For it is not merely abstract *knowing*; it is a directing of human conduct, and hence is a *doing*.

4. Wisdom, as a gift of the Holy Ghost, enables a person to judge rightly of divine things, and to judge of other things according to the divine law of charity which is in him. Wisdom presupposes charity. Since charity is expelled by mortal sin, so also is wisdom.

5. Whoever is free from mortal sin and is in the state of sanctifying grace has charity, and also has wisdom.

6. St. Augustine says that there is a special agreement or correspondence of wisdom with peacemakers. For he says (*De Serm. Dom. in Mont.*, 1): "Wisdom is becoming to peacemakers, in whom there is no movement of rebellion, but only obedience to reason." Hence the seventh beatitude, "Blessed are the peacemakers, for they shall be called the children of God," corresponds to the gift of wisdom.

46. FOLLY

1. Folly is the opposite of wisdom. Folly is the *contrary* of wisdom, whereas fatuity is the sheer *absence* of wisdom.

2. Folly is dullness in judging, especially in matters that relate to God and the good of the soul. When folly results from inordinate love and use of earthly things, it is a sin.

3. Since a man's sense is plunged into earthly things by lust more than by any other vice, folly is called "the daughter of lust."

PRUDENCE

(QUESTIONS 47 TO 56)

47. THE VIRTUE OF PRUDENCE

1. Prudence is the knowledge of how to act, how to conduct one's life rightly. St. Augustine says that prudence is "the knowledge of what to seek and what to avoid." Prudence belongs to the knowing faculty of the soul, rather than to the appetitive faculty; that is, it belongs to the intellect rather than to the will. Since intellect (as the thinking mind that enlightens the will for its choice) is called reason, prudence, properly speaking, is in reason as in its proper subject.

2. Prudence is no mere knowledge of what things are (of what is so), but of how to act (of what *to do*). Hence, prudence belongs to the practical intellect or reason, not to the speculative intellect.

3. Prudence is not just a general grasp or understanding of right procedure. It serves a man in the concrete and individual situations that make up his daily life.

4. Prudence is one of the cardinal virtues. While, as we have seen, it is, strictly speaking, in the intellect, it is a guide to right action on the part of the will, and hence it shares the nature of a *moral* virtue, that is, a will-virtue.

5. Although prudence suffuses the other moral virtues, it is a distinct and special virtue on its own account.

6. Prudence does not set up the end and purpose of the moral virtues, but regulates the means by which these virtues operate to their determinate ends. It does not indicate what the moral virtues are to do, but shows them the right way to do it.

7. Prudence discerns the mean or measure of moral virtues, and sees how their action can be reasonable, and not marred either by excess or deficiency. For prudence is the knowledge of how things ought to be done.

8. And prudence, as Aristotle says (*Ethic.* VI), gives orders. Prudence commands. It does not, indeed, take over the work of the will. It shows with certitude and authority how the will ought to choose. And, to a reasonable will, this amounts to a command. This function of *commanding* is really the chief act of prudence.

9. Prudence gives her commands in no aloof, detached fashion. Prudence is ever careful, watchful, solicitous that a person's conduct be right.

10. Prudence is not only a private virtue, looking solely to the individual good conduct of a person; it also serves the common good. St. Paul (I Cor. 10:33) indicates the social function of prudence when he says: "Not seeking that which is profitable to myself, but to many, that they may be saved."

11. Indeed, prudence is of different species according as it serves a person in his personal conduct, or serves the good of the home (domestic prudence), or the good of the commonwealth (political prudence).

12. Political prudence is itself of two kinds, for it must be in the rulers and legislators on one hand, and in the citizens on the other hand. Aristotle (*Ethic.* vi) says that prudence is like a mastercraft in rulers, and like a handicraft in those who are ruled.

13. True prudence, as a virtue, is only in the good. Serious sin casts out prudence. A sinful person in his evil life may exercise a kind of craftiness that has the outer look of prudence, but it is not the genuine article.

14. A person in the state of grace has prudence, for he has charity, and charity cannot exist without prudence. Prudence suffuses all virtues; it is a kind of bond that links them together, and it is necessary to them all.

15. Prudence is a natural virtue, too. We have been speaking chiefly of supernatural prudence, but we must notice that there is a natural prudence also. This natural prudence is called natural, not because it belongs necessarily to human nature, but because it can be acquired by the powers of human nature. It is acquired by being taught, or by learning through experience, or in both ways.

16. Prudence is not forgotten. Forgetfulness may, indeed, hinder prudent action, but the virtue itself is not lost through forgetting.

48. THE PARTS OF PRUDENCE

1. The *parts* of prudence are certain faculties, perfections, or qualities that belong to prudence, or are somehow associated with it. Among these things, some seem to be almost an element of prudence itself; these are called its *quasi-integral* parts. There are eight of these quasi-integral parts of prudence: memory, understanding, docility, shrewdness, reason, foresight, circumspection, caution. Other parts of prudence are called its *subjective* parts; these are its species or kinds of varieties, as, for example, domestic prudence, reigning prudence,

military prudence, political prudence, etc. Still other parts of prudence are called its *potential* parts; these are virtues connected with prudence, or subordinate to prudence, which produce what can be called its secondary effects; these are: good counsel, which throws a kind of headlight; synesis, which guides judgment in ordinary matters; and gnome, which guides judgment in exceptional matters.

49. THE QUASI-INTEGRAL PARTS OF PRUDENCE

1. Prudence deals with immediate situations and the means needed to guide a person through them in right and reasonable fashion. Experience serves a person here, and experience is recorded in memory. Hence, memory belongs to prudence.

2. Understanding, not as the faculty of intellect or mind, but as a knowledgeable grasp of things, is manifestly necessary for prudent action. Hence, *understanding* pertains to prudence.

3. *Docility*, or readiness to be taught, makes experience fruitful. A stubborn and opinionated person is never a prudent person. Docility serves prudence, and thus belongs to it.

4. *Shrewdness*, not in an ugly sense as low craftiness, but as the quick and ready estimate of what is suitable in a situation, belongs to prudence as a quasi-integral part.

5. *Reason*, not as the thinking mind which guides the will, but as the right use of that mind, is clearly a part of prudence.

6. *Foresight*, or the clear view of how future contingencies may bear upon the present occasion, or may depend on how the present situation is met, is a part of prudence.

7. Circumspection stands to present action as foresight stands to future contingencies. It sees what is suitable here and now in existing circumstances. Hence *circumspection* is a quasi-integral part of prudence.

8. Caution looks to avoid evil, especially evil that wears the mask of good. Hence, *caution* pertains to prudence.

50. THE SUBJECTIVE PARTS OF PRUDENCE

1. *Reigning* prudence belongs to those that legislate and exercise government. Aristotle (*Polit.* iii) says: "Prudence is a virtue proper to the person who rules."

2. *Political* prudence, in its widest meaning, includes reigning prudence. But, in a stricter sense, it is that species of prudence which guides citizens in their loyal obedience to the requirements of government.

3. *Domestic* prudence is the virtue which governs the reasonable

activities of life in a household. It stands midway between the prudence of the individual and the political prudence which guides the rule of city, state, or kingdom.

4. Scripture says (Prov. 24:6): "War is managed by due ordering, and there shall be safety where there are many counsels." Hence, there is a kind of prudence to be called *military* prudence.

51. THE POTENTIAL PARTS OF PRUDENCE

1. The potential parts of prudence are the virtues connected with prudence. One of these is good counsel. Prudence uses this virtue.

2. Good counsel is a virtue distinct from prudence itself, but closely associated with prudence. It is often called by its Greek name of *euboulia*.

3. Another virtue, called by the Greek name *synesis*, is good judgment in particular and practical matters. It follows upon *euboulia*, but is distinct from it, and from prudence. It serves prudence, and thus is called one of its parts.

4. In practical cases not covered by the common laws, a more discriminating judgment than *synesis* is required. This judgment is called *gnome*. *Gnome* is distinct from prudence, and from *euboulia* and *synesis*. It serves prudence, and is one of its potential parts.

52. THE GIFT OF COUNSEL

1. The gifts of the Holy Ghost dispose the soul to act virtuously in accordance with the movements of grace. Now, as *natural counsel* is the research of reason (that is, the thinking mind) which precedes the decision of the will, and is therefore a kind of self-advice, so *supernatural* counsel is the divine advice and guidance imparted by the Holy Ghost. Supernatural counsel is one of the seven gifts of the Holy Ghost.

2. The gifts are, as we have seen, a help to the virtues. The gift of counsel is, in a particular manner, a help to the virtue of prudence.

3. The blessed in heaven no longer need the guidance of the gift of counsel, for their end is attained. Yet the supernatural enlightenment that guided them home remains in them. Therefore, the blessed in heaven retain the gift of counsel.

4. Counsel shows the way to use means that an end may be attained. Now, the works of mercy, spiritual and corporal, are of the greatest service to man as means to get him on to heaven and his last end. Therefore, counsel is particularly concerned with the works of mercy. It is right to say that counsel corresponds to the fifth beatitude, "Blessed are the merciful, for they shall obtain mercy."

53. IMPRUDENCE

1. Imprudence is the absence or lack of prudence. When this lack is a person's own fault, it is a sin.

2. Sinful imprudence is a special sin, for it stands opposed to the special virtue of prudence. Yet, in one sense, imprudence is a general sin, for it takes in several other sins. These sins are: precipitation, thoughtlessness, inconstancy, and negligence.

3. Precipitation is an inordinate rushing into action under the impulse of will or passion. It is plain to see that this sin has the character of imprudence.

4. Thoughtlessness, as a sin of imprudence, is a willful failure to judge a situation rightly because of a contempt for, or a neglect of, the things on which right judgment depends.

5. Inconstancy, as a sin of imprudence is the unwise ceasing from, or withdrawal from, a good purpose that has been prudently taken up. Inconstancy results from appetite uncontrolled by prudent reason.

6. All these imprudences—precipitation, thoughtlessness, inconstancy—are born of appetite inordinately given to pleasures of sense, and especially lustful appetite. We may justly say that these sins of imprudence are largely from lust.

54. NEGLIGENCE

1. Negligence is a lack of due care, a culpable absence of solicitude, in meeting or performing the practical duties of life.

2. Solicitude or proper carefulness is allied to prudence. Hence, a sin against solicitude is a sin against prudence.

3. Although negligence is often a venial sin, it is possible that it may be a mortal sin; this is the case on two occasions: (a) when negligence is concerned with something necessary to salvation, and (b) when negligence is a complete remissness about the things of God.

55. CARNAL PRUDENCE

1. Carnal prudence or *prudence of the flesh* is sham prudence. It is not a virtue, but a vice which wears the mask of prudence. It is the vice of a person who regards fleshly goods as the chief end of existence. It is a sin, for it is a fundamental disorder in a person, and one that is the person's own fault.

2. To hold carnal goods as the complete end of existence would be a mortal sin. But prudence of the flesh hardly ever goes to such extremes. Commonly, it is an inordinate estimate of the importance and

value of some particular carnal good, and stands opposed to some special kind or variety of prudence. And usually it is a venial sin.

3. When a man uses trickery, or counterfeits honesty, when working for an end, he is guilty of *craftiness*. This is a special sin against prudence, distinct from carnal prudence but like it in masking itself as true prudence. St. Gregory includes carnal prudence and craftiness under the title of *worldly prudence*.

4. Craftiness is chiefly in the tricky mind of the crafty man; it is a quality of his plans and projects. But when plan or project is carried out *in fact*, then it appears as *guile*.

5. Guile may take the form of words or deeds. When it appears in deeds, it has the special name of *fraud*.

6. We are divinely instructed to rely upon God, and not to be over-anxious about material things; we are not to be over-solicitous, for this is a kind of worldly prudence, and not true prudence. In St. Matthew (6:31) we read: "Be not solicitous, therefore, saying what shall we eat, or what shall we drink, or wherewith shall we be clothed?"

7. Nor are we to be over-anxious about the future, for we read (Matt. 6:34): "Be not therefore solicitous for tomorrow; for the morrow will be solicitous for itself."

8. Carnal prudence, craftiness, guile, and fraud are sins of false prudence. And yet they are essentially contrary to *justice*. Their source is the chief of sins against justice, that is, covetousness. Although these sins are imprudences, they are called the "daughters of covetousness."

56. PRECEPTS OF PRUDENCE

1. Prudence suffuses all the moral virtues. Hence the precepts of the Decalogue, that is, the Ten Commandments, which direct virtuous acts, are all implicitly precepts of prudence.

2. Even the Old Law has definite precepts against false prudence—craftiness and allied vices—and thus, indirectly, expresses precepts of prudence.

JUSTICE

(QUESTIONS 57 TO 80)

57. RIGHT

1. *Right* means what is just. A right is what is owed. Subjectively, a right is a moral power in a person to do, to possess, or to demand something. Now, right is the object of the virtue of *justice*. Justice is the virtue that requires that right be done, and that rights in persons be observed and not violated.

2. Right is founded on law. *Natural* right rests on the natural law, which, as we have seen, is the eternal moral law as knowable by sound human reason without the aid of divine revelation. Thus an innocent man's right to life is a natural right. *Positive* right rests on positive law, that is, law enacted and set down in positive ordinance. Positive law is *divine* (as in the Ten Commandments) or *human,* as in the written code of a nation. Human law is *civil* or *ecclesiastical* according as it is the written code of state or Church; Church law is *canon* law or *diocesan* law according as it is for the whole Church or for a diocese.

3. *International* law or the law of nations expresses the rights of nations towards one another; it rests ultimately, as all laws do, on the eternal law of God. It is distinct from the natural law, for it has a different and more restricted field of application.

4. The right of *dominion* is the right of ownership, whether of *goods,* or of *jurisdiction,* that is, of justly controlling the activities of others and requiring obedience. There is a special right of control or jurisdiction called *paternal* right; this belongs to a father with reference to his children. In husband and wife, there is *domestic* right. In citizens, by reason of civil law, there is *civic* right.

58. JUSTICE

1. Justice as a virtue in a person, is a habit by which a man has the constant and perpetual will to render to everyone what is due to him. Justice is the virtue which observes the *rights* of all.

2. Justice is concerned solely about one's dealings with others. Only in a metaphorical sense can a man have justice towards himself and

from himself. In this sense, man's appetites or tendencies can be regarded as separate and independent agencies, and in their agreement and consistent action under the rule of reason there is a likeness or figure of persons getting on well together, not violating one another's rights, and therefore living in justice. Thus a just man is, first and foremost, a man who, steadfastly and always, respects the rights of others—of God, and of fellowmen. Secondarily, by the metaphor we have described, a just man is a man of virtue.

3. Justice is one of the four cardinal virtues. It is a fundamental virtue. Cicero (*De Officiis.* 1) says that good men are called good chiefly by reason of their justice, and that "the splendor of virtue shines out from justice more than from other virtues."

4. Justice is a moral virtue. That is, it is a will-virtue. It is the rectitude of the will towards the rights of others.

5. The good of any virtue has some reference, direct or indirect, to the common good of all men. Therefore, each virtue has an aspect of "to others." Now, this reference "to others" is the main characteristic of justice. What is essential to justice shines out through other virtues, and therefore justice has the character of a general virtue in addition to its own special character as an individual virtue. Justice as a general virtue regulating the common good of all under the laws that govern men is called legal justice.

6. Yet justice, as the general virtue of legal justice, and as permeating the other virtues with respect to the common good, is not *identified* with any of these virtues.

7. Justice keeps its character as an individual virtue, seeking the particular good of each man in his relations with all others.

8. The special concern of justice as a particular virtue is with external action and external things in which men communicate with one another. Aristotle says (*Ethic.* v) that particular justice has its application in matters that belong to social life.

9. Justice is not concerned, as temperance and fortitude are, with the appetites called passions of the soul, but with acts and operations which have reference to others.

10. The mean or measure of justice is in external fact. If I owe five dollars, justice fixes my duty by that fact; I must pay that amount exactly. In virtues which regulate passions, such as temperance, exact factual measurement is not always possible, or, if possible, sufficient. The measure of such a virtue must take in internal condition as well as external fact. Thus, what is temperate action for one man may be intemperate for another. As a result of all this, the mean or measure of justice is called *real*, whereas, in the passion-regulating virtues, the

mean or measure must be determined by sound reason, and is therefore called *rational*.

11. Justice seeks to preserve "the equality of proportion" in all the affairs of human life. And this equality of proportion is found when each person has what is his part, share, portion, and due. Hence, the act of justice is the rendering to each one of what he should have, and has a right to have. The motto of justice is *suum cuique*, which means, "to everyone his own."

12. Justice stands foremost among the moral virtues. Cicero (*De Officiis.* 1) says that justice is the most splendid of virtues, and that it gives its name to good men. A just man means a man that is thoroughly good.

59. INJUSTICE

1. Injustice is a special vice for it opposes the special virtue of justice. It has, however, the aspect of a general vice inasmuch as every vice strikes against the common good which justice serves.

2. A person may do an unjust thing—from ignorance, perhaps, or passion—without having the habit or *vice* of injustice. But to do what is unjust intentionally and by full choice is the mark of an unjust man, a man with the vice of injustice.

3. Injustice is found only in what is suffered against one's will.

4. In its general essential kind, or *genus*, injustice is a grave sin. In small matters, however, it is a venial sin; slight acts are not in essential conflict with the good, and with the fixed will, of the one who undergoes their effect or endures them.

60. JUDGMENT

1. Judgment, as a term used in direct connection with justice, means an authoritative statement of what is right. It is the decision and pronouncement of a judge. Aristotle says (*Ethic.* v): "Men have recourse to the judge as to one who is the personification of justice." Judgment itself is an act of justice.

2. As an act of justice, judgment is certainly lawful. One may lawfully exercise the office of judge, in civil matters or in private life, when (a) he follows justice; (b) and has authority; (c) and does his duty prudently. If a judgment fails of justice, it is unjust or perverted judgment. If it comes from one unauthorized to hand it down, it is a judgment by usurpation. If it comes from imprudence—by reason of dubious evidence, improper motive, etc.—it is called suspicion or rash judgment.

3. It is always wrong to base judgment on suspicions. St. John Chrysostom says (*In Matt.* 7:1) that our Lord in giving the command, "Judge not," means particularly that we are to abstain from "condemning others on evidence which for the most part is mere suspicion."

4. A man does an injury to his neighbor by thinking ill of him without sure and evident reasons for the bad opinion. Hence, we must judge a person good until he proves himself evil, and we must interpret what is doubtful about him in the most favorable way.

5. A thing is *right*, either by its nature or by the agreement of men expressed in human laws. In the first case, it is of *natural* right; in the second case, it is of *positive* right. True laws express and establish positive right. Hence, a judge, in matters of positive law, must make judgment according to that law.

6. A judgment by usurpation, because of the very fact that it is unauthorized, is a perverse and unjust judgment.

61. THE PARTS OF JUSTICE

1. The parts of justice are: (a) the different types or kinds of justice; (b) the directives involved in justice itself as *quasi-integral* elements; (c) the virtues connected with justice; these are called its *potential* parts. Now, there are two kinds or species of justice, namely, *commutative* justice and *distributive* justice. Commutative justice is the justice that should exist between man and man; it regulates the "give and take" of persons with persons. Distributive justice is the justice which is to be exercised by the community (state; government) towards the individual members of the community.

2. Distributive justice is administered according to "the proportion of equality" so that the person of higher merit or higher state receives more than the person of lesser merit or lower state. Thus, a greater honor and emolument is owed to the mayor than to a councilman. But commutative justice (the justice of man to man) is administered by the rule of fact, regardless of the merit or place of the persons concerned. And so the mayor, and the councilman, and the simple citizen, must each pay a debt of five dollars with five dollars. Hence, we discern a difference in the *mean* or *measure* of the two species of justice.

3. There is also a difference in the matter with which the two kinds of justice are respectively concerned. Distributive justice looks to the just *bestowal* of goods or honors; commutative justice looks to the just *exchange* of goods between parties.

4. There is a thing called *counterpassion*, which is "tit for tat" or "an eye for an eye." It means striking back when struck. It means

"getting even." Now, while there is a place for counterpassion in commutative justice (its terms are expressed in law as restitution, fines, imprisonment, penalty), there is no place for it in distributive justice.

62. RESTITUTION

1. Restitution is the act of restoring the balance or "proportion of equality" demanded by justice. Restitution is an act of commutative justice. It is occasioned by one person's having what belongs to another (with or without his consent); it is enacted by giving back what is thus possessed, or, when this is impossible, by restoring its equivalent or value, so far as may be done, to the true owner.

2. The safeguarding of justice is necessary for a man's salvation. Hence, it is necessary for one who unjustly takes, or holds, what belongs to another, to restore it. This obligation rests upon every person who has unjustly taken anything—property, good name, or any other good. The obligation binds according to the measure of possibility; no one can be bound to do what is impossible.

3. In restoring goods of fortune (that is, goods which can be priced, estimated in terms of money), the restorer is bound to give back the full value of what he took unjustly. And if a judge, in court of law, imposes a fine, over and above the amount taken, the restorer is required in conscience to pay that exact amount.

4. A man is bound to make restitution according to the extent of loss he has brought upon another. If he took an exact amount, he must restore that exact amount. If he took what is called *potential* gain from another, inasmuch as the theft prevented the rightful owner from making a profitable investment, he must make such restitution as is reasonable in view of all the conditions and circumstances of the case. But he is not required to pay all that the owner *thinks* he would have earned had his opportunity not been taken away by the theft. For, after all, the *expected* gain was never actually possessed by the victim of the theft, and the thief cannot be bound to restore what he has not taken.

5. Restitution is to be made to the person or persons from whom the thing has been taken. If this cannot be done, it must be made to the heirs of the true owners. And if this be impossible, the amount due must be expended in good works, such as gifts for the care of the poor, or orphans—that is, it must be used for *pious causes*. In no case may the unjust taker or holder keep the stolen goods. It is a maxim of justice that "no one can be justly enriched by ill-gotten gain."

6. One who takes a thing, justly or unjustly, is bound to restore it. One may take a thing justly, with the consent of the owner, by borrow-

ing. Or one may take a thing justly as a favor to the owner who wishes to commit it to his care. One takes a thing unjustly when he takes it without the consent of the owner. In every case, the thing taken is to be restored. If, however, a thing taken as a favor to the owner, is lost or destroyed without any fault on the part of the custodian, restitution is not required. When the depositor asks the favor of having his goods cared for, he takes the chance of unintended injury or loss. Of course, it he *pays* to have his goods cared for, and thus insures them, he is entitled to insurance.

7. All who have a real part in the unjust deed of taking goods without the consent of their owner, are involved in the obligation of making restitution. Those who have such a real part in the unjust deed are called *cooperators* in it. There are nine ways of cooperating in an evil deed: by counsel, by command, by consent, by flattery, by receiving, by partaking, by silence, by not preventing when possible, by not denouncing the evildoers. Those who are *always* bound to restitution by reason of their part in the theft are: (a) persons who command the theft; (b) persons who consent to it when refusal of their consent would prevent it; (c) those who receive ill-gotten goods; (d) those who actually take part in the act of thievery; (d) those who, having ability, authority, and duty to prevent the theft, fail to do so. In the other four cases (counsel, flattery, silence, not denouncing) cooperators are sometimes bound to restitution, and sometimes not, according to the real or merely *incidental* influence they exercised in the actual theft.

8. Restitution is to be made immediately if possible. To *keep* another's property, and thus to deprive him of its possession and use, is sinful, just as *taking* the property unjustly is sinful. Hence, without the permission of the owner, no delay, beyond that of sheer impossibility in making immediate restitution, is permissible.

63. RESPECT OF PERSONS

1. Respect of persons is manifested in the bestowing of a good on one person and withholding it from another, not because the receiver is qualified or worthy, but because he is this person—your friend, perhaps, or your relative, or one who can later confer a favor on you, or one whom you revere as rich or prominent. Respect of persons is an offense against distributive justice.

2. The sin of respect of persons may occur even with reference to spiritual things, as, for example, in ecclesiastical appointments, in admitting children to First Communion, in attending the sick for spiritual ministration, etc.

3. Respect of persons appears in respect and honor paid to unworthy individuals or for unjust reasons, as, for example, in honor paid to a man for the sole reason that he has money.

4. A judge who, in passing sentence, is hard upon common men and obsequious to the rich or the politically powerful, is guilty of the sin of respect of persons.

64. MURDER

1. Murder is the unjust killing of a human being by one or more private individuals. Murder is a very grave sin against commutative justice. In the necessary killing of plants and animals which we use for food, there is no offense. Only in the unjust killing of a human being is the sin of murder committed.

2. The execution, by public authority, of a person guilty of heinous crime, is not murder. Such an execution is no mere act of vengeance; it is the removal from the community, by competent authority, of one whose crime shows him to be a menace that seriously threatens the common good. As a man must sometimes have arm or leg amputated to save his life, so the body of the community must amputate seriously diseased members that threaten the whole group and its common life.

3. No private individual, or group of individuals, may justifiably take upon themselves the task of ridding the community of criminals by process of execution. Killings by such agencies are simply murders. Only the justly constituted public authority can lawfully inflict the death penalty.

4. Clerics must have no part in any killing. This is so because (a) they are to follow Christ closely in all they do, and Christ suffered without striking back or inflicting death on anyone; (b) they are the ministers of the New Law which appoints no death penalty.

5. Suicide, or self-murder, is a heinous sin against God, against nature, and against the community. To kill privately, whether the victim be oneself or another, is to usurp God's place and power, for God alone is master of life and death. Our life is given us, not to own and to dispose of as we choose, but to use for God's glory and our own salvation.

6. It is never lawful, even by public authority, to kill an innocent person, no matter what benefit may accrue to the community from his death.

7. If, in defending oneself against a murderous and unjust attack, one kills the assailant, there is no murder, but blameless self-defense. Nor is there murder in the necessary and official acts of those author-

itatively set to guard or defend the common good, such as policemen and soldiers.

8. A person who kills another by accident is without guilt if, when the fatal accident occurs, he is performing a lawful action and exercising due care.

65. MUTILATION

1. The maiming of the body is altogether unlawful and opposed to justice unless it be by way of necessary surgery competently performed, or by way of punishment for crime, under public authority. It seems clear that public authority may inflict mutilation of members as a penalty for heinous crime; the same authority may lawfully take a criminal's life, and mutilation is a much less terrible punishment than death.

2. It is not contrary to justice for parents to punish their children corporally by way of needful correction. But no person may justly strike or punish another corporally unless he has jurisdiction over him.

3. Competent public authority may lawfully detain or imprison a person by way of punishment, or even as a precaution against impending evil, provided this be done according to the order of justice. On occasion, it is permissible for an individual to restrain a person temporarily, as, for example, to prevent his jumping to death from a high place, or to hold him back from doing violent injury to someone unable to defend himself.

4. An unjust act of injuring another in his body (by maiming, striking, fettering, restraining) is made worse if the person injured is one to whom the offender owes a special reverence or respect, or with whom he is connected by some relationship.

66. THEFT AND ROBBERY

1. External goods can be lawfully *owned* by a person. Man has a natural need for such things, and for their use, and thus he has a natural right to acquire dominion over them.

2. Since man has a natural need to procure, to dispense, and to use material goods, it is lawful for him to possess such goods as his own. But in the use of such goods, man must be willing to give or share, according to reason and justice, to a neighbor in need.

3. *Theft* is the secret and unlawful taking of what belongs to another.

4. *Robbery* differs specifically from theft, for it is the open and forceful taking of another's goods.

5. Theft is a sin directly contrary to the divine commandment, "Thou

shalt not steal." Theft is opposed to justice directly, and also by the fact that it involves guile or fraud.

6. Theft, in its kind or *genus*, is a grave sin, for it opposes commutative justice and also opposes charity which is the spiritual life of the soul. For charity imposes the duty of loving one's neighbor, and theft is injury to one's neighbor. Yet the full and grave nature of theft as sin is not found in the taking of trifling things, unless, indeed, the thief *intends* serious injury by his stealing. Small thievings are, in themselves, venial sins.

7. When a person is in extreme need of material things, and there is no way of emerging from his extremity but by taking what belongs to another, the *surplus* which another possesses becomes common property, and the taker is not guilty of theft. Thus a starving man, or one whose dependents are starving, may take, openly or secretly, the food that will save human life. This, of course, is on condition that the taker of the food has no other means of getting it, and that he does not leave the person from whom he takes the food in as desperate a situation as his own.

8. Robbery involves two offenses against both justice and charity, namely, the taking of goods unlawfully, and the inflicting of violence or coercion on the victim. Robbery is, therefore, always sinful. When public authority forcefully takes over property, either as lawful penalty, or for use in an emergency such as war or public calamity, there is no robbery in the act.

9. It seems that robbery is a more grievous wrong than theft. It takes a man's goods and adds injury or ignominy to his person. Thus, it is more noticeably oppressive to a man than theft with its sly guile or fraud.

67. INJUSTICE IN A JUDGE

1. It is unlawful for a judge to pass sentence upon anyone who is not subject to his jurisdiction, whether this be *ordinary* jurisdiction (belonging to his station and office) or *delegated* jurisdiction imparted to the judge extraordinarily by competent public authority.

2. A judge in a court of law does not pronounce sentence in accordance with what he, as an individual, thinks, or even knows; he passes sentence according to the evidence brought before him. Of course, a judge may use his private knowledge to guide him in insisting on a rigorous sifting, and re-examination, of evidence, when he knows that justice is about to miscarry. But if he cannot so reject the faulty evidence, he must follow it in pronouncing sentence.

3. No judge can sentence a man who is not accused, for a judge exercises his proper office in interpreting the way of justice between two parties, accused and accuser. Scripture (Acts 25:16) indicates this fact in these words: "It is not the custom of the Romans to condemn any man, before that he who is accused have his accusers present, and have liberty to make his answer, to clear himself of the things laid to his charge."

4. The judge passes judicial sentence. Once delivered, this sentence passes from the lawful power of the judge who pronounced it. The judge is not capable of revoking the sentence or remitting the penalty it has imposed. Such remission may be made by a higher court, and especially by the highest court in a country, if thereby no injury is done to the accuser (whose cause was proved and decided) or to the common good. Of course, in things that lie within the power of the judge's discretion, and are not a matter of law applied by judicial sentence, there is room for the judge to exercise mercy.

68. UNJUST ACCUSATION

1. To *denounce* an evil-doer is to declare his fault openly in the hope that he may mend his ways. To *accuse* a man is to declare his fault for the purpose of seeing him punished. Yet even punishment looks to amendment—if not always for the one subjected to it, at least for the commonwealth. Punishment in this world is always medicinal. If a man knows of a crime against the common good, already committed or being plotted, he is obliged to make due accusation, provided he can back it with proof.

2. Accusation, to be truly lawful, must be set down in writing. Merely oral utterances are likely to be carelessly made, inaccurately understood, and readily forgotten.

3. Rash accusation is sinful, for it involves calumny, collusion, or evasion. Calumny is a false charge. Collusion is fraud or trickery on the part of accusers, when these are two or more. Evasion is the making of a charge and then trying to shift out of the inconvenience that follows for the accuser. The common good is hurt by calumny, collusion, and evasion. Hence rash accusation is always unjust.

4. An accuser who fails to prove his charge has unjustly put a man in danger of penalty. Such an accuser should be himself penalized.

69. THE DEFENDANT IN COURT

1. The accused is bound to tell the truth exacted of him according to the forms of law. If he refuses to tell what he is obliged to tell, or if

he lies, he sins, and sins gravely. But if he is asked what he is under no duty to tell, he may withhold an answer, evade the issue, or appeal it. But he is never permitted to lie.

2. Certainly, the accused person may not seek his escape by calumnies, uttered against his accusers for the purpose of discrediting them.

3. A man may justly appeal his case when he is convinced that his cause is just, and that the case has not been, or will not be, fairly decided. But a man who knows that his sentence is, or will be just, and who appeals to occasion delay in having it pronounced, is not justified in making the appeal.

4. A man justly condemned to death may not lawfully seek to defend himself by using violence against his executioners. A man unjustly condemned may rightly resist execution by every means in his power, provided his action does not work serious harm to the common good.

70. WITNESSES IN COURT

1. A man is bound to give evidence either when his duty as a citizen requires it, or when his evidence may prevent a serious miscarriage of justice. A man is not bound to come forward freely with evidence when his silence would do no harm to the common good.

2. The tested evidence of two or three witnesses is enough to enable the judge to pronounce sentence.

3. Sometimes evidence is rejected without indicating an actual fault in the witness. Extraneous reasons may detract from the value of the evidence, or render it suspect, and so cause it to be discredited.

4. To give false evidence is to commit grave sin. For this is *perjury,* which is the telling of a lie when under oath. Perjury is directly opposed to justice, and comes into flat conflict with the Eighth Commandment: "Thou shalt not bear false witness against thy neighbor." Even when the evidence as a *lie* is only a slight matter of venial sin, as testimony *falsely* sworn to, it is a serious sin.

71. THE ADVOCATE IN COURT

1. An advocate or lawyer is not bound to defend the poor without charge, except in lawsuits in which a poor man cannot be otherwise helped but by *this* lawyer at *this* time.

2. It is just that persons should be debarred from the office of advocate who have no fitness for the office.

3. An advocate is not to defend, knowingly, an unjust cause.

4. It is just for a lawyer to take a fee for his services. For a man may justly take payment for giving what he is not otherwise bound to give. An advocate is usually free from the obligation of taking up

the cases brought to him; if he accepts the task, he ought to be paid for performing it. Exorbitant fees, however, are unjust; they amount to extortion, and so are a kind of robbery.

72. INJUSTICE IN WORDS: REVILING

1. Reviling is dishonoring a person by words or deeds, but most commonly by words.

2. When it meets its definition fully, reviling is a sin against justice, and is, in its kind or *genus*, a serious sin.

3. We are sometimes required to submit in silence to reviling; this is so especially when our silence is for the good of others. And sometimes, for the sake of the reviler himself and for those who overhear his evil words, we are obliged to make answer, and thus withstand the reviling.

4. The easiest way for a person to take revenge for real or supposed injury is by using angry words. Therefore, anger is a fruitful source of reviling.

73. INJUSTICE IN WORDS: BACKBITING

1. Reviling is the open and loud dishonoring of a person. Backbiting is the secret and quiet injuring of a man's good name. Thus these two sins have a resemblance to two sins that deal with external goods, namely robbery, which is open and violent, and theft, which is secret and quiet. If the backbiting is lying, its name is *calumny* or *slander;* if it is harmful truth, its name is *detraction.*

2. Backbiting is a sin, and when it is done with full knowledge and consent and in serious matters, it is a mortal sin. Slight things said about another do not seriously injure his character, and may be venial sins.

3. Backbiting is a great evil, but it is not the most serious evil against one's neighbor. It is, for instance, less grievous than adultery or murder. But, in its *genus* or kind, backbiting is more grievous than theft, which it resembles. For Scripture says (Prov. 22:1): "A good name is better than great riches."

4. St. Jerome says (*Ep. ad Nepot.*): "Take care not to have an itching tongue, nor tingling ears; neither detract others, nor listen to backbiters." He who willingly listens to backbiting, shares its guilt.

74. INJUSTICE IN WORDS: WHISPERING

1. By whispering is meant talebearing, the spreading of gossip to the harm of a neighbor. A backbiter seeks to injure a man's good name;

a talebearer seeks to stir up trouble, or to arouse people to take action against another or others.

2. Talebearing or whispering is a greater sin than backbiting or reviling, for it seeks to rob a neighbor of his friends. And friends are a man's most precious external possessions.

75. INJUSTICE IN WORDS: DERISION

1. Derision is "making fun of a person." It is "laughing a person to scorn." In its serious form, that is, when it is not a mere bit of banter, or a light joke, it seeks to shame a man.

2. Derision, when it is a jest or half-jest, may be only a slight offense and a venial sin, or perhaps no sin at all. But in its full character, as a serious and unjust attempt to bring shame on a person, derision is a mortal sin. It seems that derision, as a grave sin, is more evil than reviling.

76. INJUSTICE IN WORDS: CURSING

1. Cursing is either a wish or a command that another be afflicted with evil. As a command, cursing is sometimes lawful; thus, a judge imposing penalty, or the Church pronouncing anathema, involves no injustice or sin. But we usually understand cursing as the wish, expressed in strong terms, that another may be afflicted with evil.

2. Cursing irrational things is, in itself, mere vain and futile speech; it is not really cursing at all. When such cursing of irrational things is actually cursing, it has reference to people. Thus when the Lord said (Gen. 3:17), "Cursed is the earth in thy work," he meant that the barrenness of the earth is a penalty put upon sinful man. And when David cursed the mountains of Gelboe (II Kings 1:21), he did so because of the people who had been slaughtered there. Likewise, when Job cursed his day (Job 3:1) he was referring to the miseries that people must endure in this world.

3. Cursing as an evil wish against other persons is a sin. It is directly contrary to charity, and it strikes against justice. Therefore, in its *genus* or kind, it is a mortal sin. But, in its actual performing, cursing is frequently mere vain speech, even when it is directed against persons. It is seldom used with attention to its meaning, or with any thought of having an evil wish fulfilled. A man who "damns" another, or tells him to "go to hell," has usually no wish at all to see the other suffer harm; he has no thought of wishing that the person addressed should undergo the punishment of hell. He is merely using a coarse, uncouth, and nearly meaningless expression that is readily learned and

habitually used to give vent to strong feeling in almost any trying situation.

4. Cursing, even when it is actually worthy of the name and is therefore sinful, is usually not so grave a sin as backbiting. Backbiting actually inflicts an injury; cursing only wishes injury to be inflicted.

77. CHEATING

1. Cheating is an injustice most commonly associated with buying and selling. It is cheating to sell a thing at an exorbitant price, and it is cheating to sell fraudulently by offering sham goods for true, or by giving short measure. The worth of a thing, which determines the just price at which it should be sold, is not only the value of the thing in itself, but the value that it has to the buyer or the seller.

2. If there is a substantial fault or flaw in goods sold, and the seller knows it and is silent, while the buyer does not discover it, the sale is unlawful, fraudulent, and unjust. Other fraudulent sales are those involving short weight or measure, and those of inferior goods sold as goods of superior quality. In cases such as these, the seller does wrong, and is bound to restitution. If, however, the seller is unaware of the fraudulent character of his sales, he does not sin, but, when he learns of the injury done, he must compensate the buyer. And if a buyer takes advantage of the ignorance or mistake of a salesman to get superior goods for the price of inferior goods, the buyer is bound to restitution.

3. If defects in goods salable are manifest (as, for instance, if a horse offered for sale has only one eye, or if apples on the market are spotted or small), the seller has no need to declare these defects. But when defects are hidden and undeclared, the sale of defective goods is fraudulent. St. Ambrose says (*De Offic.* III): "In all contracts, the defects of the salable commodity must be declared . . . otherwise, the contract is voided."

4. For a tradesman to charge more for a thing than he himself paid for it, is not cheating. His work of trading confers a benefit; he puts needed or desirable goods at the command and convenience of the buyer. For this service he deserves just recompense. But to make unreasonably great profit by overcharging is cheating.

78. USURY

1. Consumptible goods are goods which are consumed by being used—such, for instance, as food, or fuel for the fire. When such goods are borrowed, they are to be returned *in kind* and in the amount bor-

rowed. Nonconsumptible goods, such as houses, farm animals, machines, fields, articles of clothing, are not used up by being used. When such goods are borrowed, they are to be returned *themselves*. And for the service rendered by their use, their owner may charge rent or hire. Now, money is consumed in being used. Hence, to charge for its use, in addition to its substance, is to charge for something which does not exist. Money charged for the use of money is usury, and usury is unjust and unlawful. [*Note:* Moralists now say that, since the day of St. Thomas, money has taken on the character of a fruitful or quasi-fruitful commodity; they say money actually does produce money, and hence gives to the borrower more than the substance of the loan. Therefore, a reasonable charge for the use of money is lawful. Such lawful money-rent is called *interest*. Usury is excessive and unjust interest. This is the modern meaning of the terms. To St. Thomas—and rightly, in view of the place and function of money in his times—any interest at all is usury, and is unjust and forbidden.]

2. Nor can a man exact some other kind of goods than money in consideration for a money-loan. At any rate, he cannot exact goods that can be estimated in terms of money, for to demand such goods would be only to demand usury in another form.

3. If a person gets money, or other consumptibles, by usury, he must restore what he got. Yet if a man who holds a usurious commodity gets profit from it by his own effort and industry, he is not bound to restore this earned increment. Thus, if a man exacts six bushels of wheat for a loan of five bushels, he is bound to give back that one extra bushel of wheat. But if he planted all six bushels when the loan was paid back to him (that is, he planted his own five bushels, and the usuriously exacted bushel), he is not bound to restore one-sixth of his whole crop to the man upon whom he practiced the usury. He is bound to restore the one bushel he had no right to take. But if a man extorts productive goods (nonconsumptibles) by usury, such as houses or lands for instance, he is bound to restore the goods themselves and whatever profits have accrued to him by holding them.

4. A man who freely chooses to submit to usury, and borrows money at a set rate, does not sin by the action provided his purpose and intention are good.

79. THE QUASI-INTEGRAL PARTS OF JUSTICE

1. The quasi-integral parts of justice are the directives involved in the exercise of justice, namely, "do good," and "avoid evil." These directives of the natural law indicate what is requisite for the act of justice. They are therefore called "parts" or "quasi-parts" of justice

itself. Justice seeks equality of good between a man and God, a man and his neighbors as individuals, a man and his community. Now, "doing good" sets up this equality; "avoiding evil" saves the equality already set up.

2. *Transgression* violates the rule of "avoid evil." It is an act against a negative precept, a precept which says, "Thou shalt not," or has the force of such prohibition.

3. *Omission* violates the rule of "do good." It is the failure to obey a positive precept.

4. Usually, it is easier to avoid evil than to stir oneself to do good. Therefore, it is usually a graver sin to transgress than to omit, since one may, with the smaller effort, refrain from transgression.

80. THE POTENTIAL PARTS OF JUSTICE

1. The potential parts of justice are the virtues connected with justice, that is, virtues which share the character of justice, but do not perfectly conform with it in all respects. To illustrate: one such potential part of justice is the virtue of religion. This virtue has the character of justice inasmuch as it renders to God what is his due, but it cannot ever render *all* that is his due, and hence falls short of perfect justice. The potential parts of justice may be listed as follows: religion, piety, observance (that is, paying due honor and deference), gratitude, revenge (not evil revenge, but rather a *compensation*), truth, friendship, liberality, and *epikeia* or equity.

RELIGION

(QUESTIONS 81 TO 100)

81. THE VIRTUE OF RELIGION

1. Cicero thinks that the word religion derives from the Latin verb *relegere*, "to read over again," and that it suggests the propriety of reading and pondering, again and again, on what belongs to divine worship. St. Augustine thinks that the word religion comes from *religare*, "to bind, or tie up," and indicates the bond or tie between man and God. Whatever may be true of the origin of the word, religion means an ordering, a standing, a relationship between man and God.

2. Religion in a person is a virtue, that is, it is an enduring quality, a habit, which disposes him who has it to pay, steadfastly and well, the debt of honor and worship that he owes to God.

3. Religion is one virtue. For, though it has many and various acts, God is the object of them all.

4. Religion is a special virtue, distinct from other virtues, and it disposes man to give to God the special honor that is his due. Therefore, though religion serves the ends of justice, and is one of its potential parts, it has its own definite field wherein to exercise and apply justice. Thus it is not identical with justice as such. Nor is it identical with any other virtue.

5. Religion is not a theological virtue, infused like faith, hope, and charity. It is a moral virtue. The theological virtues have God himself as their object, whereas religion has as its object the honor, reverence, and worship due to God.

6. Religion is the chief of the moral virtues because its acts are directed *immediately* to God's honor and glory, while the other moral virtues direct their acts to God through the *medium* of religion. Therefore, religion is nobler and more excellent than the other moral virtues.

7. Religion is expressed essentially by internal acts of the soul; secondarily, it is expressed by suitable external acts. Man is body-and-soul; and, during earthly life, the soul has an extrinsic dependence on the body, so that, for instance, the intellect cannot grasp reality without the cooperation of bodily senses. It is inevitable, therefore, that religion which honors God and thereby perfects the faculties of the human mind and will, should also, in some sense, perfect the bodily faculties as well. Hence, these bodily faculties have some expression of religion to make; that is to say, religion will have expression, though in a secondary way, in external and bodily acts, in sensible signs, actions, and ceremonies.

8. Sanctity, which fundamentally means purity and sacredness under the law, is holiness. Now, holiness and religion come to the same thing. For it is by holiness that the human mind and will apply themselves to the service of God, and this is religion. Therefore, sanctity in a man and religion in a man are not really distinct; they are distinct by a *logical* distinction, not by a *real* distinction; that is to say, they are two distinct aspects of the same thing.

82. DEVOTION

1. Devotion, in the religious sense, is the will to give oneself steadily to the service of God.

2. Devotion is not a virtue, but the act of a virtue. Indeed, it is an

act of charity, as all the moral virtues are when they are supernatural. But specifically it is an act of the virtue of religion.

3. The extrinsic cause of devotion in a person is God. The intrinsic cause (which is in the person himself) is meditation or contemplation. When a person thinks upon God and ponders his goodness and loving kindness, he is stirred to a love of God that begets devotion. And, pondering his own insufficiency and his faults, a man is moved to turn to God and to lean upon him; out of this consideration too, devotion arises.

4. The direct and chief effect of devotion is joy in God. Its secondary and indirect effect is sorrow for one's shortcomings and sins.

83. PRAYER

1. Prayer is not an act of the appetitive power (the desiring power, the will) but of the reason, that is, of the thinking mind which enlightens and guides the will. Prayer is basically a petition, a beseeching; it is an act of reason which, as Aristotle says, "exhorts us to do what is best."

2. There are three musty errors about praying. One is that God does not rule things, and that the prayer of petition is useless. A second is that all things happen by fixed fate, and that consequently praying is a vain action. A third is that prayer attempts to make God change His providence, and is therefore foolish. We reject at once the first two of these errors as in manifest conflict with both reason and faith. As for the third, we say that we pray not to change providence, but to align ourselves with it. St. Gregory says, "By asking, men may deserve to receive what almighty God from eternity is disposed to give." Hence, it is right and reasonable to pray.

3. It is a mistake to say that prayer, as petition, seeks something from God and is therefore not an act of honoring God, and consequently is not an act of religion. For we do honor God when we confess that we need him, and proclaim his almighty power to bestow blessings. We honor God so when we pray, and therefore prayer is a true act of religion.

4. We seek God's help and blessing by prayer *directly* when we pray to God, and *indirectly* when we pray to the saints and angels to engage their cooperating prayer. In the first case, we honor God in himself; in the second, we honor God through his blessed creatures. Both types of prayer are acts of religion.

5. We rightly pray for particular favors, and not merely for blessing in general. The clear-cut petition for particular blessings suits man's nature, and stirs his devotion. Besides, when we pray, we always

have the will to leave things in God's hands; no matter how ardent are our special petitions, they are offered as subject to God's love and wisdom. Thus, in making petition with all earnestness and desire, we still do not want God to give us what would work our hurt or cause our ruin.

6. We can lawfully pray for temporal goods, so long as we do not attach to them inordinate importance, and make them the end-all and be-all of existence. For we may lawfully desire external goods, and what we may lawfully desire, we may lawfully pray for. Hence, it is not wrong, but very right, to ask God for temporal favors.

7. When we pray we should ask for what we lawfully desire, and also for what we ought to desire. Now, we ought to desire grace, and salvation, and all good things for others as well as for ourselves. Hence, we should pray for others.

8. As we are obliged to love our enemies, so we should pray for them. This prayer, like love itself, *must* be for enemies in general. It is a matter of perfection to love and pray for enemies individually.

9. The "Our Father," or Lord's Prayer is the most perfect of all prayers, not merely because Christ taught it, but because it includes in itself all that can be in a prayer. In this prayer, we ask for all that is to be desired, and in the order in which the items of desire should be listed.

10. Prayer is *proper* to rational creatures, that is, it belongs to such creatures exclusively. It is an act of reason "which exhorts us to do what is best." Irrational creatures cannot pray. And God, who is non-creatural Reason, has no occasion to pray. Therefore only rational creatures have the right and the duty to pray.

11. The saints in heaven pray for us. For prayer for others is born of charity, and the saints have greater charity than we have. And the saints are closer to God than we are; hence, their prayers are more effective than ours.

12. Prayer should find expression in audible words as well as in the silent language of the heart. Oral prayer is plainly necessary for the common prayer offered by one in the name of many. If the priest praying with his congregation did not speak out, the people would have no knowledge of the prayer. And individual man is so made that he naturally tends to put his thoughts and affections into oral speech. Even when a man prays privately, he finds it useful to put his prayer into actual speech; for this helps him (a) to fix attention and arouse devotion; (b) to give his bodily powers opportunity of joining his spiritual powers in honoring their Creator; (c) to give natural, and useful, outlet to the overflowing affection of heart and mind.

13. To be altogether perfect, oral prayer requires attention throughout. But even holy persons suffer from wandering of mind. If a person has the true intention of praying, his prayer is good and meritorious despite involuntary wanderings of mind. There are three types of attention in oral praying: attention to the words as well pronounced; attention to the meaning of the words uttered; attention to God and the things prayed for. The third sort of attention is the most necessary.

14. The cause of prayer is charity (the grace, love, and friendship of God), which ought to be in us always. We should ceaselessly have the *virtual* or *implied* intention of doing all for the glory of God. In this sense, prayer should be continuous. "And he [Christ] also told them . . . that they must always pray, and not lose heart" (Luke 18:1). Prayer, however, as actual petition to God cannot be continuous; we have many other things to consume our time; we must eat, and sleep, and attend to daily tasks, and chat with friends, and travel, and do a hundred other things. Prayer as actual and explicit petition is possible at many hours of the day; it is well that there be a few stated times for it. This actual and formal prayer ought to be long enough in time to stir fervor and desire for God and his blessings, but it ought not to be so long as to cause weariness.

15. Prayer, like any supernaturally virtuous act, proceeds from charity, and hence is meritorious. Good prayer is from charity through religion with the concurrence of humility, faith, and devotion. It is an act effective in meriting, as it is an act effective in obtaining favors from God.

16. Those who are in the state of sin can effectively beg God's blessing, for God loves the sinner even as he hates the sin. In his divine mercy, God hears the prayers of a sinner who earnestly and perseveringly asks for himself what he needs to turn from sin and save his soul. St. Augustine says (*Tract.* XLIV *super Joan.*): "If God were not to hear sinners, the publican would have vainly cried, 'O Lord, be merciful to me, a sinner.'"

17. Prayer raises the mind adoringly to God, and begs his blessings, and, with appreciative or thankful spirit, it implores divine mercy on sinful man. Hence, prayer has *parts:* adoration, petition, thanksgiving, penitential supplication.

84. EXTERIOR ACTS OF RELIGION: ADORATION

1. Divine adoration or *latria* is worship given to God alone. It is the highest type of religious reverence. The reverence we pay to the saints and angels is called *dulia*. Sometimes, especially in the older books and formulas, dulia is called adoration; but it is never called

divine adoration. And the chief act of latria or divine adoration (that is, the act of sacrifice), is never performed to express dulia, but only to express latria; sacrifice is offered to God alone. [*Note:* To Mary, the Mother of God, is offered a reverence which is higher than that offered to the other saints and to the angels; this reverence to Mary is called *hyperdulia*. It is a superior form of dulia; it is never latria. Latria is divine worship, divine adoration; it is given to no creatures, not even to the most perfect of creatures; it is given only to God.]

2. We are divinely commanded to adore God with our entire being —heart, soul, mind, strength—for we are, body and soul, God's creatures and children. Hence, there must be external or exterior acts of latria as well as internal acts. To be sure, all such exterior acts have meaning as the expression of interior adoration in the soul.

3. God is rightly adored at all times and in all places. But, for the formal exercise of external acts of latria, it is fitting, and even necessary, that there should be a special and suitable place for divine worship.

85. EXTERIOR ACTS OF RELIGION: SACRIFICE

1. The offering of *sacrifice* to God is an obligation laid on man by the natural law. Reason requires that man show signs of submission to God, as well as signs of honor paid to God. Now, man is a bodily being in a bodily world; it is reasonable that he should make the necessary signs of religion in a bodily way, using bodily things. This is done by offering sacrifice. The whole history of mankind shows that the offering of sacrifice is a universal practice. This fact confirms the truth mentioned, namely, that sacrifice to God is required of man by the natural law.

2. Sacrifice is the highest and most solemn and impressive of the acts of latria. As an official act of religion and external divine worship, it is defined as follows: sacrifice is the offering of a bodily thing (called *victim*), by a qualified person (called *priest*), in a suitable place (called *altar*), and the destruction or change of the victim (this is *immolation* or mactation) to express the supreme and unique dominion of God over all his creatures, and the absolute dependence of all creatures upon God.

3. Sacrifice is a *special* act done out of reverence for God; it therefore belongs to the virtue of religion. Sometimes acts of the other virtues are called by the name of sacrifices; thus we say that a person makes a sacrifice of time or money, or that he is a self-sacrificing person, or that he sacrifices the use of certain foods or pleasures as penance, and so on; and we say that a soldier who dies in battle makes the supreme sacrifice. Now, such things are not actually or formally sac-

rifices, but they are called so because they are a sort of offering that is, or should be, made to God; they have a resemblance, either striking or distant, to sacrifice, and thus they are given its name.

4. Using the name sacrifice in this extended meaning, we are all bound to offer to God the inward sacrifice of a devout mind, and to perform requisite acts of virtue in the spirit of sacrifice, that is, out of high reverence for God.

86. EXTERIOR ACTS OF RELIGION: OBLATIONS

1. We are all bound to make offerings, in one way or another, for the support of religion, as it exists in external and established practice according to the institution of Christ. Such offerings are oblations.

2. Offerings are made to priests (I Cor. 9:13) who are "to live by the altar." And the priest has further use for offerings or oblations than his mere livelihood; he has to obtain what belongs to the functions of external worship, and he has to dispense goods to the poor.

3. An offering or oblation is not to be made of things unjustly acquired or wrongfully possessed.

4. The Old Law required men to make an offering or oblation of "the first fruits," that is, the best of their crops and harvestings. This was to make open and practical acknowledgment that "the earth is the Lord's and the fullness thereof," and that the tiller of the soil does not create its fertility, but that all good things come from God. Even after the coming of the New Law, the offering of "first fruits" continued to be a pious custom in some countries.

87. EXTERNAL ACTS OF RELIGION: TITHES

1. The Old Law imposed the duty of paying tithes (that is, one-tenth of all revenues) for the support of religion. Certainly, the obligation of offering to the Church a decent proportion of one's income is incumbent on man, even in the light of natural reason. The paying of one's share here is an act of religion.

2. All one's material possessions come from God. Hence, some part of such things should be offered to God again, both to show that we ourselves do not create them, and to support and propagate the true religion. Such an offering is an external act of religion.

3. Since those who serve the altar, the clergy, have most serious duties to occupy all their time and energies, they must not be forced to acquire temporal necessaries for themselves. They are to be supported by offerings, by the fair contributions of all the people.

4. The clergy themselves are not required to pay tithes or to make offerings out of tithes received. But if a clergyman has property and

income of his own, as by inheritance for example, he is required to make suitable and proportionate offering out of this income for the support of religion.

88. VOWS

1. A vow is a promise, proceeding from a deliberate will, with a purpose in view. Sometimes a vow is expressed in words before witnesses; sometimes it is made silently and interiorly, with no human witness.

2. As an act of religion, a vow is a promise freely made to God to do something pleasing to him that the person promising is not already under obligation to do.

3. A vow is a promise *freely* made. No one is obliged to make a vow. But once a vow is made, it imposes obligation; it must be kept. A person must be true to his word, especially his word to God.

4. Although a vow is a promise to do what is pleasing to God, the whole benefit of the vow redounds to the person who makes it. God is not benefited or helped by our vows; no creature can confer a favor on the Creator. St. Augustine (*Ep.* 127 *ad Arment. et Paulin.*) says, "God does not grow rich on our payments, but makes those who pay him grow rich in him."

5. A vow is the directing and dedicating of the thing promised to the worship and service of God. Therefore, a vow is an act of religion. And, since vows are made to God, they are acts of *latria*, that is, of *divine* worship.

6. It is better and more meritorious to do something pleasing to God (which the performer or agent is not already obliged to do) in fulfillment of a vow, than to do the same thing without a vow. The vow itself is an act of religion, and adds its merit to the merit of the good deed which fulfills it.

7. A religious vow is *solemnized* when it is the vow of one who receives holy orders, or who enters a religious community to live under a rule approved by the Church.

8. Since a vow is essentially a free promise, a person who is lawfully subject to another is incapable of making a vow which conflicts with his duties to that other.

9. Children who have reached the use of reason can lawfully make a private vow to enter a religious community, but while they are under the age of puberty, the vow may be annulled by their parents. After puberty, according to the age determined by the Church, children can make a religious vow, simple or solemn, even without the consent of their parents.

10. A person who makes a vow makes a kind of law for himself. It may happen that this law is found to conflict with a greater good. In such a case, competent authority must decide that the vow is not to be observed. This decision is called a dispensation from the vow. If the dispensing authority imposes another obligation to take the place of the one removed, the action is called *commutation,* not dispensation.

11. The Church has power to dispense from vows, even from the vow of chastity or continency which, by ecclesiastical institution, is attached to the taking of major orders. But it seems that the solemn and perpetual vow of chastity, which belongs essentially to the religious or monastic life, admits of no dispensation.

12. Only competent Church authority can dispense from a vow or commute it.

89. OATHS

1. To take an oath is to *swear.* And to swear is to call upon God to witness that we speak the truth (*declaratory* oath), or that we will keep a promise (*promissory* oath).

2. It would be irreverent to call upon God as our witness in merely trifling matters. It is very wrong and sinful to swear to a lie, or to take oath on a promise one does not intend to keep. But it is lawful, in serious and important matters and with due caution, to take a sincere oath. Such an oath is usually an act of reverence to God.

3. The conditions necessary for a lawful oath are: truth, judgment, and justice. For Holy Writ proclaims as much when (Jer. 4:2) it says: "Thou shalt swear: As the Lord liveth, in truth, and in judgment, and in justice." We must swear *in truth:* we must never swear to a lie or to an insincere promise. We must swear *in judgment:* an oath must be made with prudence and discretion, and for no frivolous reason. We must swear *in justice:* a promissory oath must not pledge what it is unlawful to perform.

4. As we have seen, an oath, rightly made, is an act of reverence to God. It is thus an act of the virtue of religion.

5. But an oath, however reverent, indicates a lack and a deformity: it indicates a lack of trust between man and man. Hence, an oath is not desirable for its own sake. An oath is rather like a medicine: not good to take for its own sake, but only for the curing of an ailment. Therefore, oaths are not to be used more frequently than necessary. Scripture says (Ecclus. 23:12): "A man that sweareth much shall be filled with iniquity."

6. Men sometimes swear by creatures ("by my soul," "by St. George," etc.), and such expressions are really oaths if they refer, through crea-

tures, to God. Otherwise these exclamations are not truly oaths at all. Often they are part and parcel of expressions of cursing.

7. A true promissory oath that meets the conditions of justice and judgment must always be kept. But one must *not* fulfill a promissory oath that involves injustice; one cannot lawfully swear to do what is unlawful. Herod swore without judgment and justice to give to Herodias anything she might ask. When he fulfilled his oath, causing the death of St. John the Baptist, he committed a new and a greater sin. His oath itself was a sin; its fulfillment was another sin and a worse sin.

8. An oath is not more binding than a vow; on the contrary, a vow, by its nature, is more strictly binding than an oath. For a vow rests on reverence and fidelity, and to break it is a double offense. But an oath rests on reverence; to violate it does not necessarily involve infidelity.

9. An oath admits of dispensation. If a vow, with greater binding power, can be dispensed, certainly an oath, which is less binding than a vow, can be dispensed.

10. An oath is made *void* by certain conditions of person and time. Thus a minor cannot make a binding oath. And persons of great dignity, such as the king or the president of a country, are guaranteed trustworthy by their office, and are usually not required to swear; thus, in a sense, their oath is void as being unnecessary.

90. ADJURATION

1. To "adjure" a person is to put him under oath, that is, to require an oath from him. Thus the high priest required our Lord to swear that He is the Christ (Matt. 26:63): "I adjure thee by the living God that thou tell us whether thou art the Christ, the Son of God." Since it is lawful, on due conditions, to swear, it cannot be unlawful, when occasion warrants and jurisdiction exists, to demand an oath of another. In a court of law, for example, a witness is lawfully adjured, that is, he is required to swear before God that he will give full and true testimony.

2. It is a kind of *adjuring* to induce or command anyone to do a thing in the name of God. In this sense, evil spirits are *adjured* in exorcisms.

3. Sometimes irrational creatures are adjured, but only in so far as they are *instruments* of rational creatures.

91. ORAL PRAISE OF GOD

1. We use words of the lips when we speak to God, not for the purpose of making known our thoughts to One who knows them better

than we do ourselves, but to stir ourselves and our hearers to reverence for God. We need to praise God with our lips, not for His sake, but for our own. In Psalm 62 it is written: "My mouth shall praise thee with joyful lips."

2. And it is just and right that the voice of man should praise God, not alone in the spoken word, but also in song. The use of music in praising God is a means for stirring reverence for him and employing the feelings in his service; it is certainly suitable that, to such music, there should be set the words of a hymn or song or psalm.

92. VICES OPPOSED TO RELIGION: SUPERSTITION

1. Superstition is a vice opposed to religion. It offers divine worship to whom it should not, or it offers divine worship to God in an unworthy manner. The name superstition comes from the Latin *superstes* which means "a survivor." It suggests that what are called superstitions are survivors or "holdovers" from the false pre-Christian religions known collectively as paganism.

2. Superstition takes various forms: (a) *idolatry* gives divine honor to a creature; (b) *divination* consults demons, thus attributing divine powers to creatures; (c) *false observances* are outer expressions of the belief that divine powers are found in certain creatures.

93. KINDS OF SUPERSTITION

1. Sometimes the truths and practices of the true religion are misinterpreted or misused, and this is a kind of superstition. It is true doctrine, for instance, that the souls in purgatory are helped by our prayers. But it would be superstition to believe that a certain formula of prayer, or a certain number of prayers, gives absolute assurance of the deliverance of a certain soul from purgatory.

2. And the good and useful practices of Catholics—in penitential acts, for instance, and in using medals, scapulars, and other blessed objects—are sometimes turned into superstitious usages by mistaken persons who invest such practices with a kind of magical power, instead of using them, according to the mind of the Church, as means of stirring up reverence and devotion to God in their own hearts.

94. IDOLATRY

1. Idolatry is that form of superstition which sets up false gods, and pays divine honor to what is not divine. St. Augustine (*De Doct. Christ.* II) says: "Anything invented by man for making and worshiping idols, or for giving divine worship to a creature, or any part of a creature . . . is superstitious." The superstition here indicated is that of *idolatry*.

2. It is certainly a sin to worship idols, outwardly or inwardly. It is right to give honor to superiors, but not to regard them as gods. Idolatry is utterly inordinate; it is flatly contrary to reason; it conflicts with religion; it is a thing evil *in itself*. Hence, idolatry is never to be tolerated. We must reject the error of those heretics who say that, in times of persecution, it suffices to hold the true religion in the heart, and, for the sake of freedom from trouble, to take part in the outward worship of idols.

3. It is a sin, and in itself the gravest kind of sin, to practice idolatry. For it is directly against God, like hatred of God which we have called the worst sin in its kind. Idolatry would upset the order of the universe by ascribing universal control and absolute power to a creature. Some sins may be worse than idolatry by reason of the contempt for God and his law that exists in the sinner's heart; but no sin is worse *in itself*.

4. Men cause idolatry by their excessive affections, inordinate loyalties, too high an esteem for artistic objects, and also by ignorance. Scripture says (Wisd. 14:14): "By the vanity of men, they [idols] came into the world." A further cause of idolatry is found in the solicitation of demons who offer themselves to be adored.

95. DIVINATIONS

1. Divination is an effort to know the future by using superstitious means. It attributes to creatures the power of knowing, or disclosing the future absolutely, whereas this power belongs to God alone. Therefore, divination is always a sin.

2. Divination often takes the form (indeed, this is usual) of an appeal to demons or devils for knowledge of the future, or for knowledge of what one should do now to achieve good or avoid trouble in time to come.

3. There are three major classes of divinations: direct invoking of demons; reading auguries; using other means of reading the future (dreams, necromancy or pretended apparitions, utterances of the dead, etc.).

4. The invoking of demons is unlawful, for it (a) involves an implicit pact with an evil spirit; (b) results in what is prejudicial to man's salvation.

5. Divination by the stars is a vain practice, for man's future is not determined by heavenly bodies. Besides, this is a practice into which evil spirits readily enter to find gullible victims for further bad influencing. Hence, divination by the stars is sinful.

6. Divination by dreams is also unlawful. God can indeed make use

of dreams and turn them into revealing visions. But unless God make manifest the character of a dream as a revelation, it is wrong to attach to the dream a prophetic value. Of course, a man may know that when he has dreams of a certain type, he is taking cold, or some such matter. This is not divination or superstition. Only when dreams are accepted as things preternatural and prophetic are they a variety of superstition, that is, of divination.

7. Auguries, omens, use of external superstitious practices as means of getting knowledge or guidance, are all forms of divination, and share its foolish and sinful character. The evil of using such things is in the assumption that the future *depends* on them. To read the natural signs of causes now in operation is not superstitious. Thus, to predict the morrow's weather from the clouds, or currents of air, or from the cry of birds, is not divination.

8. To draw lots in the sharing of goods, or in determining the winner of a prize, is not divination. But to draw lots to determine what course of action to pursue, with the assumption that fated necessity rules lives, and that somehow the chance selection of a card or the drawing of a straw will indicate what one is fated to enjoy or endure, is divination, and, in consequence, is foolish, unreasonable, and sinful.

96. SUPERSTITIOUS OBSERVANCES

1. It is futile and sinful to dabble in what is called *magic*, and to use charms, formulas of speech, or other devices, to obtain occult knowledge or to control events by evoking occult powers. To do such things is to employ superstitious observances. Of course, the magic here mentioned is not the skilled trickery of an entertainer, often called a magician, who diverts us with prestidigitation and legerdemain; his tricks are not superstitious practices. The magic we speak of as superstition is what people commonly call *black* magic. This sort of thing debases the mind, dishonors God, and opens the door to diabolical intervention.

2. The carrying or wearing of health charms, luck pieces, and the like, is, when done with serious intent of profiting by their use, a great evil; for such practice involves a belief in some preternatural force, other than God, which gives to the objects used a magical power. This belief is superstition, and is a sin against religion.

3. Fortunetelling is a superstitious and unlawful practice, whether it be done by consulting a person, or by using cards, reading tea leaves, looking in a crystal ball, or employing other inept and futile observances. Similarly, it is superstition to give serious belief to the omens of luck, good or bad, such as horseshoes, four-leaf clovers, the

breaking of a mirror, seeing a black cat, passing under a ladder, and so on.

4. The using of incantations (recited or chanted formulas of words or sounds) and the wearing of written words on the person, in the belief that such things have a protective power, are acts of superstition. Even sacred words and blessed objects such as medals must be used in the spirit of reverence to God, and never in the way of amulets or luck pieces.

97. IRRELIGION: TEMPTING GOD

1. To tempt a person is to put him to a test. To tempt God is to try, by word or deed, to test God's knowledge or power. Sometimes, indeed, the effort is not so much to test God, as a presumptuous reliance on God to supply what a man can readily do for himself. Thus a man who refuses to take medicine when he is seriously sick, and expects God to cure him, is guilty, in some measure, of tempting God. To expect miracles when no human means are at hand to meet an extreme situation, is not to tempt God. But to expect miracles to supply for one's own lack of effort, or for the sake of enjoying a kind of spectacular exhibition, is tempting God.

2. Therefore, tempting God is a sin. It usually involves a doubt of God's knowledge and power, and seeks to be sure about these—it puts God to the test. It is manifest that there is a wild inordinateness in this spectacle of a creature setting himself up to test and judge the infinite Creator upon whom the creature essentially depends. But one must not too quickly assume that what seems at first sight to be the sin of tempting God is actually such a sin. When, for instance, the apostles asked God to confirm their words with signs (that is, with miracles) they were not tempting God; they had no doubt of his knowledge and power; they sought no proof for themselves; they wished God to make manifest his truth to unbelievers, and to accredit his messengers. The apostles' petition came from full faith, and loving reliance on God; it did not spring from ignorance, doubt, or arrogance, as the sin of tempting God always does.

3. Tempting God is a sin against the virtue of religion because it is a direct act of irreverence towards God.

4. It does not seem that tempting God is so grievous an irreverence as superstition. The person who tempts God manifests a doubt of God's knowledge and power, and this may be a passing and temporary thing. But a person given to superstition is usually steeped and confirmed in irreligious error. As lasting irreverent error is worse than passing irreverent doubt, so superstition is worse than tempting God.

98. IRRELIGION: PERJURY

1. Perjury is a lie confirmed by an oath. It is the calling upon God to witness that truth is spoken, when, in fact, truth is not spoken. We hear the term *perjury* used mostly with reference to false evidence given by a witness in a court of law. But any lie confirmed by oath, in court or out, is perjury. Perjury involves an injury to God, and therefore is a sin against religion. It is also a great sin against commutative justice, for it ruins the necessary guarantee of honesty among men.

2. Thus, by its very nature, perjury is sinful, and is essentially a sin against religion.

3. And, again by its very nature, perjury is a mortal sin. For it is not only irreverence towards God; it is contempt of God, for it invokes Him to witness what the perjurer knows is not true.

4. We should not lightly demand an oath from others merely to assure ourselves that they are telling the truth; to require an oath, a matter must be serious and important, and one in which it is essential to know the exact truth. Private individuals should never demand an oath from a known liar; his oath would be meaningless in any case, and to require it is only to furnish him an occasion of sin. But a judge in court rightly demands an oath from every witness, even if he knows that this witness or that is wholly unreliable. For the judge acts in an official capacity, not a personal one, and the common good demands a consistent procedure of supporting court testimony by oath.

99. IRRELIGION: SACRILEGE

1. Sacrilege is the violation or misuse of what is sacred. Things that belong to the worship of God have, by their purpose and use, a certain sacredness. To violate or profane such things is to be irreverent to God for whose worship the things exist.

2. Sacrilege is a special sin opposed to the virtue of religion. St. John Damascene says that when the purple has been made into a royal robe we honor it, and that he who dishonors it is punished. So also when anything is made into the instrument of divine worship, it is sacred, and he who dishonors it does a special and punishable thing.

3. Sacrilege is not only found in the profane and irreverent use of sacred things; it is also found in irreverent treatment of sacred persons, and in irreverent conduct in sacred places. The worst sacrilege against persons is that of irreverent use of our Lord in the Blessed Sacrament; this terrible sin is committed by those who misuse or profane the sacred species, and by those who deliberately receive Communion unworthily. Sacrilege against persons is also committed by those who

offer physical indignity to persons consecrated to God by vow or by holy order. Sacrilege in things is found in the irreligious use of sacred vessels, vestments, images, relics, medals, and the like. Sacrilege in places is committed by whatever profanes the altar or the house of God.

4. Sacrilege is sometimes punished by the Church through excommunication or other censure. In Catholic countries, it is sometimes punished by civil laws also.

100. IRRELIGION: SIMONY

1. Simony is the sin of trying to buy or sell something spiritual, or something connected with what is spiritual. Simony takes its name from that of Simon Magus who tried to buy from the apostles the power of calling down the Holy Ghost by the imposing of hands (*see* Acts 8:18–24). Simony is a sin, because what is spiritual cannot be estimated at a material price; because God alone owns what is spiritual, while his ministers only dispense it; because spiritual things flow freely from God and are to be freely given by his clergy (Matt. 10:8): "Freely have you received; freely give." Therefore, simony is an irreverence to God, and consequently it is a sin against the virtue of religion.

2. The priests of the Church are to be supported materially by the people to whom they minister, for those that serve the altar are to live by the altar. But no priest or prelate dare sell, or try to sell, sacrament, or Mass, or benefice, or ecclesiastical office, for this would be the sin of simony.

3. As we have said elsewhere, it is right and lawful to give something for the support of those who administer spiritual things, in accordance with the customs approved by the Church. But in such giving (and in the receiving, too) there must be no hint or thought or slightest intention of buying and selling. Nor are people to be forced into making an offering by withholding spiritual things that should be administered.

4. Things annexed to what is spiritual cannot be bought or sold unless the things can be evaluated in material terms entirely apart from their quasi-spiritual character. Thus, certain rights of patronage and benefice may be sold, if it be made clear to all parties that the spiritual element does not enter into the transaction. Similarly, blessed articles, such as blessed candles, may be sold if nothing extra is added to the price by reason of the blessing. Yet certain blessed articles lose their blessing (and attached indulgences for pious use) if they are sold, even lawfully and not simoniacally.

5. To grant something spiritual as *remuneration* for a service, is

simony. For what is *paid* for a thing is estimated, or can be estimated, in terms of money.

6. Anything acquired simoniacally must be surrendered; it cannot justly be retained. Those guilty of the sin of simony are subject to penalties set down in church law.

PIETY AND OBSERVANCE

(QUESTIONS 101 TO 122)

101. PIETY

1. Piety is the virtue which disposes a person to show due deference, honor, and veneration to those who hold a place of excellence, and who have conferred benefit upon him. Piety is paid first to God, the supreme excellence, the giver of all good gifts. Secondly, piety is honor and veneration shown to parents. Further, piety is due reverence and respect paid to kinsfolk, to superiors in Church or state, to one's government itself and its allies and friends.

2. Piety, as the reverent respect and honor paid to parents, is usually called *filial* piety. It is a virtue, and therefore consists in more than suitable outward conduct; it involves the heart and mind and will; it means looking after one's parents, lending them needed support, making sacrifice to give them care and comfort in their age, and seeing that they are well attended in illness.

3. Piety is a special virtue which springs from justice. It is specified (that is, given its character as a distinct virtue on its own account) by the fact that a special debt is owed to the principle of one's being— God first, and then parents. The same virtue extends to those that represent the principle of spiritual and political citizenship, that is, leaders in Church and government.

4. Piety and religion are two virtues. They never come into conflict, for virtue never clashes with virtue. Yet in performing the acts of virtues, a person may find himself in conflicting circumstances. In such a case, the essential worship of God must not be neglected out of a mistaken notion of piety towards parents. On the other hand, real neglect of duty to parents cannot be brushed aside in the name of religion. Thus, a man would do wrong to defer his baptism because of

parental objection. And a man would do wrong to neglect sick or needy parents so that he might send an alms to a charitable organization, or have means to enable him to attend a religious convention or congress.

102. OBSERVANCE

1. Observance, as allied to piety, is a *subordinate* yet a *distinct* virtue. By observance, one gives honor and respect to those who are in positions of *dignity*. Piety reveres excellence to which gratitude is owed. Observance reveres excellence in itself.

2. Those who occupy positions of dignity have excellence of office. And they *should* have excellence in exercising the powers of that office. On both scores, they deserve respect and honor. This respect and honor is shown them by the virtue of observance.

3. Piety is a greater virtue than observance is. For piety reverences those who are in some way akin to us (by creation, blood, or favors conferred), and with these we have stronger bonds than with others whom we are to revere by way of observance.

103. VENERATION OR DULIA

1. Honor paid to God may be wholly spiritual and in the heart, and it may also be expressed in outward acts and signs. But honor paid to creatures is external, for creatures cannot read the heart. The respect we have inwardly for creatures does not truly honor them until it is *shown* to them, and this cannot be except in external signs. We honor creatures by words, deeds, sensible signs, salutations, tributes, statues, and so on.

2. Honor or veneration is owed to persons of excellence, whether this be a general or a particular excellence, whether it be official or personal excellence.

3. The honor and veneration due to men is called by the Greek name of *dulia*. This is distinct from the honor and veneration paid to God, which is *latria*.

4. There are no essentially different kinds of *dulia,* but it may be accidentally diversified by the various human relationships on which it is founded.

104. OBEDIENCE

1. Obedience is the virtue of conforming ones conduct to the command of a superior.

2. Obedience is a special virtue. Its specific object is a command, expressed or understood. It is a moral virtue, that is, a will-virtue. Obedience is subordinate to the virtue of justice.

3. Obedience is perfectly practiced when it proceeds out of justice through charity. In measuring the greatness of obedience as a virtue, we must not fail to grasp its debt to these fundamental virtues of justice and charity. In itself, obedience is not so great a virtue as the two virtues that give it perfect effectiveness and value.

4. God is to be obeyed always and in all things. For God is the absolute lord of all, the creator and owner of every creature. Justice demands that all creatures should submit wholly to God's will.

5. Human superiors are to be obeyed within the sphere of their authority. They are not to be obeyed when their command is in conflict with the law of God.

6. Obedience to the civil law is the duty of citizens. And Christians, more than others, should understand that the civil order is necessary to man, and that it cannot be preserved without obedience to justly established human law. Yet no citizen is to obey a law that contravenes the law of God. When St. Peter and St. John were ordered by the Council to "speak no more in this name [Jesus]," they answered (Acts 4:19): "If it be just in the sight of God to hear you rather than God, judge ye." A civil law that conflicts with the law of God, is not a law at all, for a law is essentially "an ordinance of reason"; it is complete *unreason* for men to legislate against the supreme legislator.

105. DISOBEDIENCE

1. Disobedience is the refusal to conform to the command of a superior. We have seen that obedience is a virtue; it follows that disobedience is a vice. And when a just command, a requirement of law, is disregarded *with contempt,* we have disobedience of a seriously sinful character. Many acts of disobedience are venial faults, because they are done with thoughtlessness, or for some purpose other than merely contemning the law and thus practically denying man's duty to submit to law. Such acts do not show the full character of disobedience as a vice.

2. For real disobedience is *essentially* a contempt of just precept or command. A greater sin is contempt of preceptor and commander. Hence, disobedience is not so great a sin as blasphemy, for instance, or murder; these sins involve contempt for God's law, and also contempt for God himself as the supreme excellence and the master of life and death.

106. GRATITUDE

1. By the virtue of religion, we pay God due honor. By the virtue of piety, we honor God, parents, kinsfolk, and country. By observance,

we venerate persons of excellence. By *gratitude,* we give thanks to benefactors. Gratitude is a special virtue, allied to justice and subordinate to it.

2. An innocent man owes God thanks for innocence; a forgiven sinner owes God thanks for pardon. Innocence in itself is greater than forgiveness; yet to the man forgiven, forgiveness is the greater gift of the two. For forgiveness meets that man's necessity as nothing else could do. As a small but essential help given to a poor man is more to the receiver than a great gift bestowed on a man of wealth, so forgiveness is a greater gift to the penitent sinner than the gift of innocence to one who is without sin to forgive. Hence it seems that the forgiven sinner owes to the bestower of this gift a greater gratitude than an innocent person would owe.

3. We are to render thanks to every benefactor. We owe thanks to God, and, under God, to many of our fellowmen. Gratitude should be *expressed* in words and deeds according to circumstances and opportunities.

4. Gratitude makes instant acknowledgment of favors by graciousness in receiving them, and by the thankful disposition of the heart. Favors themselves are to be repaid at a time convenient to the benefactor.

5. In repaying a favor and in estimating our debt, we take into consideration the disposition of our benefactor even more than the gift he has bestowed. Seneca remarks (*De Benef.* 1) that we are sometimes under greater obligation to one who confers a small favor with a large heart, than to one who gives something greater in a grudging spirit.

6. The return of a favor, the repayment, should *exceed* in graciousness the favor received. Gratitude is due for what is freely given. An exact return of the favor received meets the moral obligation of the beneficiary, but does not include the gratitude he owes. Gratitude is something freely given over and above the amount of repayment. Hence, gratitude exceeds the favor received.

107. INGRATITUDE

1. Gratitude is a virtue. Its direct opposite is therefore a vice. Ingratitude is the vice which stands opposed to the virtue of gratitude.

2. The vice of ingratitude finds expression in sins of ingratitude. Acts or sins of ingratitude are of three types: (a) failure to return a favor received; (b) failure to express thanks for a favor; (c) failure to notice that one has received a favor at all. These types of ungrateful

acts are *degrees,* and are rated, in the order given, as bad, worse, and worst of all.

3. Conscious ingratitude is always a sin, mortal or venial, according to the nature of the ungrateful act and the conditions of its doing. When ingratitude is complete, it is combined with contempt for the duty and obligation imposed by gratitude, and this can make it a mortal sin. Usually, however, human ingratitude is a matter of negligence or carelessness.

4. We are not to refuse a favor to a person who has proved himself ungrateful. For we are the children of God, who does not cease to shower his gifts on sinners who offend him. We are meant to imitate God.

108. VENGEANCE

1. Vengeance is the inflicting of corrective punishment on an offender. We speak of vengeance here, not as an inordinate desire for revenge, which is always sinful, but as a virtue subordinate to justice. Vengeance is the virtue which restores the equality of justice upset by an offense. The perfect and permanent establishment of equality of justice will be attained at the end of time, for God says (Heb. 10:30): "Vengeance is mine; I will repay."

2. Among men, vengeance as a virtue seeks to remove harm done and to prevent its recurrence. It stems from justice, and must be suffused with charity. The parent who punishes a disobedient child exercises vengeance as a virtue; so does a judge in court imposing a suitable penalty. A person sins *by excess* when he administers vengeance with cruelty or brutality; he sins *by deficiency* when he is remiss to administer correctives that should be administered.

3. True vengeance always tends to the prevention of evil. Persons who will not be moved by positive virtue to preserve the equality of justice, must be prevented from doing evil by fear of losing what they love. Now, the things a man loves most in this world are: his life; his bodily safety and comfort; his freedom; his possessions; his country; and, his good name. Hence, civil laws exact vengeance by prescribing for offenders: death, bodily punishment, imprisonment, fines, exile and ignominy. Under fear of such evils, many who would offend are constrained to observe justice. And those who are subjected to the vengeance of the law, are taught themselves, or teach others by what they undergo, that evils are not to be done.

4. No one justly suffers vengeance save as a punishment for sinful offense. Hence, vengeance never afflicts those whose offense is in-

voluntary, and therefore not sinful. Hardship, indeed, may come heavily upon a person without fault on his part; such hardship is, under God's providence, always medicinal, and has in view the greater good or higher merit of him who suffers it. And in matters spiritual, no one is ever punished without fault. Among men, certain hardships are sometimes inflicted (such, for instance, as disqualification for an office because of a parent's fault), and indeed public order sometimes requires such things. But these hardships are not really the effects of vengeance at all.

109. TRUTHFULNESS

1. Truthfulness or veracity is the conforming of speech with fact, or, at any rate, with fact *as known*. It is the agreement of what is in the mind with what is on the lips. Truthfulness is a virtue, and a moral virtue.

2. Truthfulness is a special virtue, distinct from others. Goodness is the end and object of every moral virtue, and each special virtue is *specified,* or made a distinct virtue on its own account, by the special aspect of goodness which it seeks or serves. Now, the goodness which truthfulness specifically seeks and serves is that of agreement between thought and speech. Hence, truthfulness is a special virtue.

3. St. Jerome speaks of the truth of life, the truth of justice, and the truth of doctrine. The truth of life means the sum total of all virtues that can perfect a person; the truth of justice is justice itself; the truth of doctrine is true teaching. Truthfulness as a moral virtue is not one of these three objective types of truth; it is a subsidiary or subordinate virtue, yet a distinct one, included under justice. Justice requires balance and due equality. Now, there are balance and due equality, in a moral sense, when what is said agrees with what is known.

4. Truthfulness as a virtue inclines a person to moderate expression and avoids exaggeration. It does not demand that a man tell all he knows; it demands only that what he does tell be the truth as he knows it. Its obligation is not, in itself, a requirement to tell everything; its obligation is that a person speaking must not tell lies.

110. LYING

1. Lying or mendacity is a vice opposed to the virtue of truthfulness. A lie is the intentional telling of a falsehood. But the *intention to deceive* does not enter into the essence of a lie. Any serious statement which is opposed to the truth as known by the speaker is a lie, whether the speaker intends to deceive anyone or not. And if a speaker says

what he honestly thinks is true, but is, in fact, not true, the speaker does not tell a lie. His words make the *material* for a lie, but they lack the *form* or essential determinant of a lie. The essential determinant, or form, of a lie is the intention to speak falsely.

2. Lies are called officious, jocose, or mischievous, according as they are told for profit or convenience, for pleasure or entertainment, or for the purpose of hurting someone or causing trouble. The mischievous lie is the worst of lies; it is often called a *malicious* lie, for it is the fruit of malice or bad will.

3. A lie is always evil. For it is an inordinate and unreasonable thing, and hence an evil, to employ speech, which is the natural instrument for expressing what is in the mind, as a means of expressing what is not in the mind. It is not evil to *evade* a question; that is, it is not evil, except under extraordinary circumstances, to keep what one knows to oneself. But it is evil to tell lies. Similarly, it is not evil to elude the salesman who wishes us to buy something; it is not evil to keep one's money in one's pocket; but it is evil to buy what the salesman offers with counterfeit money. It is not evil either to speak in figurative language, provided those who hear can, or should, understand what is meant.

4. A malicious lie may be a mortal sin, for it can be a grave offense against charity and justice as well as against truthfulness. But jocose lies (when they are really lies at all) and officious lies are usually venially sinful. A jocose lie often fails to have the character of a lie because it is not a *serious* statement; those who utter such things, and those who hear, are well aware that the speaker is not manifesting his mind, his knowledge, or his convictions, but is merely jesting.

111. DISSIMULATION AND HYPOCRISY

1. What a lie is in words, dissimulation is in outward action. Hence, dissimulation has the character and evil of lying. Yet not every pretense is dissimulation; there is figurative action as well as figurative speech.

2. Hypocrisy is a kind of dissimulation. A man is a *simulator* when his actions express any falsity. He is a *hypocrite* only when the falsity which his actions express is that he is a better, or wiser, or holier person than he actually is.

3. All dissimulation is a lie in action. Hypocrisy is a type of dissimulation. Therefore hypocrisy is a lie in action, and consequently it is a sin.

4. Hypocrisy (and, indeed, all dissimulation) is a mortal or a venial sin, according to the end intended by the simulator or hypocrite.

If this end be directly opposed to charity, and is a matter of importance, the sin is mortal.

112. BOASTING

1. Boasting is the making of false claims in praise of one's own qualities or prowess; it is an attempt to lift oneself above what one really is. Boasting amounts to excessive and unjustified claims; and these, in turn, amount to lying. Hence, boasting has the evil of lying.

2. Boasting usually amounts to a jocose lie. It is so in the case of a man who "likes to hear himself talk," and who delights in bragging for its own sake. Or it may be an officious lie, as it is in a person who recommends himself for a position by making excessive claims of ability. In most cases, boasting does not exceed venial sin.

113. IRONY

1. In our present study, irony does not have its usual meaning as a kind of ridicule or mockery. It has the original Greek meaning of dissimulation of one's good qualities; it means *pretending*, not in honesty and humility but dishonestly, that one is less or worse than one actually is. Thus understood, irony has the character of dissimulation and lying.

2. One lie may be worse than another either in the *matter lied about* or in the *motive* of the liar. Now, irony and boasting deal with the same *matter*, for both are a speaker's words about himself. But the two things differ in motive. And the motive of boasting is usually viler than the motive of irony. The boaster wishes to glorify himself in the opinion of others; the ironical person rather wishes to avoid the offense of seeming prideful or snobbish. Yet sometimes irony is worse than boasting; it is so, for example, when it is used as a cunning means of deceiving persons with a view to subsequent cheating.

114. FRIENDLINESS

1. Friendliness or affability is a virtue subordinate to justice which seeks the balance and order of all things, including human relations. Friendliness thus has a special aspect of good to achieve, and is therefore a special virtue.

2. A virtue annexed to another is called a *part* or a *potential* part of that other. In this sense, friendliness or affability is a part of justice. It does not cover the whole ground of justice, and therefore is not identical with justice; it is annexed to justice, but is distinct from that virtue.

115. FLATTERY OR ADULATION

1. Friendliness or affability is a virtue which strives to make things pleasant. But there are situations in which the effort of friendliness must fail of its object: that is, particular cases in which people cannot or will not be friendly. In such situations, flattery is likely to show itself. Flattery is a sort of lying, and has the evil of lying. It is the effort to please people by praising them for good qualities they do not possess, or approving their bad qualities which should be condemned. Flattery usually has the ulterior view of getting something from those who are subjected to it.

2. Unless flattery is praise of a person's sin or is meant to draw him into sin, it is usually a venial, not a mortal sin.

116. QUARRELING

1. Quarreling is a disagreement between people, an altercation in words. When a person makes no effort to be agreeable, contradicts what people say, and gives occasion for bickering, he is quarrelsome. Quarreling is opposed to friendliness or affability.

2. Quarreling seems to be a worse evil than flattery, for the quarrelsome man causes displeasure and the flatterer tries to increase pleasure. Yet sometimes flattery, by reason of the motive behind it, is worse than quarreling.

117. LIBERALITY OR GENEROSITY

1. Liberality is a virtue, for it puts to good use the things that might be used for evil purposes—such, for instance, as money or other material things.

2. And, indeed, liberality deals, first and foremost, with money. A liberal man is an open-handed man, who is ready to "liberate" money from his own possession, and thus shows that he is not inordinately attached to it.

3. The proper act of liberality, therefore, consists in making good use of money. Liberality demands that one's debts be paid, and that suitable gifts be made. Merely to be careless with money, neglecting to save what is needed to meet expenses and to have the means of making gifts, is not liberality.

4. Parting with money by giving it to others is a greater act of virtue than parting with it in fulfilling one's own desires, that is, spending it on oneself. The liberal man is praised for *giving*.

5. Liberality seems to be allied with justice, even though it gives

more than is strictly due. Therefore, it is reckoned by many as a part of justice, that is, a virtue connected with justice but not having equal scope with it.

6. Liberality is a gracious and notable virtue, but it is not the greatest of virtues.

118. COVETOUSNESS

1. Covetousness is an inordinate love of possessing. It is in conflict with sound reason, and is therefore a sin.

2. Covetousness, as the immoderate love of getting and possessing money, is a special sin. It is a general sin inasmuch as its scope is extended to include inordinate desire of possessing anything: goods, position, knowledge.

3. As a special sin or vice, covetousness stands directly opposed to the virtue of liberality.

4. To covet riches to such a degree as to be willing to do anything whatever to possess them, is a mortal sin. Most sins of covetousness, however, are venial sins.

5. Covetousness, since it can be a venial fault, is not the greatest of sins. Yet great sins indeed may be born of the covetous spirit. The vice of covetousness is hard to cure, but it can be cured.

6. Covetousness is not a sin of the flesh, but of the spirit; it is a spiritual sin, not a carnal sin. For though the riches coveted are material things, the evil of covetousness is in the desire for satisfaction in the possession of these things, and not in the things themselves.

7. Covetousness is that "love of money" which is the root of evil. Many evils sprout from this root. It is therefore listed among the capital sins.

8. A capital sin is a source-sin, a spring from which other sins readily flow. The sins which flow most readily from covetousness, and are therefore called "daughters of covetousness," are the following: fraud, lying, perjury, dissatisfaction or restlessness, violence, and hardheartedness.

119. PRODIGALITY

1. Prodigality is an evil by excess at the points where covetousness sins by defect, and vice versa. Thus, in interior desire for riches, covetousness is excessive, prodigality is defective. But in using riches, covetousness is defective, and prodigality is excessive. For prodigality is the careless and foolish squandering of riches.

2. Prodigality is manifestly an evil, for it conflicts with right reason.

Aristotle (*Ethic.* ɪᴠ 1) says of the prodigal man that his giving is not good, nor for a good purpose, nor is it regulated by reason.

3. But prodigality, in itself, is not so grievous a fault as covetousness, because: (a) it is less unreasonable; (b) it does some good, whereas covetousness does none; (c) it is an evil more readily cured than covetousness is.

120. EQUITY

1. Equity, sometimes called by the Greek term *epikeia,* interprets the mind of the lawgiver as to the fact and extent of the law's application in a particular case. Laws have to be general; they cannot express details of every possible case that may in any manner fall under their direction. Lawgivers have their mind and intention on what ordinarily happens. Therefore, in an extraordinary case, the law, which regularly works for good, may impose an evil. It is the part of prudence and justice to interpret the true meaning of the law as touching extraordinary individual cases, and to discover the *spirit* of the law when the *letter* is of dubious or evil application. Such interpreting and applying of law are done by *epikeia* or *equity.*

2. *Epikeia* or equity is a virtue. It is a *part* of the virtue of justice.

121. PIETY AS A GIFT

1. We have seen that the *virtue* of piety disposes a person to venerate those who have excellence and who bestow benefit on him. Piety thus venerates God, parents, kinsfolk, and country. Now we speak of the supernatural piety which is a gift of the Holy Ghost. By this gift a person exercises the supernatural virtue of filial piety towards God, and worships him as the all-perfect and all-loving Father.

2. Because *meekness* removes from the soul the obstacles which obstruct the exercise of piety towards God as our Father, it is said that the gift of piety finds a special correspondence in the second beatitude: "Blessed are the meek, for they shall possess the earth" (Matt. 5:4).

122. THE PRECEPTS OF JUSTICE

1. Justice regulates our dealings with others—God and fellowman. The Ten Commandments (called the Decalogue) are therefore precepts of justice. The first three commandments regulate our activities towards God; they deal with religion, which, indeed, is the chief part of justice. The fourth commandment regulates piety, which is a part of justice. The other six commandments regulate our just dealing with other men.

2. Since man's first need is truth about God, and direction to God and away from false belief and false worship, it is right that the very first commandment of the decalogue should meet this need: "I am the Lord thy God. . . . Thou shalt not have strange gods before me" (Exod. 20:2, 3). This commandment expresses a requirement of justice.

3. The second commandment, "Thou shalt not take the name of the Lord thy God in vain" (Exod. 20:7), prohibits at once the lack of reverence which would hinder the full accord of human wills with the first commandment. This too is a precept of justice.

4. External worship is most proper in itself, and is also of the greatest value to man. It is indicated as an obligation of justice by the third commandment of the decalogue.

5. Immediately after the commandments which require just recognition of the First Principle of our being, comes the commandment which regulates our attitude and conduct towards the proximate principle of our being, our parents.

6. After the precepts of religion and piety, all of which are precepts of justice, come the six remaining precepts which belong to justice simply, and direct our duty towards all mankind.

FORTITUDE

(QUESTIONS 123 TO 140)

123. THE VIRTUE OF FORTITUDE

1. We speak of fortitude as a virtue. In another place we shall discuss the gift of the Holy Ghost which has the same name. Fortitude is the virtue which enables a person to withstand the greatest difficulties that block him from attaining his true goal.

2. It is the special business of fortitude to stand up to grave difficulties and dangers. Since it has a special business, a special aim and purpose, it serves good in a special way, and is a special virtue. This means that fortitude is specifically distinct from other virtues, and is a clear-cut virtue on its own account.

3. Fortitude puts down the paralysis of fear that would keep a person from facing up to danger. On the other hand, it moderates

daring or courage which, without it, might lead a man to wildly impulsive and ineffective action.

4. In strictest interpretation of its meaning, fortitude is the virtue of bravely facing the danger of death. A man capable of meeting with fortitude this greatest of dangers is not daunted by lesser perils.

5. Therefore, fortitude is a soldierly virtue which faces danger of death in defense of a just cause, whether in actual war, or in the warring we wage in daily life against the enemies of our soul and its salvation. Fortitude is the hero's virtue, the martyr's virtue; it faces death bravely in spite of inner fears. Fortitude strengthens the soldier in war; fortitude helps a man practice religion in the face of derision and persecution; fortitude enables a person to care for the sick or to bury the dead in spite of the serious risk of deadly infection.

6. The chief act of fortitude is that of enduring, of bearing up, of seeing the business through. It is not alone the virtue of coming to grips with danger; it is also the holding on.

7. The brave man cherishes fortitude as something good in itself, and he strives to have it, to preserve it, and to manifest it in action when occasion calls for its exercise.

8. The man of fortitude has delight of soul in his strong endurance for good. Yet he must bear threat and hardship, pain, and perhaps death; in these trials, as such, there is no delight, but sorrow.

9. Fortitude is a virtue which meets danger as it comes, and often it comes suddenly and without warning. But fortitude endures because it is seated in the soul as a habit, and therefore it involves long forethought and preparation by which a man is made ready for sudden assaults.

10. Into the action of a brave man under the stress of attack and serious danger, there enters an element of anger; not immoderate, but moderate anger.

11. Fortitude is a fundamental or *cardinal* virtue. It is an aid to every other virtue as a bulwark of steadfastness, and helps other virtues attain their ends despite what blocks and deters them.

12. Fortitude is a great and necessary virtue, but it is not the most excellent of all. Of the four cardinal virtues, the descending order of excellence is as follows: prudence is first, justice second, fortitude third, and temperance fourth.

124. MARTYRDOM

1. The Greek word *martyr* means a witness. A martyr, then, in the meaning of a person who dies for the faith, is one who bears witness to the truth, and will not withdraw his testimony even though it cost

him his life. Martyrdom is an act of virtue standing firm for truth and justice against all persecution.

2. The virtue of which martyrdom is an act is the virtue of fortitude. Some have said that martyrdom for the faith is an act of faith; some have called martyrdom an act of love for truth; some have considered martyrdom an act of the virtue of patience. But the real essence of martyrdom is its *enduring* with faith, love, and patience, the terrors and pains of deadly persecution. Therefore, primarily, martyrdom is an act of fortitude.

3. Indeed, charity or love for the cause for which a martyr suffers, is so prominent a feature of martyrdom that it makes it an act of the greatest perfection. Fortitude is not, in itself, the most excellent of virtues, and yet this act of fortitude is a most excellent act. This is so because martyrdom is suffused with charity which, as scripture says (Col. 3:14), is "the bond of perfection."

4. Martyrdom, in completeness and perfection, consists in suffering death for the sake of a cause. Christian martyrdom is dying for the sake of Christ. For, until death has ended all his acts, a man has not given full and complete demonstration of his unshakable endurance and his unchanging will.

5. All the virtuous acts of a Christian are professions of his faith. Therefore, all the virtues from which the virtuous acts come may be assigned, each in turn, as the causes of martyrdom. For a person can, under persecution, be called upon to suffer death as the alternative for clinging steadfastly to any one of the Christian virtues. Yet, in every case, it is the faith which the virtue represents that is the chief target of attack. Hence, we may say that the faith, or the truth of the faith, is the cause of the act of martyrdom in the martyr.

125. TIMIDITY OR COWARDLINESS

1. Sin puts disorder into human acts. Now, *fear* which is ordinate, and in line with right reason, helps a man shun what he ought to shun; this is a good fear, not a sinful fear. Indeed, when such ordinate fear is imparted as a supernatural dower to the soul, it is called the gift of fear; it is one of the seven gifts of the Holy Ghost. But *inordinate* fear leads a man to avoid what virtue requires him to face and endure. This is the sinful fear called cowardice or timidity.

2. Fear shrinks from what is apprehended as evil, and especially from the physical evil of death. Fortitude stands up to such evils. It is evident, therefore, that sinful fear stands opposed to the virtue of fortitude.

3. Sinful fear is often a venial sin. But it can be a mortal sin. It is mortal sin when it makes a man ready to violate divine law in serious matters in order to escape what is feared. Thus the fear that leads a man to deny the faith rather than endure martyrdom, is a mortally sinful fear.

4. Yet fear diminishes a man's responsibility somewhat, and, to that extent, excuses from sin. For fear is a stress which bears on the will and hampers its free choice. What is done from a motive of fear, however great, is indeed *simply* voluntary, but at the same time is *in some sense* involuntary, since it would not be done except for the stress of fear. Hence, an act done through fear is a mixture of voluntary and involuntary. But it is voluntary enough to make a man responsible, even for mortal sin.

126. INSENSIBILTY TO FEAR

1. If a man, from lack of love, or from pride, should be wholly without fear in any circumstance, he would be guilty of an evil. Such insensibility is in conflict with reason. If, however, insensibility comes merely from dullness of mind, which is not a man's own fault, it is not a sinful insensibility.

2. Insensibility to fear is opposed to fortitude. The virtue of fortitude regulates or moderates fear, so that a man faces grave danger in spite of it. But insensibility is a dullness, stupidity, or pride which has no fear to regulate. Fortitude faces dangers; to insensibility, there are no dangers.

127. FOOLHARDINESS

1. Foolhardiness consists in action that is overbold, unreasonably daring. It is in conflict with reason, and hence is an evil or sin.

2. Foolhardiness sins against the virtue of fortitude by excess. It is not a reasonable, and even heroic, enduring of danger, but a foolish and unreasonable rushing into dangers that need not be encountered. Fortitude regulates fears and impulses in the face of danger; foolhardiness is ill-regulated and wildly impulsive. Hence foolhardiness conflicts with fortitude.

128. THE PARTS OF FORTITUDE

1. The *parts* of a virtue are its subsidiary or associated virtues; that is, virtues aligned with it, but not coextensive with it. The parts of fortitude are listed by Cicero (*De Inv. Rhet.* III) as: (a) magnificence, or lofty undertaking, with noble purpose of mind; (b) confidence, or

firm hope in the undertaking; (c) patience, or prolonged endurance for virtue's sake; (d) perseverance, or fixed persistence in a well-considered purpose.

129. MAGNANIMITY

1. Magnanimity (which literally means large-mindedness), is a kind of stretching forth of the mind to great deeds. Now, an act or a deed is great, either (a) when it is the best use of the best things, and this is *absolute* greatness; or (b) when it is the very good use of a lesser thing, and this is *proportional* greatness.

2. Among external things, high and true honors are the best. With respect to possessing these honors and manifesting them nobly, man is said to be *magnanimous.*

3. Magnanimity shows itself in greatness of courage for obtaining or defending what is noble and honorable. It is a reasonable, regulated, and settled habit of mind; hence, it is a virtue.

4. Honor is the reward of every virtue, and therefore magnanimity has a reference to all the virtues. Yet it is a special virtue, for it focuses upon a special phase of good.

5. Magnanimity accords with fortitude in strengthening the mind and will to endure difficulty in view of a noble end. Thus magnanimity is a *part* of fortitude.

6. Cicero seems to indicate magnanimity when he assigns *confidence* as a part of fortitude. Confidence is a firm trust or hope in an assurance given, whether by the word of a man, or by the condition of affairs. Since confidence means strong hope that good will be attained despite difficulties, it is a noble expectation that appears to belong to magnanimity.

7. Security is not the same as confidence; security denotes freedom from care and fear; it consists in being strong against worry, and enemies, and misfortune. Thus, security belongs directly to fortitude, whereas confidence belongs directly to magnanimity and, through magnanimity, to fortitude.

8. In so far as goods of fortune (riches, power, friends) are honorable in themselves and are apt instruments for virtuous uses, these goods are conducive to magnanimity.

130. PRESUMPTION

1. Presumption, as we use the word here, means the immoderate and unreasonable assuming that one can do what actually lies beyond one's power to perform. Since presumption conflicts with reason, it is sinful.

2. Presumption is an evil opposed to magnanimity. For magnanimity is greatness of mind and purpose for honorable achievement which, however difficult, lies within a person's power to attain. But presumption reaches with ill-founded confidence for what lies beyond its power to grasp.

131. AMBITION

1. Desire for honors is good when it includes recognition that what is truly honorable is from God, and that the honor itself is ultimately to be referred to God. Now, the desire for honors which a man wishes for himself without referring them to God, is sinful ambition.

2. Sinful ambition is opposed to the virtue of magnanimity, because the desire or love of honors, which magnanimity regulates, is manifested without regulation in ambition.

132. VAINGLORY

1. *Glory,* in the present use of the term, means praise that is given to excellence displayed. Such praise may be from many persons, or from few, or from one, or even from oneself. Now, glory can be vain in three ways: (a) when it is praise for something unworthy; (b) when it is praise given by unworthy persons; (c) when it is praise unrelated to God directly, or indirectly as contributing to the spiritual good of man. For any of these reasons, glory is called *vainglory.* Vainglory is manifestly an inordinateness, and is therefore a sin.

2. Magnanimity refers to honors, and glory is an effect of honor; thus true glory falls into the field of magnanimity. Therefore vainglory, the opposite of true glory, is an evil opposed to magnanimity.

3. It is possible for vainglory to be a serious sin, but, for the most part, it is a venial sin. In itself, it is not necessarily opposed to charity. When, accidentally, it is brought into conflict with charity, it is a mortal sin.

4. Vainglory is not mentioned in the list of capital sins. Yet St. Gregory (*Moral.* xxxi) names it with pride. He says that pride is the greatest vice and is found in all sins, but that vainglory is an immediate offspring of pride, and should be named as one of the capital sins.

5. St. Gregory further says that vainglory, as a capital sin, gives direct rise to disobedience, boastfulness, hypocrisy, contention, obstinacy, discord, and the craze for what is new. These vices, St. Gregory calls "the daughters of vainglory."

133. FAINTHEARTEDNESS OR PUSILLANIMITY

1. Faintheartedness or pusillanimity is a culpable disposition to refuse to face up to situations of difficulty that one might well handle and overcome. By presumption, a man takes on more than he can handle; by faintheartedness, a man refuses to do what he can. This faintheartedness is a sin. The servant who buried his one talent because he was too fainthearted to engage in trade with it, was punished, as for a sin (Matt., chap. 15).

134. MAGNIFICENCE

1. The word magnificence which is commonly used to mean rich display, really means "doing great things." In this literal meaning, magnificence is a virtue.

2. Magnificence not only means the perfection of other virtues, but it is a special virtue itself. For magnificence has a special aspect of goodness in view, namely, the doing of something great—in quantity, quality, value, dignity—and thus it is specified as a virtue.

3. In external great works, magnificence requires large expenditure of money. Aristotle (*Ethic.* iv 2) says that magnificence, unlike liberality, does not belong to all uses of money, but only to the larger transactions. In splendid external matters, magnificence regulates the outlay of money: on the one hand, it curbs the love of money which would scamp the work; on the other hand, it prevents mere garish display. Thus it worthily meets the high demands of a truly great external work.

4. As a virtue, magnificence is allied with fortitude. For while magnificence does not face up to danger, it does face up to difficulty. It demands the difficult surrender of large amounts of one's possessions; it demands a lot of money.

135. MEANNESS OR LITTLENESS

1. Magnificence aspires to great things and does not shrink from paying for them. Yet it is not foolish, nor over-lavish, nor wasteful; for it is a virtue, and therefore an ordinate thing, a thing in good relation to reason. Opposed to this virtue of magnificence is the vice of littleness or meanness. This vice either (a) aspires to little things only, when greater should be attempted; or (b) exercises a pinchpenny care which refuses to noble enterprise its full greatness of execution.

2. Magnificence, to which littleness or meanness is opposed, is not the direct contrary of this vice. For magnificence stands *between* two opposed vices, namely, meanness on the one hand, and wastefulness

or prodigality on the other. A mean man spends less than his undertaking is worth; a wasteful man spends more than the work deserves.

136. PATIENCE

1. Patience is the virtue by which a man bears up against the evils that tend to make him sad and to break his spirit. St. Augustine (*De Patientia* 1) says that patience is a virtue, and a great gift of God.

2. In estimating the relative excellence of virtues, we say, first of all, that those virtues which actively incline a man to do good are greater than those which incline him to avoid evil. And, among the virtues inclining a person to avoid evil, those are greater which check the greatest and strongest impulse to evil. On these considerations, we see that patience is not the greatest of virtues. Patience ranks after the theological virtues, and after the cardinal virtues.

3. Patience, as a virtue, comes from love or charity; that is, from the grace and friendship of God. We speak, of course, of supernatural patience. For patience is possible only when the soul loves something good with a love strong enough to make it bear up under oppressing evils. Patience cannot be a *perfect* virtue unless "the love of God above all" is its core and essence.

4. Patience, as the suffering "with untroubled mind, the evils inflicted by others," is a virtue aligned with fortitude, and it is called a *part* of fortitude.

5. We bear by *patience* the heavy trials of life. We bear by *longsuffering* or longanimity continued, long enduring evils. In both virtues, our strong and steady effort manifests *constancy*. Thus, longsuffering and constancy have much in common with patience. But they are not wholly identified with it.

137. PERSEVERANCE

1. Perseverance is the virtue which disposes a person to hold steadily to a good purpose, keeping the end steadily in view, despite delays, fatigue, and temptations to indifference.

2. Perseverance is a *part* of the virtue of fortitude.

3. Constancy and perseverance agree in point of steadfastness. But these are not identical virtues. Constancy stands firm against stresses external to the virtue practiced; perseverance stands firm under the weariness that comes from the effort of the virtue itself.

4. Perseverance as a supernatural virtue requires grace. And as the act of "persevering unto the end in Christ," perseverance is a special and freely bestowed gift of God.

138. VICES OPPOSED TO PERSEVERANCE

1. Opposed to perseverance is the vice of softness or effeminacy, which tends to give way under the effort of sustained virtue, even when the stress is slight. Effeminacy takes no joy in good, and quickly wearies of it.

2. Also opposed to perseverance is pertinacity, which is the vice of headstrong, stubborn, opinionated people who want their own way rather than what is right, and who wish to humble and defeat their opponents. While effeminacy falls short of perseverance, and sins by defect or deficiency, pertinacity runs ahead of perseverance and sins by excess. Cicero (*De Inv. Rhet.* II) says that pertinacity is to perseverance as superstition is to religion.

139. THE GIFT OF FORTITUDE

1. We have considered fortitude as a virtue. We are to speak of fortitude now as one of the seven gifts of the Holy Ghost. Fortitude as a virtue disposes a person to firmness in good, despite great dangers. Fortitude as a gift of God moves a man to steadfastness in perils, and gives him confident hope of eternal life at the last. The gift makes the exercise of the virtue easier, richer, more confident.

2. The gift of fortitude moves man to virtuous living, which is difficult, and gives him a spiritual desire for "the works of justice" (as virtuous deeds in general are called). This spiritual desire is comparable to the bodily desire of a man for food and drink. Thus, the gift of fortitude stands in correspondence with the fourth beatitude (Matt. 5:6): "Blessed are they that hunger and thirst after justice."

140. THE PRECEPTS OF FORTITUDE

1. All divine laws which direct man towards heaven are precepts of fortitude inasmuch as the way to heaven is beset with temptations and dangers that a man must steadfastly overcome.

2. The virtues annexed to fortitude—patience, perseverance, magnanimity, constancy—involve laws of virtuous procedure in the face of hardships and perils, and are thus precepts of fortitude.

TEMPERANCE

(QUESTIONS 141 to 170)

141. THE VIRTUE OF TEMPERANCE

1. A virtue is a habit which disposes and inclines a person to act in accordance with reason. Now, reason indicates the need of measure and moderation; what supplies this need rightly is therefore a virtue. This is the virtue of temperance.

2. In one way temperance can be regarded as a general virtue, for ordinateness or moderation, which is the object of temperance, is found in all the moral virtues. Yet the virtue of temperance has a special phase of good in view: it holds back the appetites from inordinateness in their drive for what is most alluring. Hence, temperance is a special virtue.

3. Temperance controls desires and pleasures. It moderates the appetites for sensible and bodily delights; it also moderates the appetites that shrink from bodily evils. Fortitude controls the fear of evils. Temperance controls the pursuit of pleasurable goods, and also moderates the sorrow or distress caused by the lack of such goods.

4. Bodily goods cannot give pleasure unless they are somehow brought into contact with the bodily person of the one who enjoys them. Chief of such bodily goods are the goods of *nutriment* (food and drink) and of *sex*. Since bodily contact is involved in the use of these goods, the virtue which regulates their use, which is temperance, has to do with the tactile sense, the sense of touch or contact.

5. The principal use of the bodily and tactile goods with which temperance deals is the preserving of the human individual and the human species. And, as we have said, these goods are more a matter of the sense of touch than of sight, hearing, taste, or smell. That food, for instance, should have a pleasing taste or aroma, or that it should look attractive, is entirely a secondary matter in the service that it renders. For the essential point about food is that it supports life. Yet, since the sense of taste is closely allied with the tactile sense (for food comes into complete bodily contact with the organ of taste), the savors and flavors and amounts of food are proximately subject to regulation by the virtue of temperance.

6. Temperance regulates the use of bodily goods which belong to the order of man's natural and normal needs. This virtue, therefore, moderates and ordinates man's appetites to the end that he should use pleasurable goods according to the needs of life.

7. Since moderation, which is the characteristic of temperance, is required for virtue in general, temperance is a principal or *cardinal* virtue.

8. Temperance, in point of excellence, comes fourth in the list of cardinal virtues. These virtues, in the descending order of excellence, are: prudence, justice, fortitude, temperance.

142. VICES OPPOSED TO TEMPERANCE

1. Nature has associated pleasure with the operations necessary for life. Man is to make use of these pleasures in so far as they are required for his well-being. To reject pleasure to the extent of omitting what is necessary for preserving nature, whether in the individual or in the race, would be the vice of insensibility. Insensibility is a vice opposed to temperance. Now, insensibility is not to be confused with abstinence, which is useful and sometimes necessary even in the natural order. In the supernatural order it is right and reasonable, and hence virtuous, freely to renounce all use of sex, and much of the pleasure of the table, so that one may devote oneself more completely to the life of spiritual perfection.

2. Intemperance is the direct opposite to temperance. Aristotle calls it (*Ethic.* III 12) a *childish* vice. The adjective is justified; intemperance, like an ill-trained and unruly child, is unreasonable, headstrong, willful, wanting its own way, knowing not where to stop, and growing stronger in its disgusting qualities the more it is indulged. Finally (and still like an unruly child), intemperance is corrected only by having its tendencies curbed and restrained.

3. Intemperance is a more grievous vice than cowardice, for there is in it more of a person's own choice. It is less excusable than cowardice, for of the two vices it is the more readily cured.

4. Intemperance is the most disgraceful of vices, for it indulges pleasures that men and animals have in common; it tends to level a man to the state of a beast. And intemperance so dims the light, and weakens the control of reason, that it makes a man slave to his bodily cravings. Hence, intemperance is both inhuman and slavish; it shames and disgraces its victim in the eyes of his fellowmen.

143. THE PARTS OF TEMPERANCE

1. The integral or quasi-integral *parts* of a virtue are conditions required by its nature as that virtue. There are two such integral parts

of temperance: *shamefacedness* by which one recoils from the disgrace of intemperance, and *honesty* by which one loves the beauty of temperance. The subjective parts of a virtue are its species, kinds, or types. The subjective parts of temperance are: abstinence, sobriety, chastity, purity. The potential parts of a virtue are other virtues allied with it or subordinate to it; these parts share the character of the virtue in question, yet they are not coextensive with it in scope, and they are not species or kinds of it. The potential parts of temperance are: continence, humility, meekness (or mildness), modesty.

144. SHAMEFACEDNESS

1. Shamefacedness is a recoil from what is disgraceful; it is a drawing or shrinking back from what is base. In a broad sense, shamefacedness is a virtue. But, more strictly, it is to be called a praiseworthy passion, and not a virtue. It lacks the full perfection of a habit steadily inclining the will to good.

2. Shamefacedness has to do with action. It is not shame for the disgrace inherent in a vicious habit, but for the disgrace feared as the result of a bad deed contemplated or already performed. It is the shrinking from deserved reproach or ignominy for something vile that is proposed for doing, or for a vile thing already done.

3. A man is more likely to fear and to feel shame before those who are closest to him (his relatives, friends, and acquaintances), than before strangers. People unknown to a person, people in whose society he does not regularly move, inspire small shame; disgrace suffered before the eyes of strangers is quickly forgotten.

4. A man may become so immersed in evil that he loses shame, and may even boast of doing what is shameful. There are others in whom a lack of shame is not disgraceful, that is, people of sound virtue and aged people; these lack shame, not as by a deficiency, but they regard any shameful action as something so remote from themselves as to be negligible and worthy of no thought or concern. Of course, these persons are so disposed that if (by a well-nigh impossible supposition) they were to do a disgraceful thing, they would be ashamed of it.

145. HONESTY OR DECOROUSNESS

1. Honesty, as we use the term here, means goodness, decorousness, decency. Strictly speaking, honesty is a general term for any virtue, and for all virtues together.

2. Honesty is the same as *beauty* in the spiritual meaning of the latter word. For virtue gives the soul beauty; honesty means virtue; hence honesty and beauty of soul (that is, beauty of character, beauty of life) are the same.

3. What is *honest* has excellence in itself, and therefore deserves honor. What is *pleasing* or pleasant quiets desire and gives delight. What is *useful* is good as a means to obtain something else. Hence, there is a distinction between the honest and the pleasing, between the honest and the useful—even though it may happen that all three are found in one subject, as, for instance in the virtue of justice, which is honest, may be pleasing, and is certainly useful for righteous living. But the three things are not coextensive, and to find one is not necessarily to find all three.

4. Since temperance repels in man what is most unbecoming to him, that is, excess in animal lusts, it lends a spiritual beauty to a man, and we call that beauty honesty. Thus, honesty, the beauty-conferring expression of temperance, is a quasi-integral *part* of temperance itself.

146. ABSTINENCE

1. Abstinence is essentially a keeping away, a refraining, entirely or in some degree, from anything. Specifically, as we employ the term here, abstinence is a retrenchment in the use of food or drink. It may be a total abstaining from certain kinds of food or drink; it may be a partial abstaining from nutriment in the sense that it is observed at certain times or in certain circumstances. When abstinence is ordinate, that is, in complete accord with right reason, it is either a *virtue* (that is, an enduring good habit) or it is a *virtuous act.*

2. As a moral virtue, abstinence tends to good under a special aspect, and therefore is a special virtue.

147. FASTING

1. Abstinence, as an act, is usually the refraining from the use of certain kinds of food or drink. Fasting is the refraining for determinate periods from all use of food. To illustrate: a Catholic *abstains* when he refrains from eating meat on Friday; but he *fasts* when he refrains from food and drink altogether for a time, or, in a less complete sense of the word fasting, when he limits himself to one full meal a day. Fasting is useful for: (a) controlling the lusts of the flesh; (b) freeing the mind from bodily concerns so that it may better contemplate heavenly things; (c) penancing the body in satisfaction for sins. That fasting is a *virtuous* act is manifest from these excellent uses that it serves.

2. Fasting is an act of the virtue of abstinence.

3. Fasting for the purposes indicated above (preventing, and atoning for sin, and raising the mind to contemplation) is a duty imposed by reason, and therefore by the natural law. The positive precepts of fasting which determine its manner and extent, and the times

appointed for it, come from the Church which decides what is becoming and profitable, on this point, for her children.

4. The Church imposes the duty of fasting in general, but she makes exceptions for certain classes (the aged, the infirm, children), and grants dispensations in particular cases when this is necessary or advisable.

5. There is a notable fitness in the fasts imposed by the Church. The intensive and prolonged fasting-season of Lent comes every year, and the ember days and fasting vigils of certain feasts keep the faithful constantly in the spirit and practice of fasting, and yet without imposing great hardship upon them. And a rich symbolism attaches to the seasons of fasting, especially to the forty days of the lenten fast.

6. The eucharistic fast is the fast observed before receiving our Lord in Holy Communion. The ecclesiastical fast is the ordinary fast from food (not drink) imposed by the Church for certain days and seasons. The essence of the ecclesiastical fast seems to lie in the fact that only one full meal is taken on a fasting day.

7. The time for the one full meal permitted on a fasting day is determined by church law, even as the fast itself is so determined. The time of this meal is set for noon or the later part of the day, not the forenoon.

8. The strict fast of an earlier day, when the faithful were required to abstain from flesh meat, eggs, and milk foods (butter, cheese), has been much mitigated in later times, and for good reasons.

148. GLUTTONY

1. Gluttony is excess in eating and drinking. It is an immoderate indulgence in the delights of the palate. Gluttony is therefore inordinate, therefore unreasonable, therefore an evil.

2. Gluttony is usually not a serious sin, but it could be such a sin. It would be a mortal sin in a person so given to the delights of eating and drinking that he is ready to abandon virtue, and God himself, to obtain this pleasure.

3. Gluttony is a sin of the flesh, a *carnal* sin. Hence, in itself, it is not so great a sin as a *spiritual* sin or a sin of malice.

4. Gluttony denotes inordinate *desire* in eating and drinking. It shows itself in the avidity with which a person indulges his appetite; in his love of delicate and expensive foods; in the importance he attaches to the discerning of fine qualities in foods, vintages, cookery; in voraciousness or greediness; in eating or drinking too much. St. Isidore (*De Summ. Bon.* II) says that a gluttonous person is excessive in what, when, how, and how much he eats and drinks.

5. A capital sin is a source-sin; a spring, large or small, from which

flow many evil streams. Now gluttony leads readily to other sins, for it indulges pleasure of the flesh which is the most alluring of all pleasures. Gluttony is, therefore, a capital sin.

6. Gluttony leads to inordinate fleshly delight, to dullness of mind, to injudiciousness of speech, to levity of conduct, and to uncleanness.

149. SOBRIETY

1. Sobriety consists in the reasonable and temperate use of intoxicating drink. We call a man sober (in describing his habitual conduct) when he either drinks no intoxicants, or drinks them in such moderation that his faculties are never disordered by them. The word *sober*, and hence the word sobriety, derives from a word meaning *measure*, and therefore suggests the true meaning of the term: measure or moderation in drinking.

2. Sobriety is usually regarded as a special *part* of the virtue of temperance, and hence a special virtue.

3. No food or drink is, in itself, unlawful. Scripture says (Matt. 15:11): "That which goeth into the mouth doth not defile a man." Yet the drinking of intoxicants can be bad for several accidental reasons. Drinking becomes an evil: (a) when the person who drinks is abnormally susceptible to the influence of alcohol; (b) when a person has pledged his word not to drink; (c) when a person drinks too much; (d) when scandal (that is, bad example) is given by drinking.

4. Sobriety is a good and necessary virtue in all, and it is especially requisite for (a) the young, who readily give way to excess in pleasures, and who develop habits quickly; (b) women, whose natural refinement is quickly debased and made disgusting by intoxication; (c) teachers and pastors and parents, and all who instruct others, and all whose dignity or office demands a devout and attentive mind and the example of sober conduct.

150. DRUNKENNESS

1. St. Paul (Rom. 13:13) gives the precept that we are not to engage "in rioting and drunkenness." Drunkenness is a species of the vice of gluttony. It is a manifest evil.

2. Drunkenness is a mortal sin in the person who willingly and knowingly deprives himself of the use of reason by excessive drinking. Reason is man's guide and control for the exercise of virtue and the avoiding of sin. Foolishly and unwarrantedly to deprive oneself of reason is therefore a serious fault.

3. Drunkenness is not the worst of sins, for it is a carnal sin, and hence is not so evil in itself as spiritual sins.

4. If a man becomes intoxicated without his fault, either because he does not know that what he drinks is intoxicating, or because he underestimates its strength, or because he is affected by the drink in a manner unusual and unexpected, he is not guilty of sin, and he is excused from the responsibility for any regrettable conduct which results from his intoxication. If, however, a person becomes intoxicated by his own fault, he is at least partially responsible for any evils that result from his excessive drinking, just as he is responsible for the intoxication itself.

151. CHASTITY

1. The word chastity derives from the chastening or rebuking of concupiscence. By such chastening, chastising or curbing, passion is held in control, and is kept in alignment with right reason. Chastity, therefore, is a virtue inasmuch as it steadily tends to keep human conduct under the control of reason.

2. And chastity is a special virtue for it concerns a special aspect of good, that is, the controlling, the keeping reasonable, of the tendencies of sex.

3. Chastity is not the same as the virtue of abstinence. For chastity is concerned with the control of sex pleasures, whereas abstinence is directly concerned with the control of the pleasures of the palate.

4. The words purity and chastity are sometimes used interchangeably, but they are not perfect synonyms. Chastity *directly* regards the sexual union. Purity refers to all that is in any way *associated* with this union. Thus a person is *unchaste* if he indulges in unlawful coition. But a person is *impure* by reason of thoughts, imaginings, words, desires, and actions that have an unlawful sexual reference. Unchastity involves impurity, but impurity can exist without unchastity.

152. VIRGINITY

1. Virginity is basically derived from a word that means what is fresh, unseared, untouched by harming influence. The essential thing in virginity is not a condition of the body, but the *perpetual* refraining from the use or pleasures of sex.

2. Reason requires that external or material goods be used in a due and proportionate way. Now, the use of sex for the propagation of the race is necessary, good, natural, reasonable. But such use, while necessary for people in general, is not necessary for each individual. The race is sufficiently propagated and assured of continuance and increase, even if a very large number of individuals live singly and make no use of sex at all. Hence, virginity is not unreasonable, for it does no

harm to the common good. And if virginity is practiced for a good and holy reason, it is a most noble virtue.

3. Virginity as integrity of the flesh and freedom from sexual experience is natural to human beings from their birth. But virginity as a virtue is that virginity which is freely chosen for the purpose of serving God more completely, of giving the mind to the contemplation of divine things in the absence of family cares and with the sacrifice of family joys.

4. Virginity is directed to the good of the soul. Marriage is directed to the propagation of the race. In itself, therefore, virginity is more excellent than chaste marriage.

5. Virginity is the most excellent virtue in the *genus* or class of chastity. It surpasses the chastity of the married state, and the chastity of widowhood. But it is not the greatest of all virtues. The theological virtues of faith, hope, and charity are superior in excellence to virginity, as are the virtues of religion and the fortitude which sustains the martyr.

153. LUST

1. Lust is the vice of indulging in unlawful sexual pleasures.

2. The use of sex is not always lustful or sinful. There is a good and virtuous use of sex in marriage, when husband and wife perform their normal and natural function of sex without any inordinateness (that is, without anything that is in conflict with reason) and, therefore, without employing any unnatural or artificial means of thwarting the natural effect of their action. The only lawful and chaste use of sex is its lawful use in marriage.

3. Lust consists in disregarding the order and mode dictated by reason for the use of sex. Therefore, lust conflicts with reason, and is a sin. The habit of lust is a vice.

4. Lust is listed with the capital sins because many other sins flow from it as from their source.

5. St. Gregory (*Moral.* xxxi) enumerates "the daughters of lust" as follows: blindness of mind; thoughtlessness; rashness; inconstancy; love of self; hatred for God; worldliness; dread of a future life.

154. THE PARTS OF LUST

1. The parts of lust are the species or types of lustful sins. These parts are six: fornication, adultery, incest, seduction, rape, unnatural vice.

2. Fornication is the normal, but unlawful, use of sex by an unmarried man and an unmarried woman. Fornication is a mortal sin,

for it is a great inordinateness in the parties who are guilty of it; is opposed to the good of offspring (for only marriage establishes the home which children require, and to which they have a right), and it is plainly against the common welfare both in physical and moral effects.

3. Fornication is a grave sin of the flesh. It is not the greatest of all sins, for sins of the spirit, sins of malice, are more grievous than any carnal sin.

4. Kisses and touches that are lustful are also mortal sins.

5. Whatever occurs in sleep cannot be sinful in itself. Yet it may be sinful in its cause. If, before sleeping, a person is guilty of thoughts, desires, or deeds that are lustful, he is at least partly responsible for impurities that subsequently occur during sleep.

6. Seduction is the violation of a virgin. It is a species of lust, and is therefore a grievous sin.

7. Rape is a species of lust—and gravely sinful—in which force is employed in committing a lustful action.

8. Adultery is the normal, but unlawful, use of sex by a married and a single person, or by two married persons, who, however, are not married to each other. This grievous sin is far worse than fornication, for it violates not only chastity, but it is a gross violation of justice (committed against the true spouse of the married party, or against both spouses of the married parties). Besides, it is a more damaging offense against the common good than fornication is.

9. Incest is the use of sex by man and woman who are related by ties of blood, or by affinity, that is, by relationship arising out of a marriage. It has all the grievous character of lust, plus the violation of justice (if either party is married), and the violation of the virtue of piety.

10. Lust becomes sacrilege when it involves sacred or consecrated persons, things, or places.

11. Unnatural vice is any lustful perversion of normal and natural processes for procuring sex pleasures.

12. Unnatural vice is the worst of all sins of lust, for it is most gravely shameful as acting against the ordinance of nature. Yet *all* willful sins of lust are mortal sins.

155. CONTINENCE

1. Perfect continence is complete abstention from all sexual pleasures. But continence, in a more strict and more usual meaning of the word, is the steadfast resisting of sexual *desires.*

2. Therefore, that person is continent who refuses to surrender to

the allurements which strongly attract the passions in the matter of sex.

3. Continence is the praiseworthy and virtuous stand of the will against lustful evil tendencies. It is a moral virtue, that is, a will-virtue.

4. Continence is regarded by some as a species of temperance. In itself, it stands to temperance as imperfect to perfect. For temperance belongs to the person whose appetites are positively ruled by reason, whereas continence is the stern control of appetites that resist the rule of reason.

156. INCONTINENCE

1. Incontinence is the vice opposed directly to continence. It consists either in the *impetuosity* or the *weakness* of a soul which impulsively, and without the counsel of reason, surrenders to evil desires; or, after the counsel of reason, is weak and reluctant to accept the judgment of reason.

2. Incontinence is a sin, because it conflicts with reason, and because it plunges a person into what is shameful. It is to be remarked, however, that the word *incontinence* is often used with no implication of lust at all; it is used to express eagerness, enthusiasm, urgency in acting, even in what is blameless or in what is good. Hence, care is to be taken in interpreting this word.

3. As continence has not the full perfection and scope of temperance, so incontinence has not the full character, and is not so grave a sin, as intemperance.

4. Incontinence, as referring to evil desires, is sometimes contrasted with wild and unbridled anger. Such anger is itself often called incontinence. Now, in itself, the incontinence of lustful desire is much worse than the incontinence of anger; it is a greater deordination of reasonable life, and a thing of far greater shame than anger is. In *result*, however, the case may be different. Incontinence of anger may lead to greater evils than does the incontinence of lust. For the incontinence of lust harms the man guilty of it, whereas the incontinence of anger may break out into violence that does damage to others also.

157. CLEMENCY AND MEEKNESS

1. Clemency is the virtue which moderates the anger of a superior in punishing, or passing sentence upon, one who is subject to him. Meekness is the virtue which moderates anger in a person's own soul. Therefore clemency and meekness are not identical, although they appear very similar.

2. Moral virtues, or will-virtues, bring the appetites under the con-

trol of reason. It is clear that both clemency and meekness are moral virtues.

3. Clemency and meekness are aligned with the virtue of temperance, and are thus *parts* of that cardinal virtue.

4. Moral virtues are not so great, in point of nobility and excellence, as the theological virtues of supernatural faith, hope, and charity. Hence clemency and meekness are not the greatest of virtues. Nor are they so great as the virtues of prudence, justice, and fortitude.

158. ANGER

1. Anger, strictly speaking, is a sense-appetite and sense-passion. Since its upheaval in the sensitive part of a man may be quickly admitted (by the will) into the rational or intellective part, it is called a "passion of the soul." Anger thus exercises an influence upon reason. Now, anger can influence reason in the right direction as well as in the wrong one. Therefore, there is such a thing as just or lawful anger. Scripture says (Psalm 4:5): "Be angry, and sin not." The anger of our Lord threatening hypocrites, or driving out the men who profaned the temple, gives us an example of righteous or lawful anger. Such lawful anger is never inordinate; it never sweeps a man off his feet, or inspires outrageous words or deeds.

2. But anger, though it *can* be lawful, is more often a striking back, with unjustified desire for revenge, at someone or something that has hurt one's self-esteem. Such anger is inordinate; it is an evil; it is a sin.

3. Yet anger is not a mortal sin unless a person, by consent of will, allows it to become so fierce as to make him willing to forego his serious duty to God or fellowmen. Therefore, a person submitting, through anger, to murderous impulses or intentions, is guilty of mortal sin.

4. In itself, anger, even as mortal sin, is not so inordinate or disgraceful a sin as lust or the incontinence of lustful desires. And in comparison with the vice of hatred, anger is, as St. Augustine says in his Rule, "as the mote to the beam."

5. Aristotle classifies anger as choler, sullenness, and sternness. A *choleric* person is quick to anger; a *sullen* person angrily nurses his injuries; a *stern* or bad-tempered person clings to the angry determination to be revenged.

6. Anger is one of the capital sins. For it is the fruitful source of many evils much worse than itself, such as serious injuries and murders. Other fruits of anger are: quarrels, physical attacks, cursings, uncharitable speech.

7. St. Gregory lists the "daughters of anger" as: quarreling (in-

cluding physical encounter); vengeful thoughts and designs; clamor, or disordered and confused speech; contumely, or speech injurious to a neighbor; indignation, or bridling against what angers one as something base and unworthy; blasphemy, or offensive words directed against God.

8. A person who is wholly incapable of anger lacks something; he is in some way defective. As we have seen, there is such a thing as just and lawful anger. Were a person unable to resent evil, he would be deficient in the use of lawful anger.

159. CRUELTY

1. Cruelty is hardness of heart which makes one willing to inflict injurious or excessive punishment. It is a vice which directly opposes the virtue of clemency.

2. Cruelty differs from brutality or savagery in this: cruelty recognizes its victim as one truly deserving punishment and is excessive in inflicting it; savagery or brutality takes inhuman and even bestial delight in the torture it inflicts on a human being, regardless of the guilt or innocence of its victim.

160. MODESTY

1. Modesty is a virtue aligned with the virtue of temperance. Temperance regulates things difficult to control; modesty regulates things not difficult to control.

2. Modesty has to do with matters interior and external; it has place in the soul and character of a man, and in what he does or manifests outwardly. Modesty appears in things that belong to the virtue of humility, to studiousness (that is, the right effort after knowledge), to external movements, and to attire. We are to discuss all these matters in the pages that follow.

161. HUMILITY AS A SPECIES OF MODESTY

1. The tendencies of a man (that is to say, his appetites) need two types of virtue for their just regulation: one to support them in weakness, one to moderate them when they are inordinately impulsive or strong. Humility is of the second type. It is the virtue which restrains a man lest he be immoderate in his striving to reach high goals.

2. Humility is in the appetitive order, not the knowing order. It is a moral virtue, a will-virtue, not an intellectual virtue.

3. Humility is not a pose. The humble man does not bow to all others as though they were in all respects superior to himself. But humility does honestly recognize that all good, all excellence, is in

God, and that all creatural good comes from God. Therefore, humility sees God in every fellowman, and bows to that which is divine.

4. Humility is a virtue allied with temperance through the medium of the virtue of modesty, which is a *part* of temperance.

5. So excellent and necessary a virtue is humility that its rank is first after the theological virtues, the intellectual virtues that regard reason itself, and the virtue of justice.

6. Humility is a moral virtue, not an intellectual one. But it does involve the knowledge that we are what we are, and are not to think more of ourselves than facts warrant. And back of the act of humility is reverence for God. The inward disposition of humility has outward manifestations which, in many instances, are expressive of modesty. Some writers, like St. Benedict in his Rule, enumerate degrees of humility according to inner disposition and outer sign.

162. PRIDE

1. Pride is the habit, the vice, which disposes a man to make himself more than he is.

2. Pride is a special vice, for it has the special object of inordinate esteem for one's own excellence. Yet pride has also the character of a general vice, for it is involved, directly or indirectly, in other sins, and notably in all sins of malice.

3. Pride aspires; it tends; it desires something—not simply, but as involving some element of *difficulty*. The proud man is under pressure; he makes effort to be more than he actually is. Now, a habit that involves drive and effort (and, by that token, involves difficulty with which effort grapples) belongs to the appetitive part of man; it has its subject in the will. Pride resides in the will.

4. St. Gregory (*Moral.* xxiii 4) lists four species of pride: (a) thinking that one's good is from oneself; (b) thinking that one's good is from God but is owing to one's own deserts; (c) claiming excellence not possessed; (d) despising others and wishing to seem the exclusive possessor of what one has.

5. Pride is an assumed self-sufficiency which omits or discounts God in considering what one is. This is manifestly a very great inordinateness, and is, in its *genus* or kind, a serious or mortal evil. Yet, to be mortally sinful, an individual act of pride would have to be a conscious and fully willed misprising of God. Most acts of pride are venial sins by reason of deficiency of awareness, or lack of full consent of the will.

6. Since pride is a direct turning away from God and is a practical act of contempt for God, because it is an unwillingness to be subject

to him, it ranks with that actual hatred for God which we have called the very worst of sins.

7. Aversion from God is in all sins, but it is the very essence of pride. Other sins involve this aversion by their nature as sins; pride *is* this aversion. Aversion from God is consequent upon other sins; in pride this aversion is the sin itself. Hence the first and worst of all sins is the sin of pride; it shares this evil distinction with hatred for God.

8. Pride, as a special sin, is the source of many other sins, and is therefore listed as a capital sin. But pride, as a general sin, is not merely the source of other sins; it is actually *in* them. St. Gregory (*Moral.* xxxi 17) calls pride the queen of vices which conquers the heart of a man and delivers it to the capital sins. And therefore St. Gregory does not mention pride itself as one of the capital sins, for he considers it the mother of them all.

163. THE SIN OF THE FIRST MAN

1. Adam's sin could not have been a sin of the flesh. For in the state of innocence there was no rebellion of flesh against spirit. Therefore, the first inordinateness in the human appetite could not possibly have been a desire for any material or sensible good. The first human sin must have been connected with the desire for some spiritual good. And, since the actual desire must have been ordinate (because inordinateness did not come into man until the first sin was committed), the inordinateness must have been in the thing desired. This thing must have been something beyond the reach or above the mark of a human being. And to aspire to such a thing is pride. Hence, the first human sin was a sin of pride. The ordinate desire of the first man was made inordinate by the unsuitableness of a too-excellent object, and the desire was thus transformed into a prideful aspiring.

2. The first sin, a sin of pride, was the first man's willful desire to have something that belongs to God alone. It may be said that man, made in God's image, tried to extend unduly that image in himself. In particular, the first man wanted "knowledge of good and evil," so that, by his own natural power and without reference or deference to God, he could know what was good or evil for him to do, and could know beforehand what good and evil would happen to him. Thus, in a fashion, the first man aspired to a kind of equality with God, and so he sinned by pride, even as the fallen angels sinned by pride.

3. Was the sin of our first parent more grave than other human sins? In itself, as we have seen, pride is the greatest of sins. Yet there are degrees of pride, and many sins of pride, as acts performed, are not more than venial sins. And even in grave sins of pride there are rank

and scale: the pride of denying or blaspheming God is more grave than the pride of coveting the enlargement in oneself of the divine image. Therefore, taken simply as a *sin of pride,* the sin of Adam was not the most grievous sin of its kind. Nor was Adam's pride more grievous in itself than the pride of other men. But when we consider Adam's sin, not *simply* or absolutely, but *in relation* to the one who committed it (a perfect man, with a nature entirely untroubled by unruly passions, and dowered with most wonderful supernatural gifts and graces) we must conclude that this was indeed the most grievous of all the human sins of pride. Therefore, summing the matter up, we say: taken simply or *absolutely,* the sin of Adam was not the most grievous of human sins; taken *relatively* (that is, in relation to the state of perfection of the sinner), it was the most grievous of sins.

4. The sin of the first woman was, in itself, more grievous than the sin of the first man. For while Adam and Eve both sinned by pride, Eve believed the devil, God's enemy, and, in full awareness that what the devil suggested was against God's will, she ate the fruit to obtain the sort of knowledge that belongs to God alone. The sin of Adam did not spring from trust in the devil; Adam wanted the inordinate good and wanted it pridefully, but not inasmuch as it was clearly seen in opposition to God's will (as devil-inspired), but as aspired to by his own unaided power. Further, the woman not only sinned, but tried to lead the man to sin; she sinned both against God and neighbor. Yet it is Adam's sin, not Eve's, that brought deprivation and punishment upon the race, and is "the original sin."

164. PUNISHMENT OF THE SIN OF ADAM

1. If a person, because of a fault, is deprived of what was bestowed on him as a favor, the deprivation is a *punishment* for the fault. Now, the perfect subjection of man's lower powers to reason was a great favor bestowed on man. Out of this perfect subjection of body to spirit came soundness of health and perfection of bodily function, and the supervening gift of bodily immortality was assured. But when man sinned the great favor mentioned was withdrawn (indeed, man's sin rejected the favor), and it was withdrawn in punishment for the sin. The withdrawal of the favor meant that man was no longer immortal in his bodily life; it meant that he would die. Therefore, death is manifestly in punishment for Adam's sin. Says St. Paul (Rom. 5:12): "By one man sin entered the world, and by sin, death."

2. Scripture recounts other punishments for Adam's sin: expulsion of our first parents from Paradise; fatiguing toil; pains of childbirth; reluctance of the earth to yield fruits, etc. [*Note:* All these punish-

ments were blessings for fallen man. Once fallen, man would have
found Paradise and life as it was before Adam's sin, so delightful that
he would no longer have had thought or time for God. Fallen man
cannot stand a diet of Paradise. Were it not for the hardships and
punishments we must bear in consequence of Adam's sin, we should
all inevitably go to hell. Herein appear the infinite love and mercy of
God: when he strikes us in punishment, while we are wayfarers, his
blow turns into the caress of blessing.]

165. THE TEMPTATION OF ADAM

1. Man, dowered with free will, had to *exercise* that free will in
choosing or rejecting God. Had there been no trial, no temptation,
man would have had a kind of mechanical progress from Paradise to
heaven, and the greatest of his gifts, the gift that makes him most
like to God in his being (that is, free will) would have been a vain
and unused gift. Free human nature had to have a chance to choose
freely, and this was given in the temptation. There was no need for
Adam to succumb to the temptation. He had a perfect human nature,
and he had supernatural grace and supernatural gifts. No creature
could harm him or force his choice, against his will. That Adam sinned,
that he chose to abuse freedom instead of using it, was his own fault.

2. The manner and order of the first man's temptation were entirely
suitable. The temptation was rounded and complete. It appealed to
the intellect and will; the appeal was made through the senses; into
the whole event of the temptation there entered one of the man's own
species, the woman; one thing of the animal order, the serpent; and
one thing of the vegetal order, the tree with its fruit.

166. STUDIOUSNESS

1. Studiousness is the virtue which disposes a person to apply his
mind for the purpose of acquiring and extending knowledge.

2. The virtue of studiousness is a *part* of the virtue of temperance.
For it is the function of temperance to moderate appetite, to prevent
excess, in the use of material goods. In reference to the spiritual appetite for knowledge, studiousness has this temperance-function of
moderating desire and preventing excess. The tie-up of studiousness
with temperance is effected through the virtue of modesty (See
above, q. 160).

167. CURIOSITY

1. Curiosity, in our present use of the word, is the vice which stands
opposed to studiousness. Curiosity throws aside the moderating in-

fluence of studiousness, and disposes man to inordinateness in seeking knowledge. This inordinateness appears in a variety of ways. Thus: (a) a man may seek knowledge to take pride in it; (b) he may seek to know how to sin; (c) he may seek useless knowledge and waste effort which should be expended in learning what he needs to know; (d) he may seek knowledge from unlawful sources, as from demons; (e) he may seek creatural knowledge without referring what he knows to God; (f) he may foolishly risk error by trying to master what is beyond his capacity.

2. Curiosity appears also in the order of sense-knowledge. Inordinateness here appears in an excessive love of sight-seeing; of neglecting study to gaze idly on a meaningless spectacle; of looking needlessly on what may occasion evil thoughts; of observing the actions of others to criticize and condemn them, and so on. If, however, one is intent upon material things in an ordinate way (that is, in a way that accords with reason) one exercises studiousness, not curiosity, even in the order of sense-knowing.

168. MODESTY AS DECORUM

1. Outward activity, bodily movement or conduct, falls under the rule of virtue. For such activity is to be controlled by reason, and reason is disposed by virtue to rule ordinately. Man is meant to live rightly by inner righteousness and outer decorum. Modesty as *decorum* is the virtue which steadily disposes a person to regulate his external conduct so that it is well-ordered, fitting, and beautiful.

2. Man needs at times the relaxation of play, whether in words or deeds. For man is liable to weariness of mind and soul, as of body. He finds rest in bodily repose, and in mental divertisement. Now, the body takes rest, not only in quiet inaction, but also in games. And the soul finds an easing of tensions in lighter occupations, among which are games or play of nonathletic type. Since there is need of ordinateness or good order in necessary relaxation, there is a virtue respecting recreation and games. Aristotle (*Ethic.* IV 8) calls this virtue *eutrapelia,* which means "the habit of a pleasant and cheerful turn of mind." This virtue of *eutrapelia* finds outer manifestation in attitudes, words, and actions. The function of this virtue brings it under the head of modesty as decorum. *Eutrapelia,* the virtue of a pleasing turn for games, relaxation, and recreation, requires regulating by certain conditions: (a) games, and other modes of pleasure in recreation, must include nothing indecent or injurious; (b) a person must not be completely lost in his addiction to favorite pastimes; (c) all recreational activities must be suitably ordered with references to persons, times,

and places, and other circumstances which can influence the character and effect of human action.

3. Play goes beyond reason and sins by excess when it is either (a) discourteous, scandalous, obscene or insolent, or (b) inordinate in point of circumstances—place, time, etc. The first type of inordinateness in games or play is sinful in itself, and may easily be mortally sinful. The second type is mortally sinful if it would make a person disobey the laws of God or the Church; if, for instance, a Catholic were willing to miss Mass on Sunday rather than forgo a game in which he is avidly interested. But, for the most part, excess in games and in addiction to them is not mortally sinful.

4. It is not reasonable for a person to be wholly mirthless, and to make himself a dull burden to others in their recreation and games. Such a person is rude and boorish, and his conduct is from a vice rather than from a virtue. Lack of mirth, however, is less unreasonable than excess of mirth.

169. MODESTY IN DRESS

1. St. Ambrose (*De Offic.* i 19) says that the body should be clad and adorned appropriately, unaffectedly, simply; not in an overnice fashion, nor with costly and dazzling apparel. Modesty has a place in regulating the attire. In dress, as in all outward things, there is a reasonable and decent norm. Dress should not conflict too gaudily with established custom, provided the custom itself is decent. Nor should dress too largely absorb a person's interest and attention, for excessive pleasure in dress is vainglory. On the other hand, a person offends modesty by slovenliness in dress, and by negligence, and by want of cleanliness. A person also offends by seeking the reputation of one who is wholly unconcerned with such things as his appearance and attire; thus a man makes his very negligence a matter of vainglory.

2. Modesty in dress is particularly important for women. For a woman's attire may incite a man to lust, whereas it is quite unlikely that a man's dress should be any incitement to a woman. In point of dress and adornment, a married woman should strive, within the bounds of decency, dignity, and modesty, to please her husband. Unmarried women should avoid all that can be called lewd or extreme. For the rest, neither woman nor man should dress for mere frivolity, vanity, or display.

170. THE PRECEPTS OF TEMPERANCE

1. The Ten Commandments are precepts of temperance inasmuch as they make for moderation and right order in human conduct. In

special, the sixth and ninth commandments are precepts of temperance, for they forbid inordinateness of sex in deed and desire, and this is something directly pertinent to temperance.

2. The precepts of the virtues allied to temperance as its *parts* are also found in the Decalogue. For, though the *parts* of temperance refer directly to a man's self rather than to God and neighbor, as the Ten Commandments do, yet their *effects* reach out to others, and this fact brings them under the preceptive force of the commandments. Thus anger, for instance, may lead to murder; pride may lead to the dishonoring of parents, and to sins directly against God. Thus the effects of sins opposed to the parts of temperance may come under the commandments directly.

GRATUITOUS GRACES

(QUESTIONS 171 to 178)

171. PROPHECY

1. Prophecy is the certain foretelling of a future event by a person supernaturally informed of it, and supernaturally moved to announce it. Prophecy consists primarily in the *knowledge* of future events; this knowledge is beyond the natural power of creatures to acquire, and is imparted by God to the prophet. Secondarily, prophecy is the "expression in speech" of the divinely imparted prophetic knowledge. And, in the third place, prophecy takes it fullness and perfection from the "certainty of the message" prophetically made. This certainty will have its proof when the event prophesied comes to pass, but it is requisite for perfect prophecy to have a backing and guarantee at the time the prophet speaks. This backing and guarantee of certainty is usually afforded by the aid of miracles.

2. Naturally acquired knowledge is in a person as an intellectual *habit;* it is something he has acquired and keeps; it stays with him, and serves as a permanent mental quality which tends to make the mind better or worse in its operation. Thus natural knowledge can be used at the knower's will. But the prophet's knowledge is not something he can use at will. It is knowledge specially given, by a special divine light, and given in the measure that God wills, for utter-

ance as a divine help, guide, or warning to mankind. And, while both the prophet and the people who hear him can remember the prophecy, and in so far can make it an element of their knowledge, neither prophet nor people can work the prophecy into the common fabric of their natural knowledge to be pursued, developed, and correlated with other items of natural experience.

3. Prophetic knowledge includes more than future free events. The prophet may announce timeless things, as Isaias announced what was divinely revealed to him of the eternal perfections of God. Sometimes, indeed, a man is called a prophet when he tells of the past; so Moses prophesied when he wrote, under divine inspiration, of the creation of the world. In this way a prophecy is the certain knowledge and pronouncement of what is "remote from human knowledge." However, in its strict sense, prophecy is knowing and foretelling what is to come, that is, what is remote in time from human experience.

4. A prophet is not in possession of the whole field of prophecy; he does not know all that can possibly be prophesied. He knows what God gives him to know, and moves him to make known to others.

5. The prophet may not always be clear in his own mind about the precise line which divides the divinely revealed message from his own knowledge. But, as St. Gregory says, the Holy Ghost takes care that no erroneous human elements are mixed with the prophecy which God wills to have pronounced.

6. Nothing false, therefore, can enter into the prophecy as pronounced; it is a message from God Himself.

172. THE CAUSE OF PROPHECY

1. The knowledge of the genuine prophet cannot be accounted for by any natural power in himself. This knowledge is from God. It is revealed knowledge, not acquired knowledge, and God is its cause. St. Peter says (II Pet. 1:21): "Prophecy came not by the will of man . . . but the holy men of God spoke, inspired by the Holy Ghost."

2. In the universe of creatures, lower things are regularly directed by higher things and so up to the highest. In the world of creatural intellects, the angelic is superior to the human. It is fitting, therefore, that the knowledge to be uttered in prophecy should be conveyed to the human prophet by angels.

3. It cannot be said that God selects as prophets men of a suitable disposition for the office of prophet. God chooses as prophets whom he will, regardless of natural abilities and dispositions. The infinite

Creator can instantly produce in any man the qualifications naturally needed (as, for instance, the power to speak, or the ability to use an unfamiliar language), just as he produces the supernatural knowledge and the authority of the prophet.

4. Indeed, if God choose, the office of prophet may be exercised by a person who is not even in the state of grace. For prophecy is primarily a matter of knowledge, which pertains to the intellect, whereas grace or charity pertains primarily to the will. Yet it is most unlikely that a man of sinful and passionate life should be made a prophet.

5. The evil spirits are fallen angels; by their angelic intellect they know things that man cannot naturally know, and they can reveal these things to man. But this revelation is neither divine nor supernatural. One who proclaims knowledge acquired from demons is not, in a strict sense, a prophet; at best he is to be called "a false prophet."

6. Even such "a false prophet" may speak truth; indeed, he must offer some truth, or he would quickly be discredited, and could win no one to believe the essential falsity he wishes to propagate.

173. THE CONVEYING OF PROPHETIC KNOWLEGE

1. The prophetic vision which gives the prophet his knowledge is not the vision of God in heaven. If a prophet were to see God in the beatific vision, he would be instantly glorified and confirmed in grace, and this is impossible to man while he is a wayfarer, that is, is living this earthly life.

2. The revelation made to a prophet by divine power is sometimes an infusing of new ideas; sometimes, a new arrangement of ideas the prophet already possesses; and sometimes, a light that shows hitherto unseen implications in old ideas in their old arrangement.

7. Man forms ideas in the natural way by *abstraction* which draws *intelligible species* (that is, understandable essences) from the findings of sense represented in imagination-images or phantasms. This process is not always followed in the conveying of prophetic knowledge. Divinely imparted knowledge is sometimes directly impressed without the service of senses or phantasms. And sometimes it is an infused light which makes manifest what was not known in the natural process of human knowing.

4. It is possible that the prophet himself should not understand what the Holy Ghost means by the prophetic utterance. David understood that he had prophesied when he said (II Kings 23:2): "The spirit of the Lord hath spoken by me." But Caiphas did not understand when he prophesied (John 11:51): "And this he spoke, not of

himself, but being the high-priest of that year, he prophesied that Jesus should die for the nation."

174. TYPES OF PROPHECY

1. Prophecy is divided into prophecy of *foreknowledge* which tells what is certainly to come, and prophecy of *denunciation* which tells what will come *if* the present situation does not change. The first type is prophecy of information; the second type is prophecy of warning. When the prophet Jonas told the people of sinful Ninive that in three days their city would be destroyed, he uttered a prophecy of denunciation. He did not tell the people that their being destroyed or being spared would depend on how they received and acted upon what he prophesied; indeed, he did not know that escape from disaster was possible for them. Yet his prophecy was actually, as it turned out, conditioned upon the way the Ninivites behaved; they and their king fasted, and did penance, and called on God; in consequence, they were spared, and the dire prophecy of destruction was not fulfilled. Now, the point to remember is this: Jonas made a *true* prophecy. The causes that would destroy Ninive were in action and were to produce their effect *unless* God should intervene to stop them. When Jonas told the people that destruction was coming, it *was* coming. Jonas was given foreknowledge of destruction to come in a certain situation, but not foreknowledge of what was to come if the situation should change; and the situation did change. Therefore, in distinguishing these two types of prophecy (that is, of full knowledge, and of denunciation) we may say: prophecy of full foreknowledge *must* be fulfilled; prophecy of denunciation must be fulfilled *if* the conditions in which it is uttered remain the same. And the prophet may or may not know which type of prophecy he is uttering.

2. The most excellent of prophecies comes from the inspiration of the Holy Ghost without sensible signs, words, dreams, or visions of material things.

3. Prophecy may be typed or classified according to the fact that it is imparted by pure inspiration or by material indications. And the indications themselves are various, and can be used for further classification. And so we can speak of prophetic knowledge imparted to the prophet when he is awake, when he is asleep, by signs of truth, by words of truth, by the word of an angel, by the word of our Lord in apparition, and so on.

4. Of all the prophets Moses was the greatest. Scripture tells us that the Lord spoke to Moses "face to face," and the prophecies of

Moses were authenticated by very great miracles. In Deuteronomy (34:10, 11) we read: "There arose no more in Israel a prophet like unto Moses." Of course, when we call Moses the greatest of prophets, we are speaking of merely human prophets, divinely enlightened to speak prophecies; we do not include our Lord (who made the most wonderful of all prophecies concerning man's redemption, and the Resurrection, and the Holy Eucharist, and the Church), for our Lord is God himself as well as man, and he has no need of enlightenment about the future, for as God he knows it perfectly.

5. Prophecy has no place among the blessed in heaven. They who dwell in light itself have no need of enlightenment. Prophecy is a gratuitous grace imparted by God to help, guide, and warn man the wayfarer, that is, man living here on earth. Prophecy is meant to help get man safe home to heaven; those who are at home need no help and guide to get there.

6. Prophecies and prophets are not more and more excellent as time goes on, so that the predictions are better or greater as they near fulfillment. Moses was the greatest of the prophets, but he preceded most of the others. Indeed, it seems that the most essential and therefore the most excellent of *doctrinal* prophecies came earliest.

175. RAPTURE

1. Rapture is the state of being transported emotionally or spiritually; it is being carried out of oneself by a kind of ecstasy. In our present use, the word rapture means the uplifting of a person by the Spirit of God to things supernatural, by a movement so engrossing and powerful as to blot out the person's sense-awareness of his surroundings. St. Paul (II Cor. 12:2) tells of his being "rapt even to the third heaven."

2. Rapture is of the intellectual order rather than of the appetitive order. It deals with, and is occasioned by, revelations that enthrall the soul; and revelations are manifestations of truth to the intellect. Yet the will may so ardently desire what the intellect considers, that it contributes to the state of rapture. Besides, the intellect *beholds,* but the will *enjoys.*

3. St. Paul (II Cor. 12), speaking of himself in the third person, says he was rapt to heaven and heard secret words which it is not permitted to man to utter. Doubtless, he saw the essence of God, and had, in some way, a foretaste of the joy of heaven. But he had not the fullness of the light of glory and the beatific vision; else he would have been instantly glorified and confirmed in grace and beatitude; and, for man the wayfarer, this is impossible.

4. That St. Paul in his rapture was withdrawn from his senses is evident from the fact that he did not know whether he was in heaven in a bodily way or in vision—"whether in the body or out of the body, I know not."

5. We are not to suppose that St. Paul's soul was separated from his body during his rapture (that is, that he died, and was afterwards restored to life), but that his intellect was withdrawn from its natural operation of dealing with sense-images, and was raised, and filled supernaturally with the revelations of God.

6. As we have noted, St. Paul himself was not sure of just how his rapture was effected. He was sure of one thing: that his whole mind was supernaturally raised, and focused upon divine things to the exclusion of everything else.

176. TONGUES

1. The "gift of tongues" is the divinely imparted knowledge of a variety of languages. The apostles had this gift, and were able to speak the languages of all the peoples to whom they were sent. We read in Scripture (Acts 2:6) that when the apostles spoke to the people of many nations, "every man heard them speak in his own tongue." This was rather that they spoke in the various languages than that, speaking their own language, they were understood by all. For their own language could not, without illusion, sound differently in different ears.

2. The gift of tongues is not so great a gift (that is, a gratuitous grace) as that of prophecy. For prophetic knowledge comes by divine enlightenment. Now, it is more excellent to have knowledge than to have words to express knowledge. And prophecy is likely to be more powerful than the gift of tongues in its effect upon souls. The gift of tongues seems, sometimes, to have stirred up more astonishment than conviction.

177. THE GIFT OF WORDS

1. A gratuitous grace is one given less for the benefit of the person who receives it than for the benefit of others. Such a grace is the gift of effective speaking for the benefit and enlightenment of souls. The gift of tongues makes *understood* the knowledge that is expressed; the gift of words makes the expression *effective* in convincing and converting souls. St. Gregory (*Hom.* xxx *in Ev.*) says: "Unless the Holy Ghost fill the hearts of those who hear, the teacher's voice sounds vainly in their bodily ears."

2. The grace of the word of God to be preached publicly to the faithful of the Church, is given to men, not to women.

178. MIRACLES

1. The knowledge brought to men by prophecy, by the gift of tongues, and by the gift of words, needs to be authenticated as revealed truth. This is done by the working of miracles. The gift of performing miracles is, therefore, a gratuitous gift and grace.

2. A miracle is a wondrous fact or event, beyond the power of any creature, and produced by almighty God. In the working of a miracle, God often uses a human being as his *instrument;* in this case, the human being has the gratuitous grace and gift of miracles. Now, it is possible that the human instrument of a divine work should not be himself a holy man. For the divine work of miracles is meant to prove truth, and even a sinner can teach truth. But there are miracles which are wrought to prove the holiness of the person who is their instrument; in this case, to be sure, the truth confirmed by the miracle and the holiness of the instrument are one and the same thing.

ACTIVE AND CONTEMPLATIVE LIFE

(QUESTIONS 179 TO 182)

179. TYPES OF LIFE

1. We often call the "life" of a person that upon which he is most intent and in which he finds the greatest delight. Of one man, we say that his life is art; of another, study; of another, travel, and so on. Now, some men are especially bent upon the contemplation of truth; others are given wholeheartedly to external activity. Thus, a person's life may be described as *contemplative* or as *active.*

2. Just as the intellect is speculative or *contemplative* in knowing truth about things, and practical or *active* in its grasp of what one is to do, so life itself is suitably classified as the contemplative life and the active life.

180. THE CONTEMPLATIVE LIFE

1. The contemplative life is not one of cold study and consideration of eternal truth. It is not sheerly intellectual. It involves will and appetites; it includes love and attachment to what is studied. For the very intention to contemplate truth is an act of the will, and the contemplative person is led by all pertinent appetitive forces to love the work of contemplation and to repose happily in it.

2. The contemplative life, however, does consist essentially in the consideration of truth, and such consideration belongs to the intellect. The moral virtues (that is the will-virtues) dispose the soul for contemplation by curbing distracting passions and by allaying the disturbance caused by outward occupation, but these virtues do not enter the essence of contemplation itself. We say, therefore, that the moral virtues belong *dispositively* but not *essentially* to the contemplative life.

3. The contemplative life is not a kind of schedule of related acts; contemplation is one act. Still, the process of arriving at the truth to be contemplated involves, for man the wayfarer (that is, for man in his earthly life), a variety of acts. Thus, a man must grasp principles, and he must reason upon them to know what is implied in them. The last and perfect act, after the full discovery of truth, is contemplation, the steady gazing upon truth. This is *one* act, not several.

4. Contemplation considers God; it dwells upon the supreme intelligible Truth. The perfect contemplation which beholds the divine essence in the beatific vision is not to be had this side of heaven. Here on earth, however, we can achieve imperfect contemplation: "We see now through a glass in a dark manner" (I Cor. 13:12). Here we consider creatures in so far as they lead us to contemplate the Creator. Four things pertain, in a fixed order, to the contemplative life: (a) the disposing moral virtues; (b) preparatory acts of attention, study, reasoning; (c) contemplation of divine effects, that is, of creatures which manifest God; (d) the contemplation of divine truth itself.

5. Since, in this life, we cannot gaze directly upon the divine essence, the highest degree of contemplation possible is that which we find exemplified in the rapture of St. Paul (II Cor. 12).

6. The operation of the intellect is called a *movement*. In contemplation, the intellect's movement of fixing and focusing on a topic is called *curved* movement; the movement of reasoning or thinking a thing out in connected steps is called *straight* movement; the

union of the two movements in a movement which combines uniformity of gaze with progress through the various reasoned points, is called *oblique* movement.

7. There are in contemplation the delight of engaging in a suitable and congenial operation and the delight of knowing and gazing upon a beloved object. This spiritual delight surpasses all other human joys.

8. True contemplation is not interrupted for other sustained employments of the mind. It is continuous: perfectly so in its unchanging object, and truly so in the unabandoned purpose and effort of the contemplative person.

181. THE ACTIVE LIFE

1. The active life is given to *works* rather than to contemplation. Since the moral virtues are mainly pertinent to operation, they belong essentially to the active life.

2. And the virtue of *prudence*, which is speculative in essence and practical in many of its applications, is, as a practical or moral virtue, directly pertinent to the active life.

3. Teaching as actively exercised belongs to the active life. St. Gregory (*Hom.* xiv *in Ezech.*) says that "the active life is to feed the hungry, and to teach words of wisdom to the ignorant." Yet the teacher, considering truth in his own mind and loving it, is contemplative. Therefore teaching has a twofold aspect, one active, one contemplative.

4. The life of external action ends with earthly existence. If there be any external actions at all in heaven, they will have contemplation as their aim and end, and thus will belong to contemplation itself. St. Gregory says (*Hom.* xiv *in Ezech.*): "The active life ends with this world, but the contemplative life begins here and is perfected in heaven."

182. ACTIVE AND CONTEMPLATIVE LIFE COMPARED

1. The contemplative life, taken simply, is more excellent than the active life. Yet what is in itself more excellent is not, by that fact, more excellent in relation to every person or to all the demands and the circumstances of earthly existence. If Mary chose the best part, Martha did not choose a bad or unnecessary part. The order of human existence could not be served were all persons dedicated to contemplation and none to action.

2. The contemplative life is, in itself, more meritorious than the active life. For the contemplative life is wholly concerned with God,

whereas the active life must necessarily deal much with creatures. But it may happen that, in particular cases, one person merits more by the works of the active life than another person merits by the works of the contemplative life.

3. The active life, in so far as it demands attention to externals and care in their use and practice, hinders contemplation. But it can happen that active life contributes to the quelling of internal passions which arouse imaginings that distract and hamper the concentration of the soul; in such a case the active life itself contributes to contemplation.

4. Action precedes contemplation. For what is common to all precedes what is perfect and attainable by some. As St. Gregory points out (*Hom.* xiv *in Ezech.*), we can get to heaven without the contemplative life if we do all that we should do. But if we neglect doing what we should do (that is, if we neglect the active life), we cannot get to heaven.

STATES OF LIFE

(QUESTIONS 183 TO 189)

183. MEANING OF STATE OF LIFE

1. By a person's *state* we indicate something that establishes him with some permanence in his position and lays upon him pertinent duties. A person's state is not something mainly external and readily changeable; rather it is something internally recognized by intellect and embraced by will as lasting and in some measure binding. Thus, we do not speak of a man's being rich or poor as his state; this is his *condition*. But we do speak of a man's state as his being married or single, priest or layman or religious.

2. It is suitable that within the Church there should be various states, each with its own duties. For the Church has a variety of activities, and her beauty of order requires a scale of different offices or states to see that these activities are exercised. Says St. Paul (Eph. 4:11, 12): "He gave (that is, appointed) some apostles, and some prophets, and other some evangelists, and other some pastors and doctors, for the perfecting of the saints."

3. States with their pertinent duties differ according to the different activities assigned to each one. There is distinction of states of perfection, and distinction of active duties, and distinction of grades in each state and duty.

4. Among men who strive to cast off servitude to sin in order to serve God in justice, we distinguish the three orders of: beginners; the proficient; the perfect.

184. THE STATE OF PERFECTION

1. The perfection of Christian life consists chiefly in charity. Charity unites a person to God by grace and love and friendship. Thus charity best attains the end of Christian life, which is union with God. Says St. Paul (Col. 3:14): "Above all things, have charity, which is the bond of perfection." Charity bonds together in unity all other perfections.

2. *Absolute* perfection belongs to God alone, for what is absolutely perfect is lacking in nothing whatever, and is therefore infinite. *Relative* perfection is perfection in relation to a certain thing—person, state, condition, etc. Now, in relation to man, there is a perfection that belongs to the person who has finished his course and has attained the goal; this is the perfection of the blessed in heaven. Another perfection is that of man the wayfarer who is still engaged in making the journey of this earthly life; this perfection is possible to attain here on earth. It consists, first, in the removal from life of all mortal sin. Secondly, it consists in getting rid of every attachment or appetite which hinders a person from tending wholly to God. It is possible to have charity without this full perfection, with both its elements, but it is impossible to have charity without freedom from mortal sin. In the *proficient,* and even in *beginners,* charity exists; but the perfection of charity is in the *perfect.*

3. Primarily and essentially, perfection consists in obeying the commandments. Our Lord said that we are to love God wholly, and to love our neighbor as ourselves for God and in God. He added, "On these two commandments dependeth the whole law, and the prophets" (Matt. 22:40). Now, the love of God and neighbor is prescribed in the Ten Commandments. And, since this twofold love is the matter of charity or perfection, we rightly say that perfection consists in obeying the commandments. The counsels of poverty, chastity, and obedience to a religious superior, are instruments for the achieving of charity, but these are not prescribed for all; they are for those called by God to a special way of life. The counsels call for the giving up of good and lawful things (marriage, occupation in worldly business,

self-determination as to employment, etc.) which, none the less, can be a hindrance to charity.

4. If by the term, state of perfection, we mean the position that a person has in the Church, we see that a person can have the state without having the inner perfection. It is also possible for a person whose official status is not a state of perfection to be perfect in his spiritual life.

5. Those officially occupying the state of perfection in the Church are bishops and religious. These have bound themselves, with religious solemnity, to the unobstructed service of God.

6. Priests and others in major orders have (in the Western Church at least) the vow of chastity which belongs to the state of perfection. But for the rest, though they are bound to attain perfection in their own lives and in their own souls as all men are (and they the more so by reason of holy order), they do not hold the official status of state of perfection. Only bishops and religious are officially in the state of perfection.

7. The episcopal state (that of bishops) is more perfect than the religious state. For in spiritual things it is not lawful to look back or to descend from higher to lower status. But a man may lawfully pass from the religious to the episcopal state; hence the latter is the more perfect.

8. The religious state, in point of total dedication to the pursuit of perfection, is more perfect than the state of the diocesan or parish clergy.

185. THE EPISCOPAL STATE

1. When St. Paul says (I Tim. 3:1), "If a man desire the office of a bishop, he desireth a good work," he means what he says, namely, that the desire is for *a work*, necessary and precious, wholly indispensable. But St. Paul does not speak of the motive of the desire; he does not say that the desire is good, but that the work is good. Now, it is hardly possible for a man to desire the bishop's office without desiring what belongs to it—power to rule, a right to reverence and honor, a sufficiency of temporal goods. And, for the rest, to desire the bishop's office is likely to desire with presumption, possibly with ambition, possibly even with covetousness. For the great office of a bishop is a great burden as well, and it involves the state of perfection. But to accept the bishop's office when called to it, is always lawful, often a duty. Vainly to desire the office of bishop, or ambitiously to aspire to it, is wrong. Says the unknown author of a *Homily on Matthew* xxv: "It is good to desire a good work, but to desire primacy of honor is

vanity. Primacy seeks the one who avoids it, and eludes him who seeks it."

2. But it is not right for one appointed to the bishop's office to refuse the appointment absolutely. There is inordinateness of will in the desire to have rule over others; there is also inordinateness of will in the refusal to accept one's appointed task. St. Augustine says (*Ep.* XLVIII *ad Eudox.*): "Do not prefer your case to the needs of the Church."

3. The person chosen as bishop should have fitness for the office, and should be able to instruct, defend, and govern the faithful peacefully. It is not necessary that he be the best person for the office, but that he be a good person. For himself, a man appointed to the bishop's office need make no objection to his appointment so long as he is aware of nothing in himself that would make it unlawful for him to accept the post.

4. A bishop must remain in office as long as it is possible for him to discharge its duties well for the spiritual benefit of his subjects. When, for some good reason, he feels that he can no longer sustain the burden, he may lawfully appeal to the pope for release from his duties. Hence, it is sometimes lawful for a bishop to resign his charge.

5. A bishop binds himself to fulfill the duties of his pastoral office for the eternal welfare of his subjects. Hence, when the spiritual good of these subjects requires his presence among them, he must remain at his post, despite trials and persecutions. Yet if his subjects will suffer no essential spiritual lack because of his absence for a time, he may depart, whether because of some advantage to the Church, or because of danger to his own person.

6. It is perfectly lawful for a bishop to have property of his own. To live without owning anything of one's own is a matter of counsel, not of precept. And no one is bound to a counsel unless he has freely obligated himself to it by a vow.

7. As to the disposition of ecclesiastical goods, bishops are required to be faithful stewards or trustees; they are to use surplus goods for the benefit of the poor, for the decency of divine worship, for aid to needy clerics, and for the upbuilding of the Church in her necessary temporalities.

8. A religious who is raised to the episcopate is bound to retain such offices and duties of the religious state as are compatible with the discharge of the bishop's duties, and are helpful in that work. But he is no longer bound to such of his former observances as conflict with the demands of his new state.

186. THE RELIGIOUS STATE

1. The religious state is one in which a person seeks to adhere wholly to God. And in this is perfection. Hence, the religious life implies the state of perfection.

2. A religious is bound to make effort after perfection, and to strive to fulfill the demands of perfect charity. He must be faithful to such counsels as bind him by vow. And he must practice with fidelity the Rule he has professed.

3. For the attaining of perfect charity, the first requisite is *voluntary* poverty. By this, a person most effectively releases himself from attachment to earthly things and affection for them. Our Lord said (Matt. 19:21):"If thou wilt be perfect, go, sell what thou hast, and give to the poor . . . and come follow me."

4. Perpetual continence is also a requisite for religious perfection. For, despite the need for marriage, and the honest and honorable status of those who follow this way of life, it does involve activities and duties which can hinder a person from devoting himself entirely to God's service. St. Paul (I Cor. 7:32, 33) says: "He that is without a wife is solicitous for the things of the Lord, how he may please God: but he that is with a wife is solicitous for the things of the world, how he may please his wife." St. Paul says the very same thing of the woman who has, and who has not, a husband.

5. The religious state is a state of perfection, which means that those who embrace it must steadily strive for perfection. So that this striving may be well directed, and not, perhaps, a matter of restless and unavailing endeavor, it finds rule and regularity in full and willing obedience to a superior. Hence *obedience* is requisite for religious perfection.

6. Persons in the religious life are under obligation, freely assumed, to achieve the perfection proper to their state. Such obligation cannot be effectively assumed without a vow to observe the requisites of the religious life. In fact, religious perfection requires the vows of fulfilling its essential duties of poverty, chastity, and obedience in all lawful matters to a religious superior.

7. Indeed, it may be justly said that religious perfection consists in these three vows. For in the religious state a person strives for perfection, seeks to keep himself free from care and worry about external things, and offers himself wholly and steadfastly to God. Now, all these essential purposes of the religious life are admirably served by the vows of poverty, chastity, and obedience. The faithful practice of fulfilling these vows may rightly be said to constitute the perfection of the religious state.

8. The vow of obedience is the chief of the three vows. For (a) by obedience a person offers to God his own will, and this is something more excellent than his body which he offers by the vow of chastity, or external goods which he offers by the vow of poverty; (b) the vow of obedience *includes* the other two vows, for the religious life imposes chastity and poverty by precept; but chastity and poverty do not necessarily include the vow of religious obedience; (c) the vow of obedience, more directly than the other two vows, indicates full submission to God's will.

9. Willful and serious violation of any of the vows of the religious life is always a mortal sin. Now, the essential virtues of poverty, chastity, and obedience are subserved by a variety of observances imposed by rule. Violation of any of these observances does not exceed venial sin, unless indeed the violation comes from contempt for the rule; in this case, the violation would be a mortal sin.

10. A sin committed by one who is in the religious life is more deplorable than the same sin committed by one who is not in that state of life. Yet it may happen that a sin, not opposed to any of the religious vows, and not the occasion of scandal in any way, is no greater (and perhaps it may even be less) than the same sin committed by another who is not in the religious state of life.

187. WHAT IS FITTING FOR THOSE IN THE RELIGIOUS STATE

1. It is lawful and suitable for those in the religious state to teach and, if they are priests, to preach. For, if they have ability for such tasks, and are given jurisdiction by the right authorities, there is nothing in the works themselves to conflict with the religious state.

2. It is not lawful for those in the religious life to carry on secular business for motives of mere gain. Yet for charity, they may, with due moderation, occupy themselves with business affairs. Some measure of such work is required for the conducting of schools and orphanages. And in business connected with the Church or with the relief of a neighbor's need, there is charity, and not secular officiousness.

3. Those in the religious state are not bound to manual labor (unless there is a special precept requiring it in the Rule which they profess), any more than other people are so bound. Circumstances may, indeed, render manual labor necessary for religious, and then they are required to perform it.

4. It is certainly lawful for religious to live on alms. St. Benedict, living in a cave, and uninterruptedly intent on his spiritual growth, was supported for three years by food which a monk brought him at

intervals; he did not engage in gainful labor to support himself. Those religious who live on alms are not idlers. They sanctify themselves and others by diligently fulfilling the duties of their state, and are content to be regarded as dependents, accepting whatever is given them; thus they are helped to be humble and are made more free to attend the things of God.

5. Not only may religious live on alms given them unasked; they may also beg for the material necessaries of life. To beg is to abase oneself, and when this is done for Christ, it is a notable act of religious humility, and a potent cure for pride.

6. St. Jerome, instructing the monk Rusticus, says, "Let your sober dress show your purity of mind, and your coarse cloak show your contempt of the world." It is suitable for religious to use common and coarse attire, for such apparel befits those who do penance and contemn worldly glory.

188. VARIETIES OF RELIGIOUS LIFE

1. There are various religious orders, societies, congregations, communities. This is so because the works of charity are various, and all religous are striving to achieve perfection in charity. One religious family may be devoted to teaching, another to the care of the sick, another to the reclamation of delinquents, another to the care of orphans, and so on. Hence, various religious communities exist. And religious practice is itself marked by variety; accordingly, one religious community practices silence; another, strict abstinence; another has a special task of perfectly reciting the Divine Office, another engages in manual labor, and so on. Here again we discern a reason for the existence of various religious communities.

2. There are religious communities for the works of charity in the active life, and there are others which are devoted to the contemplative life. For, while in itself the contemplative life is the more excellent of the two types of Christian life, both active and contemplative life serve and pursue charity; for we are to love God, and neighbor for God. The contemplative life advances the soul directly in the love of God. The active life advances the soul through works that manifest the love of neighbor for the sake of God.

3. A religious community or order can exist for some special service to neighbors. Indeed, a religious order can exist for such a service as soldering. A military order cannot be established for material conquest or a worldly purpose. But it can be established for the defense of divine worship, for public safety, for defense of the poor and the oppressed.

4. An order may be founded for preaching, for catechizing, for the hearing of confessions, and for other works that make for the instruction and sanctification of human souls.

5. A religious order may justly exist for the purpose of study. For study enlightens the mind, helps to the understanding of the truths of religion, keeps the student from gross employment and the urge to base sin, prepares the teacher and preacher and writer for their tasks.

6. It follows from what has been said in several places in our studies, that an order devoted to the contemplative life is, simply considered, more excellent than an order devoted to the active life.

7. The perfection of religious life is in no way hampered or hindered by the possession of goods in common. The vow of poverty is the surrendering of personal and private ownership of material things. And the perfection of this personal sacrifice is not lessened by the fact that material things are owned by the order or community as such. The vow of poverty frees the individual religious from care and worry about privately owned property, from the love of amassing personal riches, and from the vainglory of being personally wealthy. These are the ends intended by the vow of poverty; these ends the vow achieves perfectly despite the fact that goods are owned in common.

8. Religious living in community are a help to one another in their striving for perfection. One is helped by the good example of another; one profits by the instruction of another. And the earnest religious is helped even by noting what to avoid in the unsuitable attitude or conduct of another. But when one has reached perfection in contemplation, the life of solitude is more excellent than life in community. Yet for anyone but the person who has really achieved perfection, the life of solitude is fraught with great dangers.

189. ENTRANCE INTO THE RELIGIOUS LIFE

1. The religious life is a school of perfection, and even untutored pupils may enter that school to begin their progress towards perfection. Hence, not only those who are well practiced in the observance of the commandments should enter that life, but also the unpracticed, that they may be removed from temptation, avoid sin, and work towards the attaining of perfection.

2. A good work done in fulfillment of a vow is better than the same work done without a vow. Hence, it is a praiseworthy thing for one who is called to the religious life to make a vow of entering that life.

3. Such a vow binds in conscience. It must be fulfilled accord-

ing to the measure of obligation assumed by the maker of the vow at the time he made it.

4. A person may make a vow to enter religion, and keep it by actually entering a community, and then, during his time of probation, conclude seriously that he is not called to the religious life. Such a person does not sin against his vow in leaving the order. For he fulfilled the vow when he entered the order as a candidate, and he has taken no further vow in the order itself. But a man who has passed his probation, and has freely made his solemn vows in religion, is bound to remain in the order perpetually through all his life.

5. In olden times, it was the custom of pious parents to enter little children in a religious community so that they might be trained from early youth in the duties of the religious life. This custom is no longer in vogue.

6. When parents are in need of support and cannot be fittingly cared for without the help of their children, these latter, even if they be grown up, cannot lawfully enter religion. Apart from such necessity, one who feels called to the religious state is not to be prevented from entering it because of parental disapproval or prohibition.

7. Parish priests may surrender their parochial duties to enter the religious state. For this, they need no special permission from the pope.

8. It is lawful and commendable to pass from one religious community or order to another if there are genuinely serious reasons to justify the change, and if the change is made in full observance of the pertinent laws of the Church.

9. One may lawfully urge or induce another to enter a religious community, provided there is no compulsion in the inducement, and no unholy circumstance, and no trickery.

10. A person who feels called to the religious life requires no great amount of discussion or seeking of advice. He must simply follow his vocation. With reference to which order he should enter, some consideration and counsel may be wise.

[IIIa]

THE THIRD PART

[*Questions 1-90*]

THE INCARNATION

(QUESTIONS 1 to 26)

1. FITNESS OF THE INCARNATION

1. It is most suitable that the invisible things of God should be manifested by visible things. Creatures, as St. Paul says (Rom. 1:20), prove the existence, and show the attributes of God. But the Incarnation, the coming of God himself as man, most magnificently shows forth the divine perfections. For God to become man is a work of wondrous goodness, wisdom, justice, and power; these "invisible things of God" could not be more nobly manifested than they are in the Incarnation. Now, since goodness communicates itself and spreads itself abroad, it is fitting that Infinite Goodness should communicate itself in the most perfect manner, and it does so in the Incarnation. Therefore, it is supremely fitting that God should become man.

2. The Incarnation was necessary for man's salvation. It was not *absolutely* necessary, for God is almighty, and he could have restored fallen man in other ways. But it was *relatively* necessary, that is, necessary in relation to the need of bringing redemption to man in the most noble, effective, and admirable way. Consider the surpassing excellence of the Incarnation: (a) It advances man in virtue; it enlivens his faith; it strengthens his hope; it enkindles his charity; it shows man the perfect example for good works; it gives a human being an awareness of participating in the divine nature, for, as St. Augustine says (xiii *de Temp.*): "God was made man that man might be made God." (b) The Incarnation keeps man from evil; shows him his human nobility that makes him despise the devil; makes him aware of his dignity; makes him understand the degrading effect of sin; teaches him to look humbly to Christ and not to be presumptuous; instructs him in the heartening truth that the satisfaction made by God Incarnate releases him from slavery to sin. (c) No mere man could have made satisfaction for the whole race. Yet man owed the debt that had to be paid. Only God could pay the debt, and God did not owe it. Hence it was magnificently right that the payer of the debt, the Redeemer, should be both God and man.

3. Some have taught that God, in his boundless love for us, would

have become man even if there had been no human sin and the consequent need of redemption. But this seems unlikely. All our knowledge on this point is from Holy Scripture, and scripture everywhere assigns man's sin as the reason for the Incarnation.

4. Christ who is God-made-Man, that is, God Incarnate, came to take away the evil effect of original sin, and to make it possible for man to get to heaven and so attain his true end. Christ came to give us all the means of getting rid of original sin, of obtaining pardon for actual sins, of gaining grace and staying free from actual sins. And therefore in scripture (John 1:29) Christ is called "the Lamb of God . . . who taketh away the sins of the world."

5. The time of the Incarnation was most suitable. Had God become man to redeem us immediately after the first sin was committed, human pride would not have been humbled in consequence of that sin; man would not have realized, through an impressive stretch of time, the greatness of the treasure he had lost. And it was good for man to prepare, by prayerful longing, for the redemption; thus he would gain a keen awareness of the value of redemption, and of his need for it, so that, when it came, he could ardently take advantage of it. On the other hand, it would not do to have the Incarnation too long delayed, lest human longing turn to hopelessness and despairing disappointment. Therefore, at exactly the right time, in the "fulness of time," as St. Paul says (Gal. 4:4), God became man.

6. The perfection of glory to which human nature will finally be raised by the Word Incarnate will appear when souls and bodies are united again at the end of the world in the time of the general judgment. Yet it could not be fitting to have the Incarnation deferred to that moment. For man needed remedy for sin, knowledge of God, reverence, good morals. And the Incarnation gave man these needed things: first, by hope and anticipation in those who lovingly awaited it, and then, by faith and devotion in those who actually experienced it in fact and in its fruits. None of these needed things would have come to man had the Incarnation been delayed to the end of the world. Hope and longing would have disappeared; the hearts of men would have grown cold.

2. THE UNION OF THE WORD AND THE FLESH

1. The *nature* of a thing is its essence considered as the source of operations. And the *essence* of a thing is the basic make-up of the thing; its fundamental constitution in being and kind; it is what makes the thing what it is; it is what we express by a true and exact definition of the thing. And, as we have noted, the nature of a thing is this same

essence regarded from the standpoint of what it *does*, or what it is *for*. Thus we say that man's essence, physically considered, is body and soul; man's nature is the human essence as capable of living, walking, talking, thinking, willing. Now, God's nature and essence are in all respects one and the same reality; this is because of God's perfect simplicity. And human nature (that is, the human essence with its faculties for operation, and notably its intellect and will) is a complete nature in its kind. God could not have become man by any fusion or mixing of the human nature and the divine nature; the nature of God is changeless and cannot be fused or mingled with another nature. Yet these two natures, the divine and the human, were not merely to be held side by side in an *accidental* union. There had to be a *substantial* union of God and man if God were to be incarnate. Since, as we see, the point or focus of this substantial union cannot be the natures themselves, we must seek that focus (that, precisely, in which the union took place) in *the divine Person* of the Son of God.

2. A *person* is an individual substance of rational nature, that is, equipped for understanding and willing. Whatever is to be attributed to such a being, is attributed to it *in person*. It is to *the person* of John Doe that we attribute his mind, his will, his hasty temper, his pleasant smile, his broken arm. Now, if human nature is not united to God in the *Person* of the divine Son, it is not united to the divine Son at all. Hence, we must conclude that the union of the two natures, divine and human, which we call the Incarnation, takes place in the Person of the Word of God, that is, of God the Son, the Second Person of the Eternal Trinity.

3. An individual substance with its own way of operating and acting is called a *supposit* or a *hypostasis*. Thus, a tree, or an animal, or a man, is a hypostasis. But the *part* of a substance (say, a man's arm), is indeed a substance, but it has not its own way of acting; the arm's acting is the acting of the man; if the arm be severed from the man, it does not continue (on its own, so to speak) to act as an arm. Hence, a hypostasis is a *complete* individual substance with its own way of acting. Now, when a hypostasis is equipped to act with understanding and free will, it is called a *person*. Therefore we say, "*Person* adds to *hypostasis* a determinate nature, namely the rational nature." It is manifest, then, that every person is a hypostasis, but not the other way round. Hence, a union in person must be a union in the hypostasis; else it could be a union only in point of some dignity, that is, an accidental and not a substantial union. But God actually *became* man. God therefore united human nature to the divine Nature in

the Person or hypostasis of the Son. For this reason we call the union which made the Incarnation a fact by the name of "the hypostatic union."

4. St. John Damascene (*De Fid. Orthodox.* III 3–5) says that in Christ we acknowledge two natures, but one hypostasis composed from both. This does not mean that there is any real composition or compounding in the simple divine Essence and Nature of the Son of God. It means that the Second Divine Person is now a Person in whom two natures subsist.

5. Since Christ is true man as well as true God, his human soul and human body are united substantially as these elements are united in any other man. But in Christ the substantial union of human body and human soul does not constitute a new hypostasis or person, but is substantially effected in the already existing Person of the Son of God.

6. The hypostatic union is a substantial union, not an accidental one; it is a union *of* two natures *in* one Person. If the union were only accidental, there would be two persons in Christ, whereas, in truth, there is only one Person, and that is the Person of the Eternal Word or Son. And if the union were such that the human nature would be absorbed completely into the divine Nature (were that possible), then Christ would not be true man; but he is true man as well as true God. Christ who is God Incarnate is *one* divine Person, subsisting with *two* substantially united but really distinct and unconfused natures, the nature of God and the nature of man.

7. Since God became man "in the fullness of time," the hypostatic union does not exist from eternity; it is the work or creation of God, and took place in time.

8. The Son of God *assumed* human nature in the Incarnation. This assumption of human nature is the divine action by which the hypostatic union of the two natures (that of God and that of man) was effected. Speaking precisely, then, the *assumption* is not the same as the *union*. For we can say, speaking of the *union*, either, "The divine Nature is united with the human nature," or "The human nature is united with the divine Nature." But, in speaking of the *assumption*, we refer that term to the divine Nature exclusively, and say that God assumed human nature; we cannot say that man assumed the divine Nature.

9. Because the hypostatic union is effected in the divine Person of the Son of God, it is the most excellent of unions.

10. It is correct to say that the hypostatic union took place by grace if we understand *grace* to mean the will of God doing what is well-pleasing to him, without any merit or deserving on the part of those for whose benefit it is done.

11. For the human race did not merit the redemption, nor the Incarnation which made the redemption possible. Says St. Paul (Titus 3:5): "Not by the works of justice which we have done, but according to his mercy he saved us." It may be said that the holy men of old who longed prayerfully for the Redeemer, established, by their fidelity and devotion, a claim on God's mercy and love, and thus merited the Incarnation *congruously*. But no one, or all, of the human race could merit the Incarnation *condignly* under the title of justice, as something earned, and therefore owed to man.

12. Grace was natural to the human nature of Christ in the sense that it was in him from the beginning, from the very moment of the effecting of the hypostatic union. And by reason of this union there is in the human nature of Christ a perfect and untouchable sinlessness.

3. THE PERSON ASSUMING HUMAN NATURE

1. It is fitting for a divine Person to assume human nature. In this there is no addition to the infinite God. The assumed human nature is perfected, not God who is infinitely and eternally all-perfect. Hence, in assuming human nature, a divine Person exercises a loving and merciful act, and is in no wise debased or dishonored. Hence, it is fitting for a divine Person to assume human nature.

2. Nor is there anything derogatory or unfitting to the divine Nature in the fact that a divine Person assumes human nature. For what is becoming to a divine Person is necessarily becoming to the undivided nature of God in that Person.

3. Even if we mentally focus on the divine Nature, leaving the Persons out of account, we can say that the divine Nature can fittingly assume another nature. There is no conflict or contradiction in the thought of such an assuming, and God is almighty in his divine Nature.

4. Since all the works of God's power are from the Trinity itself, the act of assuming human nature is common to the Three Persons. But the union resulting from this act is in only one divine Person, that is, the Person of the Divine Son.

5. Had it been the will of God (the undivided will of God in Trinity), the Father or the Holy Ghost might have become incarnate.

6. Indeed, the *three* Persons of the Trinity, who subsist in one divine Nature, could also subsist with one human nature, so that then the human nature would be assumed by the Three Divine Persons.

7. And there is no conflict or contradiction in the thought that one Person should assume a human nature distinct from the human nature assumed by the Son. Nor, indeed, is there contradiction in the

thought that the Son should assume another human nature distinct from the one he did assume.

8. It is most fitting, however, that the Divine Son became man to redeem us, rather than the Father or the Holy Ghost. For the Son is the Word in whom is the exemplar of every creature. Now, as a craftsman restores his broken handiwork according to the original model or exemplar, so it is suitable that the restoration of God's broken human handiwork should be accomplished through and by the Son. Again, to make men the adoptive sons of God, it was suitable that God should "send his Son into the world." And, finally, since it was man's inordinate desire for knowledge that brought ruin on himself, it is fitting that the Word of True Knowledge should come to redeem him.

4. THE NATURE ASSUMED

1. It is most fitting that human nature was assumed by God. For human nature has the dignity of being rational; it was made to know and love God; it stood in need of redemption and therefore of the Incarnation. No other nature has these points of fitness for being assumed. Irrational natures lack dignity; the rational nature of the good angels is without the need for atonement, since they have not sinned; the rational nature of fallen angels is confirmed in unrepented sin, which makes atonement and redemption impossible. Of all created natures, only human nature presents the characteristics, qualities, and conditions that make the Incarnation perfectly suitable.

2. The Son of God assumed the *nature* of man, but not the *person* of a man. In Christ the human nature is hypostatically united to the divine Nature in the one Person of God the Son. Therefore, Christ is (by the human nature assumed), truly *human,* but he is not a *human person.* He is a *divine* Person. And that Person is the Second Person of the Trinity.

3. Christ is not a man assumed by God. He is not a man *divinized* by God's boundless power. He is God himself who has assumed, not a man, but the complete nature of man.

4. It has been foolishly asserted that the Son of God ought to have assumed human nature *as such,* in an abstract way, so that Christ would not have an *individual* human nature, and would be man, but not *this* man. Now, human nature is the nature of a bodily creature; such a creature cannot really exist except in an individual way, as *this bodily thing.* Hence, the Son of God took an individual human nature, and was born as a human individual of his Virgin Mother. St. John Damascene (*De Fid. Orthodox.* III 11) says: "God the Word did not

assume a nature that exists in thought alone . . . this would have been a false and fictitious Incarnation." Therefore, God the Son did not assume human nature as it is mentally conceived in the universal idea of *man*, that is, as separated from individuals. God became man, and God-made-Man is Christ, and Christ is *this one man*, and no other. And this one man is a divine Person, not a human person.

5. Certainly, it was not suitable that the Son of God should become incarnate in *all* human individuals. This would make the whole human race one divine Person. And this would be derogatory to the divine dignity. Besides, it would make the redemptive work of Christ both needless and impossible.

6. St. Augustine (*De Trin.* xiii 18) says that God could have assumed human nature otherwise than from Adam's race; yet he chose to assume it from that race, so that he might vanquish the enemy in the nature which the enemy had vanquished. The power of God is gloriously manifested in assuming a nature that was weakened and corrupted; to stand, in that nature, perfect in purity, power, and glory.

5. ELEMENTS OF THE NATURE ASSUMED

1. The human body of Christ is a true human body, not merely an apparent body. The Son of God assumed true human nature, and to this nature a real body belongs. If the body of Christ were merely an apparent body, there would have been something fictitious in the work of redemption. For if Christ had not a real body, he could not really have died.

2. Christ's body, like every true human body, was composed of real flesh, bones, tissue, etc. It was not made of some incorruptible matter different from the structure of other human bodies.

3. And the Son of God becoming incarnate also assumed a true human soul. Without such a soul there is no human nature, and God assumed human nature.

4. To assume a human soul is to assume the faculties or powers of that soul. Hence, God in becoming man assumed a human intellect and a human will.

6. ORDER OF THE ELEMENTS ASSUMED

1. With the assuming of the human soul, complete human nature was assumed. For it is the soul which is the substantial form (or essential substantial constituent and determinant) of a living bodily man. What the soul determines and substantially constitutes is the flesh-and-blood man. Hence, we say that God the Son assumed human flesh through the medium of the human soul.

2. The human soul has a capacity for God inasmuch as it can know him, and then love him. Now, the faculty of knowing God (the fundamental act which aligns the soul with its true end or goal), is the mind or intellect. The intellect is the highest, noblest, purest faculty of the soul. Hence, through the medium of intellect, God assumed the soul; and through the medium of the soul, he assumed the flesh.

3. The human soul of Christ was not assumed separately before the flesh. For human nature demands body-and-soul, and it is human nature that was assumed.

4. Nor did the Son of God first assume the flesh, and afterwards the soul. St. John Damascene (*De Fid. Orthodox.* III 2) says: "At one and the same time, the Word of God was made flesh, and the flesh was united to a rational and intelligent soul."

5. The Son of God assumed human nature *entire*, and therefore assumed its parts. He did not assume part after part until the whole was made up; he did not assume human nature through the medium of parts, but he assumed the parts through the medium of the whole.

6. If we understand the word *grace* to mean God's free giving of Christ to redeem mankind, then grace is the effective cause of the assuming of human nature by God the Son. But even in this meaning of grace, we cannot say that grace is *a means* for effecting the union of the human nature and the divine Nature. More precisely, grace means either: (a) the grace of union, which is the very Person given freely to subsist in human nature; or (b) habitual or sanctifying grace which constitutes the human nature in holiness. Now, the grace of union cannot be *the means* for assuming human nature; this grace is Christ, the term or outcome of the assuming. Nor can habitual grace be *the means* of assuming the human nature; this grace presupposes the human nature already assumed. Therefore, we say: the human nature of Christ was not assumed by means of grace.

7. THE GRACE OF CHRIST AS A MAN

1. That the human soul of Christ had sanctifying grace, is certain. For: (a) this soul was in union with the Word of God; (b) this soul was dignified above all human souls, and was to know and love God more perfectly than any other; for such operations sanctifying or habitual grace is necessary; (c) the grace of this soul was to overflow upon others, according to scripture (John 1:10): "Of his fullness we have all received, and grace for grace."

2. Grace touches the essence of the soul; virtue belongs to the powers of the soul. As powers flow from essence, so virtues flow

from grace. From the most perfect grace of Christ's human soul the virtues flowed most perfectly. Thus, Christ had all the virtues in his human soul.

3. Christ as man, from the first moment of his conception, beheld fully the very essence of God. There was, therefore, neither need nor possibility of *faith* in our Lord. For faith is of divine things unseen, and Christ saw all divine things perfectly.

4. From the beginning of Christ's human existence, he was in full possession and enjoyment of God, and this is the object of hope. Hence, there was neither need nor possibility of the theological virtue of *hope* in Christ as man. Of course, our Lord could look forward humanly to the future events of his human life: his Resurrection, for instance, and his Ascension.

5. The gifts of the Holy Ghost are perfections of the soul's powers, which make these powers respond readily and consistently to the inspirations of God. All the gifts were most excellently present in the human soul of Christ.

6. Even the gift of fear was there, but it was neither the fear of God's punishments for sin, nor the fear of offending God by sinning. It was the deep reverence for God in the perfect human soul of Christ.

7. The gratuitous graces (such as miracles, prophecy, tongues) which are given to a man for the conversion and sanctification of others, rather than for his own sanctification, were all in Christ in the most perfect degree. Christ came to redeem us, but also *to teach* us essential divine truth; gratuitous graces are such a teacher's credentials, and they confirm his teaching. All the gratuitous graces exist most perfectly in the most perfect teacher of divine truth.

8. A prophecy is the certain proclaiming of a future or distant event; the prophet who proclaims the event must be one of the race to whom he speaks. Now, Christ is true man, and what he knows as man the comprehensor (that is, as one who beholds the beatific vision) he proclaims as man the wayfarer (that is, as one yet living in this world). Hence, in Christ is the gift of prophecy.

9. In Christ as man there is the fullness of grace *in intensity* because of his substantial union with the source of all grace. In Christ as man there is also the fullness of grace *in power,* for from him grace flows out to all others who receive it, and extends in them to its proper effects, such as virtues and gifts.

10. Among rational creatures, Christ alone (as man) has the perfect fullness of grace, in the sense that he possesses grace in its greatest excellence, its complete extent, and all the excellences of its effects.

The Blessed Mother is called "full of grace" (Luke 1:28), and St. Stephen, the first martyr, had fullness of grace (Acts 6:8). Now, the fullness of grace in all rational creatures except Christ is fullness according to capacity to receive and possess; it is fullness in *receivers;* the first and greatest of receivers, in the capacity for grace and the full dower of grace, is the Mother of God. But in Christ the fullness of grace is *on the part of grace itself*. Others with fullness of grace have all the grace *they* can receive; Christ has all the grace that *can* be received.

11. The grace of God in a human soul is a creature of God, and therefore is not infinite. Even the grace in Christ's human soul is not infinite, for that human soul is a creature, and grace itself is a creature. Of course, *the grace of union* is infinite, but this grace is the divine Person subsisting with two natures. We are speaking here of the humanity of Christ, and of his human soul with its grace; we are not speaking of the grace of union.

12. Since the fullness of grace itself is in the human soul of Christ, this grace cannot be increased. The end of grace is the uniting of a rational creature with God; Christ as man is a rational creature always perfectly united with God; he, therefore, can have no accession of grace to give him what he already possesses.

13. The habitual or sanctifying grace in the human soul of Christ follows the union effected by God's assuming of human nature. This is our way of understanding the matter: first, the union; then, grace in Christ's human soul. But this is no case of before and after, in the sense of *time*. The sanctifying grace of Christ's human soul follows the union as light follows the sun; there is no interval of time between the appearance of the sun and the luminosity of the sun.

8. THE GRACE OF CHRIST AS HEAD OF THE CHURCH

1. In the human body, the head holds the first place of dignity, perfection, and control. So, in the body of the Church, Christ as man, by reason of the union with God, holds the highest place, and is rightly called "The Head of the Church."

2. The whole humanity of Christ, body and soul, influences other human beings in body and soul. Therefore, Christ is the Head of men, not merely the Head of souls.

3. Christ is the Head of all mankind. St. Paul says (I Tim. 4:10) that Christ "is the Savior of all men." And we read (I John 2:2) that Christ is "the propitiation for our sins, and not for ours only, but also for those of the whole world." Christ is the Head of all men, and principally of all who are united to him by grace or glory.

4. Christ as man is Head of the angels. Men and angels are made for the one purpose: the glory of God, and the enjoyment of heaven. Hence, figuratively speaking, men and angels form one body; for the mystical body which is the Church consists not only of men but of angels. And of this body Christ is the Head.

5. The grace of Christ as Head of the Church, called *capital* grace, is in reality the same sanctifying or habitual grace which is in him as a human individual (that is, *personal* grace), and which constitutes that fullness of grace of which "we have all received."

6. Christ alone is the Head of the Church. On earth, the pope is his vicar, and the bishops as heads of their respective dioceses are, as St. Paul says (II Cor. 5:20), "ambassadors for Christ."

7. As prince or prelate is head of the group that constitutes his realm or charge, so the devil is the head of all the wicked. In Job (41:25) we read that the devil "is king over all the children of pride."

8. Antichrist too is the head of the wicked, but not in the same way as the devil is their head. The devil precedes Antichrist in time, and also exceeds him in the power of influencing men to evil. Antichrist is head of the wicked in the sense that he is the worst of all who are influenced by the devil.

9. KNOWLEDGE IN CHRIST

1. As God, Christ has all knowledge. As man, he has all the human perfections, including a human mind with its human or created knowledge.

2. Christ as man has the knowledge that the blessed souls enjoy in heaven, that is, the knowledge of God directly seen in beatific vision.

3. The beatific knowledge of Christ as beheld in the vision is joined in Christ as man with all possible creatural knowledge. For the human nature of Christ, because it is joined hypostatically with the divine Nature, has to be perfect in all respects. Therefore, as Scripture testifies (Col. 2:3), in Christ are "all the treasures of wisdom and knowledge."

4. In Christ as man there is *beatific* knowledge, and the fullness of *infused* knowledge. There is also *acquired* knowledge in Christ as man, for he is perfect in his human nature, and the human faculties of that nature functioned in him perfectly. Hence, even though he has perfect knowledge to begin with, he also, during his earthly life, learned things in a human way.

10. THE BEATIFIC KNOWLEDGE IN CHRIST

1. The human soul of Christ is as perfect as a human soul can be, but it is always a *finite* soul. Hence this soul, enjoying the beatific vision, does not comprehend the divine Essence in the full and accurate meaning of the word *comprehend*. For to say that the human soul of Christ *ccmprehends* the divine Essence would be to say that a finite soul perfectly compasses the infinite; and this is quite impossible.

2. Christ as man knows all things in the divine Word, for Christ *is* the divine Word as well as true and creatural man. The human mind of Christ does not itself know all things possible; here again we should have a case of finite encompassing infinite. But the human mind of Christ does know, in the Word, all that is actually said or thought or done by anyone at any time, past, present, or to come.

3. The human soul of Christ knows its own power, and all that this power can accomplish. And therefore Christ knows that his power can go on cleansing souls from sin and doing good to man, without limit; it can be said, in this sense, that Christ as man "knows infinite things."

4. The human soul of Christ is united to the Word in Person; therefore it is more fully enlightened by the Word than any other creature. Therefore, the human soul of Christ beholds the divine Essence in vision more perfectly than any other creature in heaven.

11. CHRIST'S INFUSED KNOWLEDGE

1. Christ's human intellect is enriched with the fullness of *infused* knowledge. For, by reason of the hypostatic union, the human faculties of our Lord are as perfect as such faculties can possibly be; and to have infused knowledge is a perfection of the human mind. By divinely infused knowledge, Christ as man knows all that any or all human minds can learn by the rational power (for instance, Christ perfectly knows all human sciences); he also knows all revealed truths, and all truths made known to the mind by the gifts of the Holy Ghost and the gratuitous graces. But Christ as man knows the divine Essence, not by infused knowledge, but by the direct and intuitive knowledge of the beatific vision.

2. Since our Lord as man had the beatific vision from the beginning, He could understand in its light, without turning (as men on earth must do) to the sense-images called phantasms.

3. Our Lord did not need, here on earth, to think discursively, that is, to reason things out. But he could and did use the reasoning

method in expressing his knowledge for the benefit of others, thus to make clear to them the logical nature of his teachings.

4. The infused knowledge possessed by Christ as man is more excellent than the knowledge possessed by the angels, and this, both in extent, and in the perfection of pure certitude. For the spiritual enlightenment of Christ's human soul is more excellent, by reason of the hypostatic union, than that which is shed upon any other creature, human or angelic.

5. The knowledge infused into the human mind of Christ is *habitual knowledge,* a stable possession, to be used when he pleased.

6. Since Christ's soul is a human soul with human modes of understanding, his infused knowledge is classified as constituting distinct sciences; that is, his knowledge is an *orderly* knowledge of things and classes of things knowable.

12. CHRIST'S ACQUIRED KNOWLEDGE

1. There is in Christ's human soul every perfection connatural to the soul, including an *active* intellect which renders things understandable, and an intellect *properly so called* which grasps these understandables and holds them as knowledge. Hence there is *acquired* knowledge in Christ as man. It is perfect knowledge in its kind; that is, Christ knows by his acquired knowledge whatever can be humanly known through the service of the intellect.

2. Now, the human intellect does not grasp all things intelligible in a single instant, but goes on and on, by the process called *abstraction,* forming idea after idea. Thus human acquired knowledge increases. And so of Christ it is said in scripture (Luke 2:52), that he "advanced in wisdom . . ."

3. Yet Christ was not a pupil; he was not really taught by any human being. He says (John 18:37): "For this was I born, and for this came I into the world, that I should give testimony to the truth." It was not suitable to the dignity of him who came to teach truth, that he should himself be taught by those he came to instruct.

4. Thus Christ as man was not taught by men. Neither was he taught by angels. For his acquired knowledge, the angelic ministry is not required. For his infused knowledge, the hypostatic union fills his human soul with knowledge without the mediation of angels or any creatures. Christ's human acquired knowledge is acquired and possessed as a perfection of his perfect human nature, not as a necessity for his information.

13. THE POWER OF CHRIST'S HUMAN SOUL

1. Christ as God is almighty. Our point of inquiry here has to do with Christ as man. We ask about the power of Christ's soul, which is a creature, and not almighty in itself.

2. The soul of Christ has not *of itself* the power to change a creature of one kind into something of another essential kind. Of course, the soul of Christ *as instrument* of the Godhead can perform all miracles.

3. Christ's human soul had not an almighty power over his own body. For such things as the health and growth of the body are not managed by a man's own reason and will; neither were these things subject to Christ's human reason and will.

4. Yet in the carrying out of his will, the soul of Christ had a real almightiness. For he had such wisdom that he would not will to do what was not subject to his human power as such, and he had such perfection that he actually willed all that God's power was to effect in him, for instance, his Resurrection. Thus the human soul of Christ had omnipotence in the execution of his human will, in the sense that what his will actually decreed could not but come to pass.

14. DEFICIENCIES IN THE BODY OF CHRIST

1. Christ assumed a true human body with the normal requirements of that body, and with the limitations and the deficiencies connatural to such a body, excluding those that could detract from the dignity of perfect human nature. Thus Christ could suffer in his body such things as hunger, thirst, pain, death. These hardships or defects are in themselves punishments for the sin which Christ had not. But it is suitable that he who came as man to atone for human sin should take on the *nonstaining* punishments consequent in man upon the original sin. By assuming human nature with these bodily deficiencies, our Lord both proved his true humanity, and gave to all men a most noble example of humble and patient endurance.

2. It is by natural necessity that a child of Adam has such deficiencies as the enduring of hunger, thirst, pain, death. And God chose to become man as a true child of Adam. It was by divine Will in the effecting of the incarnation that the flesh was thus allowed to do and to endure what belonged to it to do and suffer.

3. Human beings are said to *contract* the defects of human nature inasmuch as these are due to sin and are inherited by the sin-infected offspring of a sinful first parent. It is not so with the human nature of

Christ. Our Lord did not inherit sin; he did not contract or inherit the consequences of sin in his body. He assumed sinless human nature. He might have assumed human nature without any bodily deficiencies at all. Those defects which he took, he took by his own will to let natural necessity have its way in all that is not degrading—not setting this necessity aside by exercise of his divine power.

4. Christ as man did not have defects that conflict with his perfect knowledge, grace, and dignity. He was not, for instance, subject to sickness, or disease, or disfigurement, or suppurating sores, or broken bones.

15. LIMITATIONS OR DEFICIENCIES IN CHRIST'S HUMAN SOUL

1. In the human soul of Christ there can be no sin, original or actual. And, indeed, on this point our Lord challenged mankind: "Which of you," he cried, "can convict me of sin?" (John 8:46.) Sin in Christ would be sin in God, and the very mention of such a thing is an absurd self-contradiction.

2. In ordinary fallen human natures there is a readiness to sin called the *fomes* of sin. The Latin word *fomes* means touchwood or tinder or any such substance as takes fire from a mere spark. The *fomes* of sin was in no manner present in the human soul of Christ.

3. Nor was there *ignorance* in Christ. In him, as we have already seen, was the fullness of true knowledge. St. John (1:14) says he was "full of grace and truth."

4. Our Lord could suffer and he had the *passions of the soul,* but not in the way in which we have them. For: (a) in us, the passions tend sometimes to what is evil; this could not be in Christ; (b) in us, the passions tend to obscure the judgment of reason; this was not the case in our Lord; (c) in us, the passions sometimes tend to deflect us or hinder us in doing what is right; this was not so in Christ.

5. Christ endured real *pain.* Isaias said of him in prophecy (Isa. 53:4): "Surely he hath borne our infirmities and carried our sorrows."

6. And our Lord suffered *sorrow of soul* as well as pain of body. For he himself said (Matt. 26:38): "My soul is sorrowful even unto death."

7. The human soul of our Lord endured *fear* as a natural shrinking from pain. But in Christ there was no fear in the sense of uncertainty about future calamity; this sort of fear implies imperfect knowledge of things to come, and our Lord's knowledge was perfect.

8. There was *wonder* also in our Lord's acquired knowledge, in the sense of marvelling at what was new or extraordinary in his human experience; not, indeed, that he was surprised or astonished as at something unknown or unforeseen.

9. And there was *anger* in Christ; not the inordinate urge that we experience as anger, for such imperfection cannot be in the perfect Christ. His anger was *zeal* for the triumphing and prevailing of justice.

10. Our Lord was, at one and the same time, a wayfarer (that is, a human being making his way through life) and a comprehensor (that is, a man enjoying the eternal beatific vision). His soul possessed the beatific vision; his body was still to suffer before it was glorified and ready to ascend into heaven.

16. CONSEQUENCES OF THE HYPOSTATIC UNION

1. By the Incarnation God himself became man. The nature of man is assumed to the nature of God and is joined with it in the hypostatic union. Hence, the proposition *God is man* is literally true.

2. By reason of the hypostatic union, the proposition *Man is God* is also literally true. That is, of course, it is true when the word *man* is taken to mean *this man Christ;* the proposition is not true when the word *man* means any man at all or all men.

3. It is not accurate nor right to speak of Christ as a *lordly* man. Christ is not merely lordly; he is the Lord himself.

4. Following the hypostatic union in which God has assumed human nature in the unity of the divine Person of the Son, that which can be predicated of human nature can now be predicated of God. Yet we must carefully notice whether the predication refers to this one Person in his human nature, or to this one Person in his divine Nature. And thus when we predicate immortality of Christ as God, and mortality of Christ as man, we are not contradicting ourselves. We say truly that Christ is God, and that Christ died on the cross. But we cannot and do not say that God died on the cross. What we say is this: Christ who is God-made-Man died on the cross as man, or, Christ died in his human nature, but not in his divine Nature.

5. Therefore, what is proper to human nature can be predicated of God in so far as God has assumed human nature, but what is thus predicable of human nature cannot be predicated of *God as God apart from human nature.*

6. To say *God was made man* is strictly true. But this does not mean that God was *created,* or *made* simply. It means that human nature, which is a creature, was *assumed* to the eternal God. To say that *God was made man* is not to suggest that the changeless God was changed,

but that human nature was changed inasmuch as it now subsists in a divine Person without constituting a human personality.

7. It is not, however, accurate to say *Man was made God,* as though human nature were deified. The phrase would suggest that an existing human nature (and hence a human person, since human nature cannot exist except in a person, human or divine) was made into God. Now, the human nature of Christ was not in existence before it existed in Christ; the human nature of Christ, from the beginning of its existence, subsists by reason of the divine Personality of the Son.

8. We cannot say Christ is a creature unless we add *in his human nature;* for Christ is God, and when we speak of Christ simply, we think at once of God-made-man. But there is nothing misleading in saying that Christ was born, Christ suffered, Christ died and was buried; for it is manifest that we are speaking thus of Christ *as man.* When there is any possibility of doubt about the meaning of our words in reference to Christ, we should always add an explanatory phrase. Thus, when we say that Christ is one with the Father and the Holy Ghost, we know, without need of more words, that we are speaking of the divine Nature, and mean *Christ as God.* But if we say that Christ is inferior to the Father, some people may think that we are denying the Godhead of Christ; hence, we should say, rather, that Christ as man, or Christ in his human nature, is inferior to the Father.

9. To say, "This man (Christ) began to exist," is, for reasons just given, to make a misleading statement. For the term *this man* is easily interpreted as *this person.* Now, the Person of Christ is divine and eternal, and did not begin to exist. Says St. Paul (Heb. 13:8): "Jesus Christ, yesterday, today, and the same forever."

10. Therefore while it is correct to say that Christ as man is a creature, it is not right to say Christ as this man is a creature, for the phrase *Christ as this man* is usually understood to mean *Christ as this Person,* and the Person that is Christ is God the Son, the Second Person of the Blessed Trinity.

11. Nor is it correct to say Christ as man is God, for this would be to identify the human and the divine Nature in Christ; that is, it would make the two distinct natures in Christ into one nature, and this is heretical doctrine. Yet we can say Christ as *this man* is God, for, in this expression, the term *this man* means *this Person.*

12. It is not true to say that Christ as man is a hypostasis or person, for this would be to make two persons, one human and one divine, out of the one divine Person of the Son of God which subsists with two natures.

17. THE ONENESS OF THE BEING OF CHRIST

1. The dual number is used in speaking of the two natures in Christ, the divine and the human. If both natures were predicated *in the abstract* of Christ, he would be two beings and not one. The two natures are, therefore, predicated of Christ, not abstractly, but concretely, as they are concreted in one Person. And thus Christ is *one*.

2. Since *oneness* and *being* are really the same, the being of Christ is one. Human nature is not merely adjoined to the divine Nature of the Son of God, but is united to it hypostatically. Nothing new comes to the divine Person by this union, no newness or otherness of being; what occurs is *a relation* according to which the eternal Person of the Son now subsists in two natures. And thus the being of Christ is *one* being.

18. THE UNITY OF WILL IN CHRIST

1. Since nature is "essence equipped to operate," human nature is the human essence with its faculties (that is, powers for operating), and especially its noblest faculties which are the intellect and the will. Christ had a perfect human nature, and hence he had a human will. Therefore, there are two wills in Christ, the human will and the divine will. Our Lord himself contrasts these two wills when he prays (Luke 22:42): "Father, if thou wilt, remove this chalice from me; nevertheless, not my will, but thine be done." Now, as God, Christ has the divine will undividedly with the Father and the Holy Ghost. Hence, in the prayer quoted, he speaks of "my will" as his human will.

2. Human nature is not purely spiritual; it is animal too. The appetites of the flesh belong to human nature. These appetites are meant to be under the complete control of reason which experiences their urging, and thus, while they belong to the sensitive order, they are called "rational by participation." Since *reason* includes *will*, these appetites also belong to the will by participating its act, and they are called the *sensitive* will. Such a will was in Christ, because he had perfect human nature.

3. The rational human will of Christ is not itself a double, but a single faculty.

4. Christ's human will had the full perfection of such a will. Therefore it had the perfection called freedom of choice.

5. The human will has a twofold act. It tends to what is agreeable to human nature, and under the aspect of this tendency it is called "the will as nature." By this will a man wills health, and anything else

that is in itself beneficial to a human natural being. The will has another act, in exercising which it is called "the will as reason"; by this will a man chooses what he *understands* as a means to his desired end or goal, even if the thing chosen is not, in itself, desirable; such, for instance, as difficult fasting as a means to achieve grace, or bitter medicine or painful surgery as a means to health. In addition to these two acts of the rational will (that is, the will as nature, and the will as reason), there is the sensitive will or sensual will, which is the pull on the rational will exercised by the fleshly appetites. Now, our Lord by his human will *as reason,* always willed what God willed. By the rational will *as nature,* and by the *sensitive* will, he could tend away from things that God willed, such as his Passion and Death. And so, subduing the sensitive will to the rational will as reason, he said, "Not my will, but thine be done."

6. There is no contrariety or contradiction in Christ, and hence there is no conflict in him between the human will and the divine will. The tendency of *sensitive* will, or of the rational will *as nature,* never prevails in Christ, or constitutes a block to the sure and absolute rule of his will *as reason;* by this will *as reason* his whole voluntary life is in complete conformity with the divine will.

19. THE UNITY OF OPERATION IN CHRIST

1. In Christ, the human nature acts by its own power, and so does the divine Nature. But the divine Nature makes use of the human operations *as instruments* to its own operation.

2. In man, we discern three types of vital operation: the vegetal, the sensitive or animal, and the distinctively human or rational. Now, in Christ, the perfect man, the distinctively human operations prevailed, so that no sensitive movement took place without his will; even natural bodily (vegetal) operations belonged in some sense to his will, for, as St. John Damascene says (*De Fid. Orthodox* III), it was Christ's will that his flesh should do and suffer what belonged to it. Hence, there was perfect unity in the operations of Christ.

3. To *merit* is to earn, that is, to establish title to what is not yet possessed. Now, our Lord, as man, could merit or deserve of God what he did not yet possess. Before his Passion, our Lord did not yet possess the glory of body which came with the Resurrection, or the splendor of the Ascension, or the loving veneration of the faithful of his Church. As man, Christ already possessed the beatific vision, and all the excellences conferred on him by reason of the hypostatic union. Therefore, Christ as man could merit from God the excellent things not yet possessed, but he could not merit or earn

what he already had. It is fitting that Christ could merit some things, for he is the model as well as the source of merit for his rational creatures.

4. Christ could merit *for others*. He is the Head of the Church; the meriting activity of this Head reaches all the members. St. Paul speaks of our Lord's meriting for others when he says (Rom. 5:18): "As by the offence of one, to all men unto condemnation, so also by the justice of one [that is, Christ] unto all men to justification of life."

20. THE SUBJECTION OF CHRIST TO GOD THE FATHER

1. Christ is God the Son, equal with the Father and one with him in essence and nature. But Christ is also man, and as man is subject to the Father. He says (John 14:31): "As the Father hath given me commandment, so do I." And we also read (Phil. 2:8), that Christ humbled himself in obedience to the Father, "becoming obedient unto death, even to the death of the cross."

2. Christ in his human nature is subject to himself in his divine Nature.

21. THE PRAYER OF CHRIST

1. A prayer, as petition, is asking God to fulfill one's wish or will. Now, the human will of Christ is finite, and hence not capable, without divine power, of carrying out or achieving all that it wishes. Therefore, it is fitting that Christ as man should pray.

2. The sentient appetites (which we sometimes call the affections or desires of the heart) are not in themselves capable of making a prayer. For, in themselves, the sentient appetites are of the order of sense, and prayer is of the order of reason, that is, of the order of will enlightened by intellect. The will makes a prayer that the affections and desires of the heart be fulfilled, and such was Christ's prayer: "Let this chalice pass." The sensitive will made this prayer; then the will as reason made a better prayer, "Not my will, but thine be done," and so subjected all to God.

3. Christ prayed for himself: for example, when he prayed for the Resurrection (John 17:1): "Father, glorify thy Son"; and also when he prayed to be spared the suffering of the Passion. It is becoming that Christ should pray thus, for so he acknowledges the truth that God is the author of his human nature. Besides, he gives us a valuable example of making petition to God in all our needs.

4. The perfect will of Christ as man (that is, the will *as reason* in

Christ) never willed anything other than what he knew, in the fullness of his knowledge, to be the will of God. Therefore every absolute will-act of Christ as man was fulfilled; every prayer of Christ was answered.

22. THE PRIESTHOOD OF CHRIST

1. It is fitting that Christ be a priest. The office of a priest is to bestow sacred things on the people; to offer the prayers of the people to God; to make, in some manner, satisfaction for the people's sins. Our Lord exercised this priestly office; hence, he was and is a priest. And fittingly so; the priestly ministry belongs essentially to what Christ came to do. In St. Paul (Heb. 4:14) we read: "Having therefore a great high priest . . . Jesus, the Son of God."

2. Christ was not only a priest in offering sacrifice; he was the victim offered in the sacrifice. He offered himself by freely accepting suffering and death to gain us remission of sins, preservation in grace, and union with God. Says St. Paul (Eph. 5:2): "Christ hath loved us, and hath delivered himself for us, an oblation and sacrifice to God for an odor of sweetness."

3. The priesthood of Christ has power to expiate our sins. St. Paul says (Heb. 9:14): "The blood of Christ, who by the Holy Ghost offered himself unspotted unto God, shall cleanse our conscience from dead works to serve the living God." The priesthood of Christ produces the two effects needed to expiate sins: (a) it gives the sinner grace to turn to God; (b) it pays the debt of punishment due to sin.

4. The expiatory sacrifice of Christ the Priest is for others and not for himself, for he who has no sin needs no expiation. Hence, our Lord himself does not experience the effect of his priesthood.

5. The end of our Lord's priestly sacrifice is the everlasting good of those for whom the sacrifice is offered. It is the eternal bliss of the beatific vision gained for rational creatures. And thus the sacrifice is eternal, and the priesthood of Christ is eternal. Psalm 109:4 says: "Thou are a priest forever, according to the order of Melchisedech."

6. Christ's priesthood is described as "according to the order of Melchisedech." Melchisedech lived, and offered his sacrifice of bread and wine, before the Old Law was established. The priesthood of the Old Law was a figure of the priesthood of Christ, but it could not take away sins, nor was it eternal. The priesthood of Melchisedech suggests the preeminence of the priesthood of Christ over the priesthood of the Old Law.

23. THE ADOPTION OF SONS

1. Inasmuch as God, in his infinite goodness, permits men to inherit heaven, he is said to adopt them as children or sons.

2. It is the whole Trinity, not the Father alone, that adopts us as children. We often use the term *Father* in an essential and not a personal sense when we apply it to God; that is, we use the term Father for the "Tri-une" God, not for the First Person of the Trinity. We do this, for example, when we say the *Our Father*, in which we address God in unity, and not the Father as distinct from the Son and the Holy Ghost. The Triune God is the Father of us all, and adopts us as brethren of Christ for the inheritance of heaven.

3. Only rational creatures (that is, men and angels) can be adopted as children of God.

4. Our Lord himself is not an adopted child or son of God; he is the true Son of God, the Second Person of the Trinity, eternally begotten of the Father.

24. THE PREDESTINATION OF CHRIST

1. What is predestinated is something set from eternity to be done in time. Now, that God should become man was divinely ordained from eternity to take place in time. Hence, we say that Christ was predestined or predestinated.

2. And therefore our human nature was predestinated to be joined hypostatically to the divine Nature.

3. The predestinated sonship of Christ as man is the exemplar of our predestinated sonship by adoption.

4. And, indeed, the predestinated sonship of Christ as man is the cause of our predestinated sonship by adoption. For scripture says (Eph. 1:5) that God "hath predestinated us into the adoption of children through Jesus Christ."

25. THE ADORATION OF CHRIST

1. We adore Christ, God and man, with the same adoration. For what we adore is the Person called Christ. Even though this Person has two natures, the human and the divine, he is one Person, and that Person is God. Even the humanity of Christ is adored as the humanity of a Person who is God.

2. St. John Damascene (*De Fid. Orthodox,* IV 3) says that we adore the flesh of Christ, not for its own sake, but because the Word of God is united with it. And, since we give divine worship (called *latria*) to God, we give the same sort of worship to the humanity

of Christ united hypostatically with divinity. Only when we consider the humanity of Christ apart from the hypostatic union do we pay it the honor of reverence (called *dulia*) instead of the adoration of *latria*.

3. When we honor an image of Christ, we honor Christ. We do not give any honor at all to the image as a piece of painted canvas or as a carved bit of wood or marble or metal. The image is meaningful only in what it represents. And what it represents is Christ whom we worship with the adoration of *latria*.

4. The same thing is true of the honor and reverence we give to the cross on which our Lord died. What we see in the cross is not the wood of which it is made, but the whole meaning of the Crucifixion. And we adore the Word Incarnate, with the worship of *latria*, whose death for us the cross calls to our remembrance and appreciation.

5. The Blessed Mother is not venerated by *latria*, for this is divine worship and is owed to God alone. She has the reverence paid to holy creatures, saints and angels, and this is called *dulia*. Indeed, since she is the Mother of God and the queen of all angels and saints, we pay to the Blessed Virgin a special and higher type of *dulia* which belongs to her alone and is called *hyperdulia*.

6. We honor the *relics* of the saints (their bodies, bones, or things they used or had about them during life) with a true veneration that is directed to the saints themselves. And in honoring the saints we honor Christ whose members the saints are.

26. CHRIST AS MEDIATOR

1. Scripture says (I Tim. 2:5): "There is . . . one mediator of God and man, the man Christ Jesus." Christ is our mediator because by his death he reconciled the human race to God. Christ is the One Perfect Mediator. But others may participate in the mediatorship of Christ by cooperating with him in disposing men to turn to God, and in ministering to men the divinely established sacraments which unite men to God by grace.

2. Christ is the mediator of God and man; not, says St. Augustine (*De Civ. Dei*, IX 15), because he is the divine Word; he is mediator as man. For in his divinity Christ is God, not a mediator between God and man. As man, Christ stands between God and sinful human beings. He unites men to God by graces and gifts. He offers to God prayers and satisfaction for mankind. Hence, it is as man that Christ is mediator: "The man Christ Jesus."

OUR BLESSED LADY

(QUESTIONS 27 TO 30)

[*Note:* Two things are to be remembered in this and the next following treatise: (a) St. Thomas held that the human body is animated successively in the womb: first by a vegetal life-principle, then by a sentient or animal soul, and finally by a rational and spiritual soul; each soul displaces its predecessor so that in the end one rational and spiritual soul animates the human being. (b) In St. Thomas's day, the Immaculate Conception of the Blessed Virgin Mary was a question for free discussion among scholars; the doctrine had not yet been infallibly defined as of the faith. This doctrine is: the Blessed Virgin, in view of the merits of Him who was to be born of her as her true Son, was, from the first moment of her conception in the womb of St. Anne, her mother, preserved free from all stain of original sin; this privilege of Mary is called her Immaculate Conception.]

27. OUR LADY'S SANCTIFICATION

1. The Blessed Virgin was sanctified before her birth. She who was to be the Mother of God was privileged above all others, and we know from the angel's salutation (Luke 1:28) that she was "full of grace." Scripture testifies that both Jeremias and St. John the Baptist were sanctified before their birth; Mary's place was higher than theirs in God's economy of redemption, and her privileges, therefore, cannot have been less than theirs. Therefore, Mary was sanctified before her birth. [*Note:* Mary was sanctified not only before her birth, but from the very beginning of her existence; she was preserved immaculate by God's gift and grace, and thereby sanctified, from the first moment of her conception in the womb of her mother. St. John and Jeremias had original sin removed from them before their birth; Mary never had the original sin at all; it was not removed from her; she was preserved from its taint.]

2. The Blessed Virgin was sanctified when her spiritual soul had animated her body. [*Note:* See note above. See also the note at the beginning of this treatise.]

3. There is, as we have seen, a readiness in fallen human nature, a kind of flammability of the flesh by which a movement of sense-appetency is almost at once a strong and driving desire. This is called the *fomes* of sin. It is not sinful in itself, but, if unresisted, it sweeps a man on to sin. Now, in the sanctified (and immaculate) Mother of God, there was no *fomes*. This defect and blemish of fallen nature had no place in one of her high dignity and stainless birth (and conception).

4. The Blessed Virgin was, by her sanctification, fitted for the most exalted office of Mother of God. There was no sin in her, either original or actual, either mortal or venial. In her is fulfilled the prophecy (Cant. 4:7): "Thou are all fair, O my love, and there is not a spot in thee."

5. By her sanctification, the Blessed Mother received the fullness of grace; for Mary was nearest of all to Christ through whom all grace comes. Hence, her fullness of grace was greater than that of any other receiver.

6. It is fitting that the Blessed Mother should be sanctified from the first. As noted above, Jeremias and St. John the Baptist were sanctified before their birth. Of Jeremias it is written (Jer. 1:5): "Before thou camest forth out of the womb, I sanctified thee." And of St. John the Baptist scripture says (Luke 1:15): "He shall be filled with the Holy Ghost, even from his mother's womb."

28. THE VIRGINITY OF MARY

1. The Mother of Christ was a virgin in *conceiving* our Lord; Christ has no human father. It is not fitting that Christ should have a father other than the Eternal Father. And St. Augustine says (*De Sanct. Virg.*): "It is fitting that our Head, by a great miracle, should be born, in the flesh, of a virgin, to signify that his members should be born, in the Spirit, of a virgin Church."

2. The Mother of Christ was a virgin in *giving birth* to her Divine Son. She fulfills the prophecy (Isa. 7:14): "Behold a virgin shall conceive, and shall bear a son." And St. Augustine, in a Christmas sermon, declares how suitable is the Virgin Birth of Christ: "He who came to cure corruption should not, by his birth, violate integrity." Christ was born of Mary, by divine power, so that her body was not broken or violated. Nor did Mary endure birth-pangs, or need the help of kindly neighbor-women for the delivering of her Child. Painlessly, and without change in Mary's virgin body, her Son emerged from the tabernacle of her spotless womb, as he was later to emerge from the tomb, without moving the stone or breaking the seal of Pilate.

3. The Mother of God was a virgin *after* the birth of Christ. Mary
had no children other than our Lord. For: (a) The only begotten of
the Father has such dignity as God, that he must necessarily, as man,
be the only-begotten of his mother. (b) The virginal womb of Mary is
the shrine of the Holy Ghost, and should not be desecrated by a
merely human conception. (c) It is unthinkable that Mary, after the
divinely wrought conception of Christ in her womb, should choose
to forfeit the sacred virginity miraculously preserved in her during
the conception and birth of our Lord. (d) St. Joseph would never
have presumed to approach carnally one whom he knew, by the
angel's word, to have conceived of the Holy Ghost. Hence, we must
say that Mary, before, during, and after the birth of Christ, was a
virgin.

4. Mary had a vow of virginity. Her words to the angel of the Annunciation, "I know not man" (Luke 1:34), indicate as much. Besides,
works of perfection are more excellent when consecrated by a vow,
and Mary's virginity had surely the greatest excellence it could have.
Mary took a husband, as custom required, yet took with him a vow
of virginity.

29. THE ESPOUSALS OF MARY

1. Scripture says (Luke 1:27) that the angel Gabriel was sent to
"a virgin espoused to a man named Joseph." It is suitable that Christ
was born of an espoused virgin, and this for his own sake, for Mary's
sake, and for our sake. (a) *For his own sake:* lest he be thought illegitimate; so that his genealogy might be traced through a male
line; so that, as a newborn child, he might have a proper protector;
so that his miraculous birth might be hidden from the devil. (b)
For Mary's sake: lest she be stoned as an adulteress; lest she be subjected to ill fame; so that she might have the loving and holy aid of
St. Joseph. (c) *For our sake:* because St. Joseph bears witness to us
that Christ is born of a virgin; because Mary's claim to virginity is at
once rendered credible (for, if she were unespoused, it might seem
that her claim was to cover sin); because Mary typifies the virginal
Church which is espoused to Christ.

2. The espousals of Mary and Joseph constituted a true marriage.
The essence of a marriage is an inseparable union of souls, even if
this union is never brought to carnal use or fruitfulness. Scripture
calls St. Joseph the husband of Mary, and calls Mary the wife of
Joseph (Matt. 1:19, 20). Therefore, Mary and Joseph were truly
man and wife; they were truly married.

30. THE ANNUNCIATION

1. It was fitting that there should be a solemn announcement made to Mary that she was to conceive of the Holy Ghost, and that her child was to be God himself made man. Thus Mary was informed in mind, and received Christ by faith, even before she received him in her womb. Besides, the Annunciation made Mary a more certain witness of the Incarnation, for here she had God's own word for it. The Annunciation also gave to Mary the opportunity of free obedience to God's will; the angelic messenger of God waited for her reply: "Be it done to me according to thy word" (Luke 1:38). Finally, Mary's free consent to receive our Lord was, in a manner, the consent of the human race to receive the Eternal Son of God as the Redeemer.

2. It was right that an angel should be the messenger of the Annunciation. In God's order and plan, divine things are communicated to men by the ministry of angels. Further, as St. Bede the Venerable says, it was right than an angel should come to Mary to announce the restoration of man, since a fallen angel came to cajole the first man to human ruin. Besides, virginity makes one akin to angels; it is suitable that an angel be the messenger sent to the greatest of virgins.

3. The angel of the Annunciation *appeared* to Mary. He had some visible form. This is right. An invisible spirit came visibly to say that the invisible God would become visible man. It was right that Mary should have bodily testimony of a bodily conception. Lastly, the visible appearance of the angel and his audible words were a more sure and striking testimony of what was to be than an inner revelation would have been.

4. There is right order in the Annunciation. First, the angel drew Mary's attention to the greatness of his message by saluting her in a new and unusual manner. Next, he delivered his message. Then he led Mary to consent to God's will, referring to Elizabeth whose conceiving despite advanced age was an instance of the almighty power of God. Then Mary said: "Behold the handmaid of the Lord; be it done to me according to thy word."

OUR LORD JESUS CHRIST

(QUESTIONS 31 TO 59)

31. OUR LORD'S BODY

1. Our Lord came in human nature to cleanse that nature from sin. Now, the stain of sin came to human nature from Adam. Hence, the Savior assumed flesh that derived from Adam. Christ as man was a true member of Adam's race.

2. Christ's flesh was "of the seed of David." In human terms, our Lord was called the son of Abraham, and the son of David. To Abraham and to David, more than to other partriarchs, promises of the Redeemer were made, and the promises called him the seed of Abraham, and also the seed of David.

3. The genealogy of our Lord is given in two of the Gospels. St. Matthew begins with Abraham, and traces the line to Joseph. St. Luke starts with our Lord, and works back. There are points in both lists that scholars discuss with some disagreement. Yet the genealogy as it stands is suitable for its purpose. The fact that St. Matthew follows the male line from Abraham to Joseph, who was not the father of our Lord, merely indicates the invariable Jewish custom of following the male line; yet the genealogy is sufficient, for Mary, like Joseph, was "of the house and family of David"; this is the important thing, and fully indicates the fulfillment of the prophecies that the Redeemer was to be of David's seed.

4. It was suitable that the Son of God should take flesh from a woman. He came to redeem all, and, as he himself was a man, it was right that the female sex should have a place in the work of Incarnation. Hence, the Redeemer was rightly born of a human mother.

5. In the begetting of Christ, the active principle of generation was the power of God, a supernatural power. The matter from which the body of Christ was conceived was the blood of the mother. Thus the conception of our Lord's body was supernatural in the fact that God directly produced it in Mary; it was supernatural also in the fact that it took place in a virgin; but it was natural in the fact that the Child was present in Mary's womb.

6. Through the medium of Mary's body, the body of Christ is related to Adam and to the patriarchs of his line. Christ's body was in the patriarchs in the way in which Mary's body was in them, and in the way in which all their descendants were in them. Now, a descendant is not in his ancestor as a definite part of that ancestor's substance. He is in his ancestor as in his true origin, but he is not a section of the ancestor's flesh or bone or blood or tissue.

7. Christ did not assume human flesh *as subject to sin.* He assumed human flesh cleansed from all infection of sin. [*Note:* Here we discern a reason for the fact of Mary's Immaculate Conception, namely, that the immediate source of Christ's body should be virginal and immaculate.]

8. St. Paul (Heb. 7:6–9) says that Levi, the yet unborn great-grandson of Abraham, "paid tithes in Abraham" when Abraham paid tithes to Melchisedech. From this, some have falsely concluded that in Abraham our Lord paid tithes for the healing of the flesh from sin. But our Lord was not in his human ancestors in such a way as to make him inheritor of Adam's sin. He was a true child of Adam, but he was not descended by way of concupiscence and carnal or seminal power; he was conceived by the immaculate virgin under the immediate action of God's supernatural power.

32. THE CONCEPTION OF CHRIST

1. The whole Trinity effected the conception of our Lord's body. But in a special way the conception is attributed to the Holy Ghost. For Christ came because of God's great love for mankind. Scripture says (John 3:16): "God so loved the world as to give his only-begotten son." Hence, it is right that the conception of our Lord should be attributed to the Spirit of Love, that is, God the Holy Ghost.

2. We rightly say that Christ was conceived of the Holy Ghost. This suggests that the Holy Ghost is the active principle of the conceiving, and also that the One conceived is consubstantial with its active principle.

3. However, it is not right to say that the Holy Ghost is the father of Christ. St. Augustine (*Enchir.* XL) says, "Christ was born of the Holy Ghost, not as a son; he was born of Mary as a son." In his eternal personality, Christ is the Son of God by the eternal generation of the Father. He, therefore, is eternally the Son of God; he was not made the Son of God by becoming man under the active power of the Holy Ghost.

4. In the conceiving of Christ, the Blessed Mother had no active part to play beyond cooperating by giving consent that God's will

should be accomplished in her. And Mary did cooperate in God's will and work: "Be it done to me," she said to the angelic messenger, "according to thy word."

33. THE MODE OF OUR LORD'S CONCEPTION

1. St. Gregory (*Moral.* xviii) says: "As soon as the angel announced it, as soon as the Spirit came down, the Word was in the womb . . . was made flesh." The body assumed by the Word must be a body perfectly formed. Nor was it formed previously to the Annunciation and held in readiness to be assumed. It was formed and assumed in the same instant, the instant in which Mary assented to the divine Will, saying, "Be it done to me according to thy word." In that instant, "the Word was made flesh and dwelt among us" (John 1:14).

2. At the very instant that Christ was conceived, the rational and spiritual human soul animated his body. [*Note:* Recall St. Thomas's theory that the ordinary process of conception puts the conceived matter through two pre-human stages, vegetal and sentient. This, he here asserts, was not the case in the conception of our Lord.]

3. Our Lord's body was not first conceived and afterwards assumed by the Word of God. It began to exist at the precise moment in which it was assumed.

4. Our Lord's conception, in its active producing principle, was entirely miraculous and supernatural.

34. THE PERFECTION OF OUR LORD BEFORE HIS BIRTH

1. The human soul of Christ was sanctified in the first instant of his conception by its union with the Word of God. From the first, Christ as man had the fullness of grace sanctifying both his body and his soul.

2. From the first instant of his conception, Christ had a perfect human nature with complete use of reason, that is, with perfect intellect and will.

3. Therefore, the sanctification of Christ's human nature included the complete conforming of his human will to the divine will; this act is meritorious; hence, Christ merited perfectly in the first instant of his conception. And this perfect merit is complete; God made man cannot possibly *increase* in merit.

4. From the first instant of his conception Christ's human nature was taken into the unity of Person. Therefore, from the first, Christ was

a comprehensor, that is, he had perfect beatitude in the possession of the beatific vision of God.

35. THE NATIVITY OF CHRIST

1. The nativity, the being born, refers to Person rather than to nature. In an ordinary human birth, what is born is a person, not merely human nature. It is the *person who has the nature* that is born; it is the *hypostasis* that is born. So the Nativity of Christ is the birth of God the Son *as subsisting in human nature;* it is the birth of the Son of God *as man.*

2. The Son of God is *eternally* generated, or born, of the Eternal Father. *In time,* he is born as man of the Virgin Mother.

3. In its activation, the conception of Christ was God's own work. And the Nativity was effected without disturbing or violating the perfect virginity of Mary, even in the physical meaning of the word virginity. And yet Christ is true man as well as true God; he is truly Mary's Child; Mary is truly his mother.

4. Mary's Child is true God. She is the true mother of that Child. Therefore, Mary is to be called the Mother of God. It is heresy to deny this truth.

5. The *filiation* or sonship of Christ as a Subsistent Divine Relation in the Trinity is one and not multiple or manifold. If we speak of a new *filiation* or sonship of Christ with reference to the Blessed Mother, we do not mean to multiply filiations in the Son of God. We say that, in one way, there is only one real filiation in Christ, and this is in reference to the Eternal Father, and is itself *eternal.* Yet there is a *temporal* filiation of Christ with regard to his Mother.

6. Our Lord was born of Mary without opening her virginal womb. Therefore, Mary had no suffering, no pains or distress, in giving birth to her divine Son.

7. For two reasons it was fitting that Christ should be born in Bethlehem. First, he who was called by the prophets, "the seed of David," suitably chose to be born in the city of David, that is, Bethlehem, where David himself had been born. Secondly, the name *Bethlehem* is interpreted as "the house of bread," and hence it was a suitable birthplace for "the living bread which came down from heaven" (John 6:51).

8. We know that Christ was born at a fitting time, for he chose the time and he is the all-wise God. As we have noted elsewhere, the time of his coming was neither too soon, before man had learned by bitter experience the evil of the primal human rebellion against God, nor too late, when humbled pride must have sunk into despair.

36. THE MANIFESTATION OF THE NEW-BORN CHRIST

1. The birth of Christ was not manifested at once to all mankind. Had Christ been so manifested, the redemption by the cross would have been hindered; for, as St. Paul says (I Cor. 2:8): "If they had known it, they would never have crucified the Lord of glory." Moreover, universal manifestation of the birth of the Savior would have lessened the merit of faith, which is "the evidence of things that appear not" (Heb. 11:1), and the reality of his human nature would have been more easily doubted.

2. Yet the Nativity had to be manifested, even as the Resurrection had later to be manifested, "not to all the people, but to witnesses preordained by God" (Acts 10:41). If the birth had been hidden from all, it could have profited none.

3. The birth of Christ was indeed made known "to those preordained." These witnesses of the Nativity, and of the divinity of the Child, represented all nations and conditions, for they were male and female, Jew and Gentile, namely, the shepherds, the Magi, Simeon, Anna.

4. Had God directly manifested the Redeemer's birth instead of using creatures (the angels, the star), it would have been easy for people to doubt that our Lord was true man. It was much better for us all that the birth was manifested in the way in which it actually was manifested.

5. Knowledge is given by means of things familiar to those who receive it. Now, the Jews were accustomed to the receiving of divine instruction through the ministry of angels. And the Gentiles were wont to observe the course of the stars. Hence, while spiritual-minded people like Anna and Simeon received the manifestation of Christ's birth by interior revelation, the more material or worldly people had to be taught by signs and wonders.

6. Christ's birth was first made known to the shepherds; these men represent the apostles and all the believers among the Jews. Then the birth was manifested to the Gentiles in the persons of the Magi. Finally it was again manifested to the Jews represented by the holy Simeon and Anna.

7. The star of the Nativity was not a regular part of the heavenly system; it was a newly-created star, and was not in the high firmament, but near the earth. For scripture (Matt. 2:9) says that "it came and stood over where the child was." Some have taught that this star was a power endowed with reason. Some have wondered whether it were not a visible manifestation of the Holy Ghost, like the dove

that appeared in our Lord's baptism by John. Others again have believed that the angel who appeared in human form to the shepherds, appeared to the Magi in the form of the star. But it seems most just to say that the star of the Nativity was a newly-created heavenly body near the earth. Pope St. Leo says (*Serm. De Epiph.* xxxi), that the star must have been more bright and beautiful than the other stars, for its appearance instantly convinced the Magi that it had an urgent and important meaning.

8. The Magi were the "first fruits of the Gentiles." Their faith in Christ was a kind of forecast of the coming faith of all nations in the Incarnate Word. The Magi were inspired by the Holy Ghost to come and pay homage to Christ.

37. LEGAL OBSERVANCES REGARDING THE CHRIST CHILD

1. Our Lord submitted to the circumcision: (a) to prove the reality of his human nature; (b) to lend approval to a ceremony divinely instituted; (c) to show his descent from Abraham who first received the law of circumcision; (d) to remove an obstacle that would prevent Jews from believing in him; (e) to give us an example of obedience; (f) to indicate that sin is to be cured by pain of sense; (g) to take up the burden of the ceremonial law that he might relieve others of it.

2. Our Lord was called *Jesus* by divine command (Luke 1:31). The name means Savior, and it signifies the gratuitous grace bestowed on Christ as man that through him all might be saved, that is, brought safe to heaven.

3. Our Lord was presented to God in ceremonious function in the Temple at Jerusalem. This was in fulfillment of the law (Exod. 13:2) which reads, "Sanctify unto me every first-born." The presentation was a kind of official consecration or dedication of the first-born to God. Our Lord was not bound by the ceremonial law requiring the presentation, for he is God as well as man, and his divine Person is not obligated by creatural regulations, even those of divine origin. But our Lord willed to be obedient to the law, for the benefit and edification of mankind.

4. And Mary was obedient, in imitation of her divine Son, to the ceremonial law. She submitted to the requirements of the Purification, although she had no need of purifying, since there was no conveying of original sin in the conception and birth of her Son. St. Luke (2:22) says that the days of Mary's purification "according to the law

of Moses" were accomplished. St. Luke thus pointedly indicates that the requirement for the purification was on the part of the law, and not because of any need in Mary.

38. THE BAPTISM OF ST. JOHN THE BAPTIST

1. St. John, called *the Baptist* because he performed the ceremony of baptizing with water, was not following, in this matter of baptizing, any prescription of the Old Law. He was introducing something new. And this *baptism of penance* conferred by St. John (son of Zachary and Elizabeth) was apt and suitable because: (a) St. John was to baptize our Lord and thus to sanctify the ceremony of baptism; (b) he was to make manifest the divinity of Christ when our Lord came to him to be baptized; (c) he was to prepare men for the true baptism, that is, the sacrament of baptism, by making them familiar with the ceremonial part of it; (d) he was persuading men to do penance publicly and ceremoniously so that they might thus prepare for the worthy receiving of the baptism of Christ.

2. The rite of St. John's baptism was from God. For John was divinely sent to baptize, as we know from the Gospel (John 1:33). But the effect of John's baptism was not supernatural. It had not the power to confer grace.

3. For grace comes to man only through Christ. Scripture (John 1:17) says: "Grace and truth came by Jesus Christ." The baptism of St. John the Baptist was a preparation for grace, but did not give grace.

4. The baptism of St. John the Baptist was properly given to others besides our Lord, for this ceremony existed not only to manifest Christ on the occasion of his being baptized by John; it existed also to prepare men by penance for the receiving of Christian baptism.

5. Therefore, even after St. John had baptized Christ and had professed his own faith in him, he continued to baptize. And he made his ceremonial baptism of penance a means of sending people to Christ. For, as St. Bede the Venerable says, the forerunner of Christ (that is, St. John the Baptist) could not properly cease from his work until Christ was made fully manifest.

6. Of course, those who were baptized by John needed to be baptized again with Christian baptism. John's baptism was not a sacrament; it did not confer grace nor imprint a character. John the Baptist said, "I baptize with water" (John 1:26); he declared himself, and implicitly his baptism, much less than Christ and His works. Our Lord instituted the sacrament of baptism "of water and the Holy Ghost," and laid upon all the necessity of receiving it. Scripture

tells us that the apostles (Acts 19:1–5) administered tho sacrament of baptism to those who had already received the baptism of John.

39. THE BAPTIZING OF CHRIST BY ST. JOHN THE BAPTIST

1. Our Lord needed no baptism of any kind. But he received the baptism of St. John, ordering the Baptist to proceed when he humbly and reverently expressed astonishment that Christ should come to him for baptism (Matt. 3:13–15). Christ was baptized, say the fathers, to sanctify the waters that they might henceforth be worthily used for cleansing from sin in Christian baptism. And as our Lord was to make baptism a required sacrament, so now he set an example to men by receiving the outward form and figure of the reality that was to be.

2. Our Lord was baptized by St. John the Baptist to show his approval of the rite of baptism and to sanctify it.

3. It was fitting that our Lord, at the age of thirty, received the baptism of John. The age of thirty seems to have a certain perfection. Joseph, the son of Jacob, was thirty when he was made ruler of Egypt. David was thirty when he began to reign. Ezechiel was thirty when he began to prophesy. And now, our Lord at the age of thirty begins his public ministry with the receiving of John's baptism. Perhaps the perfection of *thirty* is in the fact that it is the product of *three times ten,* and suggests the perfect fulfillment of the Law (that is, the Ten Commandments) by a living faith in the Holy Trinity. In these two things the perfection of Christian life consists.

4. It was through the River Jordan that the Chosen People passed when they came into the Promised Land. It was fitting that our Lord should sanctify these waters by being baptized in them. Thus he consecrated an element for use in that sacrament which enables a man to pass into the eternal land of promise, that is, heaven.

5. At Christ's baptism by John, the heavens were opened. Scripture says (Luke 3:21): "Jesus being baptized and praying, heaven was opened." There is rich signification here, for the true baptism which Christ was to institute opens heaven to mankind in three ways: (a) by exercising heavenly power; (b) by bestowing heavenly faith; (c) by giving an entrance to heaven. And the prayer of Christ at this time suggests the continual need of prayer in those who receive the sacrament of baptism so that what that sacrament confers may not be rendered ineffective by subsequent sin.

6. When our Lord was baptized by John, "the Holy Ghost de-

scended in a bodily shape, as a dove upon him" (Luke 3:22). The visible coming of the Holy Ghost indicated what Christian baptism was to bring invisibly to the soul of the recipient. For Christian baptism was to be, not in water only, but in the Holy Ghost (Matt. 3:11).

7. The dove that came upon Christ when he received the Holy Ghost at his baptism by John was a real dove divinely created for this purpose. It was not an illusory image of a dove. But this real dove was not an incarnation of the Holy Ghost. It only indicated visibly the invisible coming of the Eternal Spirit upon Christ as man.

8. And the Eternal Father gave sensible manifestation of our Lord's divinity on the occasion of Christ's baptism by John. For there was an audible voice from heaven which proclaimed, "This is my beloved Son in whom I am well pleased" (Matt. 3:17). Here the Father's audible words, the manifestation of the Holy Ghost in the dove, and the bodily presence of Christ the Son of God, are sensible manifestations of the Three Divine Persons in whose name the Christian sacrament of baptism was to be conferred: "Going therefore, teach ye all nations; baptizing them in the name of the Father, and of the Son, and of the Holy Ghost" (Matt. 28:19).

40. OUR LORD'S LIFE

1. Our Lord came to teach men essential truth (John 18:37). Hence, his life was not passed in solitude. In his public ministry, he associated with all sorts and conditions of men. He came to save sinners, and he sought them out. He came that through him men might have access to God, and therefore he made himself accessible to men.

2. Our Lord did not discourage the many with whom he dealt by an austerity of manner, or by exacting extremely hard penances of them. He did not make himself an oddity. He truly became "all things to all men" (I Cor. 9:22), that he might win all; that is, he was moderate, and wholly virtuous, and recollected, but he was not cold or rigidly aloof. Nor were his great penances performed in the public eye: he fasted forty days alone in the desert; his long nights of continuous prayer were spent upon a solitary mountain. Hence, there was nothing in the presence of our Lord to frighten poor sinners, or make them think he would demand too much of them, or repel them with overpowering dignity of manner.

3. Our Lord is God and master of all; he might, had he so chosen, have had all that people call "advantages of wealth and position." But he came to teach us by his life as well as by his words. Now, the life of a wealthy man, or a man of social or civic power, is a life of many cares. He who is to preach God's word has not time for such

things. Christ impressed upon his disciples the need of their being free from material concerns as they went about their apostolic work (Matt. 10:9). If the disciples had been wealthy men, as St. Jerome remarks, people would have suspected them of seeking to promote some profitable scheme instead of seeking to save men's souls. Our Lord, by his voluntary poverty, merited spiritual wealth for mankind; he proved to all the world that his Godhead prevails in the spreading of his Church, not his worldly possessions or the power of money.

4. Christ conformed his conduct to the ceremonial and judicial precepts of the Old Law. Thus he showed his approval of this Law, which came from God. He obeyed it to fulfill it in every sense; that is, to meet its requirements, and to bring it to an honorable end, after which its requirements would no longer bind the consciences of men. The prophetic and figurative meanings of the Old Law emerged into factual reality in Christ. He therefore did not break violently with the Old Law, but completed it. He said that he came, not to destroy the law, but to fulfill it (Matt. 5:17).

41. THE TEMPTATION IN THE DESERT

1. Temptation is a test or trial. In special, it is an invitation or an allurement to sin which tests or manifests the moral fiber of one who experiences it. Temptation is either: (a) *external only,* and then it is an invitation or suggestion from without, with no tendency whatever, in the person tempted, to respond to it; or (b) *internal,* and then it is a weakness, passion, or tendency in the person tempted. Now the temptation of Christ in the desert (Matt., chap. 4) was entirely *external.* Our Lord's human nature was perfect and without unruly tendencies, and his Person is divine. The temptation of Christ was a test or experiment on the part of the devil. The devil wished to know for sure whether this man Christ was God Incarnate; for the divinity of Christ had been manifested to the demons only in so far as Christ willed it to be made known to them. Satan suspected; he wished to be sure. In making his proposals or temptations, Satan twice employed the phrase, "If thou be the Son of God . . ." It is interesting to note that our Lord, in rebuffing the tempter, did not tell him what he was so eager to know. Now, our Lord endured what may be called the indignity of the temptation in the desert, for good reasons: (a) to bear, at least outwardly, all that his followers have to endure; (b) to show us, and warn us, that not even perfect sanctity is immune from the assaults of the devil; (c) to set us an example of prompt and unhesitating rejection of temptation; (d) to show up, for our

benefit, the devil's method of assault, namely, first suggesting something apparently good or at least harmless ("make these stones bread"), and moving quickly on to what is most vile, even to devil-worship; (e) to assure us that all temptation can be successfully resisted, and to make us turn to him with confidence in our own temptations.

2. Christ's temptation in the desert shows us another of the devil's wiles, namely, his preferring to tempt a man when the man is alone, that is, away from where his ready help lies. Thus a man forgetful of God or negligent of prayer puts himself into a desert place where temptation lurks. Seen from Satan's angle, the world of virtue and grace-inspired works is a desert where he has nothing; he is envious of those who dwell in abundance there; he envies that abundance which cannot ever be his; he strives to tempt pious souls, therefore, and to make their lives a real desert.

3. We need penance to make us strong against temptations. Our Lord permitted Satan to approach him only after his hard penance of fasting forty days. Herein is a plain lesson for us.

4. The order of the three temptations proposed by Satan shows us his strategy and teaches us to avoid his snares. No one falls suddenly into the deepest evildoing; Satan is too shrewd to suggest to a decent person the indecency of the viler sins, until he has prepared the way for that suggestion by lesser matters. Satanic wiles begin with something of which one may say, "Why not? What harm is there in it?" Having won a first concession, the devil cleverly pursues his advantage until the grossest evils are possible.

42. THE PREACHING OF CHRIST

1. Christ's preaching, and that of his apostles, was, first of all, to the Jews. Thus: (a) he fulfilled the promise of God to the patriarchs; (b) he preached first to believers in God who were apt instruments for conveying his teaching to the "races" or "Gentiles"; (c) he thus deprived the Chosen People of any show of justice in their act of rejecting him; (d) he was ready, after the Resurrection, to extend his mission to include the Gentiles, and to send his apostles "to all nations."

2. Our Lord spoke to the Jews, not only kindly and placatingly, but with occasional sternness and words of sharp reproach. Some of the Scribes and Pharisees, leaders of the people, showed much pride and malice in their attitude towards God made man, and kept others from hearing and heeding his teaching. When our Lord rebuked them, it was not through pique or resentment, but because of his love for their souls as well as the souls they were influencing.

3. Christ spoke openly to the people. He brought essential truth to all men, not hiding its light "under a bushel," or uttering it in occult words. Even when he "spoke in parables," he explained the parables to his disciples, who would convey their meaning to all who were willing to hear.

4. Our Lord wrote no books or documents. He left that task, in so far as divine Wisdom wills to have it done, to writers inspired by God for the work. Christ spoke to people, and impressed truth in the hearts of his willing hearers.

43. THE MIRACLES OF CHRIST: IN GENERAL

1. Our Lord performed many miracles to prove his teaching true, and especially to manifest the leading truth of all his teaching, namely, that he himself is true God as well as true man. Thus he could say to the people (John 10:37, 38): "If I do not the works of my Father, believe me not. But if I do, though you will not believe me, believe the works: that you may know and believe that the Father is in me, and I in the Father."

2. The miracles of Christ, like all miracles, are works of divine power. For a miracle is, by definition, a work that surpasses all power of creatures. Christ is God, and can directly exercise the divine power in working miracles; as man, Christ is the instrument through which the miracles are wrought.

3. St. John says (2:11) that the changing of water to wine at Cana was the first of the miracles wrought by our Lord. Christ was then about thirty years of age, and was about to enter upon his public ministry. St. John Chrysostom says that it would not have been fitting for Christ to work miracles when he was young, before he was ready to begin his public life; for then men would have crucified him before his time.

4. Our Lord said (John 5:36): "The works which the Father hath given me to perfect . . . give testimony of me, that the Father hath sent me." The miracles of Christ are a full proof of his divinity: (a) by their very nature as miracles wrought for the purpose; (b) by their manner, as wrought under Christ's own authority; (c) by the fact that Christ plainly adduced them in proof of his divinity, calling people's attention to them as irrefutable evidence.

44. MIRACLES OF CHRIST: IN PARTICULAR

1. It was fitting that our Lord should cast out demons or devils by a miracle. Miracles are arguments for the faith which Christ brought to men; He rightly released, by the miracle of expelling evil spirits,

persons whose thralldom to demons prevented them from accepting the faith.

2. Our Lord wrought miracles in the heavenly bodies, as in the darkening of the sun at the hour of crucifixion (Luke 23:44, 45). This was a striking proof of his Godhead, the central truth of the faith which his miracles make manifest.

3. Our Lord showed his divine power and his saving mission to men by his miracles wrought on human beings. Scripture tells (Mark 7:37) how the people welcomed these miracles, and cried out in praise of them: "He hath done all things well; he hath made both the deaf to hear, and the dumb to speak."

4. Our Lord worked miracles on irrational earthly creatures, as when he caused the fig tree to wither away, changed water into wine, made the earth tremble and quake as he died on the cross. All these things were done for man's benefit. It was right that man should be made aware of our Lord's divinity by means of miraculous signs of his absolute control over every kind of creature: spirits, heavenly bodies, men, irrational earthly beings.

45. THE TRANSFIGURATION

1. In St. Matthew's Gospel (chap. 17) we read that our Lord was transfigured in the sight of his apostles Peter, James, and John. "And he was transfigured before them. And his face did shine as the sun, and his garments became white as snow." Thus the three apostles had a glimpse of such glory as would come to them after their life of fidelity to God, through hardships and trials. Our Lord had told the apostles of his coming Passion before he gave them this encouraging experience of seeing the Transfiguration. Christ as man had the glory of the beatific vision from the first instant of his existence in Mary's womb. But he was not to have the "overflow of heavenly glory into his body" until his Resurrection from the dead.

2. In the Transfiguration, our Lord showed by way of anticipation the clarity of his bodily glory. This was the essential clarity of true heavenly glory, here manifested in a new mode, that is, as miraculously produced. In the glory following the Resurrection, the clarity of the glorified body is not a miracle; it belongs to the glorified body as such.

3. Our Lord chose as witnesses to the Transfiguration, not only the three apostles, but Moses and Elias who appeared visibly.

4. As at the baptism of Christ by St. John, so here on the mountain of Transfiguration, the voice of God the Father proclaimed the divine Sonship of Christ. The baptism of Christ by John foretold the true baptism which brings grace; the Transfiguration foretold the

triumph of grace in glory. Both grace and glory are available to man, but only through the Son of God who became man. Hence it is notably suitable that the divinity of Christ should be divinely proclaimed on these two occasions: the baptism by John, and the Transfiguration on the mount.

46. THE PASSION OF CHRIST

1. If man was to be redeemed at all, it was necessary that God's plan for human redemption be carried out. This plan involved the suffering of God-made-man in his human nature.

2. The plan of God for man's redemption is most wondrous in every respect. Yet God could have willed to redeem mankind in some other way than by the Passion of Christ.

3. Still, there was surely no way more suitable for man's redeeming than the way of Incarnation and Passion. For here man sees how much God loves him; man has perfect and most noble example of all the virtues; man has grace made available through Christ's merits; man beholds the evil conqueror of his race subdued and vanquished by One who is truly man.

4. For many nobly symbolic reasons it was suitable that our Lord, dying for us by his own will, should have chosen the death of the cross. This mode of death was the most feared, and was considered the most degrading. To show that the upright man need fear no mode of death; to indicate that no mode of death can sully the innocent; to give full and final evidence of his love for mankind and his hatred for sin, our Lord chose the death of the cross. And since he died for all, he chose to die in the open, on an eminence, with arms outstretched to all mankind.

5. Christ did not endure all forms of human suffering. He was not, as we have seen, subject to internal ailments, to sickness or disease. His bodily suffering was externally caused. And by dying on the cross, he excluded other modes of fatal suffering, such as burning or drowning. Yet, in one sense, our Lord did endure all human suffering: (a) all types of human beings had part in afflicting him: men, women, Jews, Gentiles, friends, acquaintances, strangers, rulers, servants; (b) he endured abandonment, calumny, misrepresentation, blasphemy, insults, mockeries, despoliation even of his garments, sadness, weariness, fear, wounds, scourgings; (c) he suffered in all members of his body, and in all his bodily senses.

6. Christ's suffering was the greatest of all suffering, the keenest pain. The prophet Jeremias (Lam. 1:12) foretold this fact in the cry: "O all ye that pass by the way, attend and see if there be any sorrow

like unto my sorrow." The external pains of the scourging, the crowning with thorns, and the crucifixion, were manifestly extreme. And the sadness of his perfect soul over the sins of men was the greatest distress ever humanly experienced. Our Lord's body was most perfect, and therefore most acutely sensitive to pain. And he did not permit study or consideration on the part of reason to allay the bodily pangs in any manner. For our Lord suffered voluntarily to win for man the greatest benefits; he measured his sufferings to accord with their fruits. Thus our Lord's pain in his Passion was the very greatest, the most intense, of pains.

7. When the body is ready by suffering to be torn from the soul, the soul itself suffers. For the soul in its essence is in the body and in every part of the body. And, since the faculties or powers of the soul are rooted in its essence, these powers suffer too in the suffering of the soul. Hence, Christ, during his Passion, suffered in his whole soul.

8. Yet, despite the fact that our Lord truly suffered in his whole soul, that soul had, throughout the Passion, the uninterrupted enjoyment of the beatific vision. There is no conflict here. Things do not block each other out unless they meet on a common plane. Thus, though love and hatred are opposites, a man may love God wholeheartedly and, at the same time, hate sin wholeheartedly. For love and hatred are not here on the same plane; they are not directed to the same thing. Hence, the wholehearted suffering of Christ did not come into conflict with the higher function of reason which was uninterruptedly fixed in wholehearted fruition of the beatific vision.

9. The time of Christ's suffering was divinely arranged, and hence was most wisely chosen. Our Lord did all things in their proper season.

10. The same thing must be said of the place in which Christ willed to suffer. There is a manifest fitness in our Lord's choice of Jerusalem, the city of the great temple with its divinely prescribed sacrifices, as the place for his perfect sacrifice.

11. Our Lord who willed to be "reputed with the wicked" (Isa. 53:12) was crucified between two thieves. It belonged to the perfection of his suffering, which was the greatest, that he should bear the insult and obloquy of being publicly executed with an ordinary group of criminals as though he were one of them. The cross of Christ, with an unrepentant sinner on one side, and a converted sinner on the other, shows the divinely innocent judge of mankind on the judgment seat between "those on the right, and those on the

left," the saved and the rejectors of salvation, as the case will be on the last day.

12. The Passion of Christ was the suffering and death of our Lord as man. We cannot say that the Godhead suffered and died. It is perfectly true that he who died *is* God. But he is also man, in the unity of the divine Person of the Son. It is the divine Person *in his human nature* that suffers and dies. The Godhead lives, both in the body of the dead Christ on the cross, and in the separated soul of Christ in Limbo.

47. THE EFFECTING CAUSE OF THE PASSION

1. The persecutors of our Lord, intending to slay him, inflicted upon him what was sufficient to cause his death. Hence, these executioners actually caused his death. But our Lord could have prevented the executioners from harming him; by his divine power he could have rendered them unable to do what they did, or he could have prevented their action upon him from having any effect. He did neither. Therefore, he died by his own will. Our Lord says (John 10:18): "No man taketh my life from me, but I lay it down of myself." That is, no man can take Christ's life against Christ's will. Thus, the effecting cause of Christ's Passion is, directly and actively, the action of human persecutors and executioners; indirectly and essentially, the effecting cause of the Passion is the will of our Lord himself to suffer and die for us.

2. Our Lord died as man; he died out of obedience to God. St. Paul says (Phil. 2:8): "He humbled himself, becoming obedient unto death, even to the death of the cross." The obedience of Christ atones for the disobedience of sinful man. St. Paul (Rom. 5:19) says: "As by the disobedience of one man, many were made sinners, so also by the obedience of one, many shall be made just." The obedience of Christ enters into the cause of the Passion.

3. Our Lord suffered voluntarily out of obedience to the Eternal Father who delivered him up to suffering. Now, our Lord as God is one with the Father and the Holy Ghost, and exercises the one and undivided will of the Trinity. But *as man* he obeys this same will, which is appropriated to the Father. He obeys willingly, making his human will conform perfectly to the divine Will. With all this in mind, it is accurate to say that Christ was delivered to his executioners by the Eternal Father, of whom St. Paul says (Rom. 8.32), he "spared not even his own Son, but delivered him up for us all." This delivering of Christ to suffering enters into the cause of the Passion.

4. The fruits of the Passion came first to the Jews, and passed on to the Gentiles, for Christ died for all. And, in the Passion itself, it was fitting that the Jews should hand Christ over to the Gentiles (the Roman soldiers) for the completing of the work.

5. The persecutors of Christ did not know who he was. Surely, the learned rulers and leaders of the people knew he *must be the Messias,* for they saw in him the signs foretold by the prophets. But they did not clearly know that he is God. They would not even acknowledge what they did see; they turned away from Christ and his claims in anger, hatred, and envy; hence, their ignorance was not innocent. The common people did not even know that our Lord was the Messias. While they saw signs and wonders, and many did believe, yet the bulk of the people allowed their teachers and leaders to argue them out of accepting our Lord. This ignorance of the persecutors enters into the cause of the Passion.

6. The sin of Christ's executioners was the more grievous by reason of the malice that marked their terrible deed. Yet even their culpable ignorance was some mitigation of their crime, and our Lord made reference to it when he prayed: "Father, forgive them, for they know not what they do" (Luke 23:34). The Gentiles who had part in the Passion did not know the Law, and were therefore much more excusable than the Jews.

48. THE EFFICACY OF THE PASSION OF CHRIST

1. Christ as man suffered voluntarily to redeem mankind. He suffered for justice, and therefore grace came to him *as merited,* and this merited grace overflows into the members of Christ, the children of his Church, and indeed all men. Thus Christ by his Passion merited salvation for his members.

2. Because he suffered willingly, out of love and obedience towards God, our Lord gave back to God more than enough to compensate for the offenses of the whole human race. Hence, the Passion is a *superabundant* atonement for the sins of mankind. Scripture says (I John 2:2): "He is the propitiation for our sins; and not for ours only, but for those of the whole world."

3. A sacrifice is something acceptable to God, offered to appease him and to manifest his supreme dominion over all things. The sacrifice offered by our Lord in the Passion was the most perfect sacrifice possible.

4. And the Passion was our redemption. To redeem a man is to secure his release from captivity. Man was a captive of sin, which is the bondage of the devil; man lay also under the bondage of God's

offended justice. Now, the Passion of Christ dissolved both bonds, releasing man from the thrall of sin and Satan, and atoning to God for man's rebellion against him. Therefore, the Passion is truly a work of redemption.

5. God in Trinity is the first cause of our redemption. But the immediate cause is Christ. The life of Christ (or his blood, which makes life possible), is the price paid to redeem us. Our Lord voluntarily paid this price. Hence, in the sense of immediate action and payment, our redemption was accomplished by our Lord alone. Thus Christ alone is our Redeemer.

6. The principal effecting cause of man's salvation is God. And the humanity of Christ is the instrument of the Godhead in working out man's salvation. All that Christ as man does and suffers for us, is truly done by him instrumentally; that is, as carrying out the effectiveness rooted in, and proceeding from, the Godhead. Now, what Christ does and suffers for us is called his Passion. Therefore, the Passion of Christ is the effecting cause of man's salvation.

49. ACTUAL EFFECTS OF THE PASSION OF CHRIST

1. The first effect of the Passion is the delivering of man from sin. The Passion renders human sin *forgivable*. It furnishes a medicine which cures sin in those who take that medicine rightly. A man's individual responsibility for his acts, and his sins, is not taken away; nor is free will nullified. But the Passion removed the barrier of original sin which made heaven inaccessible to mankind, and merited the grace man needs to raise him out of actual sins and set him in the sure way to heaven. These graces man obtains through the faith by the use of the sacraments and prayer which have efficacy because of the Passion and its merits.

2. The Passion delivered man from the power of the devil. It made sin forgivable, and, through the forgiveness of sin, man can be reconciled with God and put in the way to heaven. Thus Satan is defeated, and no man need longer remain in his power. Satan overreached himself in conspiring to bring about the death of our Lord, for that death meant Satan's own defeat.

3. The Passion freed men from the punishment due to sin. Christ paid superabundantly on man's behalf. Henceforth, if a man deserve such punishment, it is his own personal and individual doing, his own actual sinning. And even such actual sin can be forgiven, and its punishment cancelled, by the forgivability of sin established by the Passion.

4. The Passion reconciled man with God. St. Paul (Rom. 5:10) says:

"We are reconciled to God by the death of his Son." The Passion, in addition to its delivering of man from the thralldom of sin, is a most pleasing sacrifice to God. So pleasing indeed, and so powerful is this sacrifice, that God is appeased by it for every human sin if the sinner makes himself one with Christ and complies with his will and his institution for removing sin and gaining grace.

5. Original sin closed the gates of heaven to all mankind. And serious actual sin also closes heaven to the sinner. Now, the Passion atoned for original sin, and so opened heaven to the whole race, and made it possible, on Christ's terms, for a man to get there. As for the personal sinner, the Passion, by making actual sin forgivable, opens heaven to the truly repentant.

6. Christ humbled himself in his Passion, and so merited to be exalted. Says scripture (Phil. 2:8, 9): "He humbled himself, becoming obedient unto death, even to the death of the cross. For which cause God also hath exalted him." Christ was exalted as man in the Resurrection, the Ascension, the placing at the right hand of God, the receiving of the homage of all rational creatures, who are to bow the knee at the mention of his name.

50. THE DEATH OF OUR LORD

1. Christ died: (a) to satisfy for man who was under sentence of death by reason of the first sin; (b) to prove that he is true man; (c) to deliver man from the fear of death; (d) to teach us to die spiritually to sin; (e) to instill in us the firm hope of rising from the dead.

2. When our Lord died, the divinity or Godhead was not separated from the body on the cross and later in the tomb. For what is bestowed by God's grace is never taken away except through fault; scripture says (Rom. 11:29): "The gifts and calling of God are without repentance." The human nature, and thus the flesh of Christ, was united hypostatically or personally with the Word of God, and this union remained permanently; it could not be disrupted by the death of Christ as man.

3. And therefore also, the Godhead or divinity was not separated from the human soul of Christ during its hours of the soul's separation from the sacred body.

4. Yet it is not correct to say that Christ was man during the period of his death; for a man means a living man, and Christ during this space of time was not living but dead. His soul did not then animate the body, for he had truly died. Christ remained really dead from the moment his soul left the body on the cross until the moment it revivified the body for the Resurrection.

5. The body which hung dead upon the cross was buried in the

tomb. This was the same body which had undergone the Passion, and which was to rise glorious and immortal. For the body of Christ, living and dead, was identically the same body. It was not, indeed, *totally* the same, for there is a difference between a body living and the same body dead. But, apart from this difference, the body in the tomb, and the body which suffered the Passion, and the body glorified at Resurrection was the same body.

6. St. Augustine (*De Trin.* IV) says that the one death of Christ in the body saved us from two deaths, that is, the death of the body and the death of the soul. We are, of course, to die a bodily death, but now it is not a victory over us: "Death is swallowed up in victory" (I Cor. 15:54). And the death of Christ destroys in us the necessity of dying in sin and being plunged into the endless death of eternal torment.

51. THE BURIAL OF OUR LORD

1. Our Lord was buried for good reasons: (a) to establish beyond all question the fact of his death; Pilate made very sure of the fact of death before permitting the body to be taken from the cross and buried; (b) to make possible the glorious Resurrection from the grave, and thus to give hope and promise to mankind of the glory in store for those that do Christ's will; (c) to indicate that we should be spiritually buried with our Lord, and hidden safe away from the rule of sin.

2. The body of our Lord was wrapped in burial bands, embalmed with a hundredweight of spices, and laid in a new grave which was hewn out of a rock. The burial was a work of reverence and love; it honored the sacred body, and was praiseworthy in all who took part in it. Such a burial put beyond all question any thought that Christ might not be truly dead.

3. There was in the perfect body of Christ no weakness that could result in decomposition or putrefaction, even after death. And scripture says (Psalm 15:10): "Nor wilt thou suffer thy holy one to see corruption." There was, therefore, no dissolution of parts, no crumbling into elements, of the body of Christ in the tomb.

4. St. Augustine (*De Trin.* IV) says that thirty-six hours elapsed from the evening of our Lord's burial to the dawn of the Ressurection. The sacred body was in the tomb one day and two nights. As each part of a day was reckoned *a day* according to prevailing Jewish usage, we say that our Lord's body was in the tomb for three days.

52. THE DESCENT INTO HELL

1. The name hell stands for an evil of penalty, as well as for an evil of guilt. At the time of our Lord, the souls who were held from

heaven (since heaven was still closed to mankind) for the *penalty* due to original sin, and, in some cases at least, for *penalty* for their own sins which were not so grave as to demand eternal punishment, were in a place and state that is called *hell*. This was not the hell of the souls who had willfully rejected God by mortal sin and were suffering everlasting penalty. This was a place and state of those who were waiting for the redemption; this place and state is called, in scriptural language, by the name of hell; to this hell, the soul of our Lord went or "descended" when it departed from the body upon the cross.

2. Therefore, our Lord did not descend locally into the hell of lost souls and demons. But he spread his power there to put the reprobates to shame for their belief and wickedness. And to the hell which we rather call *limbo,* he brought the hope and promise of glory. On those souls in Limbo who were detained there solely for original sin, he shed the glory of his Godhead.

3. Since, during the hours of our Lord's being dead, neither his soul nor his body was separated from the divine Person of the Son, we must say that wherever his soul or his body was, there was the whole Christ.

4. It seems that our Lord's soul was in limbo (or hell, as it is called) from the moment of his death on the cross to the moment of the Resurrection.

5. Christ descended into limbo, and released from its penalty the adult persons whose only reason for being detained was original sin. These he glorified by his Godhead. Thus the holy fathers were delivered from hell.

6. Christ's descent into the hell of limbo means no deliverance of any soul from the hell of the lost. For the souls in the hell of the lost either had no faith in Christ, or, if they had faith, they had no conformity of charity in his Passion. The lost are confirmed in evil, unchangeably unrepentant; there is no cleansing them from sin, for their will is fixed in sin.

7. The infants held in limbo by reason of original sin were not released by our Lord's descent, for they had not the use of reason and could not be united to Christ's Passion by faith and charity. The infants were not, of course, in any distress or pain.

8. Christ's descent into limbo did not liberate souls from purgatory, except, perhaps, in such cases as could have, through the descent, a personal application to them of satisfaction for their personal faults. The descent itself was not to make satisfaction, but to bring release "to them that were sanctified," that is, the holy fathers who were

sanctified by faith and charity, and were detained only by original sin, and not their personal sins.

53. THE RESURRECTION

1. Christ rose from the dead: (a) to manifest the divine Justice which exalts the humbled; (b) to instruct and establish us in the faith, for the Resurrection is the central truth of our faith; (c) to give us firm hope of our own resurrection; (d) to teach us to rise from the death of sin to newness of life; (e) to complete the work of our salvation, and, after enduring evil, to rise triumphant to lasting good.

2. Christ rose on the third day. He delayed the Resurrection long enough to establish the fact that he had truly died. Yet he did not delay it so long that men might fail to see it as the unquestionable proof of his Godhead. Besides, the third day commends to our notice the perfection of the number three which, as Aristotle says, is the number of everything that has beginning, middle, and end. And, mystically, since Christ's one death destroyed our two deaths, the number three is significant. The third day also indicates the three epochs of mankind in their relation to God: before the Law, under the Law, and now under grace.

3. Christ was the first to rise from the dead, to die no more. Those who had been miraculously restored to life in the Old and the New Testament, had to die again eventually. Not so with Christ who "is risen from the dead, the first fruits of them that sleep" (I Cor. 15:20); "Christ rising again from the dead, dieth now no more; death shall no more have dominion over him" (Rom. 6:9).

4. Scripture speaks of Christ (Acts 2:24) "whom God hath raised up." Yet our Lord himself says (John 10:18): "No one taketh my life from me; but I lay it down, and I take it up again." There is no conflict or contradiction here. Christ is God, and when he causes his own Resurrection it is God who raises him up. It is perfectly accurate, then, to say that Christ himself is the cause of his Resurrection from the dead.

54. THE RISEN CHRIST

1. Christ retained his own true body in and after the Resurrection. Had this not been a true body, or had it not been the body in which Christ suffered, the Resurrection would not have been real but only apparent.

2. The body of Christ was *glorified* in its rising. The saints shall rise in bodily glory; Christ's Resurrection is the cause and the exemplar of their rising; hence, his body is much greater in glory than

theirs; our Lord merited this glory by his Passion. Our Lord possessed in his soul the glory of the beatific vision from the first moment of his existence as man; yet the glory of the beatific vision was divinely prevented from overflowing into the body of Christ until after He had endured the Passion and Death for our salvation. But once that work for us was done, the glory of his soul inundated his body.

3. Flesh, blood, bones, and all the other constituents of a human body were in the body of Christ as he rose in glory. It was a complete and perfect body. Our Lord, speaking after his Resurrection to the disciples who thought he was a phantom, said: "A spirit hath not flesh and bones as you see me to have" (Luke 24:39).

4. Our Lord kept in his glorified body the marks of his wounds: (a) as an everlasting testimony of his victory; (b) as a proof that he is the same Christ who suffered and was crucified; (c) as a constant and concrete plea on our behalf to the Eternal Father; (d) as a means of upbraiding the reprobates on the last day, showing them what he did for them, thus reminding them of what they had wickedly despised and rejected.

55. THE MANIFESTATION OF THE RISEN CHRIST

1. Christ rose from the dead and was manifested to "witnesses preordained of God" (Acts 10:40). These witnesses were to make his Resurrection known to others.

2. No human eye was privileged to see our Lord in the first moment of his Resurrection. An angel was the herald of his rising glorious from the dead.

3. After the Resurrection, our Lord did not live constantly with his disciples. But he appeared to them repeatedly, and thus he proved two needful facts: the truth of the Resurrection itself, and the glory of the Risen Lord. Had our Lord lived with the disciples as he had lived with them before his Passion, it might be thought that he rose to the same life as before.

4. On the very day of the Resurrection, our Lord appeared "in another shape" to the two disciples who were journeying to Emmaus (Mark 16:12; Luke 24:13–16). After the Resurrection, Christ appeared in his *own shape* to some who were well disposed to believe in him, and in *another shape* to those who were prone to doubt. The two disciples on the way to Emmaus said that they "had hoped that it was he who should have redeemed Israel" (Luke 24:21). Their hope was, as their very words show, a thing of the past. Our Lord therefore showed himself to these disciples as he was in their own minds, that is, as a stranger.

5. Christ proved the truth of his Resurrection to his disciples, "to whom he showed himself alive after his passion, by many proofs, for forty days, appearing to them, and speaking to them of the kingdom of God" (Acts 1:3). Thus Christ strengthened the faith of the disciples, and supplied them with argument to use in carrying out their mission.

6. Our Lord's proofs of his Resurrection were perfectly adequate. He made use of the testimony of the angels, and of the scriptures. He showed that he had a true and solid body, not an apparent body, and he identified this body by the marks of his wounds. In his risen body, he ate and drank with his disciples, heard them and spoke to them, and discoursed on the scriptures. Throughout the appearances to his disciples, our Lord manifested the reality of his body and also the reality of his human soul, for he used the soul-faculty of intellect—he reasoned. Finally, our Lord showed his power and glory by entering through closed doors, and by disappearing suddenly from the presence of his disciples.

56. CAUSAL POWER OF THE RESURRECTION

1. Aristotle says (*Metaph.* IV): "Whatever is the first in any order, is the cause of what comes after it." The Resurrection of Christ was first in the order of rising from the dead: "The first fruits of them that sleep" (I Cor. 15:20). Christ's Resurrection is thus the cause of our bodily resurrection which will take place on the last day.

2. Christ's Resurrection is also the cause of the resurrection of our souls from the death of sin. The divine power which appears in the bodily Resurrection of Christ extends to human souls. St. Paul (Rom. 4:25) says that our Lord "rose again for our justification." And again he says (Rom. 6:4): "Christ is risen from the dead by the glory of the Father, so we also may walk in newness of life."

57. THE ASCENSION

1. Our Lord as man arose from the dead to an everlasting life. As soon thereafter as his divine wisdom chose, he ascended from the perishable earth to the deathless glory of heaven.

2. Christ as man ascended, by the divine power, into heaven. As God, he is everywhere, and there is no place to which he can or need ascend. Hence, Christ as man ascended into heaven, and not as God, even though Christ *is* God.

3. Our Lord ascended into heaven, primarily by the divine power, which is his own as God; secondarily, by the power of the glorified soul which moves the glorified body at will.

4. "He ascended above all the heavens" (Eph. 4:10). The glorified

body of our Risen Lord shines with greater glory than any other body. In place of dignity, it ranks highest.

5. Our Lord as man ascended into heaven to take his place, not only above all bodies, but above all spiritual creatures as well. "God set him above all Principality, and Power, and Virtue, and Dominion, and every name that is named, not only in this world but also in that which is to come" (Eph. 1:21).

6. Our Lord prepared the way for us to ascend to heaven. And his Ascension awakens in us faith, hope, charity, and reverence. Hence we can say that his Ascension is a cause of our salvation.

58. OUR LORD AT THE FATHER'S RIGHT HAND

1. To sit means to abide, to stay. It also means to occupy the throne of judgment. In both meanings of this word, it belongs to Christ to sit at the right hand of the Father, that is, to abide in the Father's glory, and to reign together with the Father.

2. It belongs to Christ as God to have, equally with the Father, the identical divine glory, beatitude, and power. This is "sitting at the right hand of the Father." The phrase does not indicate a *secondary* place, nor a place merely *next* to the Father. It means that Christ as God rules in absolute equality with the other two divine Persons.

3. And it belongs to Christ as man to sit at the Father's right hand, in the sense that Christ's humanity is dowered with the Father's gifts beyond all other creatures.

4. As God, Christ is equal with the Father, and one with him in substance; as man, Christ excels all creatures in possessing divine gifts. On both scores, Christ alone holds just title to the place at the Father's right hand.

59. OUR LORD'S POWER AS JUDGE

1. Christ, by testimony of scripture (Acts 10:42) is appointed by God to be judge of the living and the dead. Now, a judge must have, in addition to jurisdiction, a zeal for justice; he must be wise; he must know truth. The Son of God is wisdom itself eternally begotten; he is Lord and lover of justice; hence he has perfect qualifications for the function of a judge. St. Augustine (*De Vera Relig.* xxxi) says: "The Father judges no man, but has given all judgment to the son." Of course, speaking simply, the judicial power is in the Trinity. For reasons here indicated, it is *appropriated* to the Son.

2. Even as man, our Lord has power and right to judge. Scripture says (John 5:27) that the Father "hath given him power to do judgment because he is the Son of man."

3. The judicial or judiciary power belongs to Christ as man because of his divine personality, the dignity of his headship, and the fullness of his habitual grace. This power also belongs to our Lord by reason of his merit. For he who fought for God's justice, and won through to victory, though unjustly condemned, should, by divine justice, now be the judge.

4. Since, as scripture says (John 5:22), "the Father hath given all judgment to the Son," it is evident that our Lord is judge with reference to all human affairs.

5. A judgment takes place when a man dies. Scripture says (Heb. 9:27): "It is appointed unto men once to die, and after this the judgment." There will be another and *general* judgment when all human lives (and the effects of these lives that continue after the lives themselves are ended) will be perfectly and publicly judged. This judgment will take place on the last day. And Christ our Lord and God will be the judge.

6. Our Lord will also be judge of the angels. Christ has the authority to judge the angels; indeed, he delegates the authority to the apostles, and St. Paul (I Cor. 6:3) says that the apostles will exercise the delegated authority. In the beginning, Christ as the Word of God judged and sentenced the rebel angels. But there are *accidental* rewards and punishments to be meted to good and to bad angels; for these the judicial power is vested in our Lord as God Incarnate.

THE SACRAMENTS
IN GENERAL

(QUESTIONS 60 TO 65)

60. MEANING OF SACRAMENT

1. The word sacrament, in itself, means something holy or sacred, or something which is related to what is holy or sacred. But in the sense in which we are now to use the word sacrament, it means, first of all, a *sign* which expresses in a sensible manner, some sacred thing which is outside the grasp and reach of the senses.

2. A sacrament is a sign of some holy thing pertaining to man; that is, it is a sign of a thing in so far as this thing *makes men holy*.

3. A sacrament is a sign that takes in past, present, and future in its signification, for: (a) it includes reference to man's sanctification in its cause, which is the Passion of Christ; (b) it aids man's present holiness by giving grace and promoting virtue; (c) it bears in itself the promise of eternal life to come.

4. Man acquires intellectual knowledge from sense-knowledge. Therefore, sensible signs are aptly used to signify spiritual things. A sacrament is a sign that the senses can grasp; then the mind can read the intellectual and spiritual meaning which the sign is meant to convey. A sacrament is always an outer or sensible sign.

5. The signs that are sacraments are not of man's choosing. Since sacraments are for man's sanctification, they are signs instituted and chosen by the sanctifier of men, that is, our divine Lord.

6. A sign is not made a sacrament by any natural fitness or power of its own. It is made a sacrament by authentic words which give it spiritual meaning and power. Hence, *words* are necessary for constituting a sacrament.

7. Not any words that a man may choose, however apt and suitable they may be, can constitute a sign as a sacrament. As the signs themselves are divinely determined, so are the authentic words which make these signs into sacraments.

8. Any words added or omitted so as to change the essential meaning of the determinate formula of words used for a sacrament, would invalidate the sacrament itself.

61. NECESSITY OF SACRAMENTS

1. To save his soul, man needs sacraments, for: (a) human nature needs to be led by bodily and sensible things to what is spiritual; (b) man needs corporeal signs, for sin has subjected him to material things, and he is unable to apply his mind directly to what is spiritual; (c) man actively tends to material performance and outer expression; if this tendency be not directed aright, it ends in superstitious and even demoniacal practices. Sacraments, therefore, are means of instructing man in things spiritual, teaching and preserving him in essential truths and seemly practice. Hence, because of their essential service to man, we say that sacraments are necessary for man's salvation.

2. And sacraments are spiritual remedies for the wounds inflicted on the soul by sin. Indeed, while man was in the state of innocence, and was sinless, he did not need sacraments.

3. Sacred signs or sacraments were in use, by divine command, under the Old Law, before the coming of Christ. No man can be saved but through Christ. Therefore, before Christ came, people needed visible signs to testify their faith in his coming. Such signs were sacraments.

4. When Christ came and founded his Church, he established seven sacraments; these are the sacraments of the New Law; the establishing of these Christian sacraments abolishes the sacraments of the Old Law, which were ancient and holy signs prophetic of the coming of Christ and of the Christian sacraments.

62. GRACE: CHIEF EFFECT OF THE SACRAMENTS

1. The sacraments of the New Law produce grace. For the sacraments incorporate man with Christ, make man a member of Christ; and such incorporation is effected only by grace. The *principal* cause of grace is God; the sacraments are instituted to be *instrumental* causes of God's grace.

2. Grace perfects the *essence* of the soul; from grace, gifts and virtues flow into the soul's *powers*. To these normal effects of grace in the soul, and in the powers of the soul, each sacrament adds a special perfection of its own; this is the respective *sacramental grace* of each sacrament. Sacramental grace is a special divine aid bestowed on the soul by a sacrament, and meant to help that soul attain the precise end for which the sacrament is instituted.

3. Grace is in the sacraments of the New Law as a transient instrumental power.

4. The sacraments are instrumental causes of grace; therefore, they possess an instrumental power for bringing about the effects of grace.

5. The sacraments of the New Law derive their power especially from the Passion of Christ; the virtue of the Passion is in some manner communicated to the receiver of a sacrament.

6. The sacraments of the Old Law could not of themselves confer sanctifying grace; they could only signify the faith by which men are justified, that is, set in the state of sanctifying grace.

63. THE EFFECTS OF THE SACRAMENTS

1. A *character* is a lasting mark, set as a seal and a distinctive sign upon a person. Now, a sacrament is capable of imprinting a character upon the Christian soul, marking it permanently as dedicated to the worship of God. In a somewhat similar way, the uniform and insignia of a soldier is an abiding mark and indication of his allegiance, his rank, and his special duty.

2. But the character imprinted or impressed by a sacrament must be a spiritual thing, for it is a mark or seal set on the soul. It must, therefore, be one of the three things which a spiritual soul can have; that is, passion, habit, or power. It is not a passion, for a passion is not lasting; it passes quickly, whereas a character has permanence. Nor is the character a habit. It is a *spiritual* power.

3. The sacramental character is the character or mark of Christ. It is, in some way, a participation in Christ's eternal priesthood. It comes to the soul from Christ himself.

4. A *character* impressed by a sacrament of the New Law marks the Christian soul as the receiver or the bestower of things belonging to the worship of God. Now, the worship of God involves actions which come from the powers of the soul. Hence, the sacramental character has as its subject (that is, its seat, location) the *powers* of the soul, not the *essence* of the soul as such.

5. Every sanctification wrought by the priesthood of Christ is perpetual. Therefore, a character impressed by a sacrament (a character which is, in some sense, a participation in Christ's priesthood), is everlasting. It cannot be obliterated from the soul. It is an *indelible* mark and seal.

6. Not every sacrament of the New Law imprints an indelible character on the soul. Such a character is impressed by those sacraments which are ordained for divine worship and which give a person power to receive or confer other sacraments. *Baptism* empowers a person to receive other sacraments. *Confirmation* (as we shall see later) has something of this same purpose. Holy order empowers the receiver to confer sacraments on others. Therefore, these three sacraments (baptism, confirmation, holy order), imprint, respectively, a character on the soul. A property of these sacraments is that they can be received only once by the same person. Their respective characters never fade or admit of renewal.

64. SOURCE AND MINISTRATION OF THE SACRAMENTS

1. God is the cause of the sacraments, and of their effect on the soul of the recipient. The person who administers a sacrament is God's instrument. God is the *principal* cause; the minister is the *instrumental* cause of the sacraments. Now, the interior effect of a sacrament comes from the principal cause alone.

2. God alone can cause the justification of the soul by grace. Such justification is the inward effect of the sacraments. Therefore, since

only God can give to sacraments their justifying or grace-conferring power, God alone can institute a sacrament.

3. Christ, *as God,* as exercising his divine power, instituted the seven sacraments of the New Law. Yet Christ *as man* has authority over the sacraments, and is their most excellent minister.

4. Christ can impart to his priests the authority and excellence which he has in respect to the sacraments.

5. The validity of a sacrament conferred, does not depend upon the worthiness of him who administers it. The instrument cannot change the essence of what is done by the principal cause. Water is water, whether it flow through a pipe of gold or a pipe of lead. Hence, even an evil minister can validly confer a sacrament.

6. But a wicked person who administers a sacrament does wrong. He commits a sin of irreverence which, in its essential general kind or *genus,* is a mortal sin. It is called a sin of sacrilege.

7. The whole power of the sacraments comes from Christ's Passion which belongs to him as man, even though this power is not *imparted* to the sacramental signs except by Christ as God, who imparts this power in instituting the sacraments. Since Christ's suffering and death as man are the source of sacramental power, it belongs to men, rather than to angels, to administer sacraments. Yet God could give this power to angels.

8. The one who confers a sacrament must truly intend to confer it. He must employ the determinate *matter* or sign. He must mean the words (the *form*) which make the sign sacramentally significant. If the intention of the minister (that is, the person who administers the sacrament) is amiss, the sacrament is not validly conferred. [*Note:* With regard to the Holy Eucharist, it must be remembered that the minister is the consecrating priest, not the priest who distributes Holy Communion.]

9. Even should the minister lack faith, he can validly administer a sacrament, provided he use the proper sign (matter), and employ the determinate formula of words (form), and have the intention of doing what Christ and the Church intend to have done.

10. If a qualified minister intends to confer or confect a sacrament, and does all that is required to that purpose by Christ and the Church, the sacrament is true and valid. This is so, even if, by an ulterior intention, the minister's will is evil. If, for instance, a minister were to baptize a man purely for the sake of some social or personal advantage he hopes to gain from that man, the sacrament is not invalidated by this alien and evil purpose.

65. THE NUMBER OF SACRAMENTS

1. There are seven sacraments of the New Law. Man has seven bodily requirements, and, since the bodily life has a certain conformity with the spiritual life, we discern seven spiritual needs corresponding to those of the body. The seven sacraments answer these seven requirements of the soul: (a) In the bodily order, man needs first to be born; in the spiritual order, birth is baptism. (b) In the bodily order, man needs to grow to maturity and strength; in the spiritual order, this is accomplished by confirmation. (c) In the bodily order, man has constant need of nourishment to support life and strength; in the spiritual order, the soul is nourished by Holy Eucharist. (d) In the bodily order, sickness or infirmity calls for medicine and care; the soul is restored to health by penance. (e) In the bodily order, man needs full vigor, with all traces of past wounds and illnesses removed; the soul has this boon in extreme unction. (f) In the bodily order, there must be peace and seemly rule, and some must have authority to this end; this need, in the spiritual order, is supplied by holy orders. (g) In the bodily social order, man needs to propagate; in the spiritual order, this natural need finds sanctification in matrimony.

2. The fitting order to use in naming the seven sacraments is this: baptism, confirmation, Holy Eucharist, penance, extreme unction, holy order, matrimony. For first come the sacraments which perfect the individual man: (a) *directly:* baptism, confirmation, Holy Eucharist; (b) *indirectly:* by removing what is harmful: penance, extreme unction. Next come the sacraments which perfect man in society: holy orders, matrimony.

3. Absolutely speaking, the greatest of all the sacraments is Holy Eucharist, for it is our Lord and God himself. Yet, on the score of man's necessity, baptism comes first, and penance next.

4. And the necessity of which we speak is the necessity of *end.* A thing is said to have the necessity of end: (a) simply or absolutely, if the end cannot be attained without it; (b) relatively or nonabsolutely, if the end can be attained without it, but not conveniently or becomingly. Thus, if a man proposes to see a certain mountain, he must, of simple necessity, go to the place where the mountain can be seen. Some conveyance is necessary for making the journey to the place from which the mountain may be viewed, yet, despite difficulty and inconvenience, the man might be able to reach the place by walking, and so could dispense with the conveyance. But it would be a hardship. Now, of all the sacraments, baptism alone is necessary for man's salvation "by the simple necessity of end." Yet, in case a

man sins mortally after baptism, penance becomes necessary. And, as a requisite for the continuance of the Church, holy order is necessary.

BAPTISM

(QUESTIONS 66 TO 71)

66. BAPTISM

1. In the sacrament of baptism, we consider three things: (a) that which is sacrament only, that is, the sacrament as *sign;* the water used in baptizing; the washing; (b) that which is *reality* only, that is, inward grace; justification; (c) that which is *reality* and *sacrament,* that is, the sacramental character impressed by baptism on the soul of the person baptized.

2. Baptism received the power of conferring grace when Christ was baptized. This was the institution of baptism as a sacrament. But the obligation of receiving this sacrament was officially imposed on mankind by our Lord, after his Passion and Resurrection.

3. Water is the *matter* of baptism, that is, it is the material used in making the sign which is a sacrament. In St. John (3:5) we read: "Unless a man be born again of water and the Holy Ghost, he cannot enter into the kingdom of God."

4. Any true natural water may be used for baptizing. If alien substances be mingled with the water, yet not in such quantity as to destroy its nature as true water, they do not make it unavailable for baptizing.

5. In every sacrament, we distinguish *matter* and *form.* The matter, as we explained above, is the material of which the sign is constituted. The form is the authentic and determinate formula of words used in confecting the sacrament, that is, making the sign into a true sacrament. In baptism, the matter is, remotely, *water;* proximately, the matter is *water applied* in the act of baptizing. And the form, in baptism, is the set of words to be used in applying the matter, namely, the words, "I baptize thee in the name of the Father, and of the Son, and of the Holy Ghost" (Matt. 28:19).

6. We read (Acts 8:12) that the apostles baptized "in the name of Jesus Christ." This does not mean that the apostles changed the essential formula which names the Father, the Son, and the Holy

Ghost. It merely means that the apostles baptized by the authority of Christ, and that they used the name of Jesus Christ in connection with baptism. By special divine revelation, the apostles were instructed to employ the holy name of Jesus Christ to win it reverence among people, both Jew and Gentile, who had been taught to hate it. These people were to see that the Holy Ghost was given in baptism at the invocation of the holy name of Jesus.

7. The word baptism means a *washing*. Now, a washing may be done by immersion in water, by the pouring of water, and even by the sprinkling of water. Therefore, immersion is not requisite for baptism.

8. "Trine immersion" or its equivalent "threefold pouring" is used in baptism solemnly conferred according to the ceremonial of the Church. Yet this is not essential for valid baptism; one pouring suffices.

9. Baptism cannot be repeated. If a man is spiritually born by baptism, he cannot be born again spiritually. Baptism imprints on the soul of the person baptized an indelible character which, being once impressed, cannot be impressed again. And baptism *always* takes away original sin. Once original sin is taken away, it does not recur or return to the soul.

10. The essentials for baptism are: the *matter* (water applied), the *form* (the prescribed words), and the *minister* (who brings matter and form together to constitute the sacrament). For solemn baptism, the Church has surrounded these essentials with suitable ceremonies and prayers.

11. The *sacrament* of baptism is baptism conferred with water. The *effects* of the sacrament, except for the imprinting of the character, may be produced in a soul in two other ways. A person unbaptized who sheds his blood for Christ is said to have the baptism of blood. A person unable to receive baptism (because he knows nothing of it, or because his efforts to obtain it are unavailing) may be conformed to Christ by love and contrition, and thus is said to have baptism of desire. Baptism of blood and baptism of desire take away sin and give grace. But they do not imprint the sacramental character on the soul. Hence they are not truly the *sacrament* of baptism. Therefore, a survivor of bloody torture endured for Christ, and one whose desire for baptism is no longer thwarted, are to be baptized with water.

12. Baptism of blood is most excellent in its sacramental effects, for bloody suffering brings a man who has charity into union with Christ's Passion from which baptism has its efficacy. Still, it does not impress the sacramental character.

67. THE MINISTER OF BAPTISM

1. One who confects or confers a sacrament is called its *minister*. In solemn or ceremonious baptism, the priest is the *ordinary* minister. (In the older practice of the Church, a deacon was not permitted to baptize solemnly "except in cases of extreme urgency." In modern days, a deacon may baptize solemnly if there be a good reason, and the pastor or the bishop authorize the action). A deacon who baptizes solemnly, is called an *extraordinary* minister of baptism.

2. It belongs to the special office of priests (and, of course, bishops) to baptize.

3. Because of the necessity of this sacrament, it was ordained that it is to be conferred with matter easily available, namely water, and that in case of necessity when solemn or ceremonious baptism is out of question, it can be conferred by anyone who has the use of reason, and who uses the water rightly, and says the required words, and intends to baptize.

4. Women as well as men can validly baptize, youths as well as adults.

5. Even a non-baptized person can confer this sacrament validly on others.

6. Several people cannot concur in baptizing, one saying the words of the form, another or others applying the *matter*. The minister of baptism takes the place of Christ; there is only one Christ; there should be only one minister of any one baptism. If several were to concur in baptizing, applying the matter and saying the form, the first to utter the form would actually confer the sacrament. And if all spoke absolutely together, since each one would have the intention of baptizing, the baptism would be valid, but the several ministers would be guilty of improperly treating a sacrament.

7. The priest, after baptizing solemnly, turns over the newly baptized person to "his sponsor and guide." The sponsor is thus said, in an ancient phrase, "to raise the baptized person from the sacred font." That is, the sponsor receives the newly baptized person for the purpose of instructing him, and guiding him in the way of life which he takes up by being baptized.

8. The duty of sponsors is a real obligation laid upon them. St. Augustine (*Serm.* 168) says: "I admonish you, both men and women, who have raised children (that is, who have stood sponsor) in baptism, that you stand before God as sureties for those whom you have been seen to raise from the sacred font."

68. THE RECIPIENTS OF BAPTISM

1. Baptism is necessary for each person. All mankind are required to be baptized. Without baptism, there is no salvation. For baptism makes a person a member of Christ, through whom alone salvation can be attained.

2. To be saved, a man must have at least the baptism of desire. [*Note:* Desire for baptism is *explicit* in a person who knows at least something of what baptism means, and who, with Christian faith and contrition and charity, longs to receive it. Desire for baptism is *implicit* in a person who sincerely wants to do what God would have him do, and who does his honest best to live by his conscience; such a person may not even have heard of baptism, and yet may have this implied desire to receive it.] Baptism of blood has all the sacramental power of baptism of water, except for the imprinting of the character, and it remits all sin and the penalties due to sin. Baptism of desire remits sin and the eternal penalty due to it, but does not remit all the temporal penalty due.

3. Since baptism is necessary for salvation, it should be conferred promptly on infants, both because of the danger of death, and because infants have no ability to elicit a desire for baptism. Adults who wish to be baptized should be put through a time of instruction and probation so that they may receive the sacrament with understanding, reverence, and the firm will to discharge with fidelity the duties of the Christian life. Still, if adults be well instructed and disposed, they should not be made to wait for baptism. Nor should adult baptism be deferred during sickness, especially when there is danger of death.

4. An adult sinner who has no repentance and no intention of abandoning his sin is not to be baptized. A sinner who is repentant and well resolved should be baptized.

5. No kind of penance or work of satisfaction is to be imposed on an adult who is baptized, for baptism takes away all sin and all punishment due to sin. To impose a penance at baptism would be to dishonor the Passion and Death of Christ which make full satisfaction for all the sins of the person baptized.

6. An adult who is to be baptized must have some sorrow for his sins, but he is not required to confess them, beyond the general confession implied in the words of the ritual, by which he renounces Satan and all his works and pomps.

7. An adult to be baptized must have the intention of being baptized. Such a person seeks baptism at the hands of the Church; he

asks to receive it; hence he expresses his intention of receiving it.

8. To receive grace, the person to be baptized must have faith. But even in the absence of faith, a person who intends to be baptized and undergoes the rite of baptism, is actually baptized, and is marked with the sacramental character.

9. Since infants are in original sin, they need baptism. For a person capable of incurring the guilt of sin, even original sin, is capable of receiving grace. Hence, infants are to be baptized. Not only does baptism confer its wondrous and indispensable benefits on the souls of children, but it also sets them in the way of Christian living at the very beginning of their lives, and thus gives greater assurance of their persevering than would be the case if their baptism were deferred.

10. Children of Jews and other unbelievers are not to be baptized without their parents' consent. By natural justice, young children are under the rule and control of their parents. Besides, baptism is not conferred, according to the usage of the Church, on those who will have no normal opportunity of living the Christian life in conformity with the obligation imposed in baptism.

11. A child cannot be baptized while it is yet in its mother's womb. [*Note:* This is no longer true. Modern methods in medicine and surgery make it feasible to convey water to the child in the womb, so that the baptism is at least probably valid. Such a baptism is licitly conferred, under conditions set by church law, when the child is unlikely to have a normal birth, or to live until birth.]

12. Insane and imbecile persons are to be baptized, like infants, in the faith of the Church. A person who, during his normal life, manifests no desire to receive baptism, is not to be baptized if he becomes insane. Yet an insane person may have lucid intervals during which he desires to be baptized; he is not to be refused. If he lapses into madness before the sacrament can be administered, the person baptizing should wait for the next period of sanity; if such an interval is not likely to recur, or if death threatens, the sacrament should be administered at once, despite the madness of the recipient. A person who is sane, but weak-minded, is to be treated as a normal person.

69. EFFECTS OF BAPTISM

1. Baptism takes away all sin, original and actual. St. Paul says (Rom. 6:3): "All we who are baptized in Christ Jesus are baptized in his death"; and (Rom. 6:11), "So do you also reckon that you are

dead to sin, but alive unto God in Christ Jesus Our Lord." By baptism, therefore, a man dies to sin, and begins to live in the newness of grace. Thus, every sin is taken away by baptism.

2. Baptism not only takes away all sin, but cancels completely the debt of punishment due to sin. By baptism a person is incorporated in Christ suffering and dying. And scripture says (Rom. 6:8): "If we be dead with Christ, we believe that we shall live also together with Christ." Now, the Passion is satisfaction for all possible sins of all possible men. Hence, he who is baptized, and so incorporated into this perfect and plenary power of satisfaction, is freed from all debt of punishment due to his sins.

3. Baptism does not take away the penalties of sin that are to be undergone in this life. We must suffer, and endure, and die; this is for our *merit,* if we bear all hardship for God; this keeps us humble, hopeful, looking on to final resurrection, when all hardships and defects will be at an end.

4. Baptism takes away all sin and all punishment due to sin, and it confers grace and virtues on the person baptized. For baptism makes one a member of Christ; from Christ, the Head, grace and virtues flow through the members.

5. In baptism, a person is: (a) incorporated in Christ; (b) enlightened by Christ with knowledge of truth; (c) made fruitful of good works by Christ's infused grace.

6. Infants, by being incorporated with Christ through baptism, receive grace and virtues, even though their immaturity prevents the conscious exercise of acts that flow from grace and virtues.

7. Baptism, by removing guilt and the debt of punishment, takes away the obstacles that would block a man from heaven. Hence, we say that baptism "opens the gate of the heavenly kingdom" to the person baptized.

8. The essential effect of baptism (that is, the birth of a human being into spiritual life), is the same in everyone who is baptized. In adults, there is a varying degree of "newness" of life, according to the devotion and disposition they bring to the receiving of the sacrament of baptism.

9. The effect of baptism may be blocked, even though the sacrament is validly received, by what St. Augustine calls *insincerity.* A man may be insincere, with respect to baptism, in four ways: (a) when he does not believe; has not the faith; (b) when he has scorn for the sacrament; (c) when he receives baptism according to an unapproved rite; (d) when he has no devotion.

10. A man who is *insincere*, in any of these four ways, is validly baptized, and the sacramental character is impressed or imprinted on his soul. But he blocks out the grace and the virtues which the sacrament bestows. When such a man repents, and sincerely receives the sacrament of penance, his baptism will then produce its normal effects in him.

70. CIRCUMCISION

1. The rite of circumcision in the Old Law was a preparation for baptism, and a figure of baptism. For it was a proclamation of faith by which a man was aggregated to the body of the faithful.

2. Circumcision was instituted in the person of Abraham who was the first to receive the promise of the birth of Christ as of his seed or line (Gen. 22:18), and was the first to segregate himself from unbelievers.

3. Circumcision was established as a sign of faith; it was a work of the all-wise God.

4. Circumcision remitted original sin and conferred grace as a sign of faith in Christ's coming Passion. Baptism confers grace by the power of the sacrament itself as the instrument of Christ's accomplished Passion.

71. PREPARATION FOR BAPTISM

1. Instruction is to precede baptism, for our Lord said (Matt. 28:19): "Going therefore, teach ye all nations, baptizing them in the name of the Father, and of the Son, and of the Holy Ghost." Infants who are incapable of receiving personal instruction, are baptized in *the faith of the Church*. Yet the sponsor for an infant promises to use his best efforts to see that the child will be duly instructed.

2. Exorcism, which·is the casting out of evil spirits, should precede baptism. For the devil is the enemy of man's salvation, and he has a certain power over man in the fact that man is subject to sin.

3. The exorcism casts out demons lest they impede the salvation of the person baptized. In the ritual employed by the Church for solemn baptism, this exorcism is prescribed.

4. It is the work of priests to instruct and exorcise those preparing for baptism, and afterwards to baptize them.

CONFIRMATION

(QUESTION 72)

72. CONFIRMATION

1. The sacraments of the New Law are instituted to produce special effects of grace. Now, there is a special perfection in coming to full strength and maturity. To produce this effect of grace in the spiritual order, there exists a special sacrament called confirmation.

2. The *matter* of the sacrament of confirmation (that is, the material used in making the sign which is to become a sacrament), is the oil called holy chrism. Oil signifies the grace of the Holy Ghost; holy chrism is oil mingled with balm or balsam, which is a preservative with a pleasing odor. Chrism is therefore suitable *matter* for a sacrament which brings to the soul the Holy Ghost with gifts and graces, and preserves the soul in right living as "the good odor of Christ" (II Cor. 2:15).

3. The chrism used in confirmation is olive oil mingled with balsam, blessed or consecrated by a bishop previous to its use in the sacrament of confirmation.

4. Unless Scripture itself gives the *form* (that is, the determinate set of words used in confecting or conferring a sacrament), the Church prescribes that form. The Church always selects words which express precisely the meaning and reality of the sacrament. In the Latin rite the form of the sacrament of confirmation, uttered by the confirming prelate as he applies the matter by anointing the forehead of the candidate, is the following: "I sign thee with the sign of the Cross, and I confirm thee with the chrism of salvation, in the name of the Father, and of the Son, and of the Holy Ghost."

5. Confirmation imprints a *character* on the soul, as do all those sacraments which permanently fit and constitute a person for service and action in the worship of God; hence, confirmation can be received only once. As baptism permanently equips a man for living by grace, confirmation equips him for successful combat against the enemies of his soul and of the faith. Confirmation gives a man the power of the soldier of Christ. It impresses this power upon him as an indelible character.

6. The character imprinted by confirmation presupposes, of necessity, the baptismal character. For confirmation is to baptism as full growth is to birth; no one can attain maturity unless he first be born.

7. As we saw in the first part of this work (Ia, q. 43), the Holy Ghost is "sent" by way of sanctifying grace. In confirmation, the Holy Ghost is "sent" or given to those confirmed, and therefore brings them sanctifying grace.

8. The age of the body does not affect the soul. One can attain to spiritual birth by baptism even in old age. And one can attain to spiritual maturity by confirmation, even in early youth.

9. The person being confirmed is anointed with chrism on the forehead, so that he may show to all that he is a Christian, fearless of all the enemies of Christ.

10. The person confirmed is made a soldier of Christ. Now, a new soldier needs instruction in the warfare he is to wage. For this reason, the person confirmed has a sponsor to teach him. Again, since it is confirmation that gives full growth and strength, the person coming to be confirmed is still little and weak, and needs to be upheld by another; hence, he needs a sponsor.

11. The sacrament of confirmation is regularly administered by a bishop. It is, of course, within the power and jurisdiction of the pope to delegate priests to administer confirmation. Priests possess the power to confirm because of their priestly order, but they have not the right, the jurisdiction to use that power, without the delegation mentioned.

12. The rite or ceremony with which confirmation is administered is appropriate. Even in such matters, the Church manifests the guidance of the Holy Ghost.

THE HOLY EUCHARIST

(QUESTIONS 73 TO 83)

73. THE HOLY EUCHARIST

1. In the bodily order, a person must first be born, and thereafter he requires steady nourishment as long as life lasts. In the spiritual order, a person is born by baptism, matured by confirmation, and

steadily nourished by Holy Eucharist. Every sacrament is a special aid to man in his spiritual life. The Holy Eucharist is the special spiritual nourishment required by the child of God.

2. The Holy Eucharist is one sacrament, though it is both the flesh and the blood of our Lord.

3. The Holy Eucharist is the most excellent of sacraments, for it is our Lord and God himself. But, notwithstanding its surpassing excellence, it is not required for a man's salvation in the way in which baptism is required. For baptism is the beginning of the life of the soul; Holy Eucharist is the consummation of that life. Yet baptism looks on to Holy Eucharist, as beginning looks to consummation. Indeed, all the sacraments are directed to the Holy Eucharist.

4. The faithful children of the Church give to the Holy Eucharist various and reverently significant names: (a) Eucharist, which means "good grace"; (b) Communion or *Synaxis,* to indicate the union and unity of the faithful with Christ in this sacrament; (c) Viaticum, a special title, meaning "companion on the way," given to this sacrament when it is received in serious illness to be the soul's companion and support on the way to judgment; (d) Sacrifice, inasmuch as the Holy Eucharist is confected and offered in Holy Mass, which is the identical sacrifice offered by Christ on the cross, except in the manner of offering: for Christ died on the cross, but does not die in the Mass; the Mass represents his death, but does not reproduce it.

5. Our Lord instituted this great sacrament when he was about to depart from visible communication with his apostles. He would remain with them in reality, but as wrapped in the mystery of this sacrament. Again, Christ celebrated the Pasch, bringing to an end the ceremony of the Old Law, and instituting a new sacrament, which is the true Pasch. Our Lord chose the solemn moment of this Last Supper to fix this great Eucharistic mystery deep in the minds and hearts of his apostles.

6. The paschal lamb was the chief Old Testament figure of the Sacrament of Holy Eucharist. St. Paul (I Cor. 5:7) says: "Christ our pasch is sacrificed."

74. THE MATTER OF THE HOLY EUCHARIST

1. The *matter* of the Holy Eucharist is bread and wine.

2. No determinate amount of bread and wine is requisite for this sacrament. No tangible quantity of bread and wine is either too small or too large for valid use in confecting the Holy Eucharist. Reverence, and church law, determines the seemly amount of the matter to be employed.

3. The bread which is requisite as matter for the Holy Eucharist is bread made of wheaten flour.

4. True wheaten bread, leavened or unleavened, is valid matter for the Holy Eucharist. The Church decides which type of wheaten bread is to be used. In the Latin Church, unleavened bread is prescribed; in the Greek rite, leavened bread is used.

5. True wine of the grape is necessary as matter for the Holy Eucharist. At the institution of the sacrament, our Lord said (Matt. 26:29): "I will not drink henceforth of this fruit of the vine . . ."

6. At Holy Mass, a little water is mingled with the wine that is to be consecrated. This recalls the fact that water was mingled with the last drops of redeeming blood that flowed from the side of Christ as he hung upon the cross. It also suggests, as Pope Julius says, the unity of Christ and the faithful: the wine signifies Christ, and the water the people.

7. This mingling of a few drops of water with the wine to be consecrated at Mass is a requirement of strict church law, but it is not essential to the validity of the consecration.

8. Only a very small quantity of water is mingled with the wine which is used as matter for confecting the Holy Eucharist at Mass. If much water were used, the mixture could no longer be called true wine, and therefore would not be valid matter for this sacrament.

75. TRANSUBSTANTIATION

1. The words of consecration, pronounced by the priest, change bread and wine into the true body and blood of Christ. This sacrament is not a symbol or sign of Christ's body and blood; it is, in actual fact, the body and blood of Christ.

2. By the consecration, the substance of the bread and the substance of the wine cease to exist, and there remains only the substance of the living Christ.

3. The substance of the bread and the substance of the wine are not merely dissolved or disintegrated, either gradually or instantaneously; neither are these substances annihilated. They are *changed* into the body and blood of Christ.

4. The whole substance of the bread is, by divine power, changed into the whole substance of the body of Christ. And the whole substance of the wine is, by divine power, changed into the whole substance of the blood of Christ.

5. The accidentals or accidents of bread and wine (such as, size, color, shape, taste) remain after the change, which is called *transubstantiation,* has taken place. These accidentals do not become the

accidentals of Christ; they remain the accidentals of bread and wine, even though the substance of bread and the substance of wine no longer exist to be qualified by these accidentals.

6. The element in a bodily thing that makes it the kind of substance that it is, is called the *substantial form* of that thing. When a substantial form is joined with *primal matter,* it constitutes the matter as an existing bodily substance of a definite kind. Now, in transubstantiation, the substantial form of bread (that which constitutes the bread as this kind of substance and no other) is removed; it does not remain, for the substance is now not bread at all, but the substance of the living Christ. And the same is true of the substantial form of the wine; it does not remain, for, by transubstantiation, that which was wine is now not wine at all, but the substance of the living Christ.

7. Transubstantiation is an instantaneous change. There is no consuming of time, no movement of the elements (bread and wine) through successive stages or degrees as the change occurs which turns bread and wine into the body and the blood of Jesus Christ. That which infinite power accomplishes need not be worked by degrees, or with time intervals, as though some effort and skill were being applied to the work.

8. To say, "The body of Christ is made out of bread," is true when the words are rightly understood, that is, when these words are understood to mean, "Bread is changed substantially, and is now no longer bread, but the body of Christ."

76. THE REAL PRESENCE

1. In the Holy Eucharist, Christ is present whole and entire (body, blood, soul, and Godhead or divinity) under the appearances or accidentals of bread and wine. The words of consecration (which constitute the *form* of the sacrament of Holy Eucharist) bring the living Christ, God and man, truly present. The words, "This is my body," bring Christ's body truly present. This is Christ's *living* body; therefore, it has its blood, its soul, and the Godhead which assumed this body. The words, "This is my blood," bring Christ's blood truly present. This is Christ's *living* blood; therefore it is in its body, with the soul, and the divinity or Godhead which assumed this blood. Thus, the whole Christ is present under the appearances of bread, and the whole Christ is present under the appearances of wine, and the whole Christ is present under both appearances together. For, if two things are really united, wherever one is the other must be. And Christ's complete humanity (in its elements of body, blood, and soul) is really united with his divinity. Thus, by the power of this sacrament, the body of Christ is present

at the words, "This is my body," and, by the *necessity of concomitance*, the blood of Christ is present also, as is the soul, and the divinity. And the blood of Christ is present at the words, "This is my blood," and, by the necessity of concomitance, the body of Christ is present also, as is the soul, and the divinity.

2. Therefore, the whole Christ, God and man, is contained under each *species*—that is, each set of appearances, namely, the appearances of bread, and the appearances of wine.

3. And the whole Christ is present under every part or quantity of each species. As a loaf of bread is *bread,* and a slice of bread is *bread,* and a crumb of bread is *bread,* so, the Eucharistic species, in whatever quantity, is Christ. There is a difference, however, in the fact that Christ is not diminished as the bread is diminished when the loaf is taken and a slice is left, or when a slice is taken away and only a crumb is left. Christ is not made smaller as the species becomes smaller, but is whole and entire (entirely unaffected by any external dimensions) in any tangible quantity of the consecrated *matter* (that is, bread and wine).

4. The whole dimensive quantity of Christ's body is present in every particle of the Eucharistic species (every crumb, every drop), but Christ's body has not its external extension or dimensions. Nor is Christ's body measured, and "sized," according to the amounts and measurements of the species of bread and wine. The dimensions of the species are accidentals of the species; they do not become the dimensions of Christ. But the dimensions of Christ are present after the manner in which the substance of Christ is present, that is, complete in each particle, as bread is complete bread in each loaf, and slice, and crumb. The size of the sacred host is not the size of Christ; nor is Christ present in miniature, or as cramped under a quantity of the species; he is present whole and entire, and in full stature, but that stature is not *externally* measured or dimensioned.

5. Christ's body is not in this sacrament as a body is in *a place.* For a body in a place is there according to its external dimensions, and these make the body commensurate with the dimensions of the place it occupies. But Christ's body is not present in the Eucharist according to external dimensions. His body is present *quantitatively*, not in the manner of the external accidentals of measurement and dimension, but according to the manner of substance, which is complete in any quantity, large or small, that exists.

6. Our Lord is not present in a *movable* way in the Holy Eucharist. Only a body that is *located* (that is, is in a place according to external dimensions), can be moved from place to place. Hence, when the

Eucharistic species is moved, Christ is not moved. If the sacred host be dropped, Christ does not fall down. If the sacred host be moved from right to left, from left to right, or raised or lowered, Christ himself is not thus moved about. Christ is not subject to local movement, even though the sacramental species are so subject.

7. The body of Christ in the Blessed Sacrament, as the Holy Eucharist is lovingly called, cannot be seen by any eye, even the eye of a glorified body. The glorified eye sees Christ in his own proper species, as he is in heaven since the day of Ascension. No eye can see Christ as he is present in the Holy Eucharist. Christ is seen there by the mind, the intellect, illumined by faith. The *glorified* intellect (in heaven) sees all supernatural things in its view of the beatific vision of God.

8. When, by an apparition, flesh or blood is seen in the sacred host, this is not the actual flesh and blood of Christ. The actual flesh and blood of Christ is present, but invisible. The apparition is an apparition, not a reality. The blood that is seen to flow from a consecrated host (as a miraculous manifestation) is not Christ's own blood, which is never shed again after the Passion. Such a manifestation is a fearsome reminder to the observers to be aware of the *real* blood of Christ present in the host *invisibly*.

77. THE ACCIDENTS OR ACCIDENTALS OF THE HOLY EUCHARIST

1. A *substance* is a reality regularly suited to exist as *itself*, and not to exist merely as the mark or qualification or determinant of something else. An *accident*, or an accidental, is a reality regularly suited to exist, not as itself, but as the mark or qualification or determinant of something else. Thus, a man is a substance. But a man's size, age, appearance, knowledge, and so forth, exist, not as *themselves*, but as marks or qualifications *of the man;* these are accidents or accidentals of the man. Accidentals are said to *inhere in* the reality which they mark or determine or qualify. And the reality qualified by accidentals is called their *subject*. The subject of accidentals is fundamentally a substance. The substance of bread is the subject of the accidentals of bread; the substance of wine is the subject of the accidentals of wine. When, by transubstantiation, the substance of bread and the substance of wine are changed into the substance of Christ, the accidentals of bread and wine remain in existence *without* a subject. These accidentals of bread and wine remain accidentals of bread and wine; they do not inhere in the substance of Christ; they

are not accidentals of Christ. Hence, while we can say of the sacred host that it is round, and white, and brittle, and that it is two or three inches in diameter, we cannot say any of these things of the reality which the sacred host actually is, that is, the body and blood, the soul and divinity, of Jesus Christ.

2. It seems that in the Holy Eucharist, the *quantity* of the bread and of the wine endures, and that the other accidents (such as color, flavor, brittleness) exist in this quantity as in their subject.

3. The sacramental species can, by divine power (since all action ultimately depends on God as first agent), affect other bodies. Thus, we can feel the sacred species on the tongue, taste its flavor, etc.

4. The accidentals (species) of bread and wine in the Holy Eucharist are subject to corruption, that is, to spoiling, to souring. When such corruption is advanced to the degree that would make ordinary bread and wine cease to be true bread and wine, our Lord ceases to be present under the species.

5. When the sacred species are destroyed (corrupted by rotting, spoiling, souring, or mingled or melted in much water, or burned with fire), they generate other things; for instance, ashes, if the species be burned. Such corrupting does not affect the body and blood of Christ who ceases to be present as soon as corruption of the species occurs.

6. The normal effect of natural bread and wine (that is, its effect of nourishing the person who takes it in as food and drink) is in the sacred species, the accidentals of bread and wine in the Holy Eucharist. But when these species are digested by the receiver, they are corrupted, and Christ ceases to be present under them.

7. The breaking or dividing of the species is not a breaking or dividing of Christ. It is a change of quantity which is an accidental of the species, and not an accidental of the body and blood of Christ. Christ is present, whole and entire, unchanged and undiminished, in every part of the broken host, and in every separated amount of liquid in the consecrated chalice.

8. Any liquid added to the chalice that would make it other than the consecrated matter of the Eucharist, would corrupt the species, and Christ would no longer be present. If only a drop or two of liquid were so added, the presence of Christ would be withdrawn from the tiny quantity which these drops would substantially change, but would not be withdrawn from the contents of the chalice as a whole.

78. THE FORM OF THE HOLY EUCHARIST

1. The *form* of a sacrament is the authentic, authoritative, and effective set of words which constitute the *matter* (or sign) as a sacrament. The form of the Holy Eucharist is the consecrating formula of words used in Holy Mass: "This is my body . . . This is my blood."

2. The form of the Holy Eucharist is found in Holy Scripture (Matt. 26:27, 28). It consists of the words used by our Lord himself when he instituted this great sacrament.

3. The words of institution, reported by three of the four Evangelists, were words of instruction to the apostles, who employed them as the form of the sacrament of Holy Eucharist.

4. The words of consecration at Mass, uttered by a duly ordained priest who is, in this action, the instrument of Christ, actually change the bread and wine into the substance of Christ himself. Christ is the chief priest at every Mass, for he is the principal cause of transubstantiation, and his power flows through the priest (the instrumental cause) who utters the consecrating words (the *form* of Holy Eucharist) in the name and the Person of Christ.

5. The words (that is, the *form* of this sacrament) are not uttered by the consecrating priest as words of a narrative; they are not merely descriptive or historical words. The words are uttered with efficacious power to do and to accomplish what they say. The power of the words comes from the divine power of Christ, in whose Person and by whose direction and will they are uttered over bread and wine by the consecrating priest.

6. The priest pronounces the words of consecration over the bread, and afterwards over the wine. Some have mistakenly thought that the effectiveness of the words of consecration is *suspended,* so to speak, until all of them are uttered. The truth is that the words of consecration are effective the instant that they are pronounced. When the consecrating priest says, "This is my body," Christ is instantly present under the appearance of bread; and when, a moment afterwards, the priest says, "This is my blood," Christ is at once present under the appearance of wine.

79. EFFECTS OF THE HOLY EUCHARIST

1. Our Lord said (John 6:52): "The bread which I will give is my flesh for the life of the world." The life of which our Lord speaks is the spiritual life of grace. The Holy Eucharist is the richest source of grace, for it is the sacrament which is Christ himself, by whom alone grace comes to man.

2. The attaining of heaven is an effect of the sacrament of Holy Eucharist. For Christ says (John 6:52): "If any man eat of this bread, he shall live forever." Those who receive this sacrament worthily are immediately helped toward eternal glory. The Holy Eucharist is Christ, and it represents his Passion; it is only by Christ and his Passion that men can win to heaven.

3. To receive the Holy Eucharist worthily, a man must be free from mortal sin. Our Lord has prepared for us a sacrament to cleanse us from such sin. Hence, it would be sacrilegious for a person conscious of deliberate mortal sin to receive the Holy Eucharist. He must first cleanse his soul of mortal sin by receiving worthily the sacrament of penance. Although the Holy Eucharist contains all power, it was not instituted for the purpose of forgiving mortal sins.

4. Nevertheless, the Holy Eucharist does "blot out venial sins, and it wards off mortal sins from the soul," as Pope Innocent III has said. Hence, St. Ambrose declares that this daily Bread is a remedy for our daily infirmity.

5. The Holy Eucharist was not instituted for making satisfaction for sins, but for giving spiritual nourishment by uniting Christ with his members. This union, however, is effected by charity, and charity obtains forgiveness and renders satisfaction. A person who receives the Holy Eucharist worthily, does not receive full remission of the punishment due to his sins, but he does receive some remission of that punishment; the extent of this remission of punishment is measured by the devotion and fervor of the person receiving the Holy Eucharist. Also *as a sacrifice* (that is, as offered in Holy Mass), the Eucharist makes satisfaction according to the devotion "of the offerers," and "of those for whom the sacrifice is offered."

6. The Holy Eucharist is a most powerful preservative from sin. It gives a person spiritual nourishment which strengthens him against inner weakness, and it also arms him against assaults that come from without. St. John says (6:50): "This is the bread which cometh down from heaven; that if any man eat of it, he may not die." Manifestly, St. John speaks here of the spiritual death of sin.

7. Thus, the Holy Eucharist is of the greatest benefit to those who receive it. It is also of the highest benefit to those for whom it is offered in the sacrifice of the Mass.

8. Venial sins committed in the past do not hinder the effects of the Holy Eucharist, and, as we have seen, the devout receiver of the Holy Eucharist obtains remission of such sins. But venial sins that *accompany* the receiving of the Holy Eucharist partially hinder the effects of this great sacrament; yet they do not entirely block out the

sanctifying grace and charity which the sacrament bestows on a man's soul.

80. THE RECEIVING OF THE HOLY EUCHARIST

1. The Holy Eucharist, usually called the Blessed Sacrament, is received *sacramentally* by one who actually consumes the sacred species. It is received *spiritually* by one who, through faith and charity, desires to receive it sacramentally.

2. Man alone may recieve this sacrament spiritually. The angels see Christ in his own species, and they desire him so, and possess him so. Only man can desire our Lord in the Blessed Sacrament.

3. Our Lord is actually present in the Holy Eucharist; therefore, he who receives this sacrament, receives Christ. Even though a sinner receives sacrilegiously, he receives Christ. It is entirely mistaken to say that when the sacred species are touched by the lips of a sinner, Christ ceases to be present.

4. If a person conscious of mortal sin receives this sacrament, he "eateth and drinketh judgment to himself" (I Cor. 11:29). Such receiving adds to the sin already on the receiver's soul, the new mortal sin of sacrilege.

5. Unbelief and blasphemy, which involve contempt of God, are, in themselves, greater sins than the sin of receiving the Holy Eucharist unworthily. Of course, unworthy receiving of the Eucharist may be accompanied by blasphemy and contemptuous unbelief, and so it becomes the greatest of sins. But, in itself, although a very grave sin, a sacrilegious Communion is not the greatest of sins.

6. A priest is to deny the Holy Eucharist to notorious public sinners, but not to occult sinners who ask to receive this sacrament.

7. What occurs in sleep is never perfectly voluntary, and hence is not gravely sinful. Yet sometimes a sense of propriety or becomingness suggests that one refrain from receiving the Holy Eucharist after an unfortunate occurrence during sleep.

8. Except in cases of persons sick or unable to fast, it is the practice of the Church to require a fast before the receiving of Holy Eucharist.

9. People who have always been devoid of the use of reason, or who have become insane, are not to be given the Holy Eucharist. If an insane person once was sane and had faith and reverence for God, he is not to be denied the Holy Eucharist at the hour of death, provided there is no danger of his ejecting the sacred host. Feeble-minded persons who have some knowledge of the Blessed Sacrament, and some degree of devotion, are to be admitted to Holy Communion.

10. St. Augustine says (*De Verb. Dom. Serm.* 28): "This is our daily Bread; take it daily that it may perfect thee daily." Those who are properly disposed should receive the Holy Eucharist as frequently as possible.

11. No one can lawfully abstain altogether from the Holy Eucharist. The Church demands a worthy Communion at least once yearly. And our Lord himself says (John 6:54): "Except you eat the flesh of the Son of man and drink his blood, you shall not have life in you."

12. It is a wise provision of the Church that this sacrament can be received under one form only. Reverence for the sacrament, added to the difficulty of reserving and distributing the sacred species, has suggested that the faithful receive our Lord under the form of bread alone. This is the practice of the Latin Church. The sacrament is confected in bread and wine in Holy Mass, and is received under both forms by the sacrificing priest.

81. OUR LORD'S USE OF THE HOLY EUCHARIST

1. Christ instituted the sacrament of Holy Eucharist at the Last Supper, the night before he died. He gave this sacrament to his apostles in Holy Communion. And he received this sacrament himself.

2. Some have thought that Christ did not give Holy Communion to Judas. But it seems that Judas received our Lord with the other apostles.

3. When our Lord instituted the Holy Eucharist, and gave himself to his apostles under the species of bread and wine, he had not yet endured his Passion, except *in intention*. His body was not yet glorified, as it was to be glorified in the Resurrection, but was a *passible* body, that is, a body that could endure pain and death. What Christ gave to his apostles in the Holy Eucharist was his body *as it was then*, that is, at the time of the Last Supper. And yet, that body, passible in itself, was not passible in the Holy Eucharist because passibility depends on external extension, and even the passible body of Christ was unextended in the Eucharist, as this was given at the Last Supper. After the Resurrection of our Lord, his body in the Holy Eucharist is the glorified and impassible body.

4. If the Blessed Sacrament had been reserved in a tabernacle or had been consecrated by an apostle at the time of Christ's Crucifixion, our Lord would have died in the Blessed Sacrament as he died on the cross. For Christ is one and the same substantial being in his concrete bodily existence and in the Holy Eucharist.

82. THE MINISTER OF HOLY EUCHARIST

1. The Sacrament of Holy Eucharist is of such dignity that it is confected only in the Person and by the authority of Christ himself. Hence, a priest is one ordained and appointed to act as Christ's instrument, and to use Christ's own voice and authority in confecting the Holy Eucharist at Mass. Only a duly ordained priest can consecrate the elements of bread and wine and so confect the sacrament of Holy Eucharist. Only the priest can offer this sacrament as sacrifice, and he does this when he celebrates Holy Mass.

2. It is possible for several priests to consecrate one and the same host. And, at ordination, the newly ordained priests con-celebrate the Mass with the ordaining bishop. All say the words of consecration together, and jointly consecrate the host which is held in the bishop's hands.

3. Apart from cases of necessity (as, for example, when the sacred species is in danger from fire or flood or desecration), no one but the priest should touch the consecrated hosts. Therefore, the priest is not only the minister of consecration (that is, of confecting the sacrament of Holy Eucharist at Mass), but he is also the minister of distributing the Blessed Sacrament to all who receive it in Holy Communion. A deacon may distribute Holy Communion, with pastor's or bishop's permission, when there is a reasonable cause for having him do so.

4. The Holy Eucharist is both a *sacrament* and a *sacrifice*. Whoever offers a sacrifice must share in it. Hence, the priest who offers the Eucharistic Sacrifice (that is, the Mass), must receive the Eucharist as sacrament. Otherwise the sacrifice would not be complete.

5. The power of consecration, of confecting the Holy Eucharist, is given to the priest, and as often as he celebrates Mass he exercises this power. It is a power independent of the priest's own condition as virtuous or wicked. Even a priest in serious sin confects the Holy Eucharist when he offers Mass.

6. In itself, the Mass of a wicked priest is of equal value with the Mass of a good priest. In either case, it is the same sacrifice. And the prayers of a sinful priest during Mass and in all his ecclesiastical offices, are fruitful prayers inasmuch as they are offered by one set and qualified to speak officially for the Church. But the private prayers of a bad priest are not fruitful, for scripture says (Prov. 28:9): "He that turneth away his ears from hearing the law, his prayer shall be an abomination."

7. If a duly ordained priest should become a heretic, schismatic, or be excommunicated, he would still have the power to consecrate,

although he would sin gravely in using that power. Even those who are validly ordained priests outside the Church (by heretical, schismatic, or excommunicated bishops) have the power to consecrate.

8. A priest degraded and deprived of the *right* to consecrate is not deprived of the *power* to consecrate.

9. One may not lawfully assist at Mass offered by a heretical, schismatic, or excommunicated priest, nor may one lawfully receive Holy Communion at his hands. However, this prohibition applies only when the official condemnation of the Church has been pronounced, and the priest in question has been declared heretical, schismatical, or excommunicated.

10. A priest, even if he have not the care of souls, is under obligation of offering the Mass on some occasions, as for example, on the major feast days. Such obligation is in the priesthood itself, which calls for sacrifice, not only in the service of the people, but for the glory of God. If the priest never consecrated the Holy Eucharist in Mass, he would be a priest in vain. Scripture says (II Cor. 6:1): "We exhort you that you receive not the grace of God in vain."

83. THE RITE OF THE HOLY EUCHARIST

1. Christ is truly sacrificed in the Holy Eucharist at Mass, but not in a bloody manner, that is, not with the shedding of his blood and his death in consequence. St. Augustine says: "Christ was sacrificed once in himself, and yet he is sacrificed daily in the Sacrament."

2. The time of celebrating the Eucharistic Sacrifice is set by the Church.

3. Mass is to be celebrated in a suitable place, usually indoors, and with vessels that are blessed or consecrated to their sacred use.

4. Surrounding the words of Christ which are the *form* of the sacrament of Holy Eucharist, the Church, through the ages, has reverently arranged pertinent prayers of praise and adoration, of penance, of thanksgiving, of petition.

5. The action of the Mass in which the *matter* (bread and wine) of the Eucharist is offered to God, then consecrated by use of the *form,* and then received in Holy Communion, is filled with suitable ceremonies prescribed by the Church.

6. If the priest who is celebrating Mass is unable to continue because of a sudden illness, or if he dies at the altar, his Mass is not completed unless he has already consecrated the host or the host and the chalice. In this case, another priest finishes the Mass and thus completes the sacrifice.

PENANCE

(QUESTIONS 84 TO 90)

84. THE SACRAMENT OF PENANCE

1. Penance is the sacrament which takes away sins committed after baptism. A sacrament is something done, in accordance with the institution of Christ, to signify and to confer holiness. Penance is something done by the confessing sinner and the absolving priest, in accordance with Christ's institution, to signify and to confer grace or holiness. Therefore, penance is truly a sacrament.

2. The *matter* of the sacrament of penance is: (a) remotely: the sins of the penitent; (b) proximately: these sins repented and confessed with a will to make satisfaction. Thus, we say that the matter of penance consists in the "acts of the penitent," that is, contrition, confession, satisfaction.

3. The *form* of the sacrament of penance consists in the effective words of *absolution* pronounced by the priest: "I absolve thee . . ."

4. Penance is not conferred or administered by the imposing of hands, a ceremony which indicates the imparting of abundant grace and power, as in confirmation and holy order. Penance is instituted for the removal of sins from the soul. No imposition of hands is required.

5. For those who have committed serious sin after baptism, penance is necessary for salvation. [*Note:* When penance cannot be received, perfect charity, which is perfect contrition, produces its effect. The act of perfect charity embraces the full will to do all that our Lord would have one do for the removal of sins; hence, such an act involves, at least in an implied way, the will and intention of receiving the sacrament of penance. Thus, penance is still necessary to salvation, and is to be received, at least in intention, or "in vow," as the phrase is, by those guilty of mortal sin after baptism.]

6. St. Jerome calls this sacrament, "A second plank after shipwreck." It is the means of regaining the integrity bestowed by baptism and afterwards lost by mortal sin. Thus, penance is compared to a plank, or raft, or lifeboat, by which a man finds safety and survival after his ship has gone down.

7. Penance has its power and effectiveness from Christ suffering, dying, rising again. Scripture says (Luke 24:46, 47): "It behooved Christ to suffer, and to rise again from the dead the third day; and that penance and remission of sins should be preached in his name to all nations."

8. A person ought always to have a true internal sorrow for his past offences against God even after these have been forgiven. In this sense, penance should be continuous all through life. But the external acts imposed by the absolving priest as *satisfaction* are exercised for a time only.

9. We cannot be engaged in acts of penance, either internal or external, all the time. But we should always have the habitual disposition of penance; this is manifested in lasting regret for having offended God, and in watchfulness to avoid sinning again.

10. Penance is a sacrament that can be received again and again. It is always possible for man the wayfarer (that is, man making his journey through life here on earth), to lose charity; this sacrament is his divinely instituted means of recovering it. [*Note:* This sacrament is also a powerful spiritual tonic, and should be received often even by those who have not lapsed into mortal sin. The *matter* for "a confession of devotion" is venial sin, or sins of the past life already forgiven.]

85. PENANCE AS A VIRTUE

1. Penance as a *sacrament* is an outward sign instituted by Christ to take away sins and give grace. Penance as a *virtue* is a lasting disposition of soul (that is, a spiritual *habit*) to grieve for past sins, to make satisfaction for them, and to avoid committing them anew. An *act* of penance is any work or action, internal or external, by which the virtue of penance is exercised. [*Note:* The word *penance* is constantly used by Catholics in one of four meanings: penance means a sacrament; it means a virtue; it means the work of satisfaction for sins, imposed on the penitent by the confessor; it means any penitential prayer or work piously undertaken, i.e., an *act* of penance.]

2. Habits are specified by their acts. If there is a special reason requiring an act which normally comes from habit, the special habit for it exists. Hence, penance is a special virtue, not merely a general virtue.

3. Penance as a special virtue is a species of justice. Justice seeks to restore and maintain balance and order. The virtue of penance seeks to restore balance and order by removing the disorder of sins and putting the soul right with God by grace.

4. The subject of a habit, and hence the subject of a virtue, is that power or faculty in which the habit resides or is properly said to be situated. Now, the virtue of penance is a habit which consists in the steady will to repent and make amends. Therefore, the *will* is the subject of the virtue of penance.

5. Penance as a supernatural virtue is infused into the soul by almighty God; the soul, by God's grace, cooperates by acts which dispose it to receive this virtue. The soul is first stirred by a *servile* fear of punishment due to its sins; from this, the soul advances to a loving *filial* fear of God; thus it is rendered fit and ready to receive from God the supernatural virtue of penance.

6. Penance is not the first of virtues in the order of the nature of virtue. Faith, hope, and charity, come before it. But in the order of time, penance may be regarded as the first virtue, in the sense that sinful man must first turn to God, and he does this by the virtue of penance.

86. EFFECTS OF THE SACRAMENT OF PENANCE

1. The sacrament of penance cannot take away the mortal sins of those confirmed in evil, that is, of souls and demons in hell; for these beings are incapable of repentance. But it can take away all mortal sins, without exception, of man the wayfarer, that is, of man in the present earthly life.

2. Mortal sin cannot be taken away without repentance. For mortal sin is a complete turning of man's soul from God; mortal sin remains in the soul until the will turns back again to God; the will does this by repentance, that is, by exercising the supernatural virtue of penance, and, as explained above (q. 84, note), making use of the sacrament of penance.

3. One mortal sin cannot be pardoned without another; *all* are taken from the soul or *none* is taken. For every unrepented mortal sin excludes grace and pardon; if one such sin remains in the soul, grace and pardon are blocked out. Besides, no man can truly repent of one sin because it offends God, while he still has the will to offend God by another sin.

4. A sinner is under two burdens, namely, *guilt*, and *debt of punishment due*. The debt of punishment due to sin is either *eternal* or *temporal*. When mortal sin is taken away as to its guilt, the eternal punishment due to it is also taken away; yet the temporal punishment due to it may not be entirely taken away. Hence, when the guilt of mortal sin is removed by penance, some debt of temporal punishment may yet be owed by the forgiven sinner.

5. Sin leaves *remnants* or remains in the soul even after it is taken away. Sin may thus be compared to a serious sickness which, even when cured, leaves in the patient a weakness or tendency to relapse. Besides, frequently repeated sins leave a disposition, or even a habit, in the soul. The sacrament of penance which takes away sin does not necessarily take away the remains of sin or the habit of sin; yet the sacrament does diminish or weaken these things so that they do not domineer over a man or compel him to relapse into sin.

6. Penance as a virtue disposes a man to have his sins taken away, and by God's gift of this virtue, a person may obtain pardon of his guilt. Yet the most effective penance is not the virtue, but the sacrament of penance; for the sacrament directly absolves the sinner from his guilt.

87. REMISSION OF VENIAL SINS

1. No sin is forgiven without repentance or penance. Yet a more perfect penance is required for the forgiving of mortal sin; each mortal sin is to be detested and rejected. A more general grief or sorrow is sufficient in the case of venial sins.

2. Mortal sin is removed by penance (virtue and sacrament) when grace is infused into the soul to drive out and replace sin. Venial sin does not drive out grace, and hence, in one who has no mortal sin on his soul, venial sins can be forgiven without the infusion of new grace by a movement of grace or charity already in the soul. Also whenever grace is newly infused, venial sins are forgiven.

3. The pious use of holy water and the exercise of devotional acts can suffice to take away venial sins. Such pious uses and practices always *tend* to remove sin, because they can be a true movement of grace in the soul arousing love of God and detestation of what offends him.

4. A man who has both mortal and venial sins, cannot get rid of his venial sins while the mortal sins remain. For by mortal sin a man is turned completely from God, and no sanctifying grace is in him to move for the cancellation of venial sins.

88. RECURRENCE OF SINS FORGIVEN

1. A sin forgiven is forgiven. A man may, indeed, commit another sin *like* the one forgiven, but he does not fall back into forgiven sin. It is not possible for the stain of past sins, and the debt of punishment incurred by them, to return upon the forgiven sinner. A sin may be worse because of like sins previously forgiven. But the past sins themselves, once pardoned, do not return.

2. Only in the sense that a man who is pardoned returns to sins like those forgiven, and thereby shows base ingratitude to the forgiving God, is it said that forgiven sins return upon the sinner.

3. Therefore, if a man has obtained forgiveness of mortal sins, and later commits others, his ingratitude does not bring back upon him the debt of punishment due to all past mortal sins. Still, there must be some proportion in this business. The more frequent and grievous one's past mortal sins have been, the greater is the debt of punishment incurred by subsequent mortal sin.

4. We must not say that the ingratitude of a forgiven sinner who commits mortal sins anew, is a special mortal sin in itself. This ingratitude is regularly a circumstance only of the new mortal sin which the offender commits. If, however, the relapsing sinner has an actual contempt of God and the favor he received in his earlier pardon, his ingratitude is a special sin.

89. RECOVERY OF VIRTUE BY PENANCE

1. Sins are pardoned through penance, especially by means of the sacrament of penance. Now, pardon of sin means infusion of grace. And from grace all virtues flow. Hence, virtues lost by sin are recovered by penance, and notably by the sacrament of penance worthily received.

2. A man rises through penance to the virtue he lost, but he has not always the full strength of that virtue immediately upon regaining it.

3. A man is restored by penance to his former dignity; by the grace infused, he is numbered again with the children of God.

4. If a man with virtuous deeds to his credit commits mortal sin, his good deeds are rendered lifeless and ineffective, because mortal sin turns the man completely away from God and eternal life.

5. But if a man by penance recovers the grace of God, his good deeds, deadened by his sin, come to life again. Hence meritorious deeds done formerly are revived by penance. The lost merits are regained.

6. However, good works done in the state of mortal sin have not any power of merit in them when they are performed. Nor is such power infused into them when penance restores their author to grace. Dead works (that is, good and meritorious works done in the state of mortal sin), stay dead. They are not brought to life by penance.

90. PARTS OF THE SACRAMENT OF PENANCE

1. Penance is said to have *parts* inasmuch as several things are required to constitute this sacrament. This is particularly the case with regard to the *matter* of the sacrament.

2. The parts of penance are the acts of the penitent: contrition, confession, and satisfaction. We may add, as a fourth part, the *absolution* imparted by the priest.

3. An *integral* part of anything is something in and of the thing itself which gives completeness or perfection. The three acts of the penitent (contrition, confession, satisfaction), are called *integral* parts of penance. These acts must all come together to constitute the rounded perfection of penance in so far as this perfection depends on the penitent.

4. Considering penance *as a virtue,* we distinguish three types or varieties of it: penance before baptism; penance for mortal sin; penance for venial sin.

[IIIa SUPPL.]

SUPPLEMENT
TO
THE THIRD PART

[*Questions 1-99*]

PENANCE (CONTINUED)

(QUESTIONS 1 TO 28)

1. CONTRITION

1. Contrition as a *part* of penance is a supernatural sorrow for sins, stirred up in the heart by the will under grace, with a view to confessing the sins, and making satisfaction for them.

2. Contrition, in so far as it is in the will and not in the emotions merely, is an act of the virtue of penance.

3. Contrition is born of filial fear of God, and thus proceeds according to charity. Sorrow for sin which arises from servile fear of deserved punishment is a less perfect sorrow; it is called, not contrition, but *attrition*. Attrition cannot turn into contrition, for these two types of sorrow for sin are not only different in degree but different in kind. Attrition may give place to contrition, but cannot *become* contrition.

2. THE OBJECT OF CONTRITION

1. Contrition is sorrow for sin. It is not grief by reason of *punishment* due to sin, but grief for the sin *itself* which deserves punishment.

2. Contrition is sorrow in the will for what the will has done amiss. Hence, contrition does not include in its scope the original sin which the sinner has not committed by bad use of will, but has inherited by infected nature.

3. Contrition is a word which means *a crushing* of what is hard and evil out of the will. Every actual sin is a kind of hardness in the will, and this must be crushed out. Hence, we have need of contrition for every actual sin.

4. Contrition as a part of the *virtue* of penance looks to the past. A person must have contrition for the sins he has already committed, for it is these that have caused the hardness in his will which contrition crushes out. Contrition as such does not refer to future sins, yet it disposes a person to watchfulness against them. Contrition belongs to the virtue of penance; caution with regard to future sins belongs to the virtue of prudence as conjoined with penance.

5. We cannot have contrition for the sins of others, but only for our own sins. We should, indeed, grieve for the sins of others, but this grief is not contrition.

6. A person must have contrition for each mortal sin he has committed; he must confess each one and therefore he must have contrition for each one.

3. DEGREES OF CONTRITION

1. Contrition is the greatest sorrow, for it is based on the greatest charity, that is, the soul's supernatural love and friendship with God. Sin is the greatest of evils; the sorrow which crushes it out of the soul is the greatest sorrow. Contrition is, indeed, not felt as the keenest sorrow in the sensitive part of a man, but as an act of the penitent's will it is the deepest sorrow of all.

2. In the sentient order, grief for sin may be excessive. It is not right or reasonable to become emotionally distrait, even over sin. True contrition is in the will; here, it cannot be too great. But its sentient reaction must be regulated by reason, so that the sinner retains calmness and patience.

3. Sins have degrees of evil in them; one is worse than another. Therefore sorrow for one sin may, and sometimes should, be greater than sorrow for another.

4. THE TIME OR SEASON OF CONTRITION

1. As long as a person is a wayfarer (that is, as long as he lives here on earth), he is to hate what hinders his progress to God and heaven. Hence, the whole of earthly life is the time or season for contrition.

2. Since contrition cannot be too great in the will or reason, though it may be excessive in the sentient part of man, it ought to be continuous through a person's life in so far as this is compatible with the duties of life. "Blessed are they that mourn" (Matt. 5:5).

3. The time or season of contrition ends with this life. The souls in heaven have no grief, but supreme joy. The souls in purgatory have grief, but no longer have need to crush out hardness from their will, for it is not there. Besides, the souls in purgatory have passed their time for meriting, and true supernatural contrition is always meritorious.

5. THE EFFECT OF CONTRITION

1. Contrition, when it is a perfect act of the supernatural virtue of penance, blots out sin. As part of the sacrament of penance, con-

trition operates instrumentally for the forgiveness of sin, which is effected by this sacrament.

2. Contrition or sorrow for sin may be so perfect as to take away all punishment due to sin as well as the guilt of the sin itself.

3. Sorrow which is true and perfect contrition blots out sin. The want of sensible sorrow (that is, the feeling or emotion of sorrow) is no hindrance to the perfection of contrition, for contrition belongs essentially to the will and not to the feelings.

6. CONFESSION

1. Confession of sins is necessary for the normal reception of the sacrament of penance. As penance is necessary for the salvation of one who has committed mortal sin after baptism, so also confession of these sins is necessary.

2. Confession is not a requirement born of the natural law, but is requisite by the supernatural institution of Christ. Our Lord gave his priest the power to forgive sins, setting up the sacrament as a kind of judgment in which testimony (or confession) indicates whether sins are to be forgiven or retained.

3. All who are bound to contrition and satisfaction are bound to confession. And, since all who have sinned are bound to contrition and satisfaction, all who have sinned are required to confess. The Church, by her law, imposes on all her children the duty of confession.

4. Confession is to be made in truth and sincerity. Hence, a man would do wrong, no matter what his motive, if he were to confess a sin he had not committed.

5. A person who has committed mortal sin should confess it as soon as he reasonably can do so. But we cannot say that he is strictly obliged to take the *earliest* opportunity of confessing.

6. Confession is required of all adult children of the Church. There is no such thing as dispensation from the duty of confessing.

7. THE NATURE OF CONFESSION

1. St. Augustine describes confession as an act which lays bare the hidden evil and disease with the hope of cure and pardon.

2. Since confession is a true manifestation of conscience in which the heart and the lips agree, it is an act of virtue.

3. The virtue exercised by confession is the virtue of penance.

8. THE MINISTER OF CONFESSION

1. Confession is to be made to a duly ordained priest, for to no other is given the power to absolve from sins. St. James indicates this

wondrous power which Christ gave to men, when he says (James 5:16): "Confess your sins, one to another." St. James knew and preached the divine institution of the sacrament of penance; here he directs the faithful to confess to their brethren who are priests.

2. Confession to a layman when no priest is available would indicate the strong desire of the penitent to receive the sacrament of penance; it would show his eagerness to do his part. Some have held that, in such a circumstance, Christ, the great High Priest, confers absolution. But this is not revealed, and the Church does not approve confession to one who cannot give absolution. Confession to a layman would generally be an imprudent act, and could be spiritually dangerous to both penitent and lay-confessor.

3. Some have held that it is expedient to confess venial sins to a layman if no priest is available. This is not an approved procedure, for it is not necessary to confess venial sins at all, though it is useful and pious to confess them in making regular confession to a priest, and therefore it is certainly not necessary to confess them to a layman. Venial sins can be remitted by contrite prayer, pious practices, and devout use of sacramentals.

4. The law of annual confession (which is a precept of the Church) once required each parishioner to confess to his own parish priest. But now a penitent may fulfill this duty by confessing to any approved priest.

5. A priest receives approval and jurisdiction for the hearing of confessions—in a definite place, or of definite persons—from his bishop or from his religious superior or from those who hold or share the ordinary jurisdiction in a diocese or religious community.

6. A penitent who is at death's door may be absolved, from sins and censures, by any priest whatever. The Church herself supplies jurisdiction to the confessor in such a case.

7. Before absolving a penitent, the confessor imposes upon him a work of *satisfaction* (some prayer or pious exercise), which the penitent accepts and agrees to perform. This imposed duty is commonly called "a penance," and the penitent in performing it says that he is "doing his penance." In imposing such a penance, the priest is guided by the gravity of the sins confessed, and by circumstances which indicate in each case what is prudent and salutary.

9. THE QUALITY OF CONFESSION

1. Confession of sins is to be made with true supernatural sorrow and sincerity of heart. Otherwise, the absolution of the priest cannot

be effective. Nor does the effect of absolution take place in a penitent who confesses without sorrow and *afterwards* repents.

2. Confession is to be entire; that is, all mortal sins in kind and number, according as they are remembered by the penitent, are to be confessed. Otherwise, the confession would savor of hypocrisy. And even one remembered mortal sin left unconfessed would keep the soul from union with God, and it would render the confession sacrilegious.

3. Confession is made by the penitent sinner in person, not by sending another as agent or proxy, or by mailing a letter. The penitent is to confess his own sins, manifesting them to the priest in some intelligible manner.

4. The requisite qualities of confession, therefore, are that it should be humble, sincere, and entire.

10. THE EFFECT OF CONFESSION

1. Confession is a *part* of the sacrament of penance, and therefore shares the effect of the sacrament itself; it delivers the penitent from sin when it is made with perfect contrition and with the qualities mentioned above, that is, when it is humble, sincere, and entire. If confession is made with imperfect, but supernatural, contrition, it does not deliver the penitent from sin, but disposes him proximately for the absolution which removes his sins.

2. Confession with absolution takes away the guilt of mortal sins and the eternal punishment that is due to them; it also lessens, in greater or smaller degree, the temporal punishment owed to forgiven mortal sins and to venial sins.

3. The power of forgiving sins, imparted by Christ to his priests, is called "the power of the keys." For the sacrament of penance, rightly received, opens the gate of heaven to the forgiven sinner. Hence we rightly speak of penance as the key or keys to heaven, and of the power of conferring this sacrament as the power of the keys.

4. We hope for forgiveness through Christ. By confessing, we submit ourselves to the power of the keys which has its efficacy from the Passion of Christ. Hence, an effect of confession is the renewed hope of heaven.

5. A man must confess all mortal sins that he remembers committing. If there be other mortal sins not remembered, they should be included in a general way in the confession, by use of some such phrase as, "For these sins that I have confessed, and for any others that I may have committed, I am sorry, and seek absolution from them all."

11. THE SEAL OF CONFESSION

1. The priest who hears confessions is most strictly bound to hold in perfect secrecy all sins confessed to him. This obligation incumbent on the confessor is called the "seal of confession."

2. The *seal* extends to everything connected with the sins confessed. That is, it obliges the confessor to complete silence about any circumstance that might reveal, or cause to be suspected, the identity of the sinner who has confessed to him.

3. The priest hearing a confession, and he alone, is bound by the seal of confession. One who overhears a penitent accusing himself, is seriously bound to secrecy, but is not, strictly speaking, under the seal of confession.

4. If the penitent, for good and serious reason, voluntarily asks the priest to reveal to another what he confesses, the priest is freed from the seal in the precise matter indicated by the request. Yet the priest will not, except under most pressing need, accede to such a request on the part of the penitent. The priest will rather require the penitent to tell him again, apart from the sacrament of penance, what he wishes to be revealed. And thus there will be no danger of scandal, no suspicion that the priest has broken the sacred seal.

5. What a priest knows from a source other than confession does not come under the seal. Thus, if a priest saw a man commit a robbery, he could testify to the fact, even though the robber had, in the meantime, confessed the sin to him. For while the sin as confessed is under the seal, the sin as observed apart from confession is not under the seal.

12. SATISFACTION

1. Satisfaction is something done to make up for the evil of an offence, even when the offence is already forgiven. It is an act of the virtue of penance.

2. Satisfaction is also an act of the virtue of justice, for justice demands an equality in things, an order and balance; such order and balance, satisfaction seeks to restore.

3. St. Augustine says (*De Eccl. Dogm.* 54) that satisfaction is to root out the causes of sin and to give no opportunity for its recurrence.

13. POSSIBILITY OF SATISFACTION

1. Absolutely speaking, man cannot make to God satisfaction for sin. Sin offends an infinite God, and has, therefore, something of infinity about itself. Man is finite; he can in no wise, of himself, render

infinite satisfaction. Still, man should do *what he can* in the way of satisfaction for sin; justice and penance (the virtue) demand as much. If a man cannot make *equivalent* satisfaction, he may be able to make *sufficient* satisfaction.

2. One man can make satisfaction for another, as is manifest from the doctrine of the Communion of Saints. But in so far as satisfaction is *remedial*, and is meant for the cure of the person performing it, it cannot be rendered by anyone but that person. Similarly, a man fined by a judge may have his fine paid by a friend. But if the judge imposes a personal penalty to teach the offender a lesson, no friend can step up and pay this penalty. One person cannot discharge the obligation of penance imposed on another by a confessor, unless the confessor says so.

14. THE QUALITY OF SATISFACTION

1. A man in mortal sin cannot render satisfaction for his other sins; for he cannot hold on to one or to some mortal sins while effectively satisfying for others. Yet a man who has the duty of performing a penance imposed in confession is not freed from this obligation by reason of a mortal sin committed before the imposed penance is fully performed.

2. St. Paul (I Cor. 13:3) says: "If I should distribute all my goods to feed the poor, and if I should deliver my body to be burned, and have not charity, if profiteth me nothing." Charity is impossible to hold without the grace of God, and a man in mortal sin has forfeited that grace. He is without charity. Hence, his works have no value as satisfaction, even if offered as satisfaction for old and forgiven sins from which he was absolved before his lapse into the present mortal sin that stains his soul.

3. Nor do works of satisfaction which are ineffective or dead because their author is in the state of mortal sin, come to life and exist as true works of satisfaction when he is restored to grace. Dead works lack the power of satisfaction when performed and ever afterwards. Yet the performing of good works is valuable to a man in sin; not, indeed, as satisfaction, but as disposing him to repentance, and as setting up a congruous claim for the grace of contrition.

4. Works done without charity (which is love and friendship existing by grace between God and the soul) are not only without satisfactory power, but they are without meritorious value. Such works cannot merit *condignly* either eternal life or temporal good. Yet, as has been said, they may make fitting or congruous the extending of God's mercy to raise their author from sin.

5. Good works done in the state of mortal sin may be said to diminish the pains of hell in the sense that they indicate something of good disposition in the sinner; such works at least keep their author from doing what would settle him more deeply in hell than he now deserves to be settled.

15. MEANS OF MAKING SATISFACTION

1. Since hardship or punishment is the remedy for sins, it is the means for making satisfaction for sins. For satisfaction looks to the future as well as to the past; it seeks to remedy harm done and to prevent it from being done anew. For both purposes, penal works, works involving some sort of pain, are to be used.

2. Submitting with patience to the trials and hardships of life that come upon us in the way of Providence, is a good and profitable way of making satisfaction for sins.

3. Satisfaction should take something away from us (goods, comfort, convenience, etc.) for the honor of God. By giving *alms,* we take material things from ourselves to honor God in our fellowmen. By *praying* we submit all we are and all we have to God. By *fasting* we deprive the body of its comfort and convenience. Here, then, are suitable means of making satisfaction: almsgiving, prayer, fasting.

16. THOSE WHO HAVE THE VIRTUE OF PENANCE

1. As a man is *curable* by reason of his sound health, even though he never had a disease, so a man may have the virtue of penance, even though he has never sinned actually. The virtue of penance is infused by God with the other supernatural virtues.

2. The virtue of penance is a *part* of justice, and justice will remain in the soul in heaven. Hence the virtue of penance also will remain in the soul. But in heaven the act of the virtue of penance will not be grief for sin, but joyous thanksgiving to God for his mercy in pardoning sin.

3. There can be no virtue of penance in the angels, for the good angels have not committed sin, nor are they capable now of committing it. And the evil angels are fixed and determined in their sinful will, and cannot be repentant.

17. THE POWER OF THE KEYS

1. The gate of heaven, always open to mankind since the day of Ascension, is closed upon that individual man who is burdened by the *guilt* of mortal sin and the debt of *eternal punishment* due to it. Whatever takes away these two things from that man's soul, opens the

gate of heaven to him. Now, what opens a gate is fittingly called a
key. The power to remove sin, both as to guilt and debt of eternal
punishment, is bestowed by Christ on his Church and on the priest
of his Church; this power, especially exercised in the sacrament of
penance, is figuratively called "the power of the keys."

2. The "keys" are the power of binding and loosing given to the
Church by our Lord; more specifically, the "keys" are the power given
to priests to forgive sins.

3. Now, there are two keys, and they are distinguished from each
other by their respective acts: the one is the *key of judging* whether
sins are to be forgiven or retained; the other is the *key of absolving*
from sin. When these two keys are used (when the penitent is judged
worthy and is absolved from his sins) the gate of heaven is opened to
the penitent.

18. THE EFFECT OF THE KEYS

1. The power of the keys remits the *guilt* of sins, for grace is given
by the sacrament of penance, and grace removes guilt.

2. The power of the keys, through the priest's absolution, takes
away the eternal *punishment* owed to sin in strict justice; the power
of the keys also takes away at least part of the temporal punishment
due to sins.

3. The priest exercises the *binding* power of the keys (the power
that keeps the gate locked), when he judges that absolution must
not be given to the confessing sinner, and therefore refuses to give it.
The *binding* power of the keys is also exercised in the imposing of
"a penance" on the forgiven sinner; for here, while the keys open
heaven to the forgiven sinner, they lock him into the obligation of
performing a work of satisfaction.

4. The priest in confession does not exercise the power of the keys
as he chooses, or according to his personal likes, dislikes, or prejudices.
The priest exercises the power of the keys in his office as God's minister,
wielding in the sacrament of penance God's own authority and power,
and hence he acts with care, discretion, and reverence, prudently consulting the sacredness of the sacrament on the one hand, and, on
the other, the disposition and the needs of the confessing sinner.

19. THE MINISTER OF THE KEYS

1. The priesthood of the Old Law was not dowered with the power
of the keys. But the priest of the Old Law had powers which fore-
shadowed and prefigured the power of the keys.

2. Before all others, our Lord himself has most excellently the

power of the keys. He owns this power as God; he merits it as man. And this wondrous power he conferred on the priests of his Church.

3. The power of the keys pertains to holy order, and exclusively to priests. [*Note*: Sometimes the phrase "the power of the keys" is used, by extension of meaning, for the power of jurisdiction in Church or diocese; that is, the power and right to rule, to authorize, to excommunicate. But this use of the phrase is not common.]

4. No matter how holy a layman may be, he has not the power of the keys, nor can he, as a layman, acquire it.

5. The power of the keys belongs to the priesthood as such. It does not depend for its effect on the state of soul (grace or sin) of the priest who exercises it.

6. Schismatical, heretical, and excommunicated priests retain the essence of the power of the keys, but they lack the right to use it, that is, they lack jurisdiction. The Church, by withdrawing jurisdiction from priests who are outside her pale, removes all true penitents from such confessors. No penitent could sincerely present himself to such confessors; if he did so knowingly he would sin, and no man can obtain absolution from sin by sinning.

20. USE OF THE POWER OF THE KEYS

1. A priest may exercise the power of the keys according to the jurisdiction imparted to him by his authentic ecclesiastical superiors, whether the jurisdiction extends to certain places or certain persons or both. Usually a priest is appointed by his bishop to hear the confessions of the faithful in any place in the diocese. Lawfully to exercise this power in another diocese than his own, a priest requires the approval of the authorities in that diocese.

2. By the power received in his ordination, a priest can absolve from any sin. But the power of jurisdiction, that is the right to *use* the power of the keys, is limited by the terms of the priest's assignment to duty. The bishop or acting ordinary (that is, the authentic ruling head of diocese, vicariate, or other ecclesiastical district) may *reserve* to himself the right to absolve from certain sins, as, for example, those to which excommunication is attached, or certain heinous evils.

3. All who have the use of reason in the Church, clergy and laity from highest to lowest, need the grace of the sacrament of penance. All must go to confession and seek absolution. And, since no one can absolve himself, ecclesiastical superiors, including the soverign pontiff, seek absolution at the hands of their priest-subjects. The highest prelate may be absolved by any priest, even the youngest, who is qualified by jurisdiction to hear confessions.

21. EXCOMMUNICATION

1. Excommunication means: (a) separation from the family of the faithful; (b) loss of the right to share in the prayers and general good works of the Church; (c) loss of the right to receive the sacraments.

2. The Church imposes this stern penalty of excommunication only when the reasons demanding it are most grave. And the Church always hopes that her stern action will humble the pride of the person excommunicated, and so bring him to repentance and amendment, and thus win him back to his place among her children. The Church hopes also, by imposing the censure of excommunication, to prevent or lessen the bad effect exercised on others by the excommunicated person's evil example.

3. The reason for excommunication is always a grave sin, in which the sinner is obstinate. Sometimes even temporal things can enter into grave and stubbornly persistent sin; bodily integrity, for instance, or liberty, or valuable property. And so it is possible that a person may incur excommunication for inflicting even temporal harm.

4. Excommunication is effective; that is, it produces the sad effects mentioned in the first paragraph above. However, it is not actually effective if it should be imposed by mistake or error.

22. PERSONS CONCERNED IN EXCOMMUNICATION

1. The right of excommunicating is lawfully exercised only by those who hold the greater and more general judicial power in the Church, that is, bishops and major prelates.

2. It can happen that the major jurisdiction required for excommunicating should exist in one who is not a bishop, or even a priest, as, for example, in a papal legate who is a layman, or in a designated bishop-elect who has not yet been ordained to the priesthood.

3. A person who is himself excommunicated, or one who is a cleric suspended from ecclesiastical office, cannot excommunicate. Such persons, being deprived of jurisdiction by the penalty imposed on themselves, cannot exercise that jurisdiction over others.

4. Excommunication is a penalty imposed by a superior. Therefore, a person cannot excommunicate himself, his equal, or his superior.

5. Excommunication is never imposed on a group as such, although each member of a group may be excommunicated individually at the same time.

6. A person may labor under multiple excommunication, for this penalty may be imposed as often as serious reasons demand it. The effect of a second, third, and fourth excommunication is to remove

the excommunicated person further and further from the spiritual helps which the Church gives her children in her general prayers and good works.

23. DEALING WITH EXCOMMUNICATED PERSONS

1. If a person labors under full excommunication, having been officially declared by name as one to be shunned, the faithful can have no dealings with him whatever. In other cases, it is not forbidden to deal with excommunicated persons in temporal matters, such as business transactions or casual social encounters.

2. It may happen, according to the canonical terms of the penalty of excommunication as imposed, that one who deliberately and perversely disobeys the law by dealing with "an excommunicated person named as one to be shunned," is himself subject to excommunication.

3. It is a sin to disobey the command of the Church by dealing in matters not permissible with an excommunicated person. This offence is a mortal sin: (a) if it involves a sharing of the cause for which the penalty and censure of excommunication was imposed; or (b) if it deals with religion; or (c) if it implies contempt for the Church.

24. ABSOLUTION FROM EXCOMMUNICATION

1. The absolution we speak of here is not the absolution which is a part of the sacrament of penance. *That* absolution is the removing of sins from the soul of the penitent; the absolution of which we now speak is the release of an excommunicated person from his censure. Absolution from sin is, indeed, usually required for the rehabilitation of an excommunicated person, for the reason for his expulsion from the community of the faithful is grave sin, and he must be rid of that sin to be properly returned to the soul and body of the Church. But the specific release of an excommunicated person from the ecclesiastical ban, censure, and penalty of excommunication, is the *absolution* of which we now speak. Excommunication is imposed by ecclesiastical authority; therefore, only competent ecclesiastical authority can remove it; only an ecclesiastic with jurisdiction can absolve from it. In some cases of excommunication, a priest cannot absolve without obtaining jurisdiction from his bishop. In a few cases, in which excommunication has been imposed for most serious offences, the excommunicated person cannot be absolved from his censure by any priest except one who has received delegation of jurisdiction from the pope.

2. Excommunication can be absolved, even when the excommunicated person does not seek absolution, or is opposed to it. For excommunication is imposed as a penalty for fault, but not as a fault itself. Now, while no fault can be forgiven without the contrite will of the offender, penalty can be removed at the will of the one who imposed it, regardless of the will of him on whom it was imposed.

3. Just as it is possible for a person to have excommunication added to excommunication, so also it is possible for such a person to have one excommunication absolved while others remain.

25. INDULGENCES

1. An indulgence is the remission, in whole or in part, of the temporal punishment due to sin. The Church draws from her spiritual treasury (which consists of the inexhaustible meriting of Christ and the superabundant merits which the saints gained through Christ) to pay the temporal debt of sin, which, otherwise, the sinner would have to pay by trials and sufferings in this life or in purgatory. For the performing of certain designated good works, or the reciting of assigned prayers, the Church, in her power of loosing and binding, releases the well-disposed person from the temporal punishment due to his sins—and this, completely or partially. This is called "granting an indulgence."

2. The Church has at her disposal the limitless spiritual treasure of Christ's merits, to which are added the superabundant merits of Mary and the saints, and therefore she has unlimited means for cancelling the debt of temporal punishment due to human sins. If the indulgence be authoritatively proclaimed, and if the person seeking to obtain it is in the state of grace and has true piety as his motive, the indulgence can be perfectly gained.

3. Indulgences are sometimes attached by the Church to the reciting of certain prayers, sometimes to the performing of good deeds, such as almsgiving, or the making of pious pilgrimages.

26. THE GRANTING OF INDULGENCES

1. Indulgences are granted by the pope, and by the bishop for his subjects, and by the official who exercises the bishop's jurisdiction in a diocese. Indulgences cannot be granted by others, such as abbots, or parish priests.

2. Sometimes a person who is not in holy orders can grant an indulgence; for example, a layman who has been designated bishop, has not yet been ordained or consecrated, but who has taken over the rule of his diocese. The power of granting indulgences does not

belong to the sacrament of holy orders, but to jurisdiction or authoritative rule in the Church.

3. The fullness of power to grant indulgences resides in him who has the fullness of jurisdiction in the Church, that is, the pope. This power is shared, in the measure of the pope's wishes, to the bishops of the Church.

4. A man in mortal sin cannot gain an indulgence. But a man with jurisdiction, who is himself in mortal sin, can grant an indulgence to be gained by those disposed to gain it. For this remission of temporal punishment due to sin is not accomplished through the holiness of the person who grants an indulgence, but by the objective application of merits drawn from the spiritual treasury of the Church.

27. THE GAINING OF INDULGENCES

1. A person in the state of mortal sin deserves, in strict justice, the eternal pains of hell. To relieve such a man of temporal punishment would be meaningless. Hence, to gain an indulgence, a person must be in the state of sanctifying grace.

2. Any person in the state of grace (layman, cleric, or religious) can gain an indulgence if he meets the conditions prescribed by the Church for gaining it, and if he has the right disposition, that is, if he has piety as his motive.

3. An indulgence is not gained except upon due fulfillment of all conditions set for its gaining by the prelate who grants it.

4. Anyone who meets all requirements can gain an indulgence, even the prelate who grants it. But such a prelate cannot grant an indulgence for his own private benefit.

28. PUBLIC PENANCE

1. For some very grave sins which are committed, so to speak, in the eye of the public, and are therefore likely to cause great spiritual harm because of the bad example they set to the faithful (that is, because of the *scandal* they cause), the Church imposes public and solemn penance.

2. Such public penance is very rarely imposed. And it seems that it should not be imposed more than once on any individual, even if the individual sins publicly again.

3. Public penance "not imposed in the solemn form" may be repeated. It may be imposed on laymen or clerics. Public and solemn penance, which can be imposed but once, is never imposed on clerics because of the scandal that would be involved in the very performing of the penance by such a person. Public and solemn penance may be imposed by a bishop, but not by a parish priest.

EXTREME UNCTION

(QUESTIONS 29 TO 33)

29. EXTREME UNCTION

1. Extreme unction is a sacrament which, through the anointing and prayer performed by a priest, gives forgiveness and grace to the soul, and sometimes confers health on the body of a person in danger of death from sickness, injury, or accident.

2. Extreme unction is a true sacrament instituted by Christ. And it is *one* sacrament, although it involves the anointing of the several senses.

3. Scripture does not give us the time nor the manner in which Christ instituted the sacrament of extreme unction. But the Church from earliest times has used this sacrament, and has recognized the fact that it is not within her power to abrogate it. And therefore it is certainly a sacrament instituted by the divine Founder of the Church.

4. Scripture speaks of extreme unction as a fact. In the Epistle of St. James (5:14) the *matter* of this sacrament is indicated as oil. This is olive oil, specially blessed, or *consecrated* as the usual term is, by a bishop for use in this sacrament. This oil is called *oleum infirmorum* or "oil of the sick."

5. It is right that oil should be consecrated for use in extreme unction, for in all sacraments the *matter* is blessed, and so is dedicated to a sacred use.

6. All sacraments which involve anointings—confirmation, holy order, extreme unction, and solemnly conferred baptism—require oil consecrated by a bishop.

7. The *form* of extreme unction consists of prescribed words which express and apply the matter as this sacrament is conferred.

8. The priest in administering extreme unction anoints the eyes, ears, nostrils, lips, hands, and feet of the sick person. At each anointing, he says, "Through this holy anointing and his most tender mercy, may the Lord forgive whatever thou has done amiss through . . . ," naming the pertinent sense or sense-function: sight; hearing; smell; taste and speech; touch; walking.

9. The prescribed *form* of extreme unction is suitable. It expresses: (a) the matter or sign: "this holy anointing"; (b) the cause of effectiveness in the sacrament: "may the Lord . . ."; (c) the actual effect of the sacrament: "forgive . . ."

30. THE EFFECT OF EXTREME UNCTION

1. The chief effect of extreme unction is in the soul of the recipient, and is by way of bringing grace. Now, grace is not compatible with sin. Hence, if there be sin on the soul of the recipient, mortal or venial, extreme unction takes it away, provided the recipient does not block this effect by his own bad will. Further, extreme unction removes from the soul the remains of sin, that is, the weaknesses consequent upon sin, such as the readiness to relapse into it. Thus this sacrament achieves its main purpose, which is to fortify the soul, to strengthen it and hearten it for the stresses of its last earthly hours, so that it may face death and judgment with resolution and confidence.

2. Bodily healing is an effect of extreme unction when the good of the sick person's soul requires it. Otherwise, extreme unction has no curative effect upon the body.

3. The sacraments which give a person Christian existence (baptism), or set and equip him for a special sacred task and duty (confirmation, holy orders), imprint an indelible *character* upon the soul. Extreme unction is not one of these sacraments, and it therefore imprints no character.

31. THE MINISTER OF EXTREME UNCTION

1. Since the remission of actual sins comes by extreme unction, and since the office of forgiving sins is proper to Christ's priesthood, no lay person can administer this sacrament.

2. Nor can a deacon administer it. Scripture says (James 5:14) with reference to extreme unction: "Is any man sick among you? Let him bring in the priests of the church . . ."

3. The conferring of extreme unction is not reserved to bishops; this sacrament is regularly conferred by any priest within the parish or district assigned to his care by competent ecclesiastical authority.

32. THE CONFERRING OF EXTREME UNCTION

1. Extreme unction is a sacrament of spiritual healing and strengthening. This is signified by the bodily healing which sometimes accompanies its use, and *may* accompany it in any instance of its being administered. Hence, this sacrament is not for those who are in health, but for the sick. And Scripture indicates as much: "Is any man

sick among you? Let him bring in the priests of the church, and let them pray over him, anointing him with oil in the name of the Lord" (James 5:14).

2. Extreme unction is not to be conferred in slight illnesses. It is a proximate preparation of the soul for death, and judgment, and heaven. Its name indicates the fact that it is to be administered in extremity; it is *extreme* unction. This sacrament is conferred upon a person seriously ill, not necessarily near to death, but suffering an illness that may prove fatal.

3. Extreme unction is sometimes conferred upon a person who has lapsed into unconsciousness. It is not refused to an unconscious patient whose previous life has indicated, at least implicitly, that he would wish to be fortified with the sacraments when he comes to die. Hence, extreme unction is not conferred upon lifelong imbeciles or insane persons; their previous life could contain no evidence of desire for this sacrament.

4. The sacrament of extreme unction requires, in the recipient, real devotion, actual or habitual. Hence, it is not given to infants, who have not come to the use of reason. Besides, a baptized child under the age of reason has neither sin nor remains of sin on his soul.

5. In administering extreme unction, the priest anoints, not the whole body, but special parts of the body, namely, those that serve a person constantly and directly in his daily life.

6. These parts are: eyes, ears, nostrils, lips, hands, and feet.

7. Deformity in a bodily member to be anointed is no bar to the anointing. Absence of members does not prevent the patient from receiving extreme unction.

33. THE REPEATING OF EXTREME UNCTION

1. Extreme unction prepares a sick person to face his judgment. If a person who has received this sacrament recovers from his sickness, he must some day come again into danger of death. And he will need again the strengthening of soul afforded by extreme unction. Thus the sacrament of extreme unction can be received more than once.

2. But a person does not receive extreme unction more than once while he is in the *same danger*. He may receive it more than once in the *same sickness*, for a sickness may continue for a long time, with only now and again a period of real peril. A sick person, therefore, may receive extreme unction in each new danger. Indeed, it is the practice of the Church, in case of a person continuing in serious illness without showing much change, to permit the administering of

extreme unction once a month. For, after a month of serious sickness with no marked improvement, a person may well be considered to be in a new danger, a more immediate peril of death.

ORDER

(QUESTIONS 34 TO 40)

34. THE SACRAMENT OF ORDERS

1. Orders, or holy orders as it is more generally called, is the sacrament by which bishops, priests, and deacons are given the power to perform their sacred functions.

2. Peter the Lombard defines the sacrament of orders as: "A seal of the Church by which spiritual power is conferred on the person ordained." Rightly understood, this is a good description of orders. The sacrament is a sign or seal. It is "of the Church" in the sense that Christ instituted it and consigned it to the Church for administering; our Lord did this with all the sacraments; hence it is common to hear the expression, "the sacraments of the Church," even though the Church cannot institute or abrogate any sacrament. The definition of Peter the Lombard indicates the effect of this sacrament in the recipient, namely, *spiritual power*.

3. A sacrament is an outward sign instituted by Christ, while he was here on earth before his Ascension into heaven, which both signifies and confers an inward grace. The sacrament of orders squares with this definition. It is therefore a true sacrament.

4 & 5. This sacrament is conferred by the imposing of the bishop's hands upon the recipient (this constitutes the *matter* of the sacrament) followed by prescribed prayers (the *form*) which indicate the meaning of the matter or sign, and constitute it a sacrament.

35. THE EFFECT OF THE SACRAMENT OF ORDERS

1. The sacrament of orders confers sanctifying grace, as all sacraments do. And it is notably suitable that the sacrament which empowers a person to confect and dispense the sacraments as means of grace should itself bring grace to its recipient.

2. Since any sacred order which pertains to the sacrament of orders (that is, episcopate, priesthood, diaconate) sets a man in a place of

power with reference to the dispensing of the sacraments, it marks him for this duty by an indelible character impressed upon his soul.

3. The character of orders presupposes the baptismal character as already on the soul. It is the character impressed by baptism that renders a person capable of receiving the other sacraments.

4. The character of orders does not, of necessity, presuppose the character imprinted in the soul by confirmation. But it is most suitable that confirmation be received before orders are conferred; for a man should come to ordination with all perfections he can manage to receive. Therefore, the Church requires that the candidate for orders be confirmed before he presents himself for ordination.

5. The character of orders is impressed as the sacrament is received, without dependence on the proper sequence of ordinations. Thus, if a man were to be ordained priest without having first been ordained deacon, his priesthood would be valid. But the order of deaconship would be supplied by the proper ordination. The Church requires, however, that orders be received in due succession.

36. QUALITIES IN THOSE TO BE ORDAINED

1. A man who receives the sacrament of orders is set to lead others. Therefore, he should be a man of holy and exemplary life. Yet this is a requirement of precept and of propriety; it is not of the essence of the sacrament. Even a sinful man who receives orders is validly ordained, although he does great wrong in accepting ordination.

2. A candidate for orders should have knowledge adequate for the proper discharge of his sacred duties. He must have a sufficiency of knowledge of the scriptures, and know the doctrines of the faith, and the requirements of Christian morality.

3. The personal holiness of an ordained man has nothing to do with the sacrament itself; an ordained man does not advance in degree of orders as he advances in personal holiness.

4. A prelate who knowingly ordains a candidate wholly unworthy of the office he assumed, commits a grave sin, and shows himself an unworthy servant of the Lord.

5. A man in orders who, apart from necessity, exercises his office while he is in the state of mortal sin, is guilty of another grievous sin every time he performs a sacred function.

37. THE DISTINCTION OF ORDERS: THE CHARACTER

1. "As in one body we have many members, but all the members have not the same office" (Rom. 12:4), so in the Church there are various orders appointed to their respective sacred offices.

2. The distinction of orders is derived basically from their varying

reference to the Holy Eucharist. There is: (a) the *priest*, who offers the Eucharistic Sacrifice; (b) the *deacon*, who assists the priest; (c) the *subdeacon*, who assists the priest and deacon and attends the sacred vessels of the Eucharistic sacrifice; (d) the *acolyte*, who proffers the matter (bread and wine) for the sacrifice; (e) the *exorcist*, who expels evil spirits which render a person unworthy to receive the Holy Eucharist; (f) the *lector* or reader, who imparts sacred instruction to those who come to Mass and Communion; (g) the *porter* or doorkeeper, who attends the bells and portals, and welcomes the faithful to the sacrifice and excludes those who should not be admitted.

3. These seven orders are classified as *major* orders and *minor* orders. The major orders are three: subdeaconship, deaconship, priesthood. Deaconship and priesthood belong to the sacrament of holy orders. The bishop's office, the episcopate, is the fullness of priesthood. The minor orders are: doorkeeper, lector, exorcist, acolyte.

4. Each of the orders has its proper acts and many incidental functions. These, as we have noted, are all directed in some manner to the divine center and core of our religion—our Lord himself in the Holy Eucharist.

5. The *character* impressed upon the soul by the sacrament of orders is given when the sacrament is conferred.

38. THE MINISTER OF HOLY ORDERS

1. The bishop alone has the power to confer the sacrament of orders.

2. This power is not taken from a bishop. He retains it always. Even should he lapse into heresy or schism, he does not lose this power. A heretical or schismatical bishop would sin gravely by exercising the power to confer holy order.

39. IMPEDIMENTS TO ORDERS

1. No woman may receive the sacrament of orders. St. Paul says (I Tim. 2:12): "I suffer not a woman to teach (in the Church)." The nature of this sacrament, the example of Christ, and the constant law and practice of the Church, make it abundantly evident that the female sex is an absolute impediment to the receiving of the sacrament of orders.

2. The Church sets a definite age for the ordaining of candidates. As regards minor orders, very young boys might be validly ordained. Prudence and reverence demand, however, that the candidate for any order be old enough to discharge its duties with seemliness and with an appreciation of the dignity and the responsibility it lays upon

him. [*Note:* The canonical age is the age set by the laws or canons of the Church as minimal for ordination. For example, a man is not ordained to the priesthood until he has entered his twenty-fifth year, that is, has passed his twenty-fourth birthday.]

3. One who is *enslaved* cannot lawfully be raised to orders. Yet, if he be actually ordained, the ordination is valid. The same is true of those who are under the burden of heavy debts, and of those who are bound to the exacting care of others.

4. One who has been guilty of homicide, though penitent and pardoned, cannot lawfully be ordained. Still, if he were ordained, the ordination, though illicit, would be valid.

5. Legitimate birth is required in the candidate for lawful ordination. Here again, the impediment is one of licitness, not of validity. For lawful ordination, an illegitimate person must first be dispensed by the Church from his impediment of illegitimacy.

6. Any notable and noticeable deformity of body is an impediment to lawful ordination.

40. MATTERS PERTINENT TO THE SACRAMENT OF ORDERS

1. The wearing of the *tonsure* (that is, having the head shaved in the form of a crown) is a fitting practice for those in orders.

2. The conferring of tonsure is a ceremony which officially sets a man in the ranks of the clergy. It is not an order, not even one of the minor orders which do not belong to the sacrament itself. The tonsuring of a candidate for orders is a preliminary ceremony, and it regularly precedes the receiving of the first minor order; it is then called the *prima tonsura* or first tonsuring.

3. Tonsure is not a ceremony of renunciation by which a man gives up temporal goods. It is a ceremony of dedication to the service of God before all else. Hence the cleric (that is, the tonsured man) is not to be unduly or excessively occupied with temporal goods, but he is not forbidden their ownership and use.

4. There is need of the office of bishop. The bishop presides over others, and makes orderly all the divine ministries. He has the fullness of the priesthood, and to him belongs the power and duty of ordaining candidates who are prepared to receive orders.

5. The office of bishop (that is, the episcopate) is not a special order. It is the order of priesthood in its fullness.

6. The pope as supreme pontiff and vicar of Christ is above all other bishops by divine right and appointment. His is not only the

fullness of the priestly office and order, but the fullness of universal jurisdiction in the Church. He is also the supreme and infallible teacher of the universal Church in matters of faith and morals.

7. Special vestments are properly used by the clergy in their official religious functions. These vestments, mostly ancient in origin, are full of symbolical meaning, and their use reverently manifests the faith of clergy and people.

MATRIMONY

(QUESTIONS 41 TO 68)

41. MATRIMONY

1. Man is by nature both gregarious and political. And, as Aristotle says (*Ethic.* VIII 12), he is more strongly inclined by nature to connubial society than to political society. In a word, man has not only a tendency (as all living bodies have) to propagate his kind, and (as herd animals do) to live with his kind, he has a tendency to the stable unions of *marriage, family,* and *state.* Thus, marriage belongs to the domain of the natural law. The conjugal union of marriage is an institution of nature.

2. The majority of men are called to this conjugal union, but it is not imposed upon each individual as a duty. That many should marry is necessary for the common good. Yet the same common good requires that some should be devoted to the contemplative life, to which marriage with its duties is a great obstacle. Besides, we have ample teaching in scripture of the excellence of virginity; chastity is one of the counsels of perfection. Hence, not all individuals are required to marry. The natural law is observed if a sufficient number marry to maintain and propagate the race.

3. The conjugal act of man and wife is by no means sinful. Scripture (I Cor. 7:3) says: "Let the husband render the debt to his wife." The opinion that the marital action is sinful is both mistaken and heretical.

4. The marital act rightly performed by man and wife is an act of virtue, and therefore is a meritorious act.

42. MATRIMONY AS A SACRAMENT

1. A sacrament is a sensible sign, instituted by Christ, to signify and confer grace. Matrimony meets the requirements of this definition. Hence, it is truly a sacrament.

2. Matrimony is instituted for the begetting of children according to God's providence and law. It was established from the beginning, before the fall of man, as a holy institution of nature. It was raised to supernatural rank by our Lord when he made it a sacrament.

3. Like every sacrament, matrimony confers grace upon those who receive it worthily. It also confers the special sacramental grace which helps the spouses to be faithful in the performing of all their duties.

4. The actual use of marital action is not an integral element in the sacrament of matrimony.

43. BETROTHAL

1. A betrothal is a promise of future marriage. It is not a marriage, but a pledge or promise of marriage.

2. It is possible for a betrothal to be contracted for a child who has at least some understanding of a contract, even though he be unable to make a contract of his own accord. [*Note:* The Church urges pastors and parents to use all effort to avoid and prevent any sort of nuptial agreement or promise before the parties are themselves old enough to marry.]

3. A betrothal is a contract, but not an indissoluble one. It can be dissolved by the mutual consent of the parties it binds; or by the fact of one party's entering religion; or by one party's marrying another than the betrothed; and also in other ways. If the betrothal has been formally made as a religious rite, it should not be dissolved without appeal for the judgment of the Church.

44. DEFINITION OF MATRIMONY

1. Matrimony is a joining. It unites spouses in the task of begetting and rearing children, and it dedicates them to one common life.

2. Matrimony, as a word, derives from *mater* which means *mother*, and, perhaps, from *munus* which means *duty*. Matrimony is sometimes called nuptials; this word comes from *nubere* which means *to veil*, for it was an ancient custom to veil the heads of spouses. Matrimony constitutes a man and wife as a *conjugal* society, and this word comes from *conjugium* which means *a joining*, or *a yoking*.

3. Peter the Lombard describes matrimony as "the marital union

of a man and a woman, which involves their living together in undivided partnership."

45. MARRIAGE CONSENT

1. The effecting cause of matrimony is the consent of the parties making the matrimonial contract, which is a sacramental contract as well.

2. This essential consent must be manifested outwardly, by words if possible, or at least by unmistakable signs.

3. The consent must be expressed in the present tense. Expressions of future agreement may make a betrothal or engagement, but not a marriage.

4. The outwardly manifested consent must express a true inner will and intention. Consent given falsely or jestingly does not make a true marriage.

5. Nor can the consent be secret. There must be witnesses to it. Secret consent of parties to a contract can make a true contract, but not a true and sacramental marriage. According to the institution of Christ, sacraments are to be administered by the Church. The Church cannot make or abrogate a sacrament; but the Church can, and indeed must, determine the conditions in which a sacrament can be received. The laws of the Church concerning sacraments are, on the one hand, a shield against irreverent use of most holy things; on the other hand, these laws consult the true good of the faithful. Therefore, the Church has decreed most wisely that the secret consent of parties to a marriage (that is, clandestine marriage) cannot constitute the sacrament of matrimony.

46. CONSENT UNDER SPECIAL ASPECTS

1. We have seen that marriage consent cannot be expressed in the future tense; the spouses must accept each other here and now when they utter their consent. This is so even if an oath is added to the words of promise. For a promise, with or without an added oath, expresses what has not yet happened. A marriage happens at the moment consent is given and expressed.

2. A consent to future marriage, even with an oath, and even if followed by carnal use or marital rights, does not make a true marriage.

47. COMPULSORY AND CONDITIONAL CONSENT

1. Consent is a voluntary or free-will act. Now, as we have seen elsewhere in these studies (Ia IIae, q. 6), an act may be voluntary

and yet have in it an element of involuntariness Thus, the captain of a ship who throws overboard a valuable cargo in time of storm, *wills* to perform the act, but does not *wish* to perform it; he would *not* perform it were he not afraid of losing both ship and cargo if he retained the goods on board. Therefore, it appears that a kind of compulsion can be back of a free consent. There is such a thing as a compulsory consent, or a contract made under duress, but the stress of circumstance which compels the consent is, in contracts, from other people and not from storms or irrational creatures. Now, a contract made under duress is a contract, but, in both civil and ecclesiastical law, it is a *voidable* contract.

2. It is possible for a normal person, and even a person of steady and reliable character, to be so moved by *fear* as to consent to a contract under its stress.

3. Consent given under stress of fear invalidates the marriage contract. Marriage is a permanent bond; it involves "a lifelong bargain." Now, a person who is moved by fear to consent to a situation, does so to escape a danger, but hardly intends to bear the unpleasant situation permanently after the danger is past. Hence, it is unlikely that consent under compelling fear is really a consent sufficient for marriage. In any event, the Church, which has the right of legislating upon the essential conditions for receiving a sacrament, has declared compulsory consent insufficient for the sacrament of matrimony.

4. Some have thought that the party who uses compulsion to make the other party marry him is truly married; for there can be no question of *his* free will and full consent in the contract. But this is quite impossible; marriage means the joining of two wills in a common consent. A man cannot be the true husband of one who is not his wife; nor can a woman be the wife of a man who is not her husband. What prevents true consent for one of the parties prevents the marriage.

5. A *condition* attached to the consent does not necessarily prevent a true marriage, unless it be a *future* condition, or a condition that conflicts with the very nature of marriage. Thus, there is no marriage if one party says, "I take you for my true husband (wife) on condition that you will not drink any more." Nor is there a marriage if the consent is given on condition that there will be no children.

6. Parents cannot compel their children to marry.

48. OBJECT OF THE CONSENT IN MARRIAGE

1. The consent that makes a marriage is, implicitly, the consent to the use of marital rights.

2. The essential end of marriage is the begetting and rearing of

children, and the control of fleshly tendencies. The parties may have many other accidental or nonessential ends in view, good or bad. Thus a person may marry for wealth, or for social position, or to prevent another from getting the person espoused, or to reform the person married, or for a variety of other reasons. But the essential end of marriage is in marriage itself, and those who assume the marital state assume *what that state is,* no matter what their individual purposes and intentions may be. The accidental ends (the personal or individual purposes and intentions of the spouses) cannot prevent their marriage from being a true one. Thus a woman who marries for social position is a married woman, despite her unworthy purpose in marrying. A man who marries for wealth is a married man, notwithstanding his personal objective in taking a wife.

49. THE BLESSINGS OF MARRIAGE

1. The disorder brought into human life by original sin has made the generative act so intensely emotional as to remove it from the ready control of reason. Hence, to justify this act in fallen man, some compensating goods or blessings must attach to marriage.

2. Such goods are listed by Peter the Lombard (IV *Sent. D.* 31) as: fidelity, offspring, sacrament. Fidelity keeps the man and wife true to one another exclusively in the performing of their marital act. Offspring is the good fruit of the marital act, and belongs to it in intention even if the marriage proves unfruitful. Sacrament is the holiness of the state and duties of spouses.

3. Of the three marriage goods or blessings, sacrament is the most excellent. For that which makes marriage a divinely instituted and supernatural state is its most notable and essential blessing.

4. Since the three marriage goods or blessings—sacrament, fidelity, offspring—are the things that make the marriage act different from the lawless use of sex, it follows that these three blessings justify and sanctify the marriage act, and remove it entirely from the category of sin.

5. Therefore, without the marriage blessings or goods, the marriage act could not be justified as a good act.

6. Yet a spouse, seeking only pleasure in the marital action, would not be guilty of serious sin unless his quest were such as to involve a will and intention to illicit indulgence were lawful means unavailable to him.

50. IMPEDIMENTS TO MATRIMONY

1. What hinders or prevents a marriage between certain persons is called an *impediment.* Some impediments hinder marriage; they

prevent it if it has not yet been contracted, yet do not dissolve it if it has already occurred. Other impediments absolutely prevent marriage between the parties, thus making it impossible for them to enter upon a valid contract of marriage, at least without dispensation. The first type of impediment is called *prohibiting;* the second type is called *diriment.* The word *diriment* means "utterly destroying."

51. ERROR AS AN IMPEDIMENT TO MARRIAGE

1. An error concerned with the persons or the particulars of a marriage is a lack of knowledge in one or both of the parties to the contract, and therefore it is a hindrance to consent; for consent is a *knowing* acceptance of a situation; one cannot enter upon a free agreement without sufficient knowledge.

2. Yet an error which can render a marriage void must be an error in *essentials.* If a man marries the wrong twin, being assured deceivingly that it is the right one, there is no marriage. But if a man marries a woman who has falsely informed him about her age, or fortune, or nationality, the marriage stands.

52. SLAVERY AS AN IMPEDIMENT

1. The condition of a slave prevents him from rightly fulfilling the duties of marriage. For a slave has not free control of his person, and therefore cannot properly transfer that control to another. Still, if a person knows that the other party is a slave, and marries him none the less, the marriage is valid.

2. And indeed, since, as St. Paul says (Gal. 3:2, 28), "In Christ Jesus . . . there is neither bond nor free," a slave has as much right to marry as a freeman.

3. A husband who sells himself into slavery does not, by this fact, break his marriage. For nothing that happens after a true and valid marriage is contracted can dissolve it.

4. Various human customs and civil laws prevail about the children of a father who is a slave. It seems most reasonable to say that, on the score of freedom or bondage, the children inherit the condition of the mother. [*Note:* This discussion is now irrelevant.]

53. VOWS AND ORDER AS IMPEDIMENTS

1. A *simple* vow which is in conflict with the state and duties of marriage is a prohibiting impediment, but does not annul a marriage. However, a person with such a simple vow sins by marrying unless he has first obtained dispensation from his vow at the hands of the proper ecclesiastical authorities.

2. A *solemn* vow of chastity in a religious order or congregation is a

diriment impediment of matrimony. Once the vow is formally taken, it renders a subsequent marriage invalid.

3. A man who has received subdeaconship has solemnly taken upon himself the obligation of celibacy. Therefore, he cannot thereafter contract a valid marriage. In some Eastern rites, a married man can be ordained; but it is a general ecclesiastical law that no ordained man can (after subdeaconship) enter the married state.

4. The fact that a true marriage exists does not necessarily bar a man from sacred orders. If the wife dies, or if she freely consents to release her husband permanently from the marital obligation, the husband can be ordained; he receives with his ordination to subdeaconship the obligation of perfect and perpetual celibacy.

54. BLOOD RELATIONSHIP AS IMPEDIMENT

1. Blood relationship or *consanguinity* is established by natural descent from a common ancestor.

2. Degrees of consanguinity are distinguished according to *lines*. The ascending and descending line (father, son, grandson, great-grandson) is the *direct* line. The lines on the various levels of the ascending and descending line are called *lateral* or collateral lines (brother, sister, first cousins, second cousins, and so on).

3. Consanguinity is, by natural law, an impediment to marriage between certain closely related persons. It would be contrary to the ends of marriage, chief of which is the welfare of offspring, if inbreeding were practiced. What was necessary in the beginning of the race is not needed now. The voice of nature, as well as the voice of human experience, proclaims the unlawfulness of marriage between near relatives.

4. The Church, by her disciplinary or regulative laws (canons), fixes the degrees of consanguinity within which marriage is forbidden.

55. AFFINITY AS IMPEDIMENT

1. Affinity is the relationship of a married person with in-laws. By becoming one flesh through marriage, each of the two spouses contracts a relationship with all the blood relatives of the other spouse. And this is affinity.

2. Affinity sets up a lasting relationship. It does not cease to exist for a husband whose wife dies, nor for a widow with reference to her late husband's relatives.

3. Formerly, unlawful carnal intercourse established affinity, but this is so no longer. Affinity arises out of valid marriage only.

4. Affinity is not contracted by betrothal or engagement, but arises only out of true and valid marriage.

5. Affinity does not cause affinity. Relatives of one spouse are not related by affinity to relatives of the other spouse. Affinity exists only between a husband and the blood relatives of his wife, and between a wife and the blood relatives of her husband. A sister of one spouse is free to marry a brother of the other spouse. And a man who marries a widow does not contract affinity with the relatives of her late husband; nor does a woman who marries a widower contract affinity with the relatives of his late wife.

6. Affinity voids marriage throughout the whole direct line. It is a diriment impediment. Thus a widow or widower cannot marry parent or grandparent of the deceased spouse. Affinity voids marriage (and therefore is a diriment impediment) in the lateral line to the second degree inclusive. Thus a widower cannot marry his late wife's sister or niece.

7. Degrees of affinity are computed according to degrees of consanguinity. Affinity has no degrees of its own. Thus a person related by blood in the second degree to one spouse, is related by affinity in the second degree to the other spouse.

8. Degrees of affinity are thus *coextensive* with degrees of consanguinity. A husband stands in the first degree of affinity with his wife's sister (collateral line), because the wife stands in the first degree of consanguinity with her own sister (collateral line). A wife stands in the second degree, collateral, of affinity with her husband's nephew; for that is the line and the degree of blood relationship which the husband has with his own nephew.

9. Affinity of kind and degree sufficient to nullify marriage makes marriage impossible (without dispensation, which is sometimes obtainable), and when such a union is submitted to the judgment of the Church, she pronounces it no marriage.

10. In the official process of pronouncing on a union that is submitted to the Church for judgment, the method of charge and proof is followed.

11. In such processes, witnesses are called, and evidence is taken, as in other judicial procedures, so that the fact (if fact it be) of nullifying affinity or consanguinity, is indubitably known and established.

56 SPIRITUAL RELATIONSHIP AS IMPEDIMENT

1 & 2. Spiritual relationship is a bond arising, by church law, from the administering and receiving of the sacrament of baptism. It exists between the person baptizing and the person baptized, and also between the sponsors and the person baptized, but not between one sponsor and the other sponsor. It is a diriment impediment of marriage.

3. In an older day it was commonly considered that a spiritual relationship could arise from standing sponsor at confirmation, and even from giving catechetical instructions. But the Church has definitely settled the matter, as explained above.

4. The spiritual relationship of a godfather to the person baptized does not pass to his wife so as to make her also a spiritual relative of the person for whom her husband stood sponsor. The same is to be said of a godmother and her husband.

5. Nor does spiritual relationship pass to the children of a sponsor.

57. LEGAL RELATIONSHIP AS IMPEDIMENT

1. Legal relationship is a bond arising out of adoption. Adoption is an act by which, under due process of civil law, a person takes another who is not his child, to be in fact, his child; or, at any rate, takes another to be a true member of the family or household.

2. Legal relationship is an impediment to marriage, and is regularly considered so in civil law as well as in church law. It is not seemly or suitable for those who live together as a family to intermarry.

3. Legal relationship exists between adopting parent and adopted child; also between adopted child and the natural children of the adopting parent; also between the adopting parent and the natural parents of the adopted child. Legal relationship is an impediment to marriage in all cases. But this impediment, as existing between the person adopted and the natural children of the one adopting, ceases when the adopting person dies, or when the children concerned come of age. In cases of legal relationship, the law of the Church follows the civil law of the country. Where civil law makes legal relationship a diriment or nullifying impediment to marriage, so does the Church regard it; where civil law makes this impediment only prohibitive, it is only prohibitive in church law.

58. CERTAIN OTHER IMPEDIMENTS

1. Impotence is physical inability to perform the marriage function. If this inability exists before marriage, and is incurable (that is, perpetual), it renders marriage impossible; it is a diriment impediment.

2. Inability to perform the marital act is diriment to marriage (if it occur *before* the valid marriage and is incurable) even if it come from preternatural causes, such as demons, and constitutes a kind of spell or bewitchment.

3. Insanity is an impediment to marriage, for madmen cannot freely and knowingly make a valid contract. If it comes after marriage, of course, insanity does not affect the marriage bond. If insanity is not

constant, so that the afflicted person has intervals of sanity, he is capable of marrying at such times; yet it is most unwise for him to do so.

4. Incest committed by a spouse is a reason for which the other spouse may refuse marriage rights; but it does not dissolve a marriage.

5. Defect of age is an impediment to marriage. Girls under fourteen and boys under sixteen are debarred by church law from marrying. By the natural law, marriage is invalid for persons who have not attained puberty.

59. DISPARITY OF WORSHIP AS IMPEDIMENT

1. Disparity of worship exists between a baptized child of the Church and one who has not been baptized. It is a diriment impediment to marriage, by church law, and with good reason; for the chief end of marriage is the welfare of offspring. Parents divided upon the basic truth of life cannot well concur in the proper education of children, that is, cannot rightly attend to the welfare of their offspring.

2. Unbaptized persons can be validly married to each other.

3. A husband, converted to the faith and baptized, does well to remain with his wife even if she be unwilling to be converted also.

4. But if the nonbaptized spouse will not live in peace with the converted and baptized spouse, or live without offending God and doing spiritual harm to the baptized party, then the convert-spouse (who by baptism died to his former life and was reborn in Christ) may put away the unbaptized spouse as no longer his true and validly married mate. This fact is known from scripture (I Cor. 7:12–15).

5. Once the free status of such a spouse (who puts away his mate for reasons given above) is officially established by decision of the ecclesiastical tribunal, he can marry anew.

6. No other cause than unbelief and recalcitrance in the precise circumstances mentioned can nullify a marriage, and no cause can nullify a valid marriage between Catholics.

60. UXORICIDE AS IMPEDIMENT

1. Uxoricide is wife-murder. This most horrible crime never has justification, even if a husband discovers his wife in the very act of committing adultery.

2. A man who kills his wife with the moral or physical concurrence of another woman whom he intends to marry, incurs a diriment impediment (of *crime*) which makes the proposed marriage impossible. The same is true of a wife who plots and acts with an unlawful lover to cause her husband's death.

61. SOLEMN VOWS AS IMPEDIMENT

1. A person who has contracted marriage validly (and thus has had his marriage *ratified*) and has also performed the marital act (thus making the ratified marriage a *consummated* marriage) is bound to the married state of life, and cannot, without the free consent of his spouse, leave it to enter religion and take solemn vows in an order.

2. Yet if the marriage is ratified only, and not consummated, a spouse may leave it and enter religion, taking solemn vows, whether the other spouse consents or not. For until marriage is consummated, only a spiritual bond exists between the spouses; by consummation, a carnal bond is established, and the spouses are thenceforth really two in one flesh, Now, a purely spiritual bond may be dissolved by the spiritual death which a person undergoes in dying to the world by taking solemn vows in religion. But the carnal bond is not dissolved so.

3. When a spouse, after a ratified but not consummated marriage, takes solemn vows in religion, the other spouse is free to marry anew. Yet all this must be subjected to the ecclesiastical court for examination, judgment and official declaration of the free status of the abandoned spouse. Otherwise, a new marriage is not lawful.

62. INFIDELITY

1. A spouse may seek lawful separation from bed and board if the other spouse be guilty of infidelity, that is, commits adultery. This is not the case, however, if the spouse seeking separation is also guilty of adultery. Nor is it the case if the spouse now seeking separation has already forgiven the infidelity by using the marriage right with the offending party. Nor is it true in any case except that of actual, recognized, freely committed adultery.

2. No spouse, however, is *bound* to seek separation by reason of adultery on the part of the other spouse, unless the offending party be determined to continue committing this same sin. In this case, there is a duty to separate.

3. No spouse can, by private authority, effect a separation from bed and board. One spouse, truly injured by the adultery of the other, may indeed effect a separation from bed. But for full separation, the injured party must appeal for the judgment of the ecclesiastical court.

4. In all matters touching fidelity in marriage, husband and wife are on a par. Nothing is lawful for one and unlawful for the other.

5. Separation allowed by reason of infidelity does not dissolve mar-

riage. The separated spouses are still husband and wife; neither can marry anew while the other lives.

6. Separated spouses should strive to be reconciled and to take up decent married life together, if and when this becomes at all possible.

63. SUCCESSIVE MARRIAGES

1. At the death of either spouse, the marriage tie ceases to exist for the other. Widowed spouses are free to marry again.

2. The Christian marriage of a widowed person is a true sacrament. All the essentials of sacramental marriage are present. There is nothing to detract from the perfection of the present marriage in the fact that another or others preceded it.

64. IMPLICATIONS OF MARRIAGE

1. Marriage brings to the spouses the mutual obligation of rendering *the debt*, as it is called; that is, of surrendering the body to the generative act.

2. This sacred duty is to be rendered by either spouse at the will of the other, whether this will be expressed explicitly or indicated implicitly.

3. In the rendering of the marriage debt, husband and wife are on a plane of perfect equality; both are equally in command; both are equally held to obey.

4. Since marriage involves the duty of rendering the debt, neither spouse, without the full and free consent of the other, is free to make a vow which conflicts with marriage duty. If one spouse should make such a vow without the consent of the other, he sins. Nor must he keep the vow. Instead, he must do penance for a vow unlawfully made.

5. It is wise and prudent, if there be no danger of concupiscence, for spouses to abstain sometimes from the use of the marital act, for instance, on holy days.

6. Yet there is no serious obligation on spouses of practicing such abstention. And one spouse cannot justly enforce abstention on the other, even at times when it seems suitable for reasons of piety or religion. Recurrent physical inconvenience on the part of the wife makes it most suitable that the husband abstain, but if the marriage debt be demanded, even in these seasons, it is not to be refused.

7. The Church has wisely decreed that marriage (which may be lawfully enacted at any time) is not to be ceremoniously celebrated, with nuptial Mass and blessing, during the seasons of penance called Advent and Lent.

65. PLURALITY OF WIVES

1. The natural law is, as we have said many times, the eternal law of God for right human conduct, inasmuch as this law can be known by sound reason without divine revelation. It may be called man's natural awareness of what is right and fitting. Whatever upsets the normal proportion of an action or state, with reference to its end or purpose, is contrary to the natural law. Now, a simultaneous plurality of wives upsets the sane balance and proportion of marriage with reference to its end; at least it does so in a secondary way. For, though children may be begotten of many wives, and well reared too, yet a peaceful and united family life, which pertains to the welfare of offspring (the chief end of marriage), is rendered impossible in such circumstances. Besides, simultaneous plurality of wives destroys that blessing of marriage called *fidelity*, which is the exclusive use of marital rights by one husband and one wife. Further, if there be several wives, spouses cannot really be two in one flesh. For all these reasons, we say that simultaneous plurality of wives is in conflict with the natural law.

2. And yet this conflict with the natural law does not touch that law in its primary precepts, but in secondary ones. And, before the institution of matrimony as a sacrament, God, in the Old Law, permitted to some a plurality of wives—this, by way of exception. The primary requirement of the natural law respecting marriage is that offspring be generated, born, and well reared; this is the essential good of offspring; this *can* be attained even with plurality of wives.

3. It is certainly contrary to the natural law, as it is in conflict with Christian morality, for a man to have a concubine or mistress as well as a wife.

4. It is unquestionably a mortal sin for a man to make use of a concubine; this is plainly the terrible sin of adultery.

5. In the Old Testament, in cases where, by divine dispensation, plurality of wives was permitted, these wives were often called concubines, yet they were not really so in the accurate meaning of that term.

66. BIGAMY AS CAUSE OF IRREGULARITY

1. An *irregularity*, in the technical sense in which we use the term here, is any physical or moral defect which, by decree of the Church, prevents a man from receiving the sacrament of holy orders. Now, bigamy (that is, a plurality of wives, a plurality of marriages) makes a man irregular. For he who is to administer the sacraments, must not himself be deficient with reference to the sacrament of matrimony.

For marriage as a *sacrament* signifies the union of Christ with the Church, and this is a union of One with one.

2. A man who has one wife *in law*, and another *in fact*, is a bigamist, and incurs the irregularity mentioned above.

3. One who marries a non-virgin is adjudged irregular.

4. Baptism does not remove the fact of bigamy, nor the irregularity consequent upon bigamy.

5. In certain cases, it is possible for a bigamist to be dispensed from irregularity. [*Note:* Most of this discussion of irregularity from a cause of bigamy is wholly irrelevant or meaningless today.]

67. DIVORCE

1. To achieve its full natural end, essential and secondary, marriage requires the permanent union of husband and wife. Therefore, permanence in marriage is a requirement of the natural law, at least in the secondary precepts of that law. And what is required by the natural law is required of all men without exception, Christian and pagan, Greek and Roman, Jew and Gentile. It is not just a requirement of church law that a man should cleave to his wife in permanent and unbroken wedlock.

2. It sometimes happened in the Old Law, that a man put his wife away by "a bill of divorcement," and that this exceptional act was sanctioned by Mosaic precept. But such a severance of the marriage bond is not possible when the marriage is also the sacrament of matrimony.

3. Our Lord himself tells us (Matt. 19:8) that the Mosaic permission for divorcing a wife was granted on account of the hardness of the hearts of the people, and adds, "From the beginning it was not so." It seems that this Mosaic permission amounted to a dispensation from the marriage bond to prevent the terrible crime of wife-murder to which the people were prone.

4. Yet it is not clear that the Mosaic "bill of divorce" permitted the separated spouses to marry again.

5. But it is clear that a husband, having repudiated his wife by a "bill of divorce," could never take her back again.

6. Doubtless, hatred of a wife, and whatever gave rise to that hatred, could be adduced as reasons for giving her the "bill of divorce," but it seems that these reasons had value only because they could lead directly to wife-murder.

7. The causes of the severance of spouses were not given in detail in a Mosaic "bill of divorce," but were expressed in a general way.

68. ILLEGITIMACY

1. A child born out of true wedlock is called illegitimate.

2. An illegitimate child suffers inconveniences, such as being debarred from certain offices and dignities, and also with reference to inheritance. Both parents of illegitimate children are bound, by the natural law itself, to provide for them.

3. The positive or statute law establishes illegitimacy, and therefore the same law can remove it. Hence, illegitimate children can be legitimized by due process of law.

THE
GENERAL RESURRECTION

(QUESTIONS 69 to 86)

69. THE PLACE OF DEPARTED SOULS

1. Souls that depart from their bodies at death are assigned to certain corporeal places. However, these souls are not present in a place by *quantity* or *dimension,* as bodies are, for the souls are spirits and have no quantity or dimensions of their own. But a spirit can be in a place in a manner proper to itself. We rightly say that the souls of the departed are in heaven and purgatory and hell. And these terms mean places as well as states.

2. The assignment of a departed soul to its place occurs at the instant it is severed from its body. Souls fit for heaven, go there; souls in mortal sin are, by their own free choice and decision, assigned to hell; souls in God's grace but unready for heaven are detained in purgatory. For it may be, and doubtless often is, that a soul at the moment of death, even if free from mortal sin, is in venial sin, or has yet to pay some temporal punishment due to forgiven sins, and perhaps has upon it the remains of sin. Now, the soul that labors under these burdens is not fit for heaven (which is for those without spot or wrinkle, and is the place and state into which nothing defiled can

enter), and still such a soul does not deserve the eternal pains of hell. Such a soul labors under an obstacle that must be first removed before it can enter heaven. As a body lighter than air tends to fly upward, but is prevented from reaching its true level by an overhanging obstacle, so the soul in purgatory is blocked by its burdens from ascending into heaven; it remains in purgatory until the preventing obstacle is removed by enduring the penalties of its state or by prayers and suffrages offered on its behalf.

3. Heaven, hell, and purgatory are places and states. No soul in heaven or in hell may ever leave its *state*, but it is possible by divine dispensation that a soul may leave its *place* and come in apparition before the eyes of people on earth.

4. Before the redemption, all the departed souls were said to be in hell. This was a general term, like our own expression, "the hereafter." Or we may say that the hell of the older time had two departments: the limbo of the just, and the hell of lost souls.

5. The limbo of the just was known as "the limbo of the fathers," that is of holy men (such as the patriarchs, and Job, and St. Joseph) who died before our Lord's Resurrection and Ascension. It is possible that the limbo of the fathers and the hell of eternal punishment were in the same *place*, but they were not the same *state*. For the fathers suffered only their unfulfilled longing for heaven, and not a pain of sense.

6. The limbo of children is the state and place of unbaptized children who have original sin only. As to *place*, this may be the same as the limbo of the fathers, but it is not the same *state*. In the limbo of children there is no suffering whatever.

7. Thus we distinguish the abodes of departed souls: heaven, hell, purgatory, the limbo of children. The limbo of the fathers ceased to exist when our Lord ascended into heaven carrying with him the souls of all the just who were awaiting that glad hour in the limbo of the fathers.

70. QUALITY OF THE SEPARATED SOUL

1. The soul, separated from its body, can no longer exercise the powers of sense, for these require the service of bodily members. But the soul is still the root-principle of sense-action and retains its fitness for activating sense-organs. Hence, we may say that the sentient powers belong *radically* (or *in root*) to the separated soul.

2. Certainly, sense-action itself is not within the power of the separated soul.

3. Although the fire of hell be a bodily fire, it can afflict a spirit

thus far at least, that it can *detain* it, and hinder its movement according to its own will.

71. SUFFRAGES FOR THE DEAD

1. The word *suffrage* really means *a vote*. A suffrage is a vote, or a request to God, that some good act of ours have its merit bestowed on another. A suffrage is a good deed cast, like a ballot, in favor of someone. All the faithful are members of one body which is the Church. And, as in a living body, one member may be assisted by another. Such assistance is a *suffrage*. So much we know from the doctrine called the "Communion of Saints." But one member cannot actually replace another; one member of the Church cannot save the soul of another. One member may, and should, help another, not only by giving him good example and praying for him, but by performing good and meritorious deeds, and ascribing the benefit of these to another.

2. The prayers and suffrages of the living, offered for the souls in purgatory, are of benefit to these souls. This we know from the infallible teaching of the Church, and also from scripture (II Machabees 12:46): "It is a holy and wholesome thought to pray for the dead that they may be loosed from their sins."

3. Even those who are in the state of mortal sin may do something for the souls in purgatory. For the *deed done* may have a value apart from the status of the *doer* of the deed.

4. Suffrages offered by the living on behalf of the souls in purgatory are deeds of charity, and, as such, they confer a benefit upon those who perform them. Says Psalm 34: "My prayer shall be turned into my bosom."

5. Suffrages, however, can be of no benefit whatever to those who are in hell. The lost souls are changelessly beyond all aid. They are under debt of eternal punishment, and no suffrage with its gift of temporal satisfaction, can be of any avail.

6. It is a point of the faith itself that the suffrages of the living help the souls in purgatory to pay their temporal debt. For purgatory does the work of satisfaction that a person could have done in this life, but died without doing, or without completing. Temporal punishment can be paid off; we on earth can help pay it for our brethren in purgatory who can merit no longer for themselves.

7. Infants in limbo cannot be aided by suffrages. For these infants are not under any debt of punishment for actual sins. We cannot relieve temporal suffering where there is no suffering to relieve.

8. Suffrages are called so because they *help,* just as a vote helps to

elect a man. Now, we cannot help those who have achieved the glory of heaven. One cannot help another to get home if he is already at home. So we do not offer suffrages on behalf of the saints.

9. The Holy Sacrifice of the Mass, the share we have in the general prayer of the Church, and almsgiving, are notable works of charity; therefore, these are powerful suffrages.

10. Indulgences granted by the Church and made applicable to the souls in purgatory can be gained by the faithful on earth for the benefit of the holy souls. And indulgences thus gained are suffrages.

11. St. Augustine says that the burial service for the dead, with its solemn ceremonies, is rather a consolation for the survivors than a help for the departed. And yet the burial service as prescribed by the Church contains many prayers for the dead, and even Holy Mass which is offered for the departed soul. Further, the ceremonies themselves may stir observers to pious thoughts, and lead them to pray and offer suffrages for the dead. And thus, "to bury the dead," is indeed a work of mercy. And as such a work, it is a suffrage.

12. It seems most reasonable to suppose that suffrages offered for one definite person are a help to him rather than to another who is perhaps more worthy of help. For the suffrage offered derives its value not only from the deed done, but from the intention of the doer of the deed.

13. Suffrages offered for several souls are divided among the souls. It is quite unreasonable to think or say, as some have done, that such suffrages are of as much value for each of the several souls as if they were offered for that one soul alone.

14. General suffrages (those offered in general for the souls in purgatory) are certainly of profit to the holy souls. But here again it is unreasonable to say that neglected souls find in general suffrages such help as makes up to them all they have been deprived of through neglect on the part of those who should help them.

72. PRAYERS TO THE SAINTS

1. The saints are all the human beings who have reached heaven. They enjoy the beatific vision, seeing, directly and intuitively, God in his essence. They behold in God all that they ought to know about themselves and about their glory. Now, it is part of their glory to assist others, and help them serve God and reach heaven. Thus the saints cooperate with God; thus they are made godlike. But the saints cannot assist others unless they know these others and understand their needs. Therefore, the saints *know in God* the devotions, prayers, and promises of people on earth who pray to the saints.

2. It is right to pray to the saints for their aid. We pray for one another here on earth. St. Paul, great apostle as he was, asked humbly for prayers (Rom. 15:30). Our brethren with God in heaven are in far better position to offer our petitions to him than are our brethren on earth. Besides, the Church prays to the saints, as, for example, in the solemn Litany of the Saints.

3. The prayers of the saints for us are effective. The saints pray in complete conformity with God's most loving will towards us, and they ask favors for us according to that will. Thus, their prayers are always granted.

73. SIGNS PRECEDING GENERAL RESURRECTION AND JUDGMENT

1. When our Lord comes in glory to judge the world at the end of time, certain signs shall herald his coming. These signs will be such as to forewarn all people and bring them into reverent subjection to God's will if they will heed. Just what the signs of Christ's second coming will be, we do not know. Those signs mentioned in scripture refer not only to his coming to judge mankind, but to his coming continually to visit his Church; some of them refer to the coming of divine justice upon unfaithful Jerusalem.

2. The actual darkening of the sun and moon may precede the coming of the Judge, and may stir sinners to fear and repentance. But it is not likely that the Day of Judgment will be dark. Our Lord will come in glory as scripture says (Isa. 30:26): "The light of the moon shall be as the light of the sun, and the light of the sun shall be sevenfold."

3. "The virtues of heaven shall be moved," says scripture, referring to the day of general judgment (Matt. 24:29). This prediction probably refers to the angels, either in general, or to the particular order of angels called *Virtues*. The end of time means a change in the temporal assignment of angels who have charge of earthly things.

74. THE FIRE OF JUDGMENT DAY

1. At the end of time sin and all uncleanness on the earth shall cease. Those who are voluntarily and irrevocably given to evil will all be in hell. The earth where man has sinned will be cleansed and purified.

2. It appears that the cleansing agency for the bodily world will be fire. We read in scripture (I Peter 3:12): "The heavens being on fire will be dissolved, and the elements shall melt with the burning heat."

3. The cleansing final fire will doubtless be the same kind of fire as the natural sort with which we are familiar. As natural water washed

the sinful world in the great flood, so natural fire will cleanse it at the last day.

4. The heavenly bodies are not subject to contamination by man's sin. They need nothing to fit them for the state of glory but to have their local movement set at rest by divine decree.

5. It seems that after the cleansing by fire, the substances of air, earth, fire, and water will remain, but as *purified*, and no longer in natural conflict with one another.

6. Therefore, all earthly substances, including fire itself, will be purified and cleansed in the final fire.

7. The cleansing fire will precede the judgment: "A fire shall go before him" (Ps. 96). Yet the special action of fire which will engulf the wicked will follow upon their judgment.

8. The final fire will act on men as the instrument of divine justice. It will reduce or change all bodies; but it will pain the wicked, and not the good, except in so far as temporal punishment may still be needed for the cleansing of the good.

9. With the purifying of the world by fire, all that is evil and ugly will be cast into hell with the wicked; all that is beautiful and noble will be taken up to heaven for the glory of the elect.

75. THE RESURRECTION OF THE BODY

1. The body will rise again. Says scripture (Job 19:25, 26): "I know that my Redeemer liveth, and in the last day I shall rise out of the earth, and I shall be clothed again with my skin, and in my flesh I shall see my God." Since man is one substance composed of soul and body, the ultimate state of man must involve the body as well as the soul. Hence, the body will rise again.

2. This, therefore, is true of all men without exception; for all are of the same *species,* that is, the same complete essential kind. No human soul will remain forever separated from its own body.

3. The resurrection of the body is *natural* in the sense that it is natural for the soul to have its body. But there is no power resident in soul or body to bring them together once they have been separated by death. Hence, the agency which actually joins souls with their respective bodies is wholly *supernatural.*

70. THE CAUSE OF THE RESURRECTION OF THE BODY

1. It was the divinity or Godhead of Christ (which is one in the three divine Persons of the Blessed Trinity), which raised him from the dead. And scripture says (Rom. 8:11): "He that raised up Jesus

Christ from the dead shall quicken also your mortal bodies." We are to rise in the likeness of the Resurrection of our Lord, and indeed in virtue of that Resurrection. God is the cause of the resurrection of bodies; the Resurrection of Christ can be called the quasi-instrumental cause through which God will raise us up.

2. On the last day, the appearance of Christ in his glory will summon all men to resurrection and judgment. His voice will be as the trumpet to rouse and summon all.

3. The angels will come with the Judge, ministering to him, and preparing for the bodily resurrection of mankind. But the actual reuniting of souls and bodies will not be done by angels, but will be the immediate work of God himself.

77. TIME AND MANNER OF THE RESURRECTION OF THE BODY

1. The resurrection of the body will take place at the end of the world, not previously.

2. The time of the end of the world, and of the concomitant rising of men, is not humanly known; nor will it be known. Scripture says (Matt. 24:36): "Of that day and hour no man knoweth; no, not the angels of heaven." When the apostles asked our Lord about the time of the world's ending (Acts 1:7), he said to them: "It is not for you to know the times or moments which the Father hath put in his own power."

3. As to the *hour* of the bodily resurrection, many think that because Christ rose from the dead in the early part of the day while it was yet dark, the resurrection of men's bodies will be in the nighttime.

4. The resurrection of the body will take place in an instant, and not by degrees. St. Paul, speaking of the bodily resurrection, says (I Cor. 15:51–52): "We shall all indeed rise again . . . in a moment, in the twinkling of an eye."

78. THE STARTING POINT OF THE BODILY RESURRECTION

1. Every movement has its starting point and its goal, and the movement itself consists in the transit or "going over" from the first of these to the second. Now, the movement of the bodies of men to life in the final resurrection, has its beginning or starting point in the state of death. Therefore, all men must die. Those who are alive on earth when the last day comes will die, and then rise in the general resurrection.

2. All human beings shall rise from the dust and ashes to which death and decay (or the final fire) reduces them. Scripture says (Gen. 3:19): "Dust thou art, and into dust thou shalt return."

3. There is, in the dust and ashes to which bodies are reduced, no tendency towards reconstruction as human bodies. The divine plan and the divine power bring about the resurrection, uniting each soul with the dust and ashes which, by reason of the union, is constituted as the proper body of the vivifying soul.

79. THE RISEN BODY

1. In the resurrection, each soul will be united with its own body. For in a real resurrection, that which falls is that which rises again. If the soul be not joined substantially with its own body, then there is not a resurrection, but an assuming of a new body.

2. The selfsame man who dies will rise again. For, by the resurrection, a man is to live again, not to be turned into someone else.

3. However, it is *the soul* that constitutes the material element of man as his living body and gives it its personal identity in the body-soul compound that we call a man. By uniting substantially with matter, the soul constitutes that matter as its own body, holding it in continuous identity, notwithstanding the flow and change of bodily particles all through life. Perhaps, in the risen body will be present some of the actual physical particles which the living body used at some stage of earthly life.

80. INTEGRITY OF THE RISEN BODY

1. The human body will rise complete and perfect with all its members. In the elect, the perfected soul will animate its body and cause that body to be perfect.

2. Even in such things as belong to the body more as ornaments than necessary members, such as hair and nails, the risen body will be perfectly complete.

3. Man's risen body will lack nothing that belongs to the integrity (that is, the complete and rounded perfection) of human nature. The risen body will need none of the processes that merely preserve it, or make it grow, or propagate. But the body will have all that makes it enduring, mature, and perfect.

4. The risen body will have all that belongs to true human bodily nature; it will have all this in the most perfect and suitable mode and degree.

5. As noted heretofore, the actual material particles which flow through and in the human body during its term of earthly existence will not all be found in the risen body.

81. THE QUALITY OF THOSE RISEN FROM THE DEAD

1. Those who rise will not have the imperfections of immaturity or old age. All will rise in the most perfect stage of human nature, which is the age of youth; that is, of youth just arrived at maturity and full development.

2. However, all arisen bodies will not be the same in size. Variety on this point is no defect in nature. We know only that risen bodies will not be deficient in any natural perfection. Each person's body will be of the size most suitable to him.

3. Human beings, then, will rise with perfect bodies, all in full maturity, none with infantile or childish imperfection, none bent with age. They will be perfect men and perfect women, with bodies of suitable size perfectly proportioned.

4. Risen bodies will not require the things they needed on earth to sustain them, preserve them, and move them to development or further perfection. Risen bodies will not eat, or drink, or sleep, or beget offspring, or feel the pull of fleshly appetites or passions.

82. THE IMPASSIBILITY OF RISEN BODIES

1. To be *impassible* is to be immune to suffering and change.

2. The bodies of the just will not be capable of suffering any pain whatever, nor will they ever undergo substantial change. The bodies of the damned will endure pains in hell, and hence are not impassible; yet these bodies will not undergo substantial change. St. Paul (I Cor. 15:42) says: "It [the body] is sown in corruption, it shall rise in incorruption."

3. Impassibility in the risen bodies of the just does not mean numbness or insensibility. It means immunity to what is contrary to human nature and painful to it. The risen body will have sensation (that is, its senses will operate and bring in sense-findings or sense-knowledge), and it will have movement; these things belong to the perfection of the body.

4. The senses of the risen bodies of the just will find in the overflow of glory, which comes upon them from the soul, their complete and enduring perfection. The senses will be perfectly and satisfyingly in operation, and they will possess their objects, and not merely tend to these objects, or be in a state of readiness to perceive them.

83. THE SUBTLETY OF RISEN BODIES

1. The risen body will be, in all organic action, perfectly subject to the soul, and instantly responsive to the will, needing withal no material sustenance. This spirit-like quality of the risen body is called *subtlety* or *subtility*.

2. The subtlety of a glorified body will not enable it to occupy the same place with another body, unless this be done by a miracle.

3. Now, there is no contradiction in the thought of two bodies being in the same place simultaneously, even though there is nothing in the nature of a body capable of producing this effect. What keeps bodies from compenetration is their external extension, and this is not of the essence or nature of bodies, but is an effect of quantity, which, in turn, is only a proper accidental of bodies and not their essence. Hence, there is no conflict or contradiction in the notion of compenetration of bodies; therefore, since the thing is conceivable, it might be done by a miracle.

4. However, the subtlety of the glorified body does not make this compenetration possible without a miracle. Besides, in heaven, distinctness of bodily being will be a perfection; if several bodies were to occupy the same place, this distinctness of being would be obscured.

5. The glorified body, just as the natural body on earth, will occupy space, and will be in a place according to its dimensions.

6. There will be nothing ghostlike in the risen body. It will be a true body. But it will have spiritual or spirit-like qualities. It will be something that can be touched and felt. When our Lord in his risen and glorified body came in, through closed doors, to his disciples, he told them he was not a spirit or ghost, and said (Luke 24:39): "Handle and see: for a spirit hath not flesh and bones, as you see me to have."

84. THE AGILITY OF RISEN BODIES

1. The glorified body will be able to move with the quickness of thought from place to place under the direction of the soul and the command of the free will. This quality of the risen body is called *agility*.

2. The risen body in heaven will move about. Scripture says (Isa. 40:31): "They shall run and not be weary"; and (Wisd. 3:7), "[The just] shall run to and fro like sparks among the reeds." But this swift and untiring movement will not deprive the just of the beatific vision or diminish their happiness.

3. The movement of the glorified body will not be strictly instantaneous; it will take a moment of time, yet this moment will be so short as to be imperceptible.

85. THE CLARITY OF RISEN BODIES

1. The risen body in glory will have a measure of lightsomeness and splendor, according to the soul's degree of glory. Says scripture (Matt. 13:43): "The just shall shine as the sun in the kingdom of their Father." This shining and splendid quality of the risen body is called its *clarity*.

2. The clarity of the blessed in heaven will be visible to the non-glorified eye of the damned. For clarity is naturally visible, as it was to the eyes of the three apostles who beheld it in our Lord's body at the time of the Transfiguration.

3. Yet the glorified body is not *necessarily* visible; it will appear or disappear as the soul wills. It will be like our Lord's glorified body at Emmaus, that is, capable of being seen, but also capable of being withdrawn from the sight of men.

86. THE RISEN BODIES OF THE DAMNED

1. The bodies of all men will rise in natural perfection without deficiency or defect. But the bodies of the damned will lack the qualities of the glorified bodies: agility, clarity, subtlety, impassibility.

2. The bodies of the damned will not be corruptible. Scripture says (Apoc. 9:6): "Men shall seek death and shall not find it, and they shall desire to die and death shall fly from them."

3. As noted, the bodies of the damned will be passible, that is, capable of enduring suffering. Retribution must come to man, body and soul. And punishment of body involves passibility.

THE LAST THINGS

(QUESTIONS 87 TO 99)

87. KNOWLEDGE IN RISEN MAN

1. When a man rises from the dead and comes to the general judgment, he will know all the sins he has committed in his lifetime. St. Augustine says this complete remembrance of all one's sins will be conferred on each person by God's power; it will be a special gift for

the occasion. The judgment will be most perfect, and therefore the accuser, the witness, the defendant must know all that is to be judged. Each man's conscience is like a book that contains an accurate and detailed record of his life. And at judgment, the books will be opened (Apoc. 20:12).

2. At the last judgment, each person will know, not only his own sins, but the sins of every other person. For in this judgment, God's justice is to be manifested to all.

3. This special knowledge of one's sins and the sins of all mankind will not be acquired by some time-consuming process, but will be as knowledge that is acquired at a glance.

88. TIME AND PLACE OF THE GENERAL JUDGMENT

1. Each soul is judged, in what is called the particular judgment, the instant it leaves its body; that is, each man is judged immediately after death. The general judgment of the last day will not reverse or change any sentence passed in the particular judgment; the purpose of the general judgment is to manifest to all rational creatures the justice of God, as well as his goodness and mercy.

2. It seems likely that the general judgment will take place without words. For all will be judged at once; each will know his own sins and the sins of all others; each, then, will know at once the justice of the judgment in each case. Hence, it seems that the general judgment will be conducted without word-of-mouth discussions. Indeed, it is most probable that the whole judgment will be enacted and received mentally, not audibly.

3. God alone knows the day and the hour of the end of the world and the last judgment. Scripture says (Mark 13:32): "Of that day or hour, no man knoweth"; and (I Thess. 5:2), "The day of the Lord shall so come as a thief in the night."

4. The prophet Joel says (3:2): "I will gather together all nations . . . into the valley of Josephat, and I will plead with them there." This prophecy is usually taken to indicate the place in which the last or general judgment will be held. The valley of Josephat is near Jerusalem, and is overlooked by Mount Olivet from which our Lord ascended into heaven.

89. PERSONS TO BE PRESENT AT THE LAST JUDGMENT

1. Christ our Lord will come to judge all men. Scripture says (John 5:22): "The Father hath given all judgment to the Son." Yet there will be holy men associated with our Lord, and these are said *to judge*, but

the active and effectual judgment will be that of Christ alone. The apostles, for instance, are thus to sit in judgment with our Lord, for scripture says (Matt. 19:28): "You [apostles] also shall sit on twelve seats judging the twelve tribes of Israel."

2. Those saints who will be privileged to sit with Christ the judge, and thus to judge with him, will all be saints notable for the virtue of voluntary poverty. For this virtue makes a man free from all creatural influence, and therefore disposes him well for the office of a judge.

3. The angels, who have not man's nature, will not be judges of men. But they will minister to the Judge by gathering all men before his judgment seat (Matt. 13:41).

4. The fallen angels will carry out upon the damned, the sentence of the Judge; for sinners, by their sin, subject themselves voluntarily to the devil and his minions, and it is fitting that they should be punished by the same evil spirits.

5. All human beings without exception, will be present at the general judgment. For we read in scripture (Apoc. 1:7): "Behold, he cometh with the clouds, and every eye shall see him."

6. The good who love God perfectly will be submitted to no judgment beyond being assigned to their reward. The good who are imperfect will be judged as to their imperfections, but will be saved.

7. The evil will be judged and sentenced to eternal punishment of a degree and intensity determined by the degree of their guilt.

8. The angels will not be judged at the general judgment of mankind. For the judgment of angels has already occurred. Scripture says (John 16:11): "The prince of this world [that is, the devil, a fallen angel] is already judged."

90. CHRIST, THE JUDGE

1. Christ *as man* will judge mankind at the last day. Our Lord is God the Son who became man by assuming human nature. When His true humanity is emphasized, scripture calls him "the Son of man." And we read (John 5:27): "He hath given him power to do judgment because he is the Son of man." Christ is our Lord and master because he is God; but he is also our Lord and master because he redeemed us by dying for us *as man*. Hence, as man he has authority to judge us.

2. Christ will come "with great power and majesty" (Luke 21:27) to judge mankind. He will come in the glorified body in which he appeared after his Resurrection. He who came in weakness and "in the body of our lowness" (Phil. 3:21) to be our redeemer, will come in strength and majesty to be our judge.

3. At the final judgment the wicked will behold Christ as man, and, at the same time, will thoroughly realize that he is God. But they will not behold his divinity directly, for, if they did, they would be filled with joy, which is contrary to their condition and their perverse will.

91. THE WORLD AFTER THE LAST JUDGMENT

1. In Isaias we read (65:17): "Behold, I create new heavens and a new earth, and the former things shall not be in remembrance." And the Apocalypse says (21:1): "I saw a new heaven and a new earth. For the first heaven, and the first earth was gone." The earth will be renewed after the last or general judgment. All bodily things were created for man, and when man is renewed in the resurrection of the body, the earth should receive a splendor of renewal for renewed man.

2. "Time shall be no longer," says the Apocalypse (10:6). It appears then that the movement of the heavenly bodies must cease, for it is this movement which enables man to measure time; the movement itself is the *reality* of time.

3. After the last judgment, the renewal of the earth will find its counterpart in a new splendor of the heavenly bodies. Isaias says (30:26): "The light of the moon shall be as the light of the sun, and the light of the sun shall be sevenfold."

4. As we have noted, all bodily things are for men and will somehow reflect his glory in heaven. There will be brightness in all common things. Earth will gain a transparency; water will be as crystal; fire will have the beauty of the most wondrous stars.

5. Plants and animals will have no place in the renewed world; no living things except those that are deathless will be there.

92. HEAVEN: THE BEATIFIC VISION

1. In heaven the blessed will directly see the very essence of God. "We shall see him as he is" (I John 3:2). God is supremely intelligible or understandable, and is himself the *determining* of the creatural intellect to know him in his essence. To know God thus is to behold the beatific vision.

2. After the general resurrection when bodies and souls will be reunited, the blessed will not behold God's essence with their *bodily* eyes. For bodily eyes, even when they are glorified, behold bodily things, and God's essence is not bodily. Those that see God in heaven (before or after the resurrection of the body) see him with the mind, the intellect—strengthened, elevated, and illumined by the Light of Glory.

3. No creature can know God exhaustively, so as to know all that

God knows. This would mean the encompassing of the infinite by a finite understanding; this is utterly impossible. Therefore, the blessed see God in his essence, but they do not see all that God sees. Even the angels "who know all things in God," do not know all that God knows. The term "all things" means "all that they know."

93. HAPPINESS OF HEAVEN: MANSIONS

1. After the resurrection of the body, the blessed in heaven will find an increase of happiness. For then their happiness will be that of the complete man, body and soul, and not of the soul alone.

2. The degrees of heavenly happiness are called mansions. A mansion is literally *a remaining*. It is a goal attained in which the attainer rests or remains. It is the reaching of the home for which one strives and is a remaining in it, a dwelling there. Now the heavenly city or kingdom has "many mansions," as our Lord says (John 14:2). Each of the blessed finds his mansion in the degree of reward and happiness which he attains in heaven.

3. The various mansions of heaven are distinguished according to the degrees of charity (which is love and friendship with God by grace) in the blessed themselves. For in each of the saints or blessed, their degree of charity determines the measure of the light of glory which is imparted to them; this, in turn, determines their degree of reward and happiness, that is, their mansion.

94. THE SAVED AND THE DAMNED

1. The sufferings of the damned will be perfectly known to the saints or blessed in heaven, and will only make them the more thankful to God for his great mercy towards themselves.

2. There can, however, be no pity in the saints with reference to the damned. For, on the other hand, they know that the damned are suffering what they chose and still perversely choose. On the other hand, pity is painful in the one who experiences it, and there can be nothing painful in heaven.

3. The blessed are in full conformity with the will of God who wills justice. The saints rejoice in the accomplishment of God's justice. To this extent it can be said that they joy in the pains of the damned.

95. THE ENDOWMENTS OF THE BLESSED

1. When the blessed, or the saints—for the names mean the same here—are brought to the glory of heaven, they are dowered with suitable gifts.

2. These endowments do not constitute beatitude. Beatitude is per-

fect happiness in the beatific vision; this happiness or beatitude is what the soul has merited through Christ and by his grace. But endowments are gifts that are not merited in any sense.

3. Christ our Lord as man has all possible perfections and every gift and endowment, for his humanity is united to Godhead. Still, strictly speaking, it is not proper to say that Christ as man is adorned with gifts and endowments. For Christ is God as well as man; endowments are his to give, not to receive.

4. Now, an endowment is a dowry, and a dowry suggests a wedding and a bride. Human nature is wedded to the divine nature in Christ; Christ himself is wedded to the Church. Hence, when speaking of human beings, we may use the term dowry or endowment with propriety to indicate the perfections of the blessed. But this is not the case when we speak of angels, for the metaphor of marriage and bride does not apply in their case. Of course, angels have all the perfections that can adorn a rational being in heaven. The point we make here is merely that the term dowry or the term endowment is not suitably employed to express angelic perfection.

5. The dowries or endowments of the blessed are: vision, love, and fruition. These gifts may be said to correspond, respectively, to the theological virtues of faith, hope, and charity. Faith is fulfilled in vision; hope, in loving possession; charity, in the fruition or full enjoyment of what is loved.

96. SPECIAL HEAVENLY REWARDS

1. The essential reward of heaven is called the *aurea*, that is, the golden crown. All the blessed have this aurea. Now, it seems that some saints—by reason of the special type of victory they won in saving their souls: by martyrdom, by virginity, by notable teaching of the truths of faith—have a special crown or *aureola* in addition to the aurea. *Aureola* means a little golden crown; sometimes it is called *nimbus* or halo. Christian art often depicts any saint, and even our Lord, with the nimbus or halo. But the precise meaning of *aureola* is not something general and to be attributed to all the blessed, but something special, bestowed in recognition of a particular excellence, on certain saints.

2. In addition to the *aurea*, which all the blessed possess, and also in addition to the *aureola* which certain saints have, there is a special gift called *fruit* which belongs as a reward to certain saints. We may say: (a) the *aurea* is the joy that all the blessed have in God, who is their reward exceeding great; (b) the *aureola* is the special joy that some saints have in the perfection of their works done on earth;

(c) *fruit* is a special joy that some saints have in the disposition, that marked their lives on earth, to be fertile fields for the seed of God's word.

3. The fruit of fertility for the implanted seed of God's word belongs especially to those saints whose lives were characterized by continence.

4. Scripture (Matt. 13:8) tells of the planting of the seed of God's words in human souls, and "they brought forth fruit, some a hundredfold, some sixtyfold, and some thirtyfold." The three fruits fittingly apply to the three types of continence, namely, the continence of virgins, the continence of widowed people, and the continence of married people. The continence of virgins is complete and perpetual and receives the *fruit* called "a hundredfold." The continence of widowed people is like that of virgins, but was not always so; it receives the *fruit* called "sixtyfold." The continence of married people is the lawful use of sex under the rule of reason and God's law; it receives the *fruit* called "thirtyfold."

5. Fruit, then, is the special heavenly reward of virgins, widowed persons, and faithful spouses. Virginity has both fruit and aureola. The virginity that has the reward of the aureola is not the virginity of the innocent who never knew temptation, but is rather the award for shining victory in the war where "the flesh lusteth against the spirit" (Gal. 5:17).

6. An aureola is assigned to martyrs. For martyrdom is the gaining of victory under special difficulties. It is a notable triumph. And so it has its special little crown.

7. Those who have been notable teachers of God's truth have gained much, not alone for themselves but for all who profitably heard their teaching or preaching. Such teachers are the saints called holy doctors. A special reward or aureola rightly marks their victory over error.

8. Since the *aureola* is the mark and reward of those who *shared* the victory of Christ, it is not properly assigned or ascribed to him who won the perfect victory, that is, to Christ himself. The aurea belongs to the perfect humanity of our Lord. But the aureola would indicate rather a failure to award Christ his due than to express his perfection. The aureola means participation in the work of Christ; it means conforming by grace to the perfection of Christ. But Christ does not merely participate or conform with himself and his perfect works.

9. Angels have not an *aureola;* at least, not in the sense in which this award is found in certain saints. For an angel has by its nature as confirmed in grace what the haloed saints have by reason of their brave warring against contrary forces.

10. The *aureola* is a reward possessed by the soul of a saint; it is not an ornament to appear in the risen body, although the risen body may be the more beautiful by reason of the overflow of joy from the *aureola*. The symbols in Christian art which indicate the *aurea* (glow of light about the head) or the *aureola* (circle of gold, halo) are not actual pictures of these heavenly rewards, for, as we have said, the rewards are spiritual.

11. It is suitable that *aureolas* should be assigned to virgins, martyrs, and doctors. These three types of saints represent, each in its own way, a special and notable conformity with Christ.

12. Speaking generally, or in the abstract, we may say that the ranking order of the *aureolas* seems to be this: first and greatest, that of martyrs; second, that of doctors; third, that of virgins. Yet in concrete particular cases, a virgin's *aureola* might be more excellent than a martyr's, or a doctor's *aureola* might be greater than that of either virgin or martyr.

13. The rank of the *aureola* in excellence depends, in individual cases, upon the greatness of the act or reality (with all implied in it —purposes, circumstances, and conditions) for which the aureola is conferred as a reward.

97. THE PUNISHMENT OF THE DAMNED

1. Those who undergo the punishment of hell are tormented by fire and also by other afflicting agencies. As the person condemned to hell has, in earthly life, put various material things in the place of God, he is justly punished by a variety of afflictions.

2. "The worm that dieth not" will afflict the condemned soul in hell. This means that remorse of conscience (but not repentance), will incessantly trouble that soul.

3. The "weeping" that will be in hell after the bodily resurrection will not be the shedding of tears (for there will be no bodily alteration in hell), but will be a steady affliction of the head and the eyes.

4. The darkness of hell is a true and material darkness. After the resurrection of bodies, this darkness will afflict the bodily vision of the damned. The fire of hell, as St. Basil says, will have heat but not light for those punished by it.

5. The fire of hell is a bodily fire which now afflicts and detains lost souls; after the resurrection it will torture the bodies of the damned in hell.

6. It seems that the fire of hell is essentially the same as the fire we know on earth, although it doubtlessly has different properties, since it needs no fuel and does not consume what is cast into it.

7. No one can say for certain where hell is located. It seems, however, to be suggested by some passages in scripture that hell is "under the earth," that is, that it is located somewhere in the interior of the earth, under the earth's surface.

98. THE WILL AND THE INTELLECT OF THE DAMNED

1. The will of a person in hell is, by its own perverse choice, confirmed in evil, and is changelessly and wholly devoted to evil. Every act of such a will is a sin.

2. Repentance in the true meaning of that word, is a hatred of sin as such. There is no repentance of this kind in hell. But if repentance be taken to mean merely the regret that sin causes suffering, and hatred of sin merely as the cause of suffering, then we can say that there is repentance in hell.

3. The condemned in hell cannot wish to be annihilated, for this wish is in conflict with the nature of every being. But doubtless the damned wish for some kind of sleep or death or extinction of consciousness that would bring surcease of suffering.

4. As in heaven there is perfect charity, and happiness in the fact of each soul's being saved, so in hell there is perfect hatred and envy, and malicious desire to see others suffer the pains of hell.

5. The damned hate God (not in himself, for this is impossible) in the effects of his justice which they have perversely brought upon themselves.

6. Strictly speaking, there is no meriting or demeriting in either heaven or hell. For the time of meriting and demeriting is the time of life on earth.

7. Knowledge acquired during earthly life will remain in the damned and will be a factor in their suffering.

8. The condemned who are in hell will never think upon God directly, but only in so far as the thought of him is involved in the thought of the divine justice which afflicts them.

9. The damned have knowledge of the glory of the blessed in heaven. When the resurrection of the body restores bodily eyes, the damned will look in vain to see the glorified bodies of the saints. But they will know of heaven, and they will feel the punishment of not being worthy even to look at it.

99. GOD'S MERCY AND JUSTICE TOWARDS THE DAMNED

1. Scripture repeatedly tells us that the punishment of hell is everlasting. For instance, St. Matthew says (25:46) that "the wicked shall go into everlasting punishment." As reward is measured to meet merit, so punishment is measured to meet guilt. But the guilt of mortal sin is the guilt of completely rejecting God and offending him whose majesty is infinite. The guilt of such a sin deserves unending punishment.

2. There is no place for mercy in hell, for mercy cannot be exercised upon what, by its very nature, rejects it. The perverse will of both men and fallen angels in hell is ceaselessly opposed to any mercy that might be shown them. Further, if mercy were to bring an end to retribution, justice would bring an end to the happiness of heaven.

3. Despite God's wondrous mercy, the fallen angels and lost human souls, cast themselves into hell. While they hate their torments, they still retain their perverse will against God. Sorrow for sin, in the sense of rejecting evil and turning to God, is utterly impossible in hell. Hence, even the mercy of the all-merciful God cannot penetrate the rebel wills of the lost and bring them relief.

4. Christians who go to hell are there eternally, just as non-Christians are. Indeed, Christians who *knew* more than many others who are in hell, are more deserving than those others of endless torment.

5. It cannot be said that those who perform works of mercy during life on earth will necessarily escape the punishments of hell. Even great sinners may sometimes do remarkable deeds of mercy. During earthly life, such deeds may be the means of winning (congruously) contrition for the one who performs them, but they are no guarantee that contrition will be accepted, or that it will endure to the end of life, and so enable the performer of the good deeds to escape hell.

APPENDIX I

THE INNOCENTS IN LIMBO

Only the guilt of actual sin calls for painful punishment, that is, for the affliction of the senses by fire or other bodily agency. Those who die in original sin only, are not afflicted by the pain of sense. Therefore, unbaptized children who are in the limbo of children suffer no pain.

Nor do they suffer any spiritual affliction. For their powers of soul (their intellect and will) have never been disordered by actual sin. Therefore, the infants in the limbo of children will suffer neither pain of sense nor affliction of mind.

These infants are not wholly separated from God; they are united to him by their nature and its gifts. They continually rejoice in God by natural knowledge and love.

APPENDIX II

TWO NOTES ON PURGATORY

Note One

It seems that the pains of purgatory are greater than all pains of this life. The pain of loss (that is, the pain of delay in coming to the beatific vision) is the greater of the two types of pain in purgatory. The lesser is the pain of sense.

The greater love and desire one has for what is, at least temporarily, out of one's reach, the greater is the pain of being deprived of it. Now, the souls in purgatory have a keen awareness of the great Good which they desire; their love and longing for it surpass anything experienced in this life; hence, their pain is the greater. And the pain of sense, directly imposed on the soul itself as the root principle of sensation, is more keenly felt than pain experienced through bodily members.

The souls in purgatory patiently submit to their penalties, but they long to be freed from them and to be purified from all that blocks them out of heaven.

The devils in hell have no power to afflict the souls in purgatory. Indeed, the souls in purgatory have conquered the demons by avoiding mortal sin or by being contrite for it. The souls in purgatory have actually won heaven, and wait only till they are conditioned to enter it. The holy souls are the victors, and the demons are the vanquished. The vanquished cannot torment or afflict the victors.

The punishments of purgatory purge the souls there of venial sins and cancel the debt owed for venial guilt. Not all venial sins are cleansed from a soul simultaneously; the more persistent or habitual venial sins are more slowly wiped out both as to guilt and punishment. Thus one soul may be liberated from purgatory more quickly than another soul which has committed the same factual venial sins; only the soul first liberated had not committed the sins with the persistency or intensity of the other.

Note Two

Those who deny purgatory are actually speaking against the justice of God. For a soul may depart this life in venial sin, and with the remains of forgiven sin upon it. Justice requires these things to be removed by penalty or punishment. But this penalty cannot be the eternal punishment of hell; that punishment would go beyond the requirements of justice. The punishment required must be temporal. Now, temporal punishment after death means purgatory.

It seems likely enough that the fires of punishment of hell and of purgatory are in the same place. Just as the same fire can be used to purify gold and to burn dross, so the one type of punishing fire may purify souls from venial sin and merely afflict souls in mortal sin. Still, no one can say for sure that the one fire afflicts both the souls in purgatory and the damned in hell. Nor can anyone say with certainty just where purgatory is located.

INDEX

457

Index

Fate, 95
Father as applied to God, 32
Fast, Eucharistic, 386
Fasting, 276
Fear, 132 ff., 198 f.: insensibility to, 267; and human acts, 106
Filial fear, 198 f.
Final impenitence, 195
Final perseverance, 184
Fire of hell, 451
Firmament, creation of, 57
First man, intellect of, 79 f.
First principles, 66
Flattery, 261 f.
Folly, 215
Foolhardiness, 267
Form, accidental, 86
Fortitude, 264-72: gift of, 272; parts of, 267 f.; precepts of, 272; virtue of, 264 f.
Fraternal correction, 209
Free will and predestination, 26
Freedom and the will, 69
Friendliness, 260 f.
Fruits of the Holy Ghost, 150 f.
Future, angelic knowledge of, 49

Generosity, 261 f.
Gift as name of the Holy Ghost, 34
Gifts of the Holy Ghost, 149 f.
Glory of the angels, 53 f.
Gluttony, 277 f.
God
    attributes, 3-28
    beatitude, 27 f.
    changelessness of, 11
    distinctions in, 29
    essence of, 34 ff.
    eternity of, 11 f.
    exemplar of things, 40
    existence of, 4 f.
    existence in things, 10
    and evil, 43 f.
    first cause, 39 f.
    goodness of, 9
    ideas in, 19
    immutability of, 11
    infinity of, 9 f.
    justice of, 24
    knowledge of, 13 f.
    his knowledge, 16 f.
    life of, 21 f.
    his love, 24
    meaning of term, 16
    mercy of, 24
    movement of creatures, 86 ff.

God (*continued*)
    names of, 14 ff.
    perfections of, 8
    persons in, 30, 34 ff.
    plurality of persons, 30
    potentiality in, 26
    power of, 26 f.
    presence of, 46
    procession in, 28
    providence of, 25
    relations in, 29 f.
    self-existent, 8
    simplicity of, 6 f.
    terms for unity of, 31
    trinity as applied to, 31
    unity of, 12 f.
    will of, 22 f.
Good, meaning of, 42
Goodness: and being, 8; and final cause, 8 f.; of God, 9
Grace, 178-84
    of angels, 53 f.
    cause of, 181 f.
    effects of, 182 f.
    essence of, 180
    final perseverance, 184
    in first man, 80
    gratuitous, 181, 291-97
    and justification, 182
    necessity of, 178 f.
    prevenient, 180
    sanctifying, 180
    subsequent, 180
Gratitude, 255 f.
Gratuitous graces, 181, 291-97
Gregory, St.; on the angels, 91; on cardinal virtues, 144
Guardian angels, 93

Habits, 137-40: intellectual, 74; synderesis, 66 f.
Happiness of man, 100-105
Hatred, 434 f., 447-51
Heaven, 434 f., 447-51
    creation of, 57 f.
    endowments of blessed, 448 f.
    fruits of blessed in, 449 ff.
    mansions in, 448
    special rewards, 449 ff.
Heavenly bodies, 58
Hell, 434 f.: kind of fire, 451; punishment of the damned, 451 f.; St. Basil on, 451
Hell (Limbo), 357 f.
Heresy, 194 f.

Index

Index

Man (*continued*)
grades of life, 61
happiness of, 100-105
image of God, 78 f.
intellect of, 64-67
last end, 99-105
primal matter in, 62
production of body, 96
production of soul, 96
self-knowledge, 74
sentient faculty of, 64
soul of, 60 f.
substantial form of, 62
and *synderesis*, 66
union of soul and body, 60 f.
vegetal faculty of, 64

Mansions in heaven, 448
Martyrdom, 265
Mary, Blessed Virgin, 334 ff.
Annunciation, 337
espousals, 336
sanctification, 334 f.
veneration of, 333
virginity, 335 f.

Mass: con-celebration, 388; consecration, 384
Material things: angelic knowledge of, 48 f.; intellect and, 73; knowledge of, 73
Matrimony, 420-34
betrothal, 421
bigamy, 432 f.
blessings, 424
closed seasons, 431
consent, 422 ff.
definition, 421 f.
divorce, 433 f.
error in, 425
illegitimacy, 434
impediments, 424-30
infidelity, 430 f.
plurality of wives, 432
as sacrament, 421
successive, 431
witnesses, 422

Matter; primal, 86; principle of individuation, 45; secondary, 86
Meanness, 270
Meekness, 282 f.
Memory, intellectual, 65
Mercy; corporal works of, 207 f.; of God, 24; spiritual works of, 207 f.
Merit, 183 f.
Minister of the Holy Eucharist, 388 f.
Miracles, 87 f., 297: by angels, 91; of Christ, 349

Modesty, 284: as decorum, 289: in dress, 290
Money, use of, 261 f.
Moral precepts of the Old Law, 172 ff.
Moral principles, 66
Morality: in acts of the will, 116 f.; of external acts, 117 f.; of human acts, 114 ff.; of passions, 120 f.; of pleasure, 128
"Morning knowledge" of the angels, 50
Mortal sin, 43
Moses as prophet, 295
Multitude and unity, 12
Murder, 228
Mutilation, 229

Names
analogous, 15
equivocal, 15
of God, 14 ff.
univocal, 15
use of, 15
Negligence, 220
New Law, the, 176-84
Notional acts, 36

Oaths, 245
Obedience, 254 f.
Old Law, the, 171-76: ceremonial precepts of, 174 f.; Decalogue, 173; judicial precepts of, 175 f.; moral precepts of, 172 ff.
Ontological truth, 19
Orders of angels, 89 ff.
Orders, Holy, 416-20
age for, 419
character, 417
effects of, 416 f.
impediments, 418 f.
major, 418
minister, 418
minor, 418
Peter Lombard on, 416
priests, 418
qualities of recipients, 417
tonsure, 419
Orders, religious, 305 ff.
Original sin, 160

Pain, 128-31
Pandects of Justinian, 170
Passio, meaning of, 80
Passion of Christ, 351-58: actual effects, 355 f.; cause of, 353: efficacy of, 354 f.

463

Index

ESSENTIAL CATHOLIC READING

At your bookdealer or direct from the Publisher.

ESSENTIAL CATHOLIC READING

Sermons on Our Lady.................... St. Francis de Sales
Confession of a Roman Catholic .... Paul Whitcomb
The Catholic Church Has the Answer .... Paul Whitcomb
The Sinner's Guide .... Ven. Louis of Granada
True Devotion to Mary .... St. Louis De Montfort
Life of St. Anthony Mary Claret .... Fanchón Royer
Autobiography of St. Anthony Mary Claret ... St. A. M. Claret
I Wait for You .... Sr. Josefa Menendez
Words of Love ... Srs. Menendez, Betrone, Mary of the Trinity
Little Lives of the Great Saints .... John O'Kane Murray
The Rhine Flows into the Tiber .... Fr. Ralph Wiltgen
Prayer—The Key to Salvation............ Fr. Michael Müller
The Victories of the Martyrs........... St. Alphonsus Liguori
Canons and Decrees of the Council of Trent....... Schroeder
St. Dominic's Family .... Sr. Mary Jean Dorcy
Sermons for Every Sunday............. St. Alphonsus Liguori
What Faith Really Means .... Fr. Henry Graham
A Catechism of Modernism................ Fr. J. B. Lemius
What Catholics Believe .... Fr. Lawrence Lovasik
Alexandrina—The Agony and the Glory .... Francis Johnston
Blessed Margaret of Castello........... Fr. William Bonniwell
The Ways of Mental Prayer .... Dom Vitalis Lehodey
Who Is Teresa Neumann? .... Fr. Charles Carty
Summa of the Christian Life. 3 Vols. .. Ven. Louis of Granada
Fr. Paul of Moll—A Flemish Benedictine .... van Speybrouck
St. Francis of Paola....................... Simi and Segreti
Communion Under Both Kinds .... Michael Davies
Abortion: Yes or No?.................. John L. Grady, M.D.
The Story of the Church .... Johnson, Hannan, Dominica
Religious Liberty .... Michael Davies
Hell Quizzes.......................... Radio Replies Press
Indulgence Quizzes..................... Radio Replies Press
Purgatory Quizzes...................... Radio Replies Press
Virgin and Statue Worship Quizzes....... Radio Replies Press
The Holy Eucharist .... St. Alphonsus
The Way of Salvation and of Perfection .... St. Alphonsus
The True Spouse of Jesus Christ............... St. Alphonsus
Textual Concordance of The Holy Scriptures..... Fr. Williams
Douay-Rheims Bible....................... Leatherbound

At your bookdealer or direct from the Publisher.